Hana-Kimi
For You in Full Blossom

To get close to her favorite athlete, Izumi Sano, Japanese-American Mizuki Ashiya moved to Japan...and enrolled in an all-male high school! Now Mizuki and Sano are roommates...but can Mizuki keep up her pretense of being a boy?

SHALL WE DANCE?
The Christmas dance party begins, and Mizuki looks for a chance to give Sano a present. Later, Mizuki flies home for New Year's and an unexpected reunion with Gilbert, her first love. Though time has passed and her romantic hopes are now focused on Sano, Mizuki discovers that this old flame hasn't been completely snuffed out in her heart!

$9.99 USA/$13.95 CAN

ISBN-13: 978-1-4215-0542-8
ISBN-10:   1-4215-0542-8

This book reads from right to left.

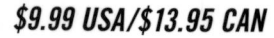
media

50999

9 781421 505428

Hey! You're
Reading in the
Wrong Direction!

This is the *end* of this graphic novel!

To properly enjoy this VIZ graphic novel, please turn it around and begin reading from **right to left.** Unlike English, Japanese is read right to left, so Japanese comics are read in reverse order from the way English comics are typically read.

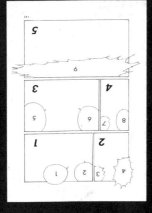

Follow the action this way

This book has been printed in the original Japanese format in order to preserve the orientation of the original artwork. Have fun with it!

CONTENTS

Hana-Kimi Chapter 62.....................5

Hana-Kimi Chapter 63.................40

Hana-Kimi Chapter 64.................71

Hana-Kimi Chapter 65...............101

Hana-Kimi Chapter 66...............131

Hana-Kimi Chapter 67...............155

Let's go to a voice-over session! ..185

About the Author 189

In the Next Volume 190

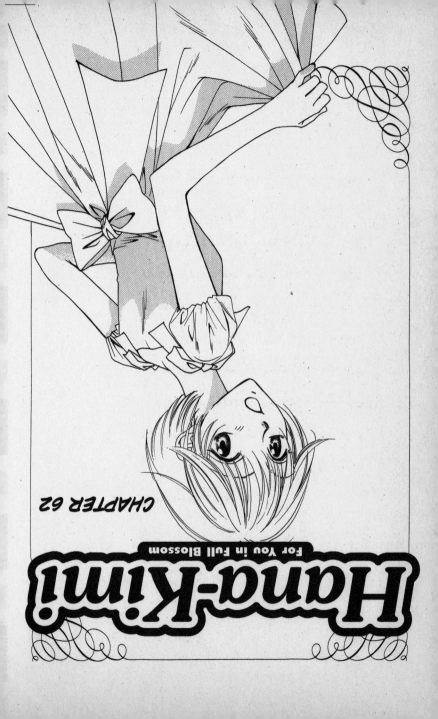

CHAPTER 62

For You in Full Blossom

Hana-Kimi!

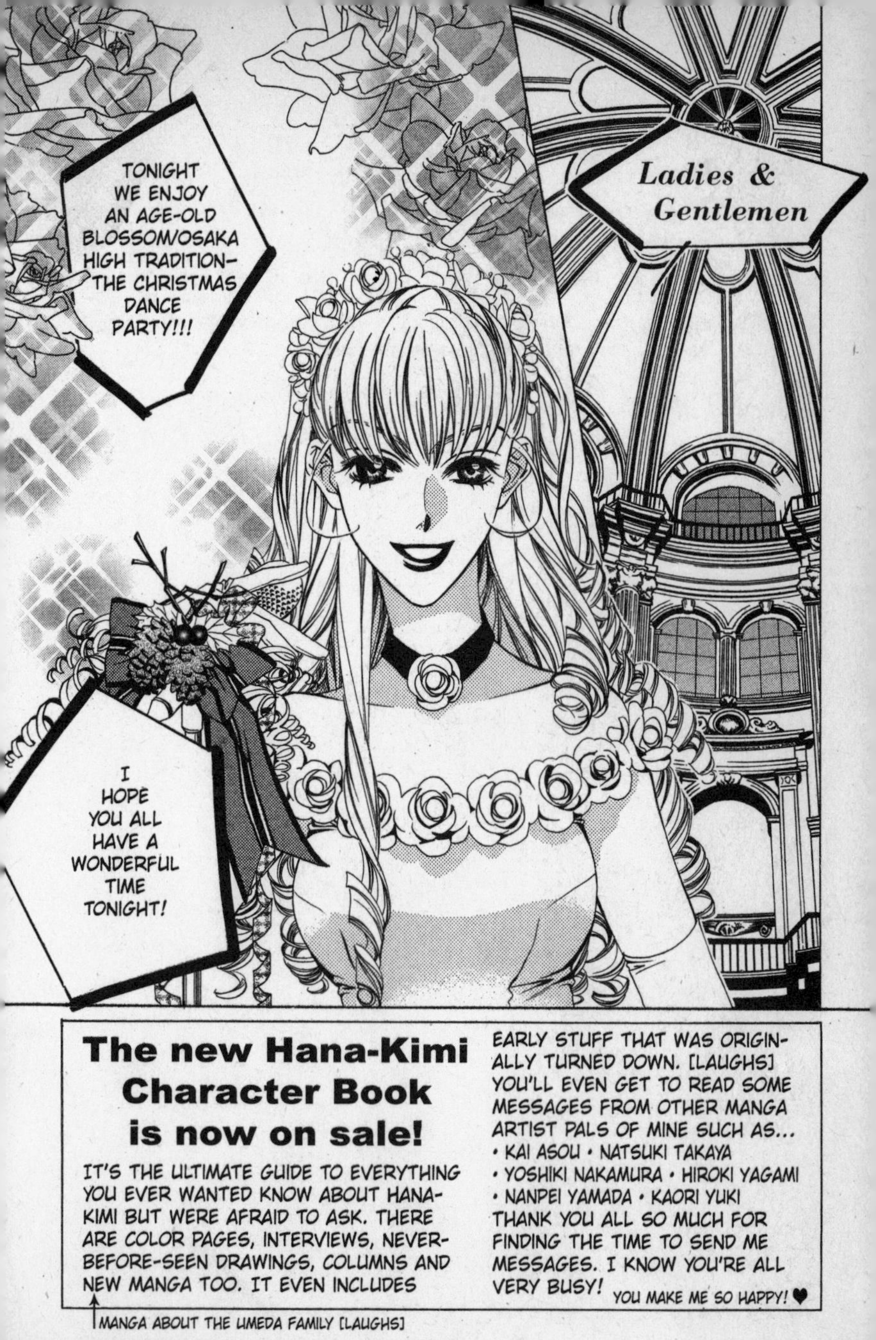
Ladies & Gentlemen
TONIGHT WE ENJOY AN AGE-OLD BLOSSOM/OSAKA HIGH TRADITION—THE CHRISTMAS DANCE PARTY!!!
I HOPE YOU ALL HAVE A WONDERFUL TIME TONIGHT!

The new Hana-Kimi Character Book is now on sale!

IT'S THE ULTIMATE GUIDE TO EVERYTHING YOU EVER WANTED KNOW ABOUT HANA-KIMI BUT WERE AFRAID TO ASK. THERE ARE COLOR PAGES, INTERVIEWS, NEVER-BEFORE-SEEN DRAWINGS, COLUMNS AND NEW MANGA TOO. IT EVEN INCLUDES EARLY STUFF THAT WAS ORIGINALLY TURNED DOWN. [LAUGHS] YOU'LL EVEN GET TO READ SOME MESSAGES FROM OTHER MANGA ARTIST PALS OF MINE SUCH AS...

- KAI ASOU • NATSUKI TAKAYA
- YOSHIKI NAKAMURA • HIROKI YAGAMI
- NANPEI YAMADA • KAORI YUKI

THANK YOU ALL SO MUCH FOR FINDING THE TIME TO SEND ME MESSAGES. I KNOW YOU'RE ALL VERY BUSY! YOU MAKE ME SO HAPPY! ♥

↑MANGA ABOUT THE UMEDA FAMILY [LAUGHS]

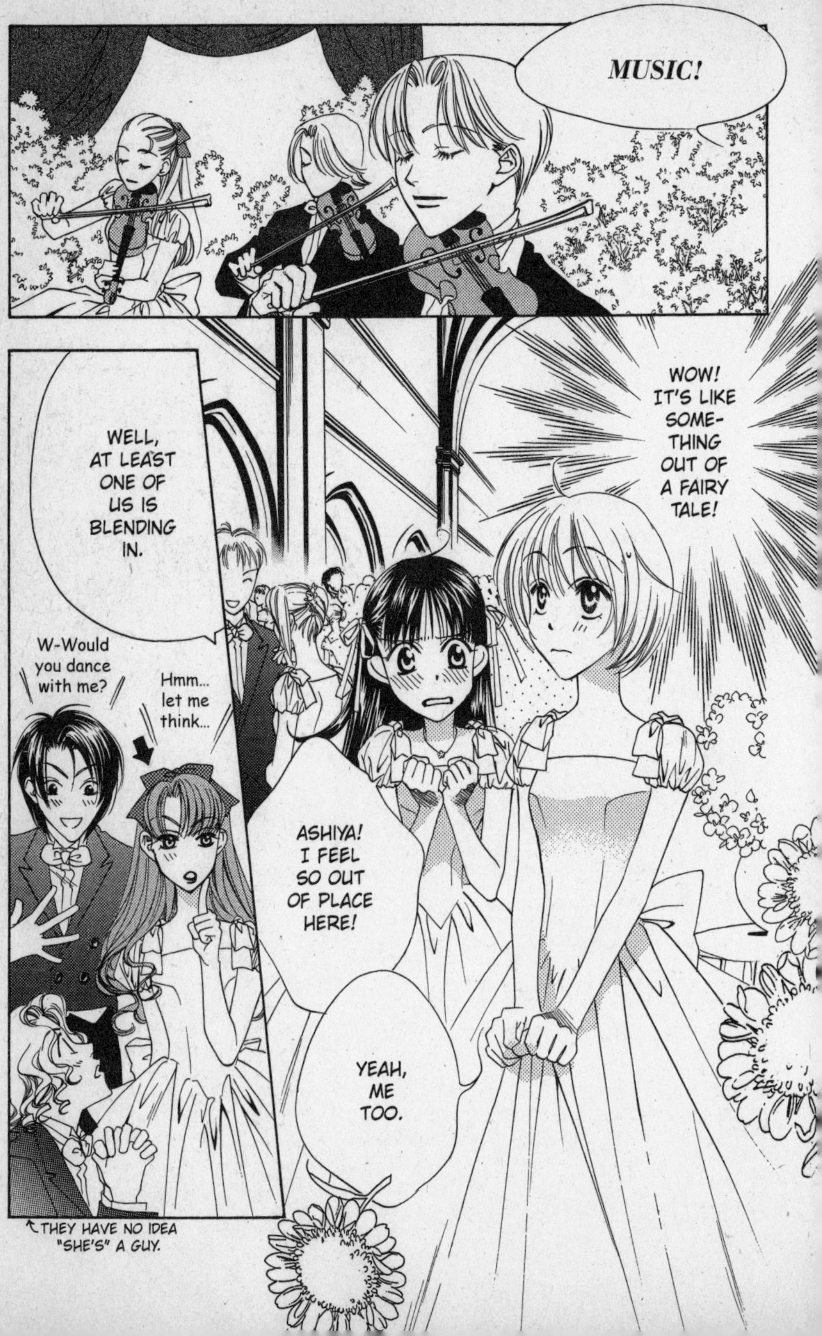
MUSIC!
WOW! IT'S LIKE SOME-THING OUT OF A FAIRY TALE!
ASHIYA! I FEEL SO OUT OF PLACE HERE!
YEAH, ME TOO.
WELL, AT LEAST ONE OF US IS BLENDING IN.
W-Would you dance with me?
Hmm... let me think...
THEY HAVE NO IDEA "SHE'S" A GUY.

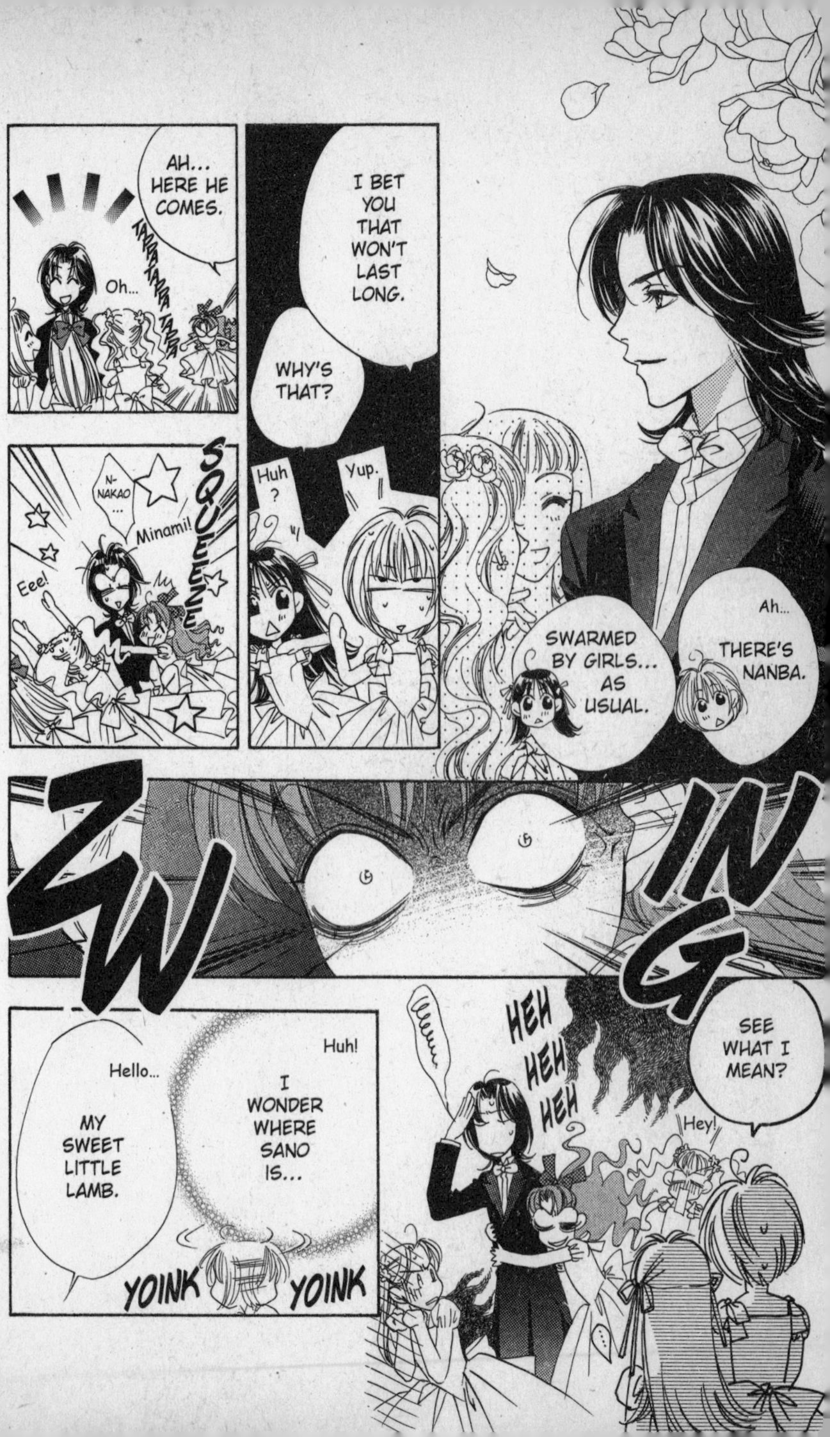
Ah...
THERE'S NANBA.
SWARMED BY GIRLS... AS USUAL.
I BET YOU THAT WON'T LAST LONG.
WHY'S THAT?
Huh?
Yup.
AH... HERE HE COMES.
TAPPA TAPPA TAPPA
Oh...
SQUEEEEZE
N-NAKAO...
Minami!
Eee!
ZWING
SEE WHAT I MEAN?
HEH HEH HEH
Hey!
Huh!
I WONDER WHERE SANO IS...
Hello...
MY SWEET LITTLE LAMB.
YOINK YOINK

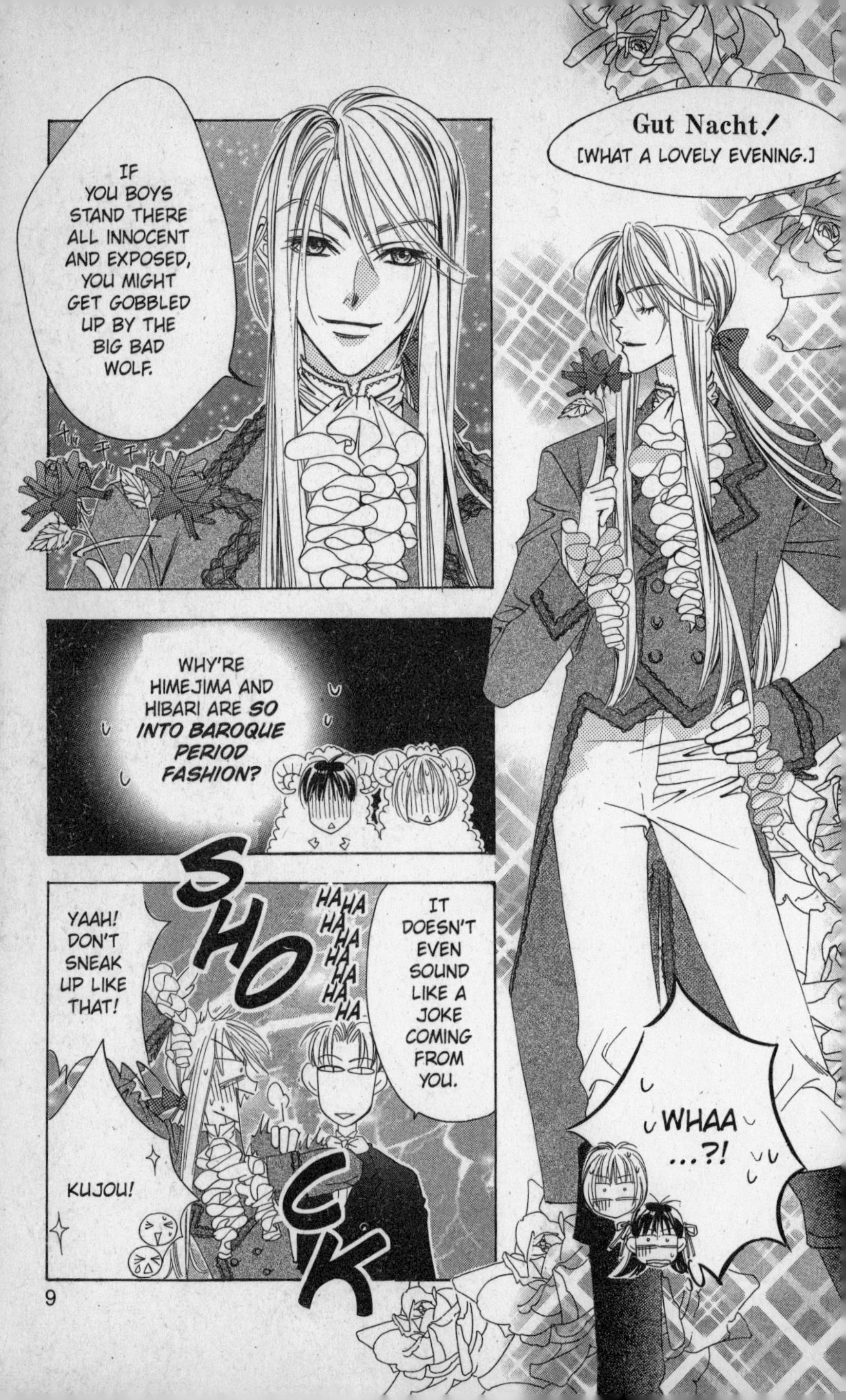
Gut Nacht!
[WHAT A LOVELY EVENING.]
WHAA ...?!
IF YOU BOYS STAND THERE ALL INNOCENT AND EXPOSED, YOU MIGHT GET GOBBLED UP BY THE BIG BAD WOLF.
WHY'RE HIMEJIMA AND HIBARI ARE SO INTO BAROQUE PERIOD FASHION?
SHOCK
IT DOESN'T EVEN SOUND LIKE A JOKE COMING FROM YOU.
HAHA HA HA HA HA HA HA
YAAH! DON'T SNEAK UP LIKE THAT!
KUJOU!

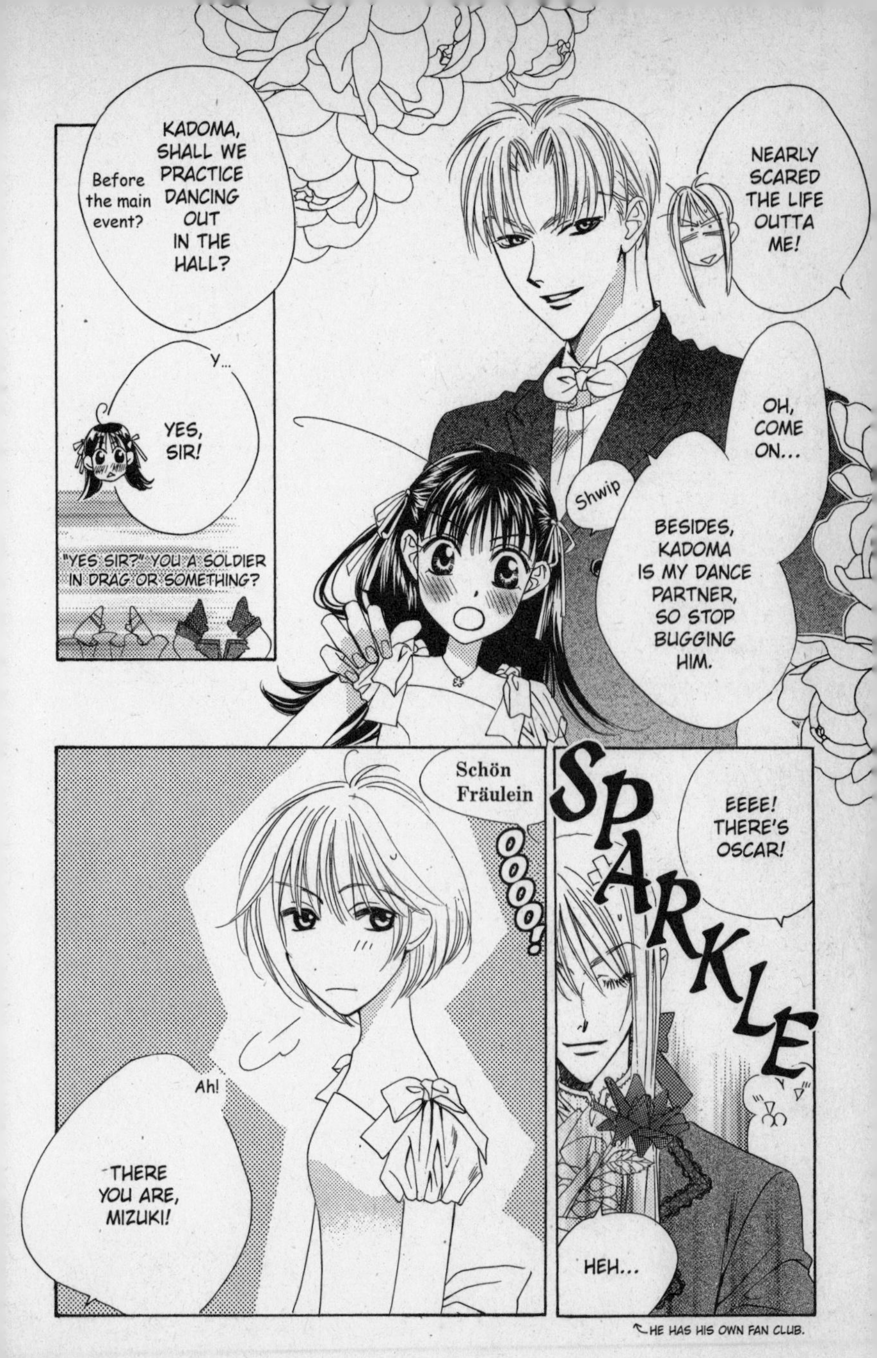
NEARLY SCARED THE LIFE OUTTA ME!
KADOMA, SHALL WE PRACTICE DANCING OUT IN THE HALL?
Before the main event?
OH, COME ON...
Shwip
BESIDES, KADOMA IS MY DANCE PARTNER, SO STOP BUGGING HIM.
Y...
YES, SIR!
"YES SIR?" YOU A SOLDIER IN DRAG OR SOMETHING?
EEEE! THERE'S OSCAR!
SPARKLE
HEH...
HE HAS HIS OWN FAN CLUB.
Schön Fräulein
OOOO!
Ah!
THERE YOU ARE, MIZUKI!

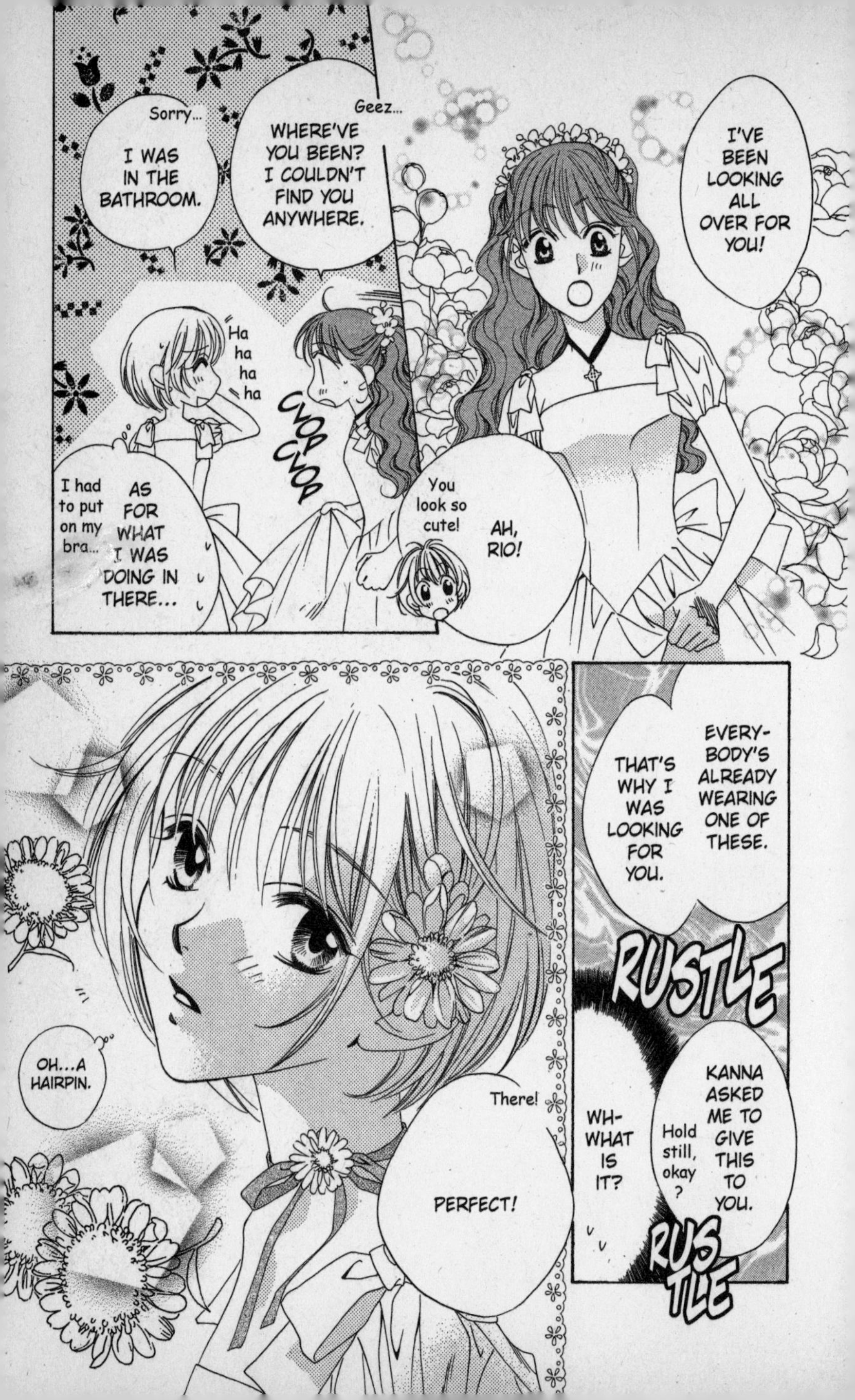
I'VE BEEN LOOKING ALL OVER FOR YOU!
Geez...
WHERE'VE YOU BEEN? I COULDN'T FIND YOU ANYWHERE.
Sorry...
I WAS IN THE BATHROOM.
Ha ha ha ha
CLOP CLOP
AH, RIO!
You look so cute!
AS FOR WHAT I WAS DOING IN THERE...
I had to put on my bra...
EVERYBODY'S ALREADY WEARING ONE OF THESE.
THAT'S WHY I WAS LOOKING FOR YOU.
RUSTLE
KANNA ASKED ME TO GIVE THIS TO YOU.
Hold still, okay?
WH-WHAT IS IT?
RUSTLE
There!
PERFECT!
OH...A HAIRPIN.

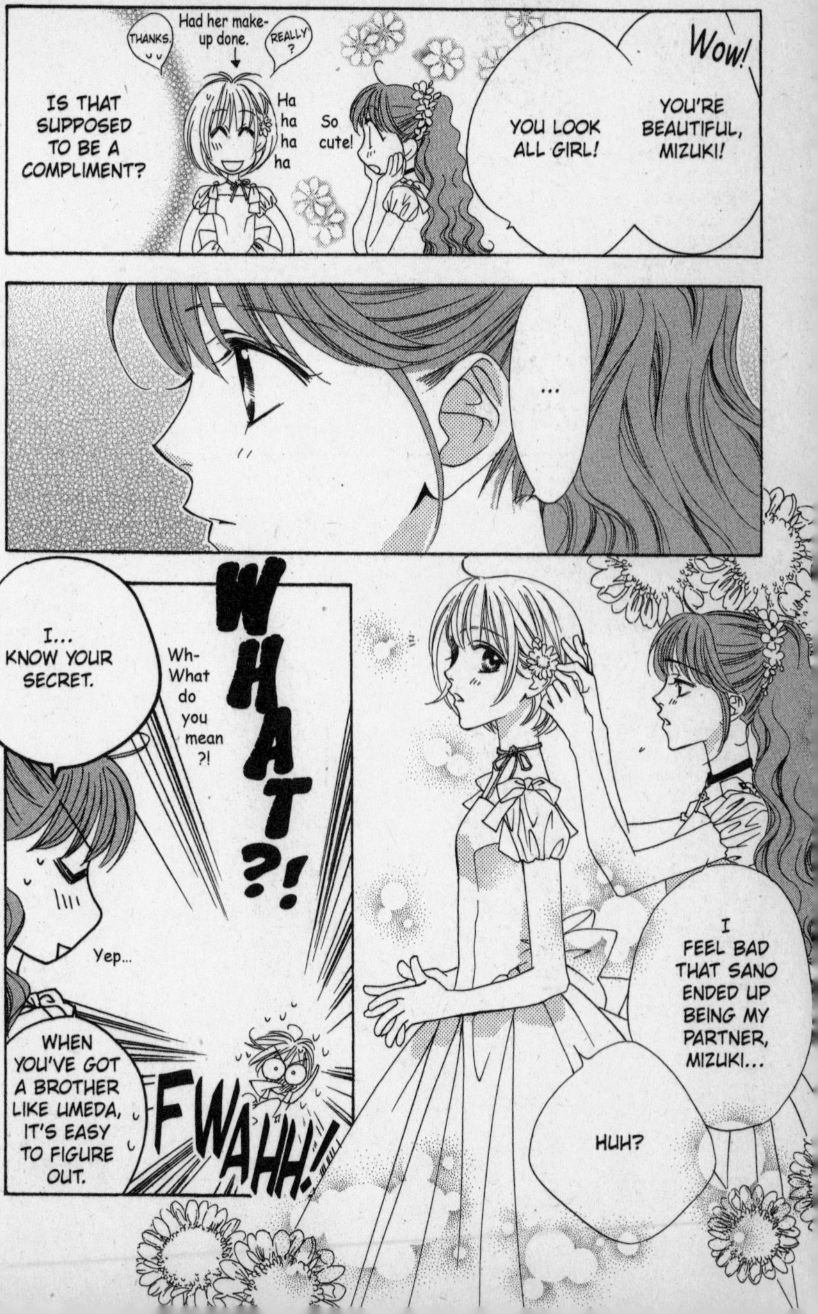
Wow!
YOU'RE BEAUTIFUL, MIZUKI!
YOU LOOK ALL GIRL!
So cute!
Ha ha ha ha
REALLY?
Had her make-up done.
THANKS.
IS THAT SUPPOSED TO BE A COMPLIMENT?
...
I FEEL BAD THAT SANO ENDED UP BEING MY PARTNER, MIZUKI...
HUH?
I... KNOW YOUR SECRET.
WHAT?!
Wh- What do you mean?!
Yep...
WHEN YOU'VE GOT A BROTHER LIKE UMEDA, IT'S EASY TO FIGURE OUT.
FWAHH!

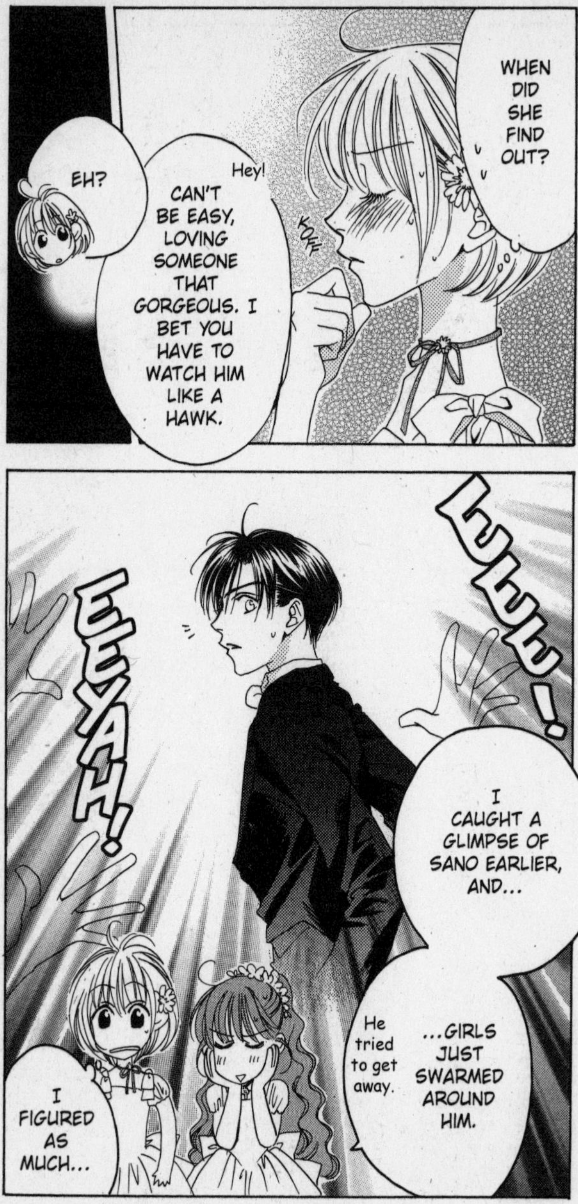
WHEN DID SHE FIND OUT?
KOFF
Hey!
CAN'T BE EASY, LOVING SOMEONE THAT GORGEOUS. I BET YOU HAVE TO WATCH HIM LIKE A HAWK.
EH?
EEEE!
I CAUGHT A GLIMPSE OF SANO EARLIER, AND...
EEYAH!
...GIRLS JUST SWARMED AROUND HIM.
He tried to get away.
I FIGURED AS MUCH...

12

HELLO THERE. [LAUGHS] IT'S HANA-KIMI BOOK 12! THE DANCE PARTY EPISODE IS ALMOST OVER. I'VE ADDED SEVERAL PAGES HERE, SINCE I WASN'T ABLE TO INCLUDE THEM IN THE ORIGINAL. (UM...THAT IS, I WAS SICK.) SORRY TO BE SUCH AN IRRESPONSIBLE MANGA ARTIST. I'VE GOTTA GET A NEW ATTITUDE. BY THE WAY, GIL IS ON THE COVER! REMEMBER HIM? SOME PEOPLE PROBABLY THOUGHT I'D PUT HIBARI ON THE COVER. [LAUGHS] DID ANYBODY GUESS IT WOULD BE GIL? THE IMAGE FLOWER IS CALLED A TOAD LILY. I THINK IT'S REALLY CUTE WHEN LOTS OF SMALL FLOWERS BLOOM, AND FORM A LITTLE BALL. I LOVE IT!

12

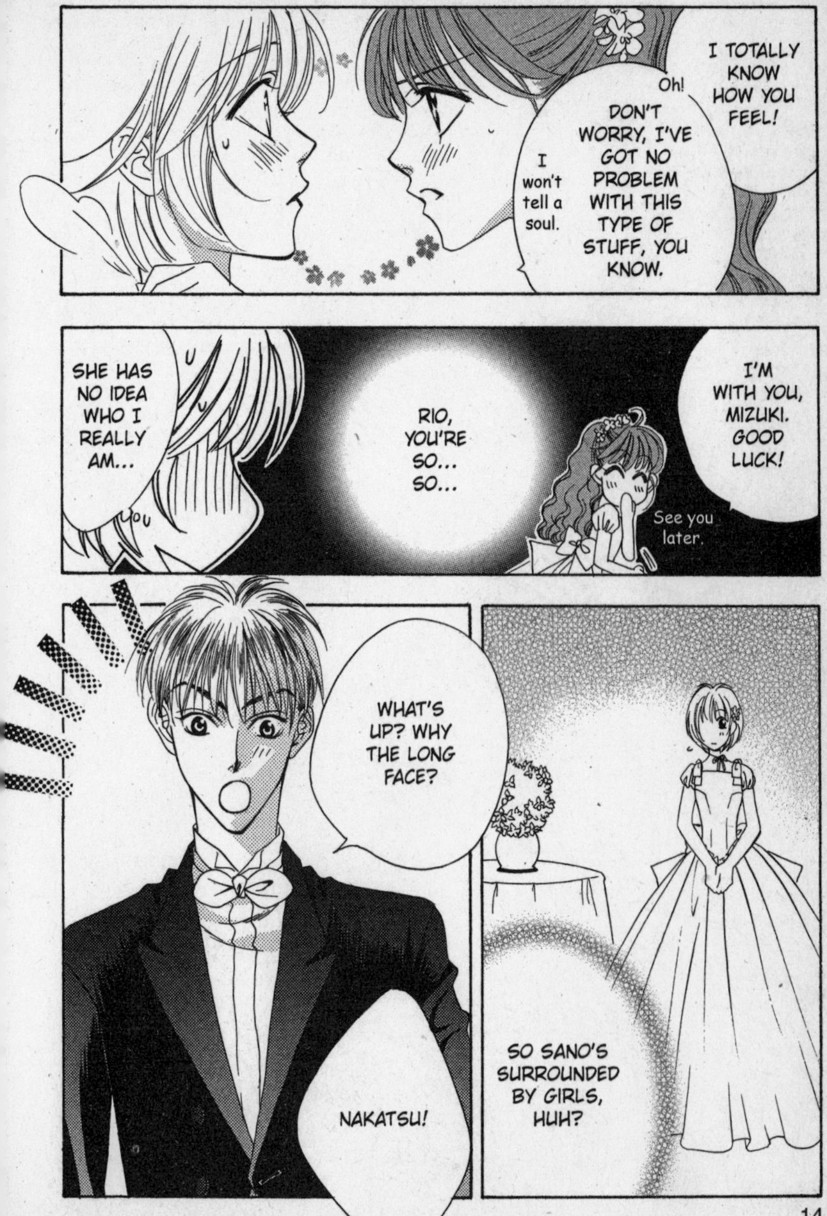
I TOTALLY KNOW HOW YOU FEEL!
Oh!
DON'T WORRY, I'VE GOT NO PROBLEM WITH THIS TYPE OF STUFF, YOU KNOW.
I won't tell a soul.
I'M WITH YOU, MIZUKI. GOOD LUCK!
See you later.
RIO, YOU'RE SO... SO...
SHE HAS NO IDEA WHO I REALLY AM...
SO SANO'S SURROUNDED BY GIRLS, HUH?
NAKATSU!
WHAT'S UP? WHY THE LONG FACE?

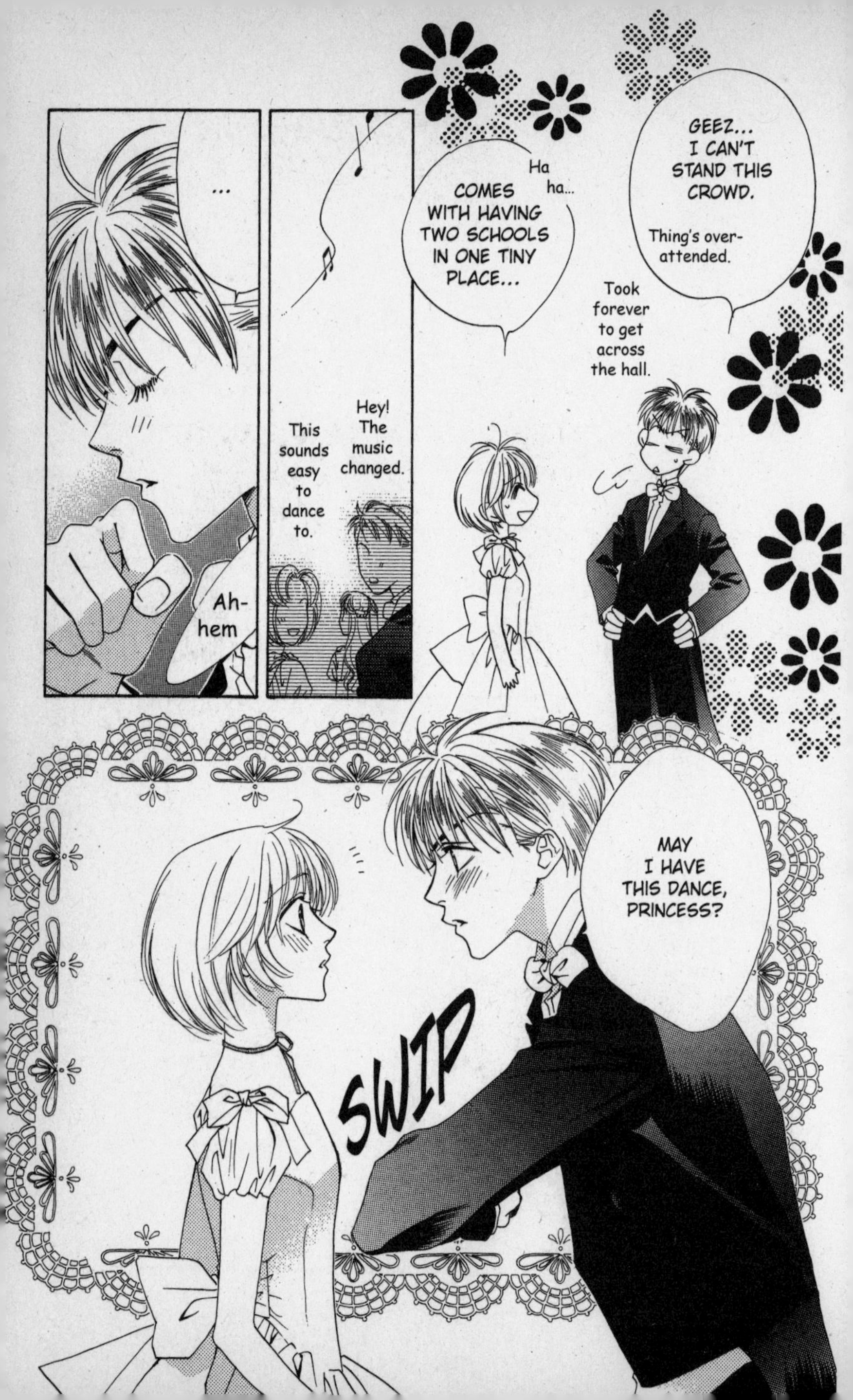
GEEZ... I CAN'T STAND THIS CROWD.
Thing's over-attended.
Took forever to get across the hall.
Ha ha...
COMES WITH HAVING TWO SCHOOLS IN ONE TINY PLACE...
Hey! The music changed.
This sounds easy to dance to.
...
Ah-hem
MAY I HAVE THIS DANCE, PRINCESS?
SWIP

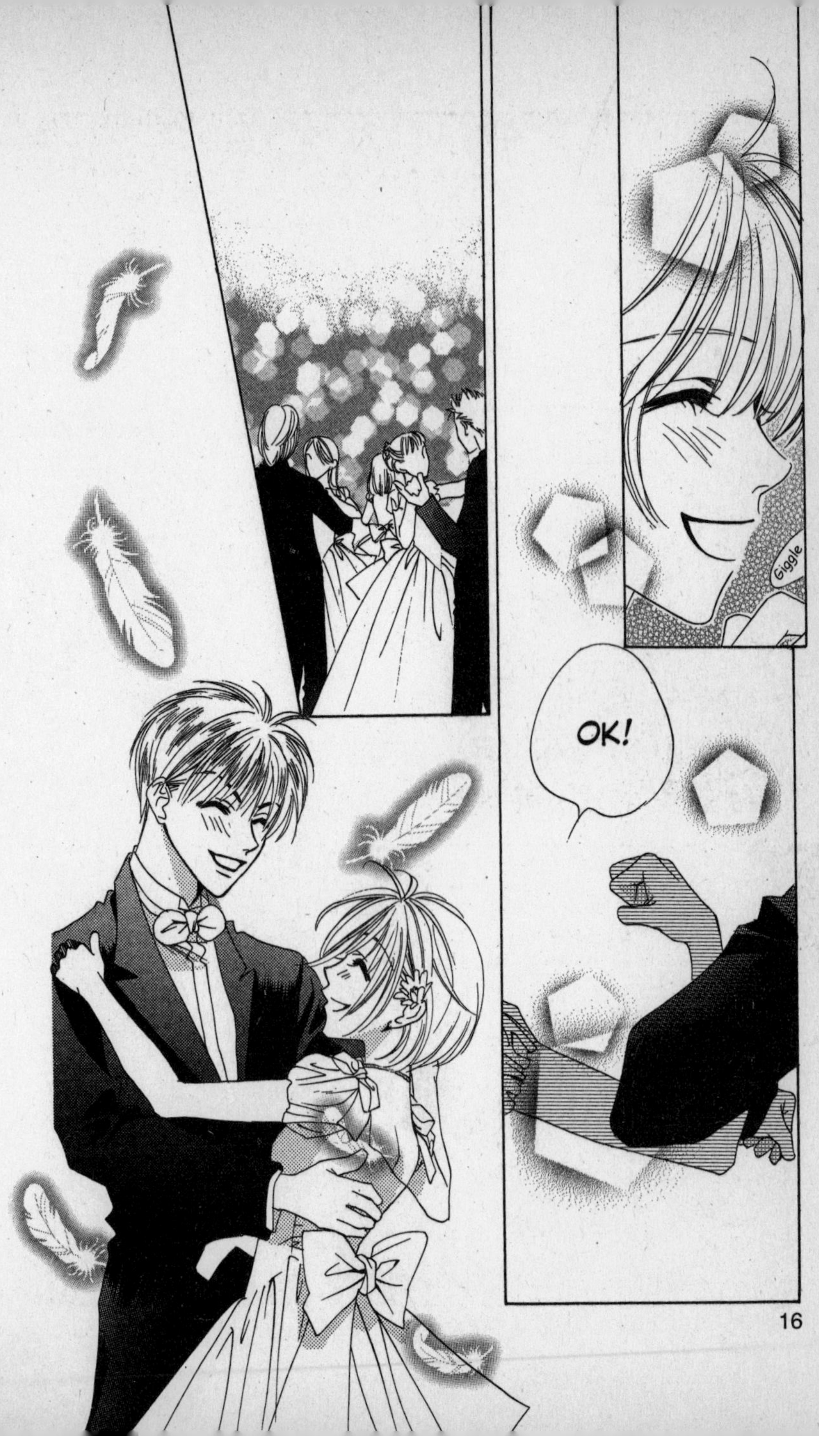
Giggle
OK!

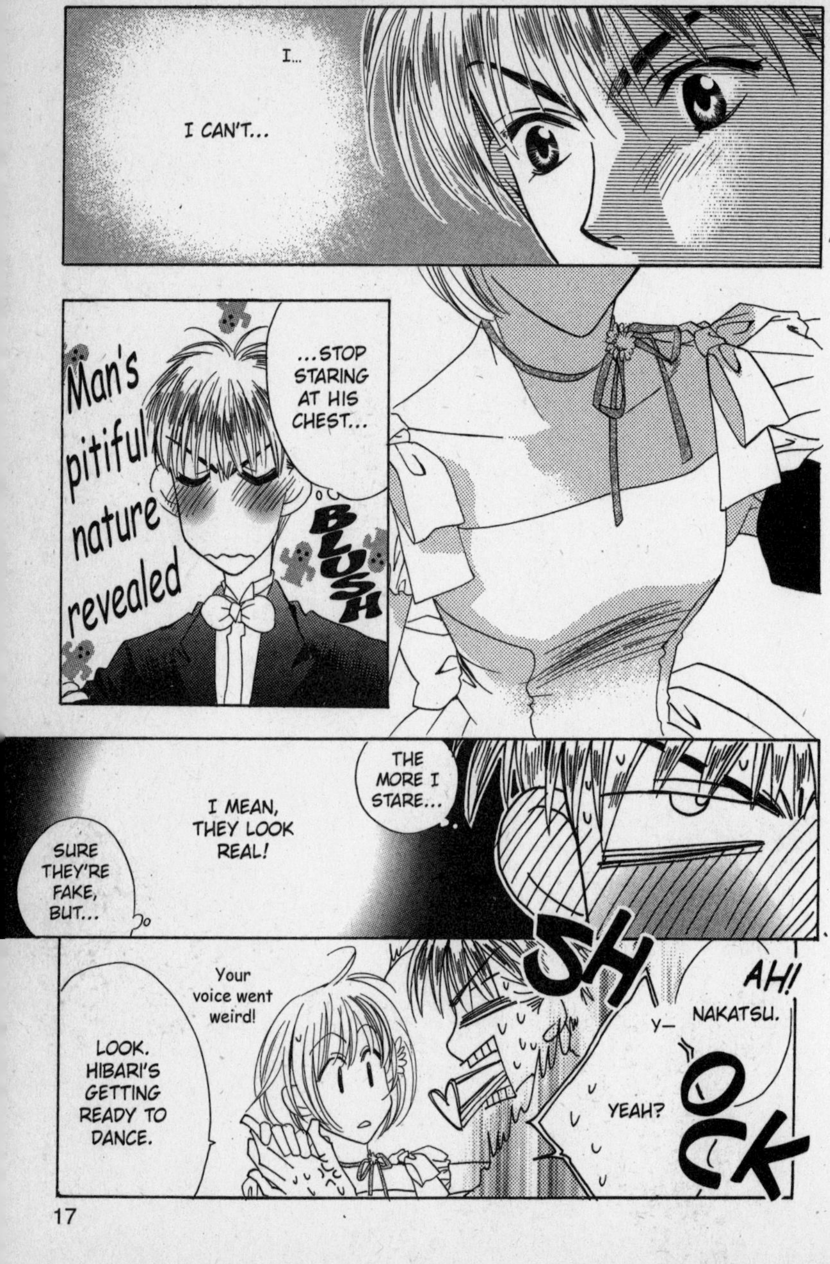
I...
I CAN'T...
...STOP STARING AT HIS CHEST...
BLUSH
Man's pitiful nature revealed
THE MORE I STARE...
I MEAN, THEY LOOK REAL!
SURE THEY'RE FAKE, BUT...
SH
OCK
AH! NAKATSU.
Y—
YEAH?
Your voice went weird!
LOOK. HIBARI'S GETTING READY TO DANCE.

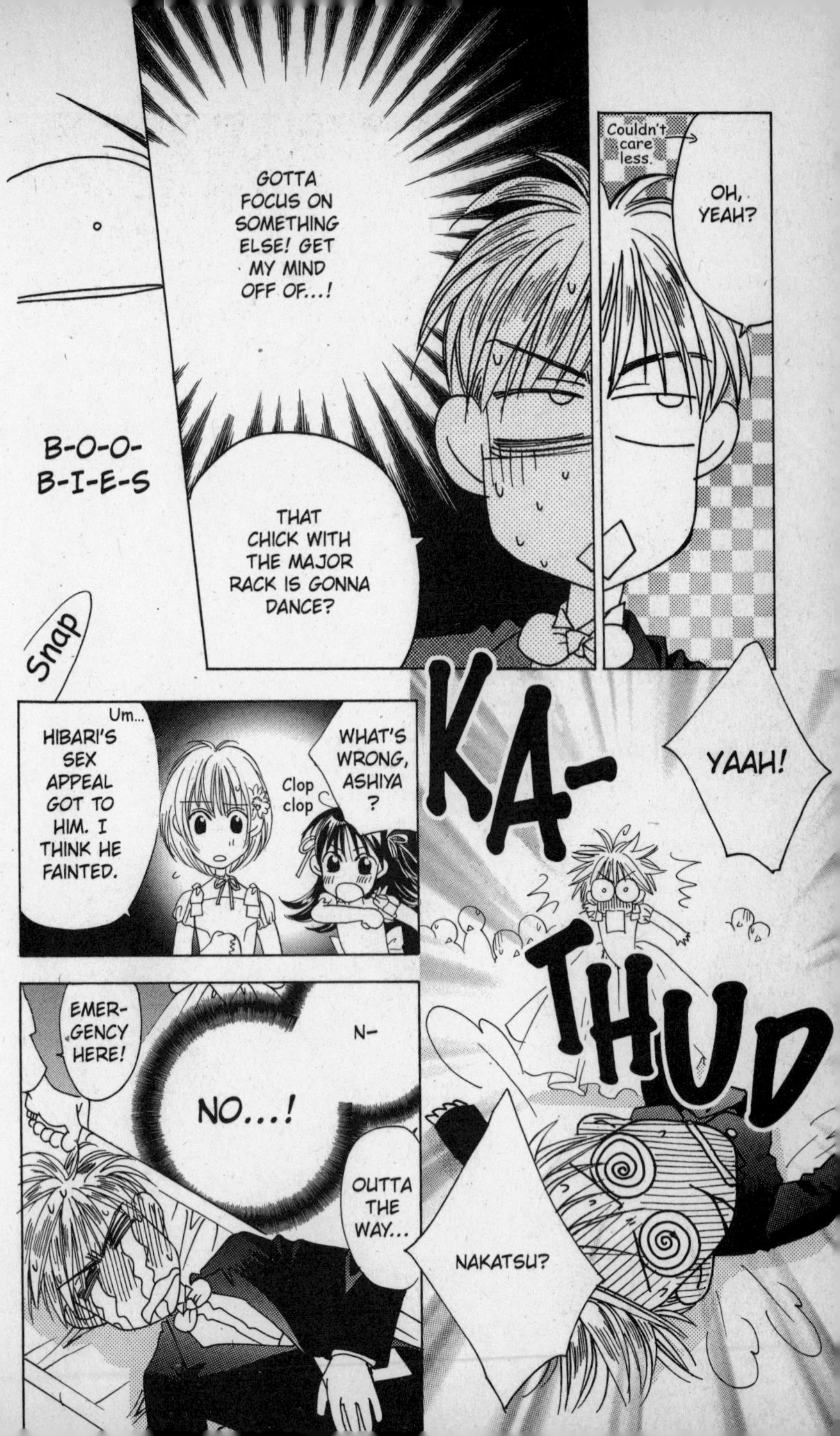
OH, YEAH?
Couldn't care less.
GOTTA FOCUS ON SOMETHING ELSE! GET MY MIND OFF OF...!
THAT CHICK WITH THE MAJOR RACK IS GONNA DANCE?
B-O-O-B-I-E-S
Snap
YAAH!
KA-THUD
WHAT'S WRONG, ASHIYA?
Clop clop
Um... HIBARI'S SEX APPEAL GOT TO HIM. I THINK HE FAINTED.
NAKATSU?
OUTTA THE WAY...
N-
NO...!
EMER-GENCY HERE!

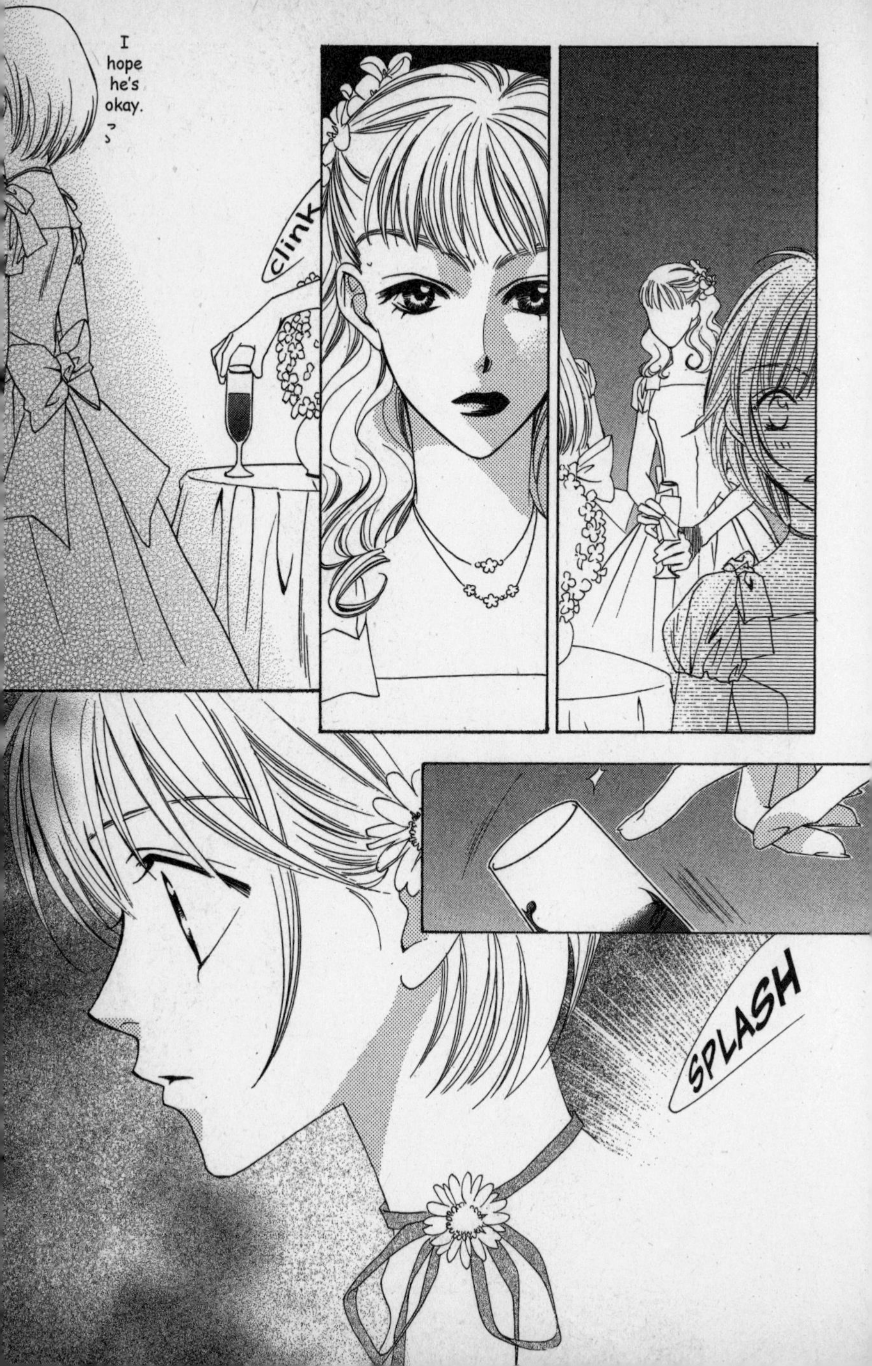
clink
I hope he's okay.
SPLASH

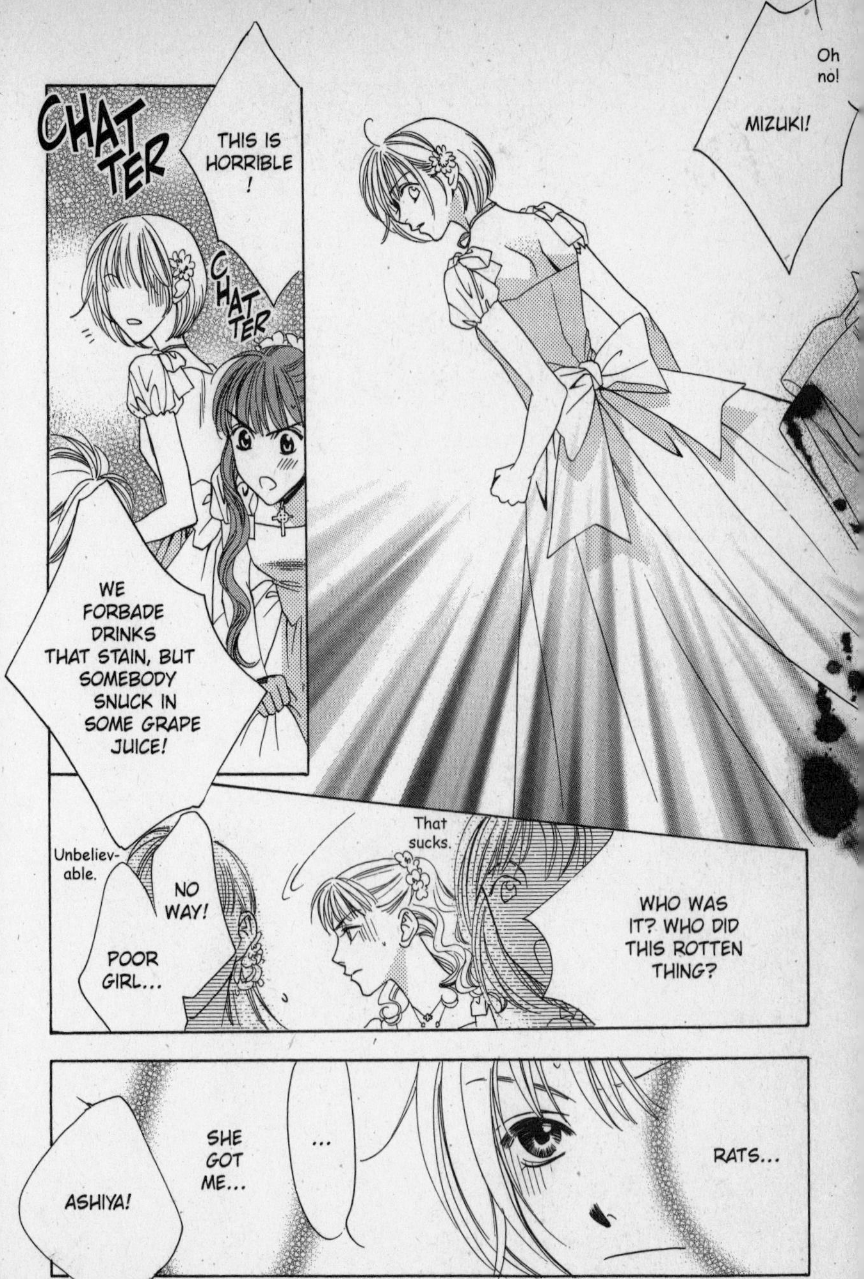
Oh no!
MIZUKI!
CHATTER
THIS IS HORRIBLE!
CHATTER
WE FORBADE DRINKS THAT STAIN, BUT SOMEBODY SNUCK IN SOME GRAPE JUICE!
WHO WAS IT? WHO DID THIS ROTTEN THING?
That sucks.
NO WAY!
Unbelievable.
POOR GIRL...
RATS...
...
SHE GOT ME...
ASHIYA!

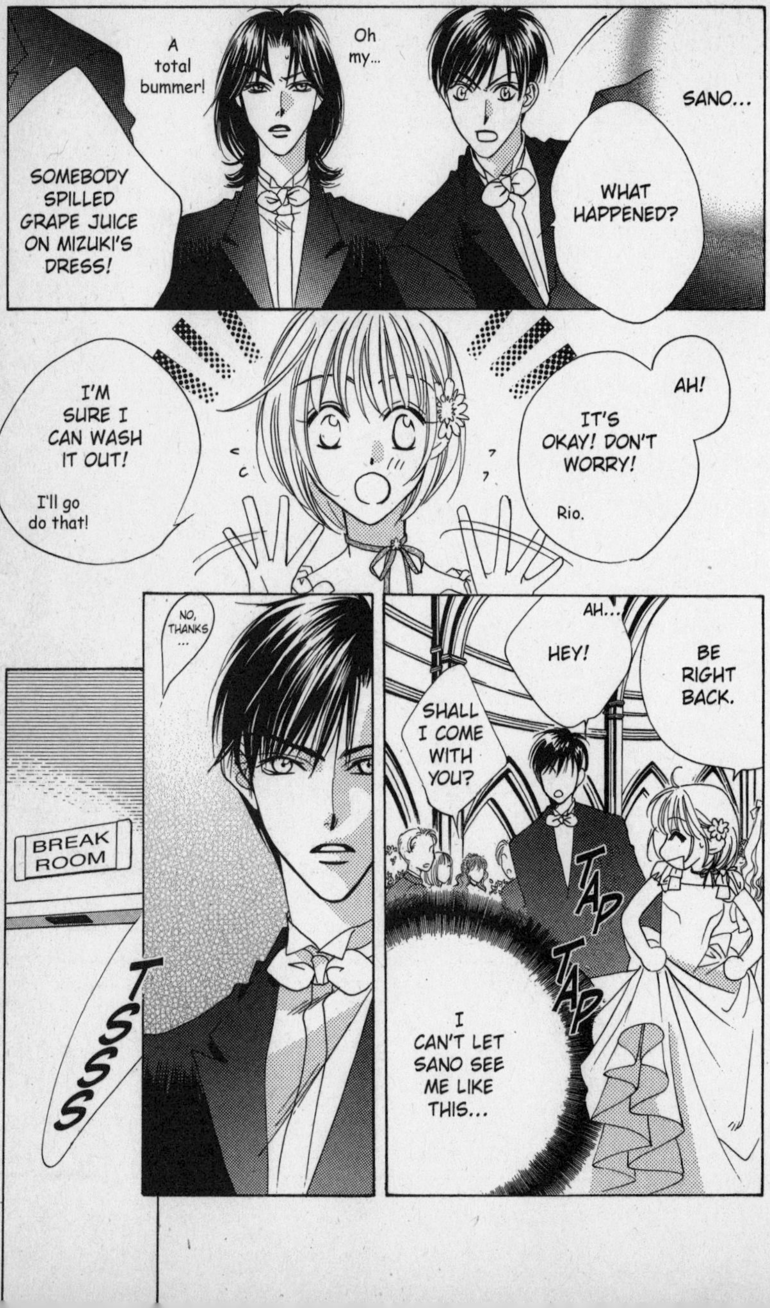
SANO...
WHAT HAPPENED?
Oh my...
A total bummer!
SOMEBODY SPILLED GRAPE JUICE ON MIZUKI'S DRESS!
AH!
IT'S OKAY! DON'T WORRY!
Rio.
I'M SURE I CAN WASH IT OUT!
I'll go do that!
BE RIGHT BACK.
AH...
HEY!
SHALL I COME WITH YOU?
TAP TAP
I CAN'T LET SANO SEE ME LIKE THIS...
NO, THANKS...
BREAK ROOM
TSSS

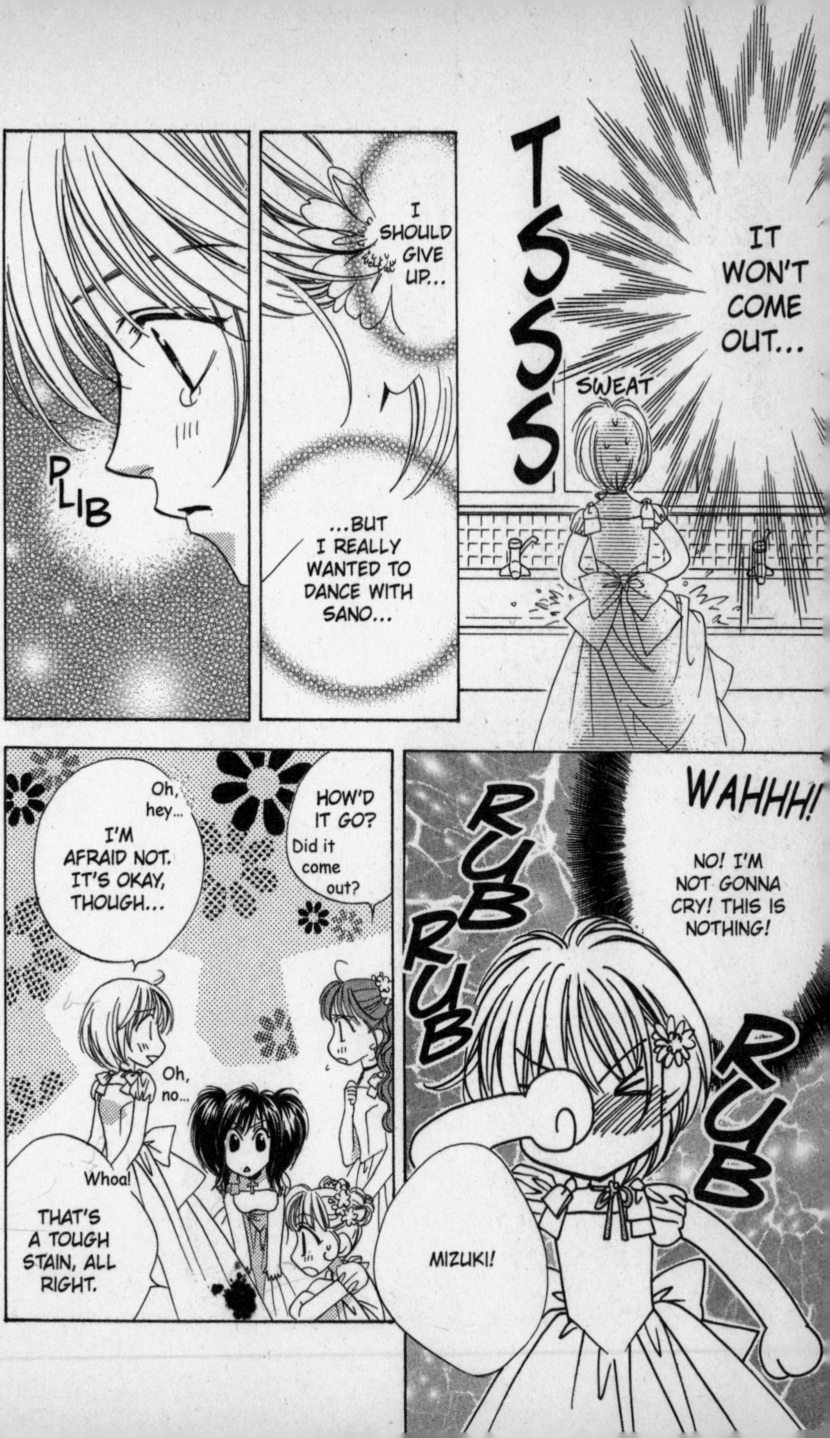
IT WON'T COME OUT...
TSSS
SWEAT
I SHOULD GIVE UP...
...BUT I REALLY WANTED TO DANCE WITH SANO...
PLIB
WAHHH!
NO! I'M NOT GONNA CRY! THIS IS NOTHING!
RUB RUB RUB RUB
MIZUKI!
HOW'D IT GO? Did it come out?
Oh, hey... I'M AFRAID NOT. IT'S OKAY, THOUGH...
Oh, no...
Whoa!
THAT'S A TOUGH STAIN, ALL RIGHT.

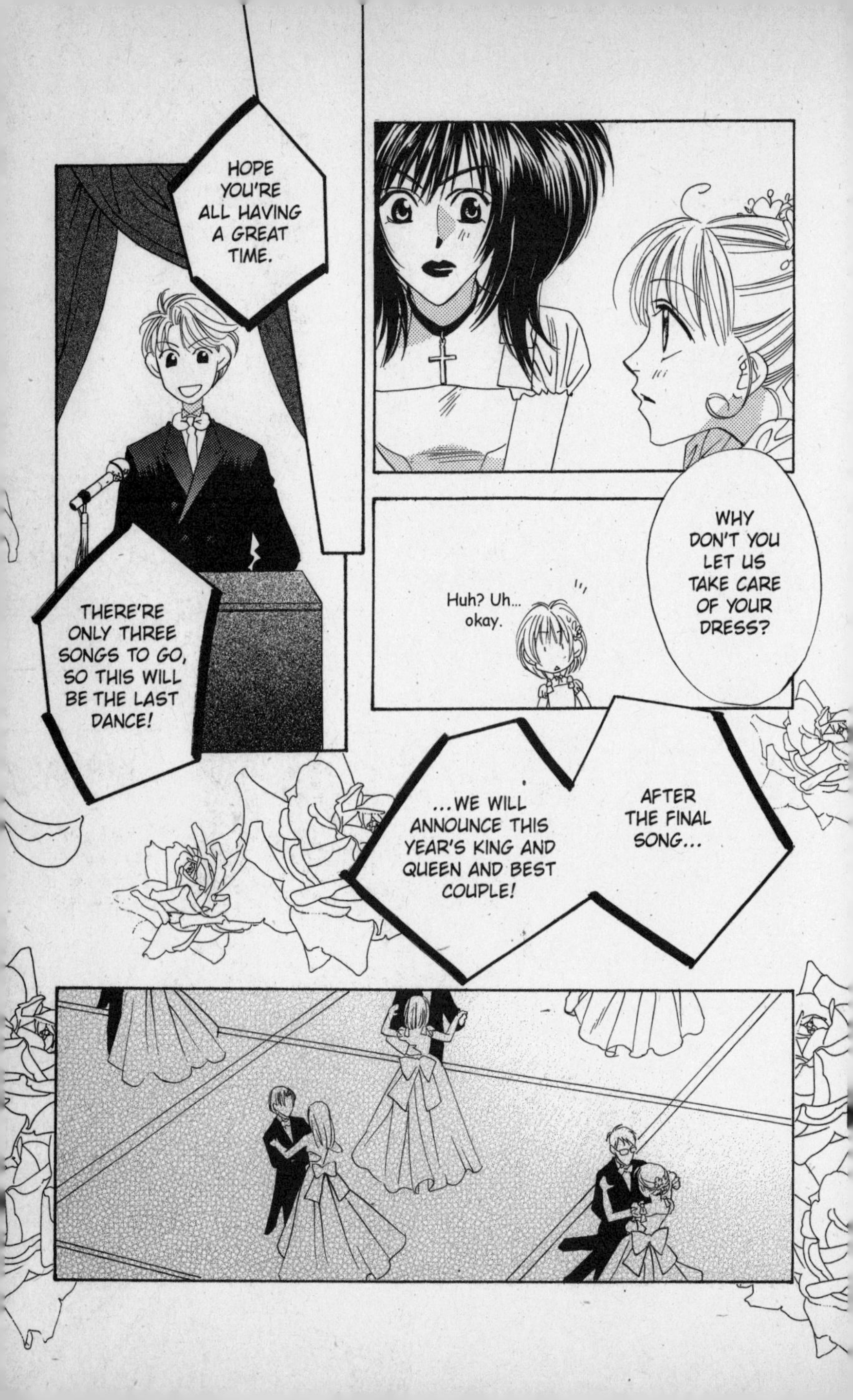
WHY DON'T YOU LET US TAKE CARE OF YOUR DRESS?
Huh? Uh... okay.
HOPE YOU'RE ALL HAVING A GREAT TIME.
THERE'RE ONLY THREE SONGS TO GO, SO THIS WILL BE THE LAST DANCE!
AFTER THE FINAL SONG...
...WE WILL ANNOUNCE THIS YEAR'S KING AND QUEEN AND BEST COUPLE!

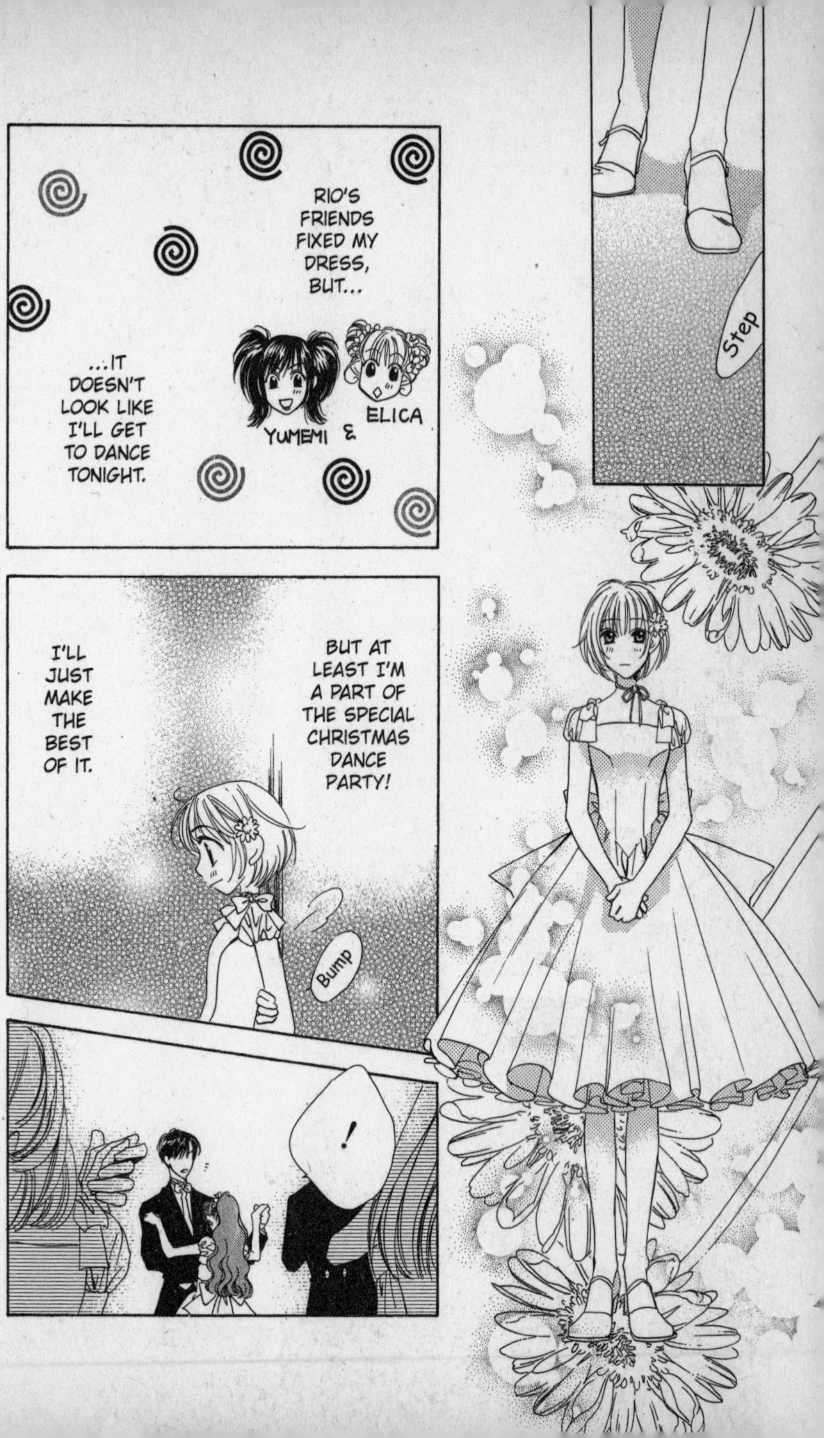
Step
RIO'S FRIENDS FIXED MY DRESS, BUT...
YUMEMI & ELICA
...IT DOESN'T LOOK LIKE I'LL GET TO DANCE TONIGHT.
BUT AT LEAST I'M A PART OF THE SPECIAL CHRISTMAS DANCE PARTY!
I'LL JUST MAKE THE BEST OF IT.
Bump
!

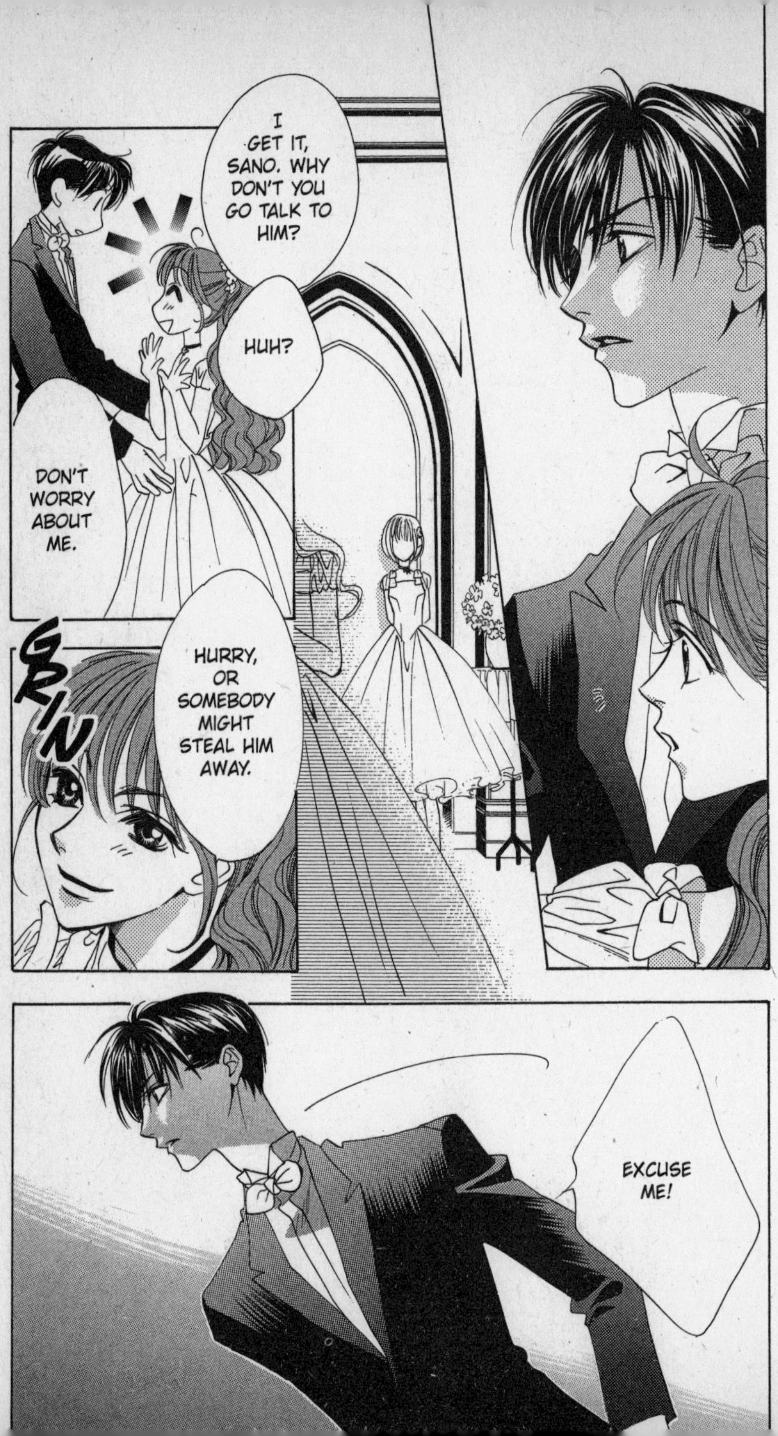
I GET IT, SANO. WHY DON'T YOU GO TALK TO HIM?
HUH?
DON'T WORRY ABOUT ME.
HURRY, OR SOMEBODY MIGHT STEAL HIM AWAY.
GRIN
EXCUSE ME!

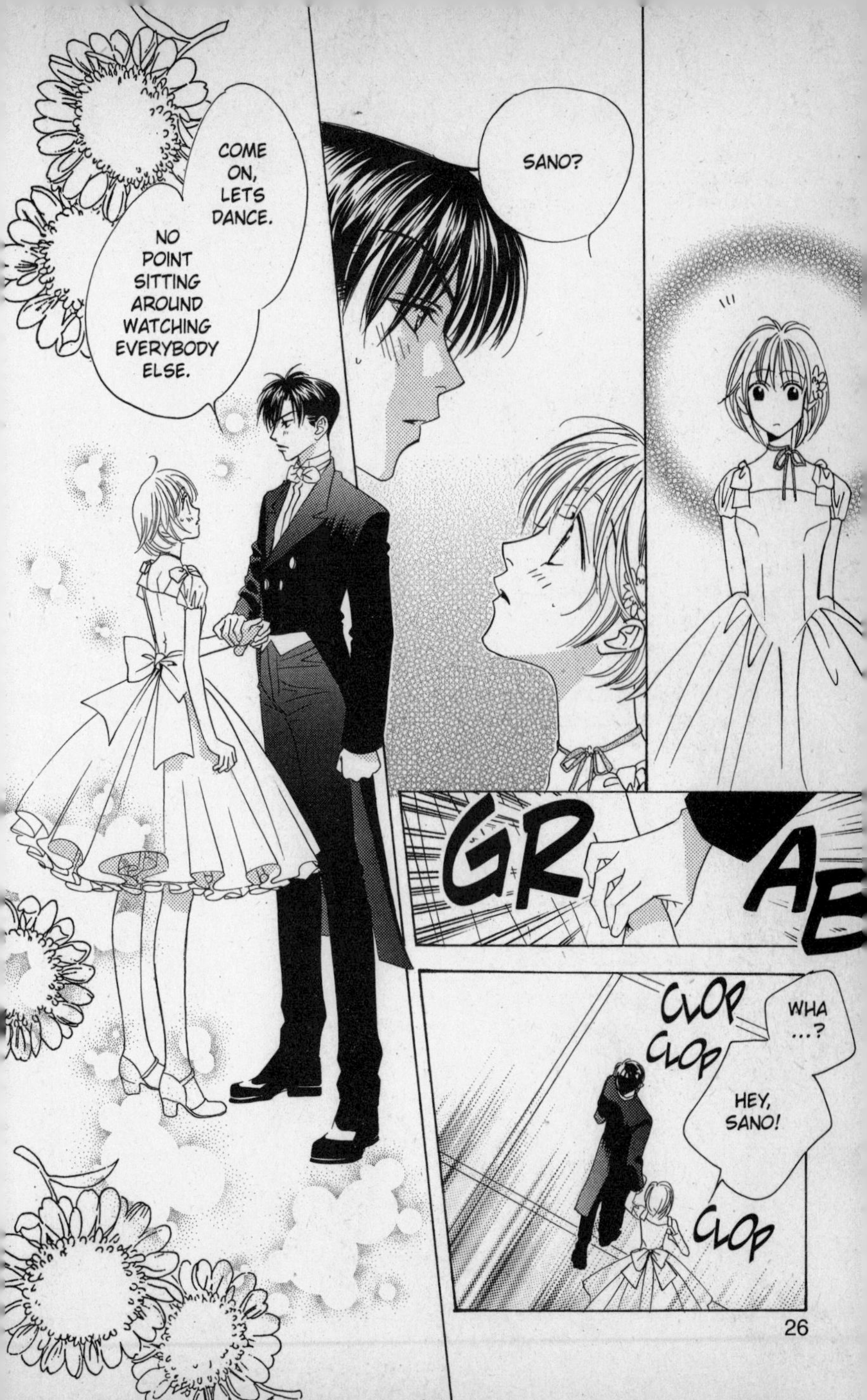
SANO?
GR AB
WHA ...?
CLOP CLOP
HEY, SANO!
CLOP
COME ON, LETS DANCE.
NO POINT SITTING AROUND WATCHING EVERYBODY ELSE.

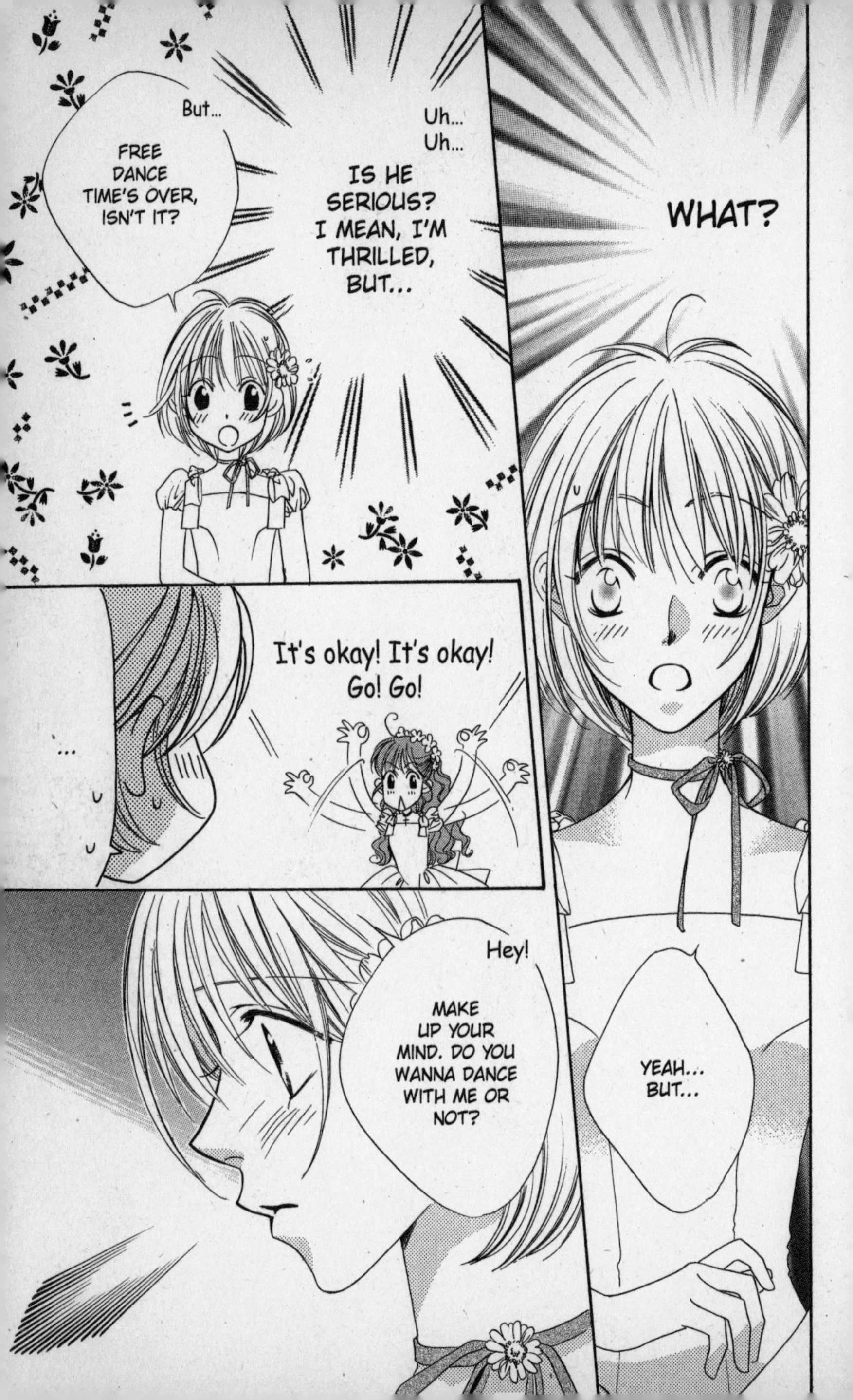
WHAT?
YEAH... BUT...
Uh... Uh...
IS HE SERIOUS? I MEAN, I'M THRILLED, BUT...
But...
FREE DANCE TIME'S OVER, ISN'T IT?
It's okay! It's okay! Go! Go!
...
Hey!
MAKE UP YOUR MIND. DO YOU WANNA DANCE WITH ME OR NOT?

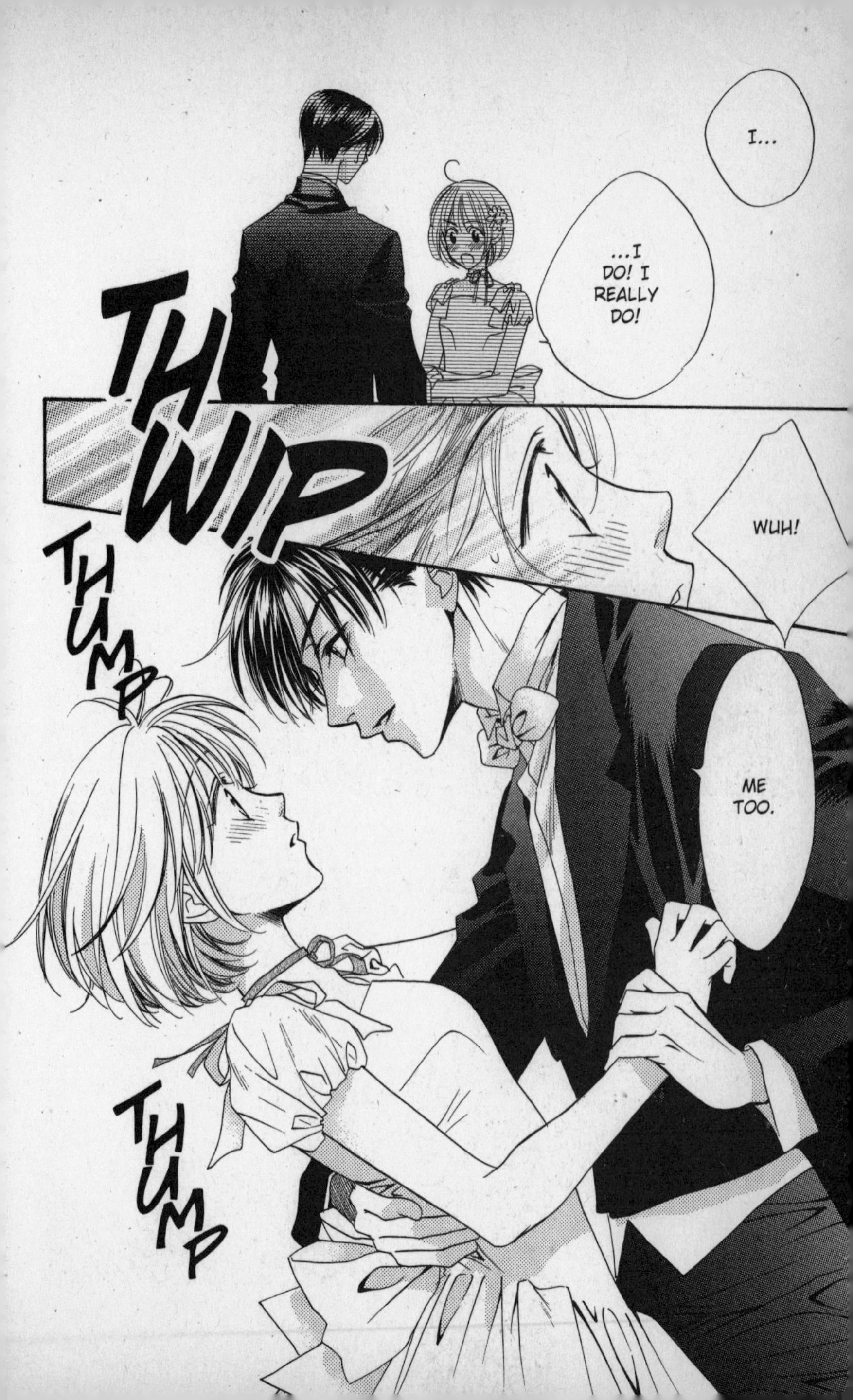
I...
...I DO! I REALLY DO!
THWIP
WUH!
ME TOO.
THUMP
THUMP

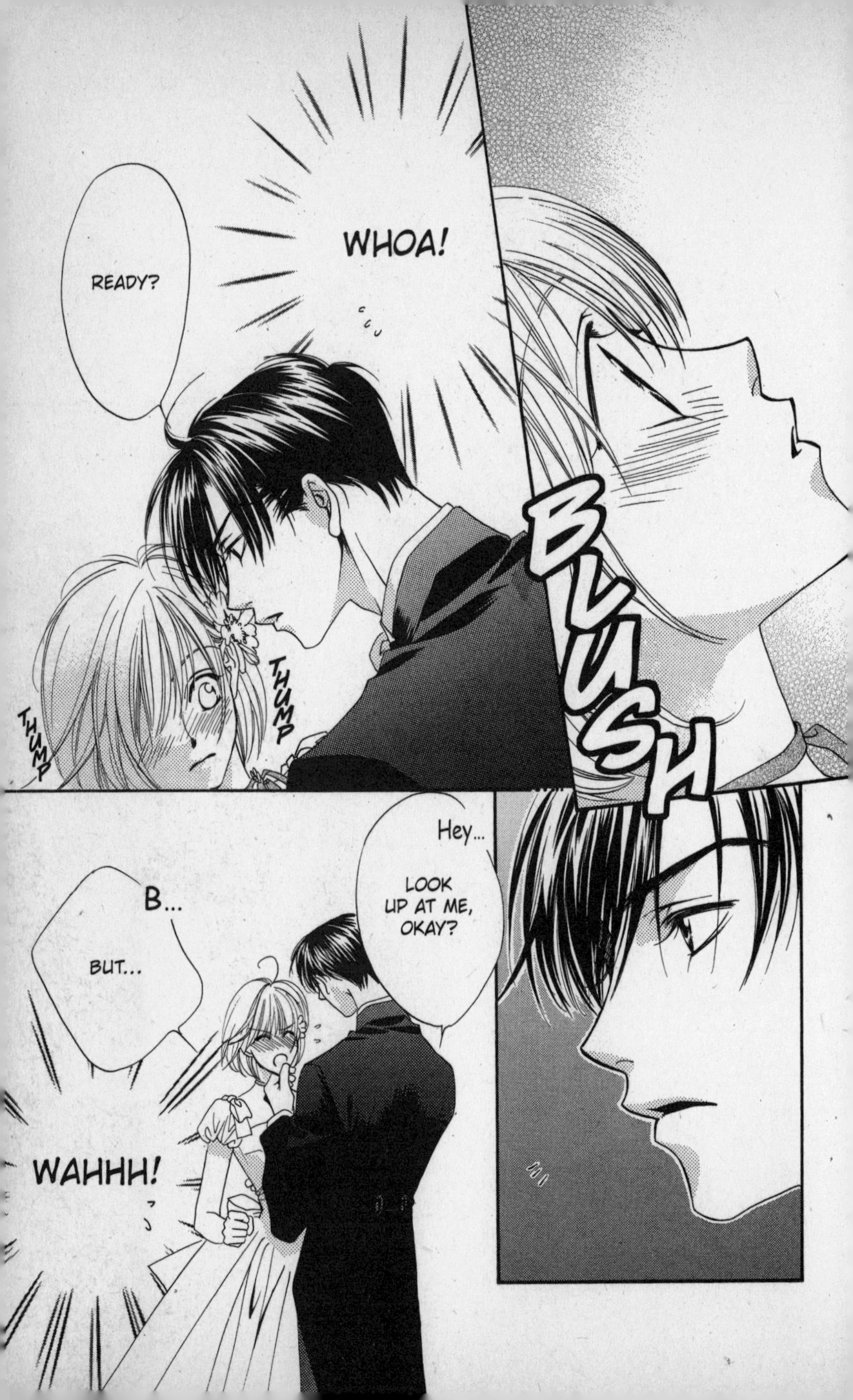
BLUSH
READY?
WHOA!
THUMP
THUMP
Hey...
LOOK UP AT ME, OKAY?
B... BUT...
WAHHH!

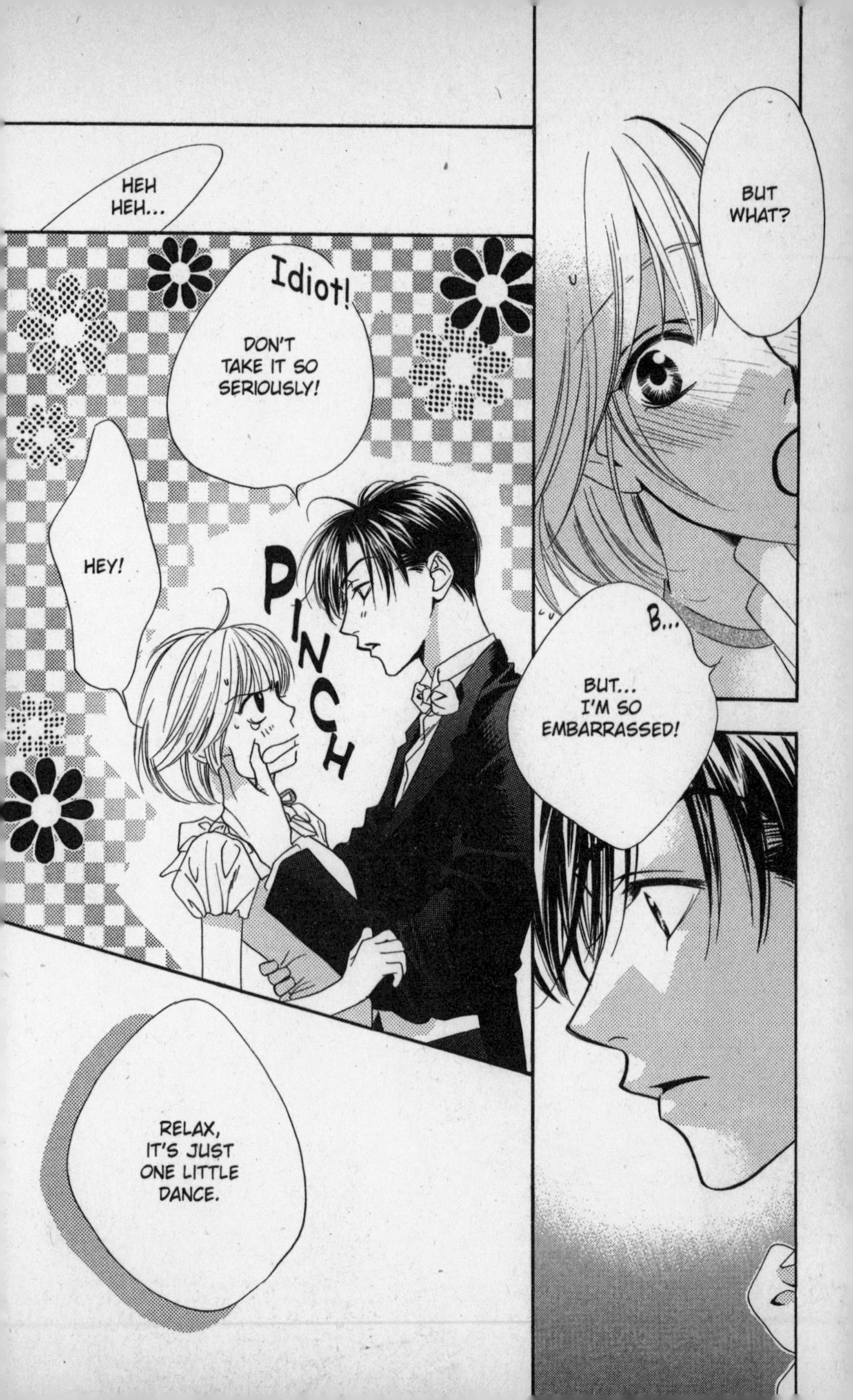
BUT WHAT?
B...
BUT... I'M SO EMBARRASSED!
HEH HEH...
Idiot!
DON'T TAKE IT SO SERIOUSLY!
HEY!
PINCH
RELAX, IT'S JUST ONE LITTLE DANCE.

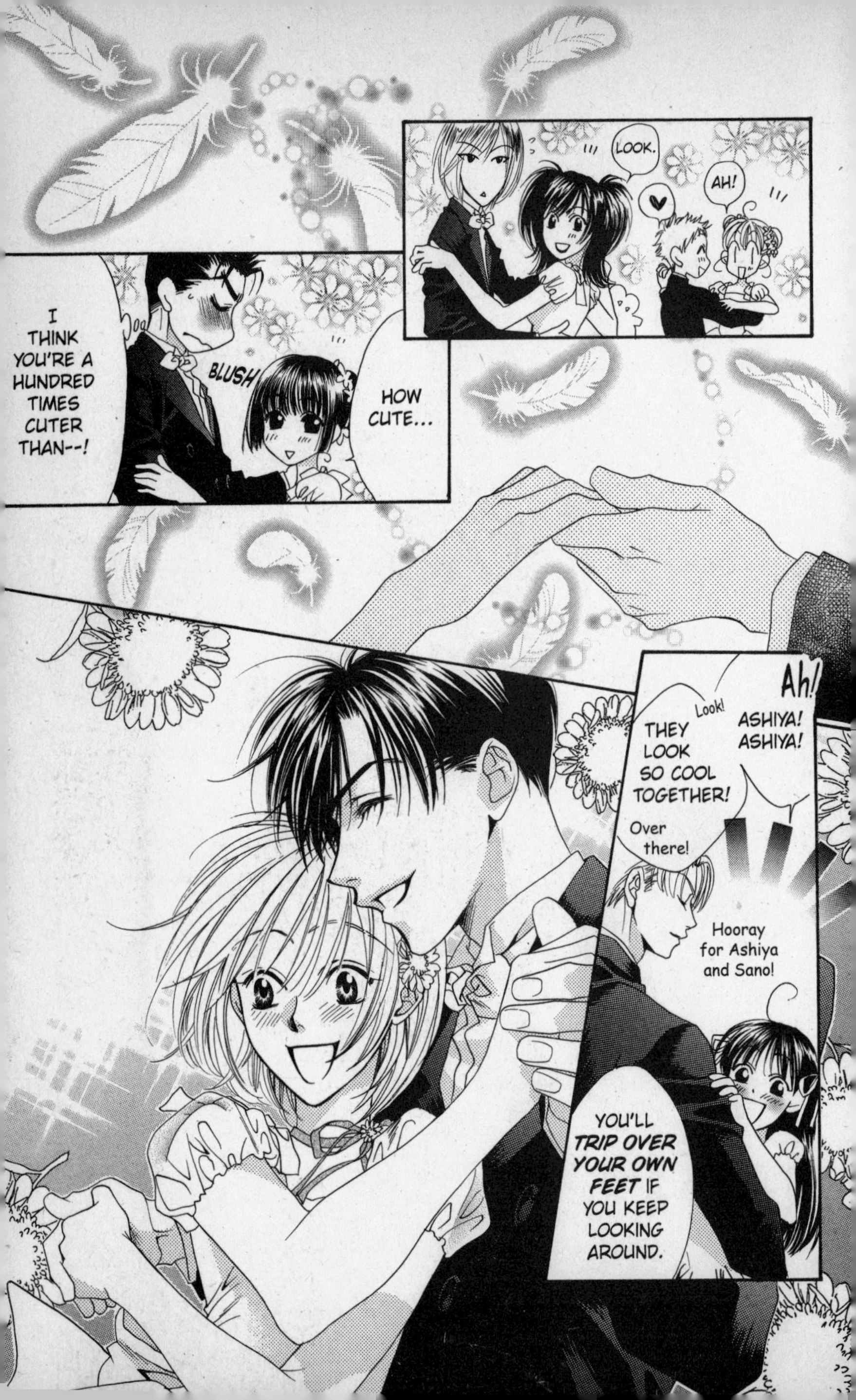
LOOK.
AH!
HOW CUTE...
BLUSH
I THINK YOU'RE A HUNDRED TIMES CUTER THAN--!
Ah!
ASHIYA! ASHIYA!
Look!
THEY LOOK SO COOL TOGETHER!
Over there!
Hooray for Ashiya and Sano!
YOU'LL TRIP OVER YOUR OWN FEET IF YOU KEEP LOOKING AROUND.

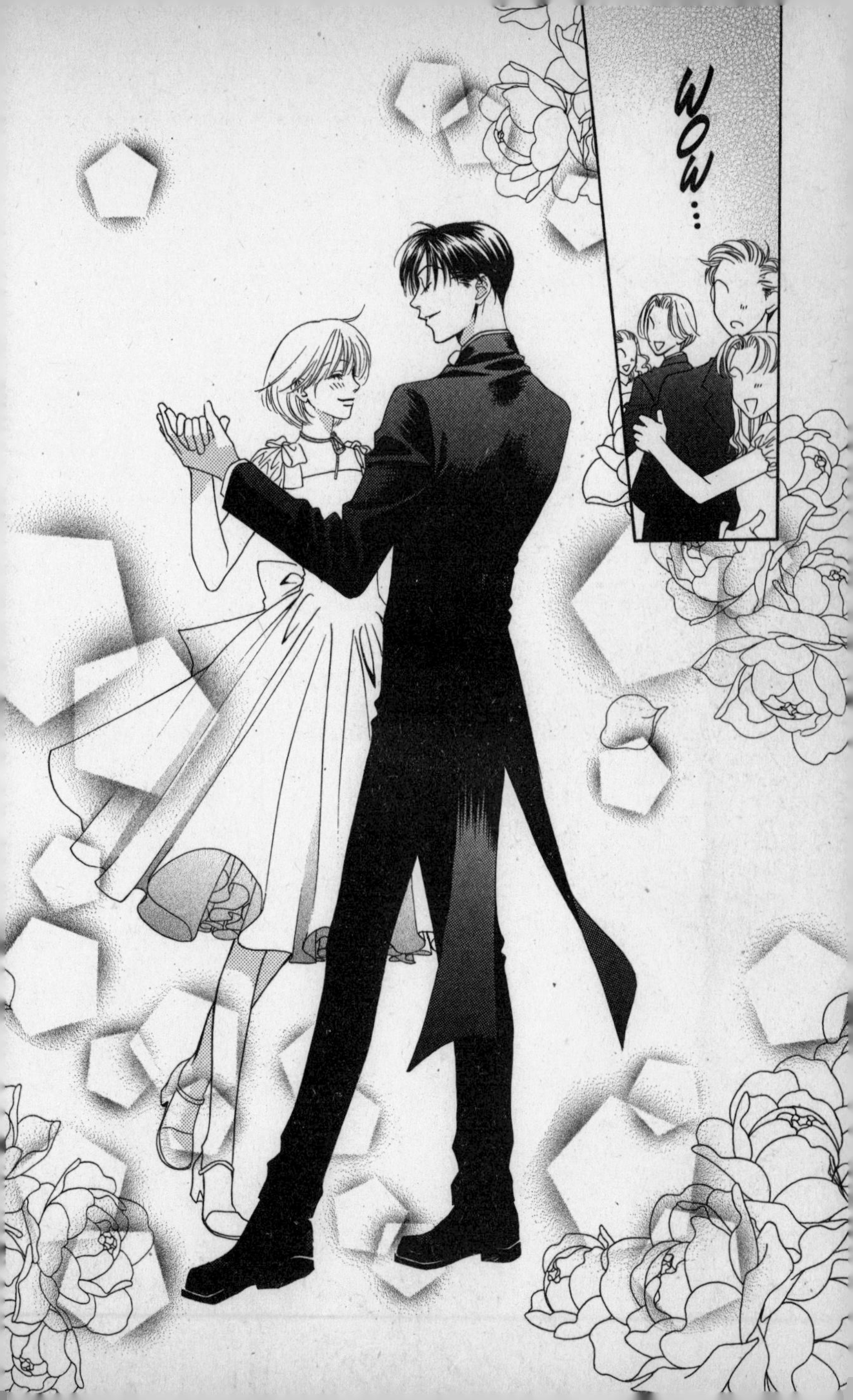
WOW...

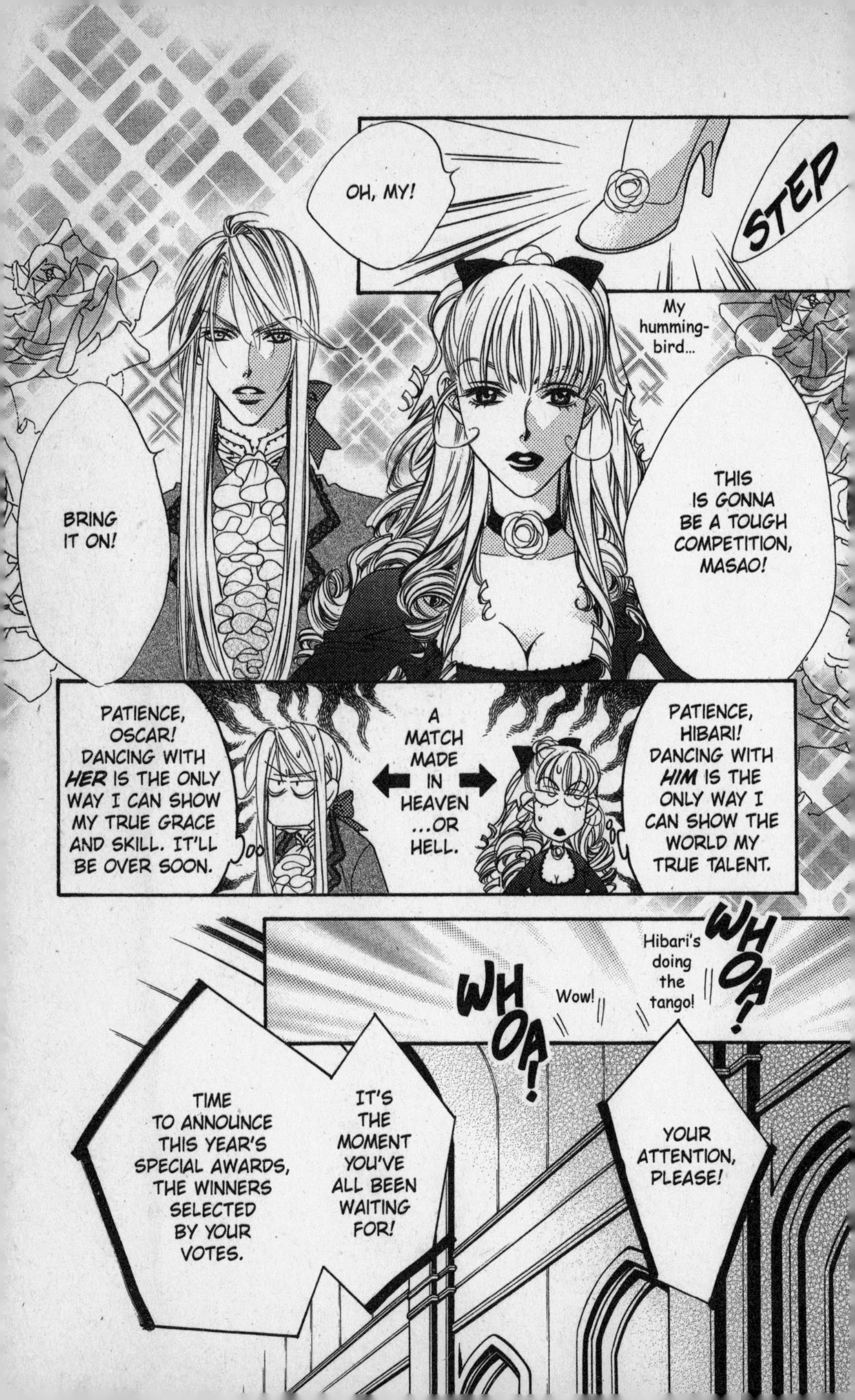
STEP
OH, MY!
My humming-bird...
THIS IS GONNA BE A TOUGH COMPETITION, MASAO!
BRING IT ON!
PATIENCE, HIBARI! DANCING WITH HIM IS THE ONLY WAY I CAN SHOW THE WORLD MY TRUE TALENT.
A MATCH MADE IN HEAVEN ...OR HELL.
PATIENCE, OSCAR! DANCING WITH HER IS THE ONLY WAY I CAN SHOW MY TRUE GRACE AND SKILL. IT'LL BE OVER SOON.
WHOA!
Hibari's doing the tango!
Wow!
WHOA!
YOUR ATTENTION, PLEASE!
IT'S THE MOMENT YOU'VE ALL BEEN WAITING FOR!
TIME TO ANNOUNCE THIS YEAR'S SPECIAL AWARDS, THE WINNERS SELECTED BY YOUR VOTES.

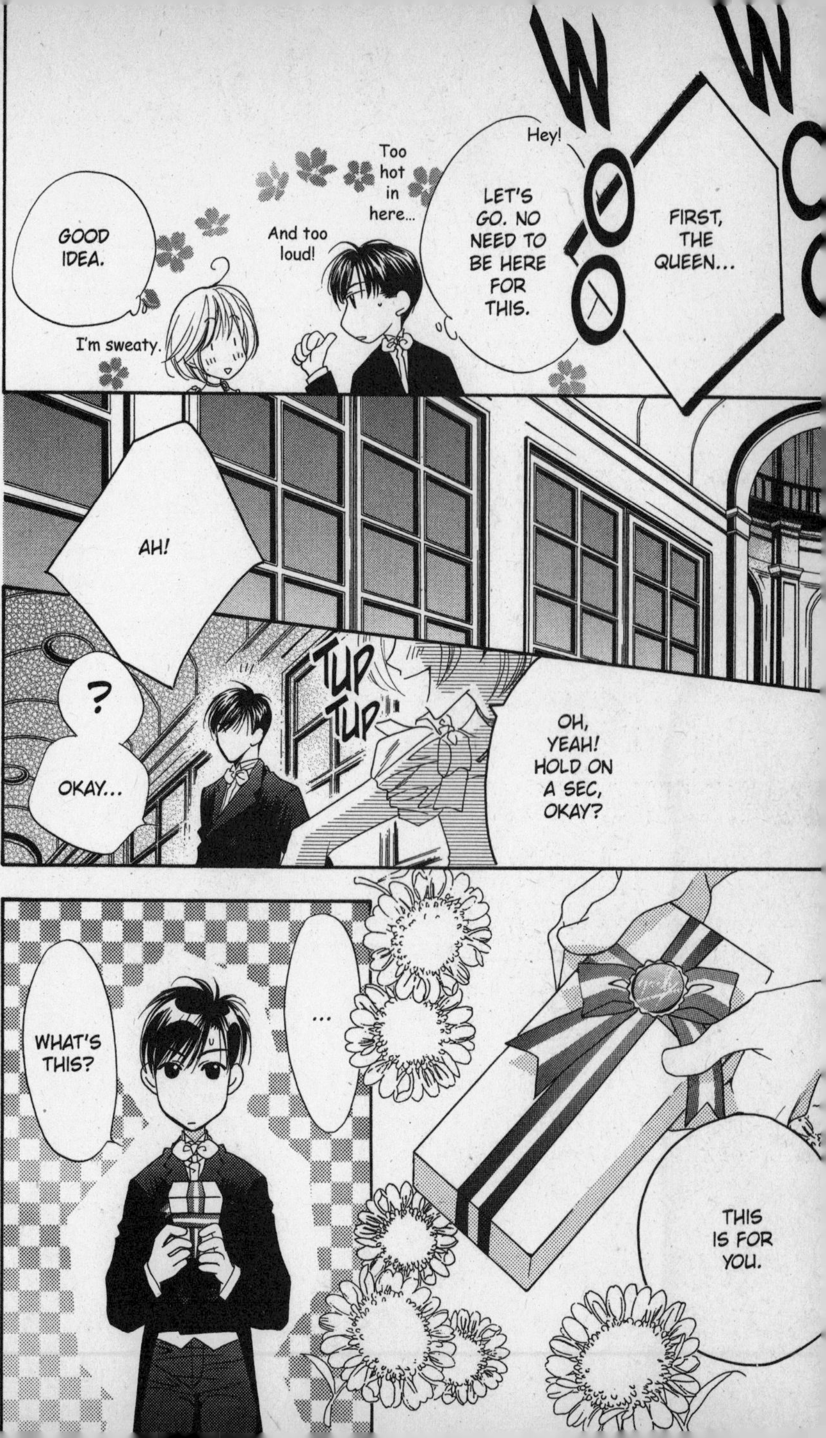
WOOOO
FIRST, THE QUEEN...
Hey!
LET'S GO. NO NEED TO BE HERE FOR THIS.
Too hot in here...
And too loud!
GOOD IDEA.
I'm sweaty.
AH!
OH, YEAH! HOLD ON A SEC, OKAY?
TUP TUP
?
OKAY...
THIS IS FOR YOU.
...
WHAT'S THIS?

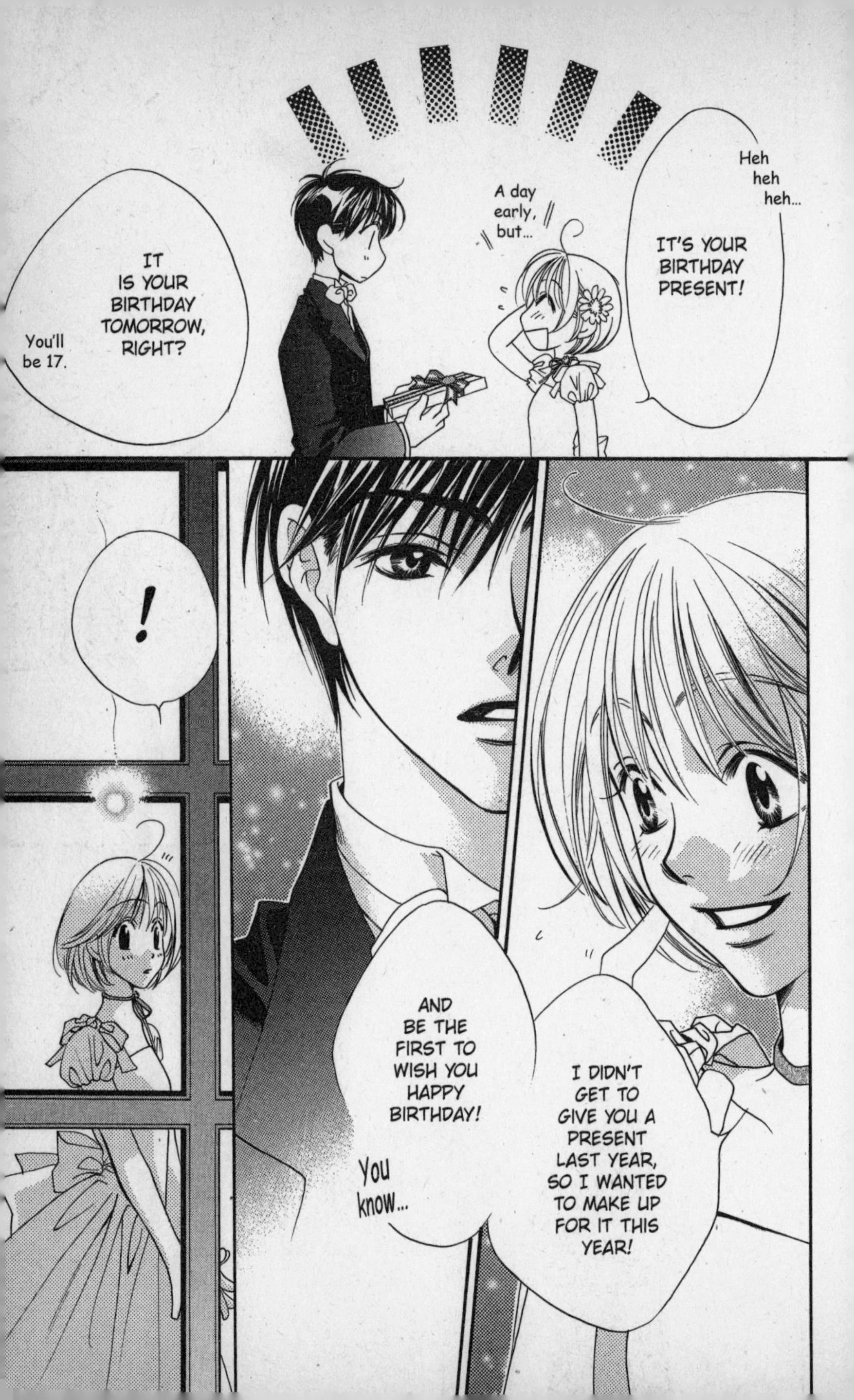
Heh heh heh...
IT'S YOUR BIRTHDAY PRESENT!
A day early, but...
IT IS YOUR BIRTHDAY TOMORROW, RIGHT?
You'll be 17.
I DIDN'T GET TO GIVE YOU A PRESENT LAST YEAR, SO I WANTED TO MAKE UP FOR IT THIS YEAR!
You know...
AND BE THE FIRST TO WISH YOU HAPPY BIRTHDAY!
!

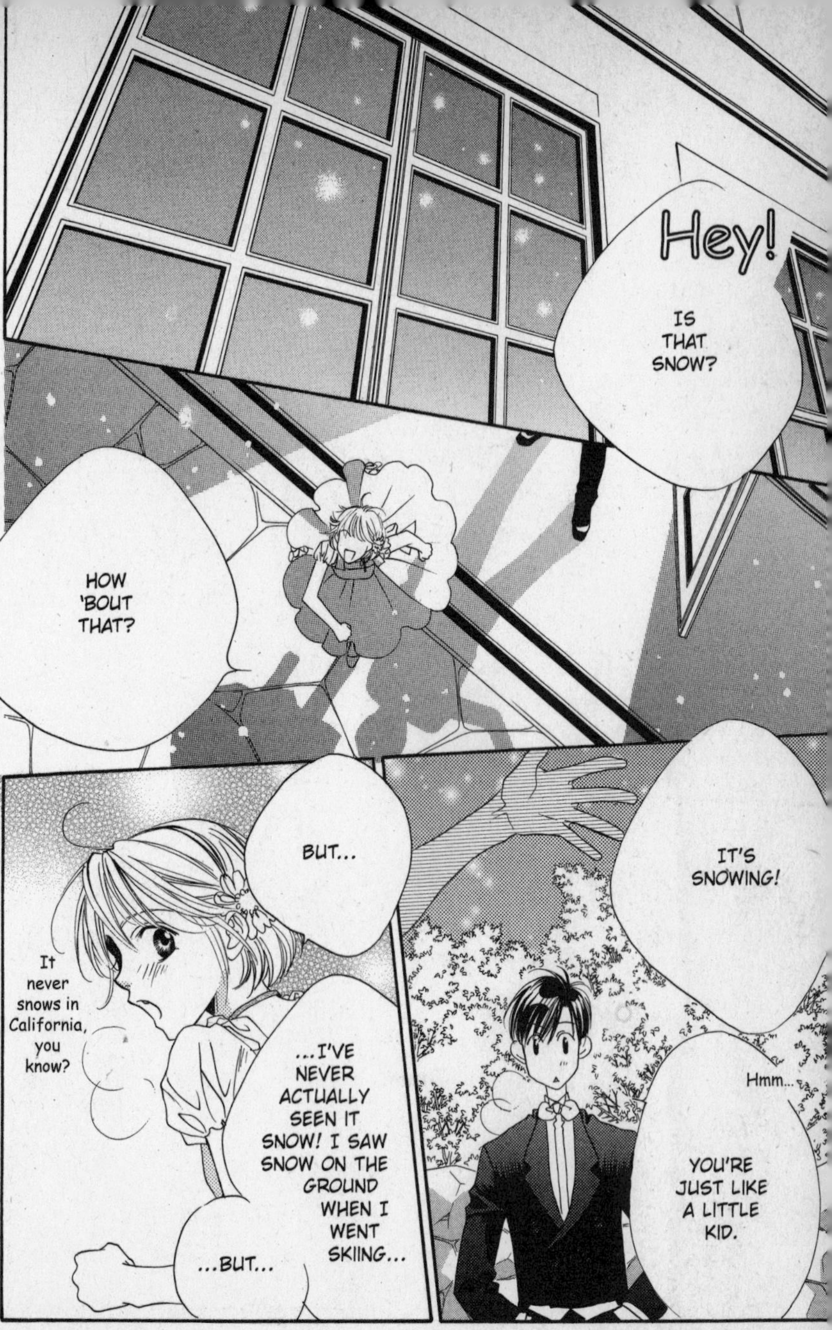
Hey!
IS THAT SNOW?
HOW 'BOUT THAT?
IT'S SNOWING!
Hmm...
YOU'RE JUST LIKE A LITTLE KID.
BUT...
It never snows in California, you know?
...I'VE NEVER ACTUALLY SEEN IT SNOW! I SAW SNOW ON THE GROUND WHEN I WENT SKIING...
...BUT...

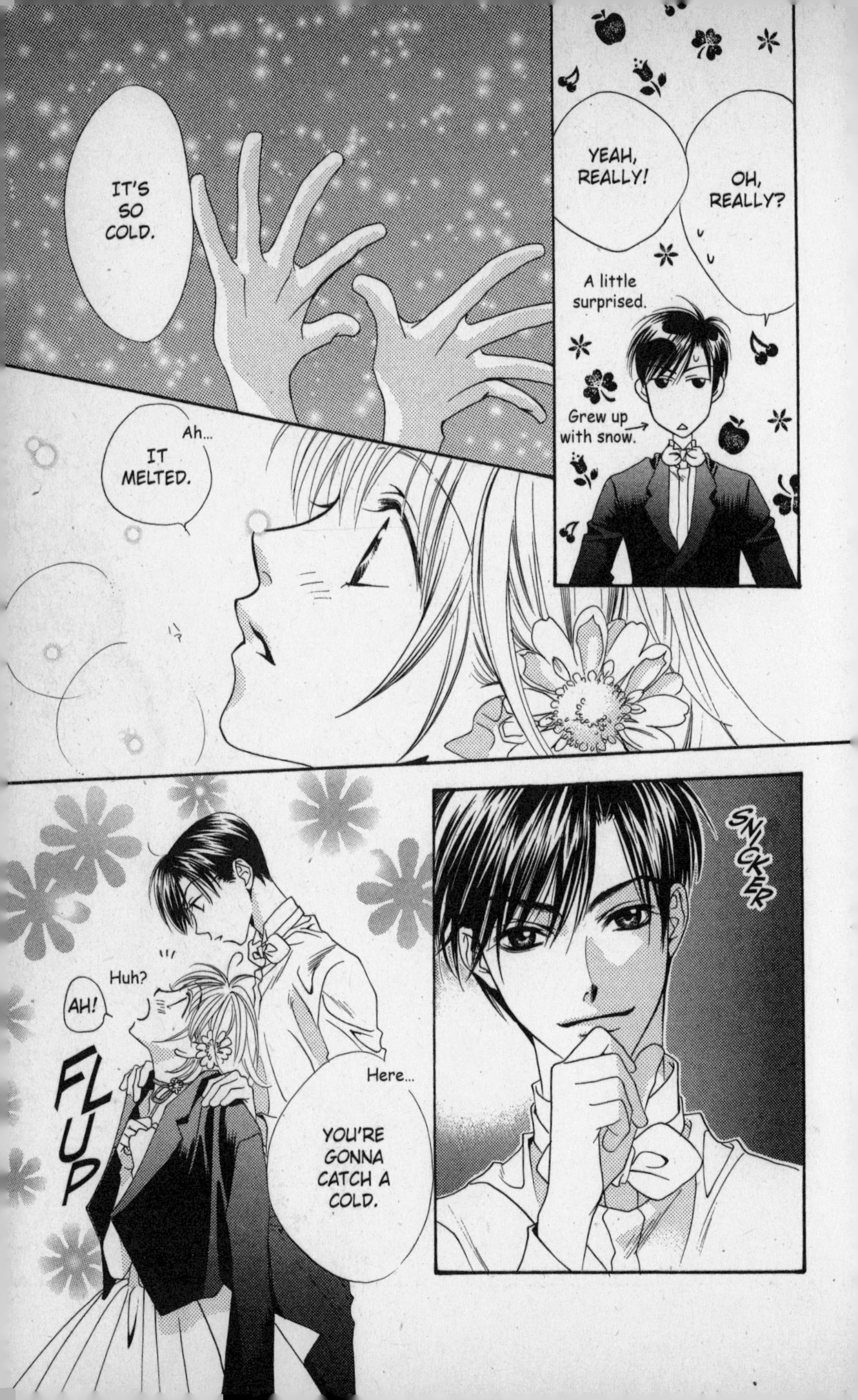
OH, REALLY?
YEAH, REALLY!
A little surprised.
Grew up with snow.
IT'S SO COLD.
Ah... IT MELTED.
SNICKER
Here...
YOU'RE GONNA CATCH A COLD.
FLUP
Huh?
AH!

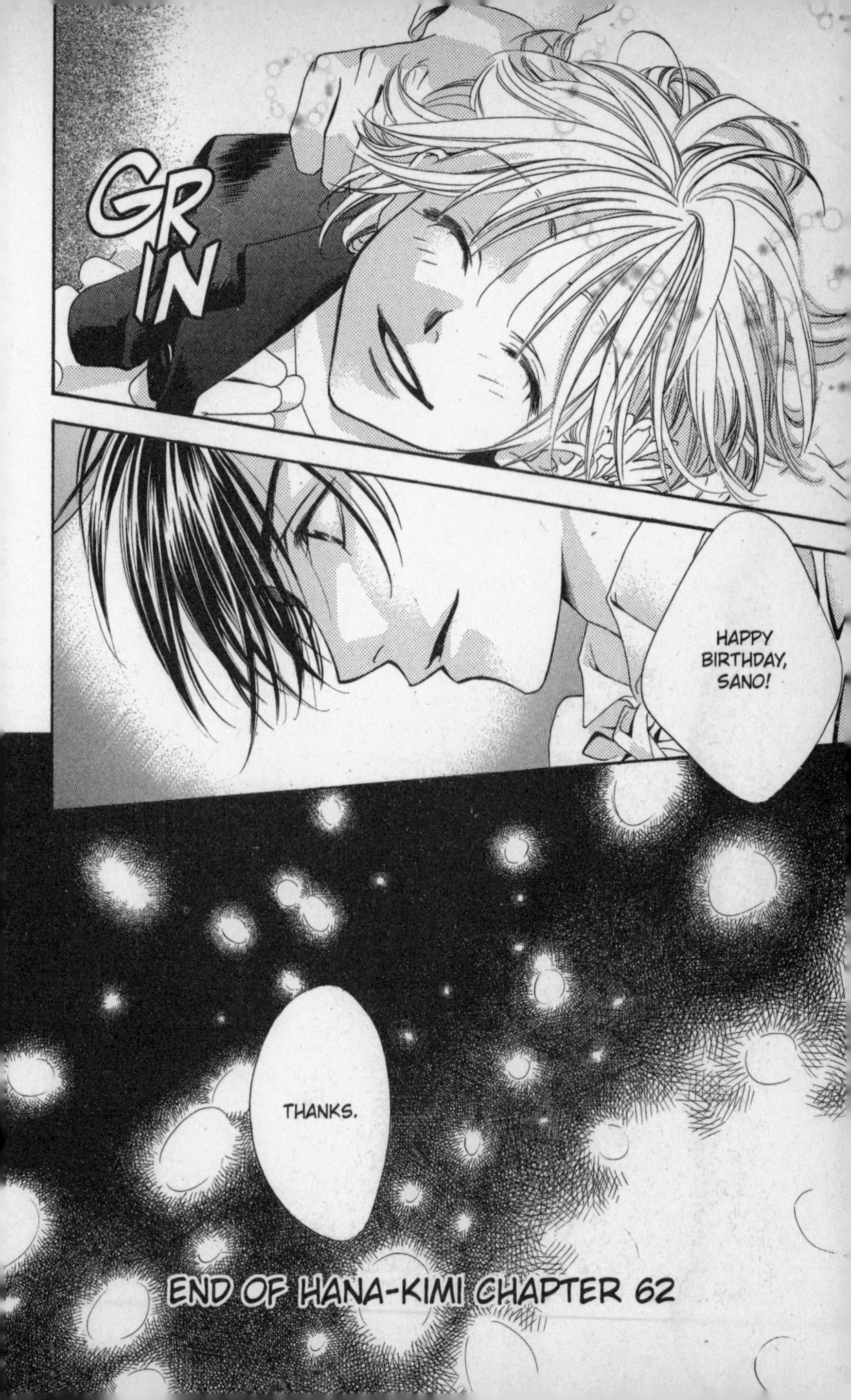
GRIN
HAPPY BIRTHDAY, SANO!
THANKS.
END OF HANA-KIMI CHAPTER 62

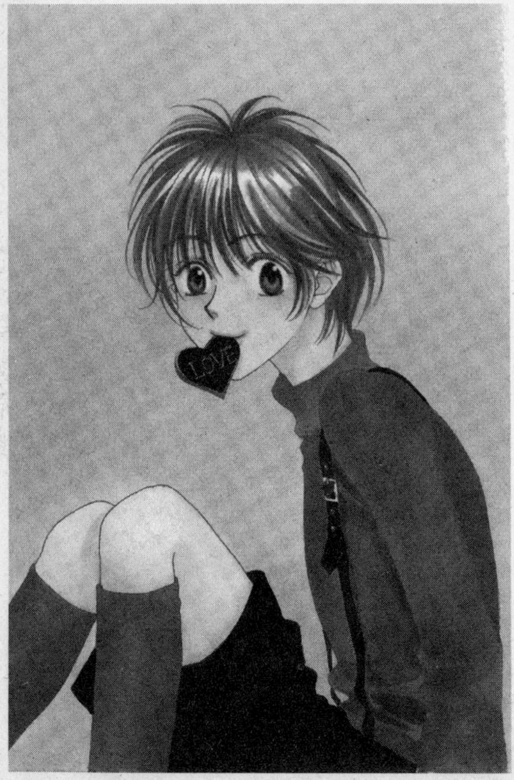
LOVE

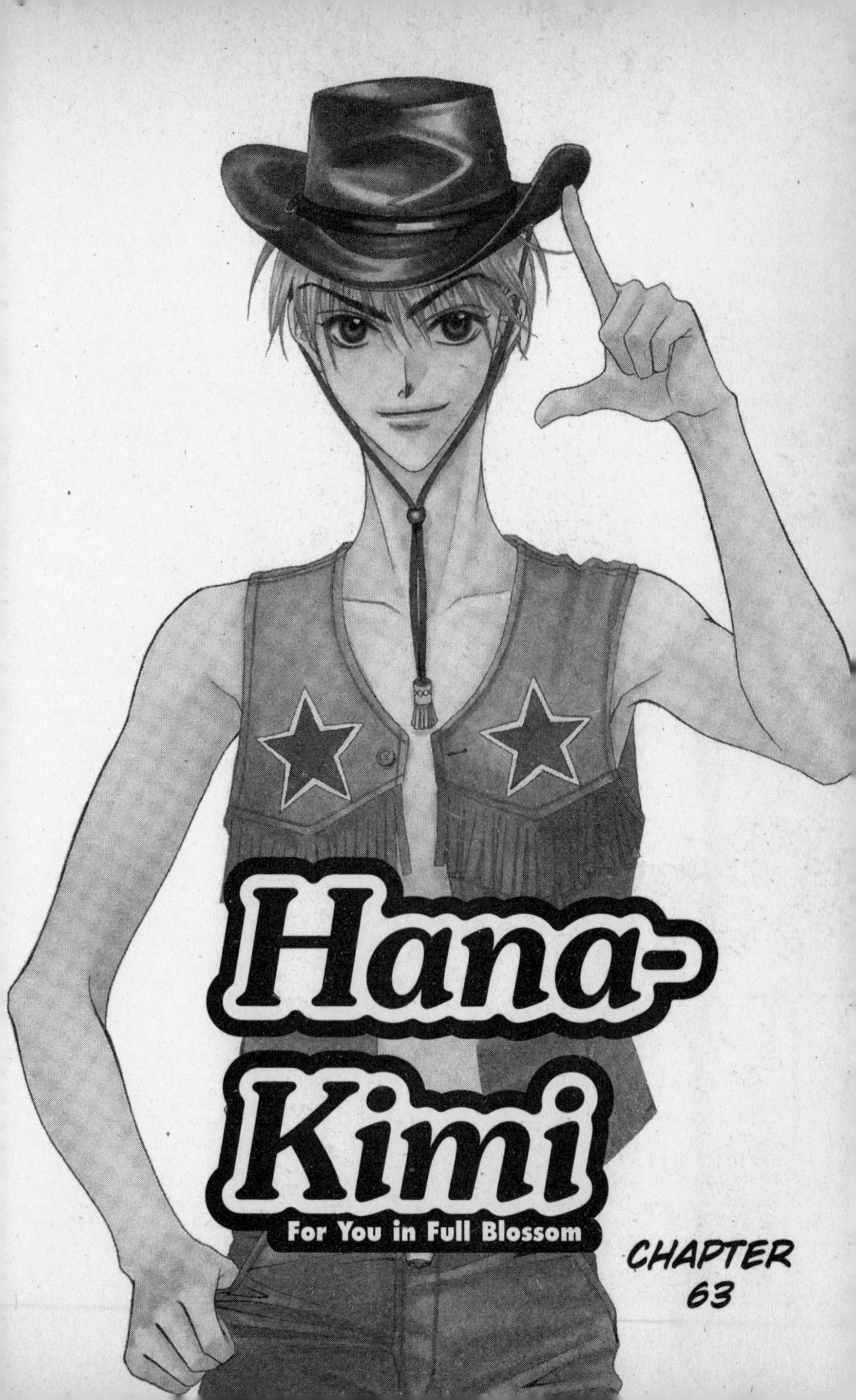
Hana-
Kimi
For You in Full Blossom
CHAPTER
63

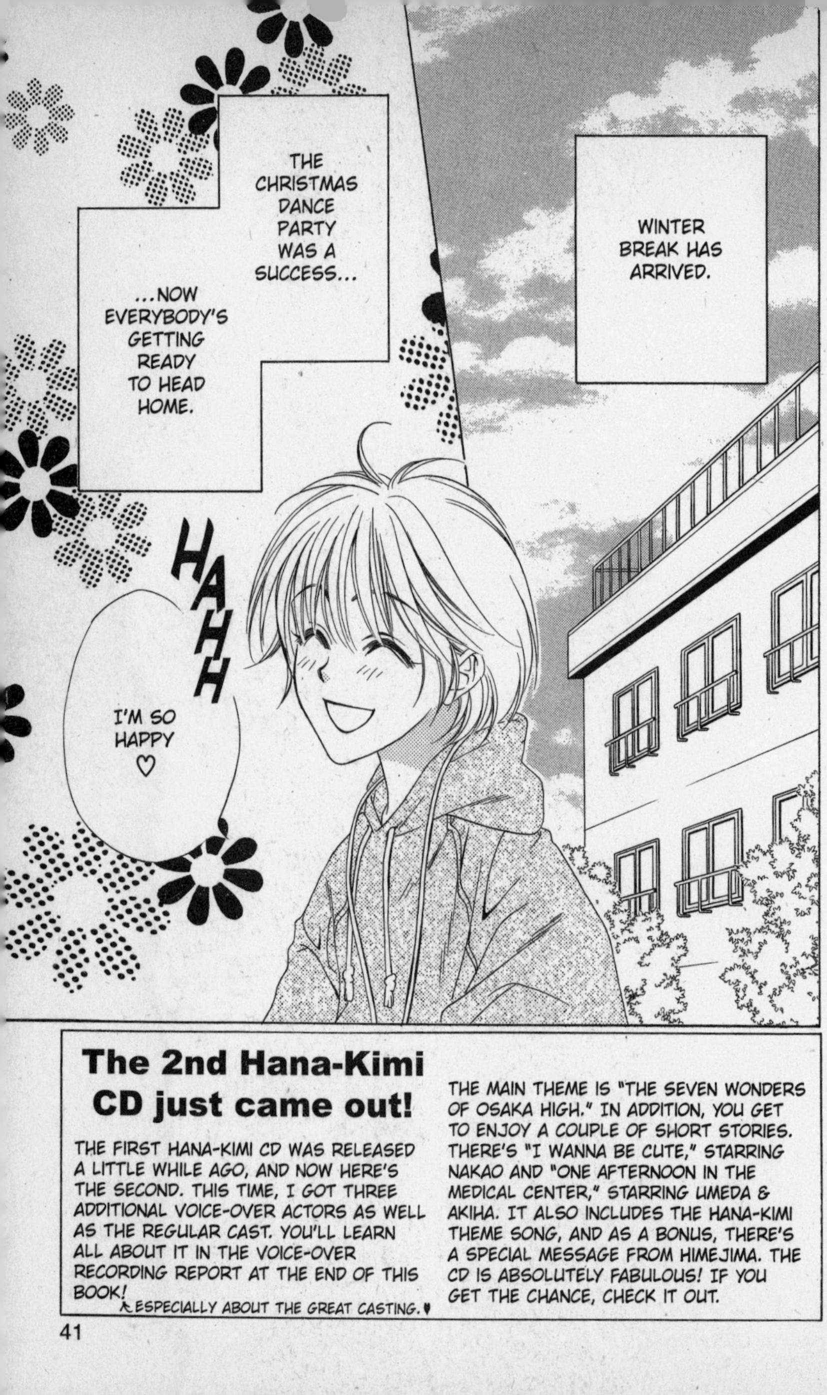
WINTER BREAK HAS ARRIVED.
THE CHRISTMAS DANCE PARTY WAS A SUCCESS...
...NOW EVERYBODY'S GETTING READY TO HEAD HOME.
HAHHH
I'M SO HAPPY ♡

The 2nd Hana-Kimi CD just came out!

THE FIRST HANA-KIMI CD WAS RELEASED A LITTLE WHILE AGO, AND NOW HERE'S THE SECOND. THIS TIME, I GOT THREE ADDITIONAL VOICE-OVER ACTORS AS WELL AS THE REGULAR CAST. YOU'LL LEARN ALL ABOUT IT IN THE VOICE-OVER RECORDING REPORT AT THE END OF THIS BOOK!

ESPECIALLY ABOUT THE GREAT CASTING. ♥

THE MAIN THEME IS "THE SEVEN WONDERS OF OSAKA HIGH." IN ADDITION, YOU GET TO ENJOY A COUPLE OF SHORT STORIES. THERE'S "I WANNA BE CUTE," STARRING NAKAO AND "ONE AFTERNOON IN THE MEDICAL CENTER," STARRING UMEDA & AKIHA. IT ALSO INCLUDES THE HANA-KIMI THEME SONG, AND AS A BONUS, THERE'S A SPECIAL MESSAGE FROM HIMEJIMA. THE CD IS ABSOLUTELY FABULOUS! IF YOU GET THE CHANCE, CHECK IT OUT.

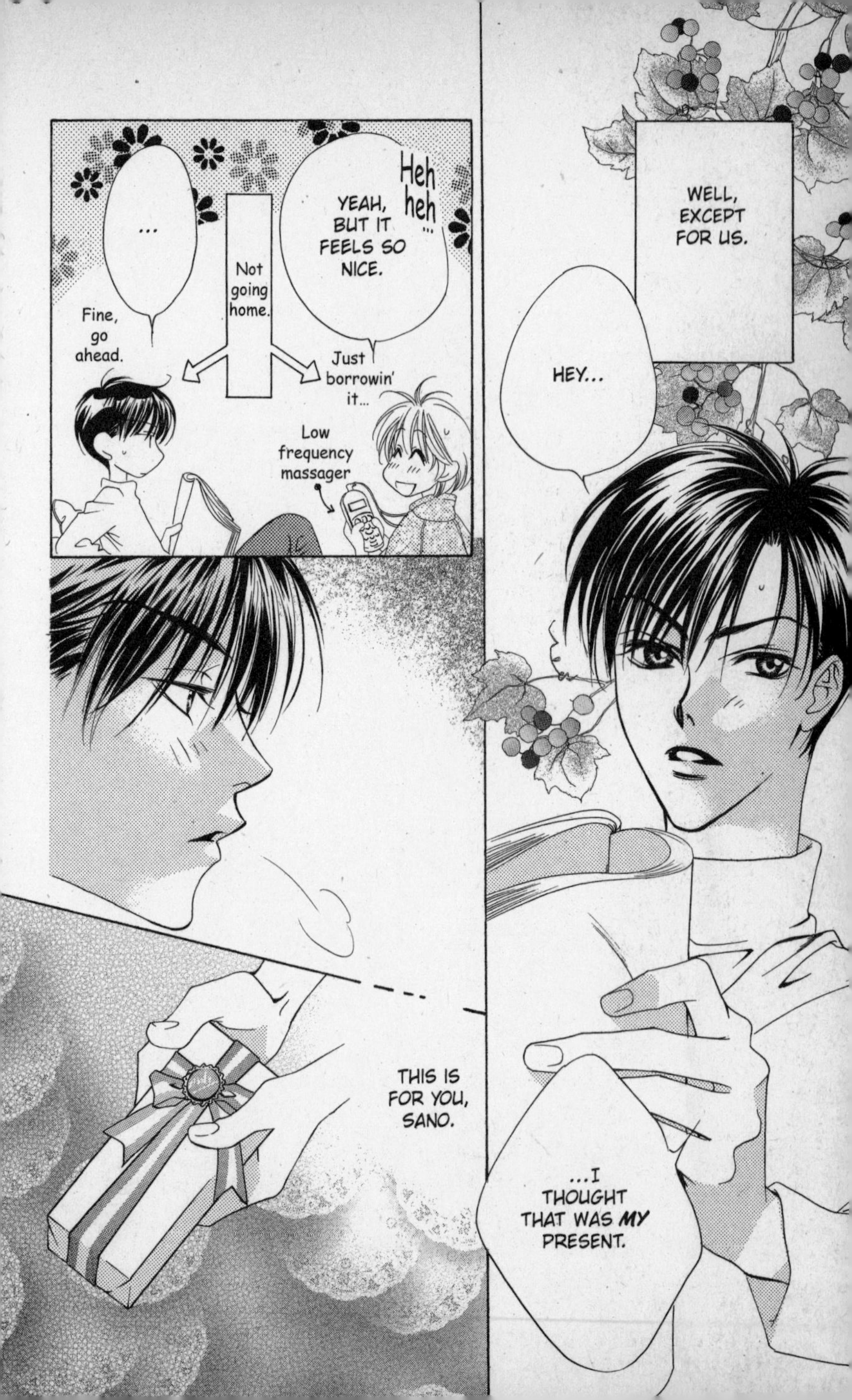
WELL, EXCEPT FOR US.
HEY...
...I THOUGHT THAT WAS *MY* PRESENT.
YEAH, BUT IT FEELS SO NICE.
Heh heh...
Just borrowin' it...
Low frequency massager
Not going home.
...
Fine, go ahead.
THIS IS FOR YOU, SANO.

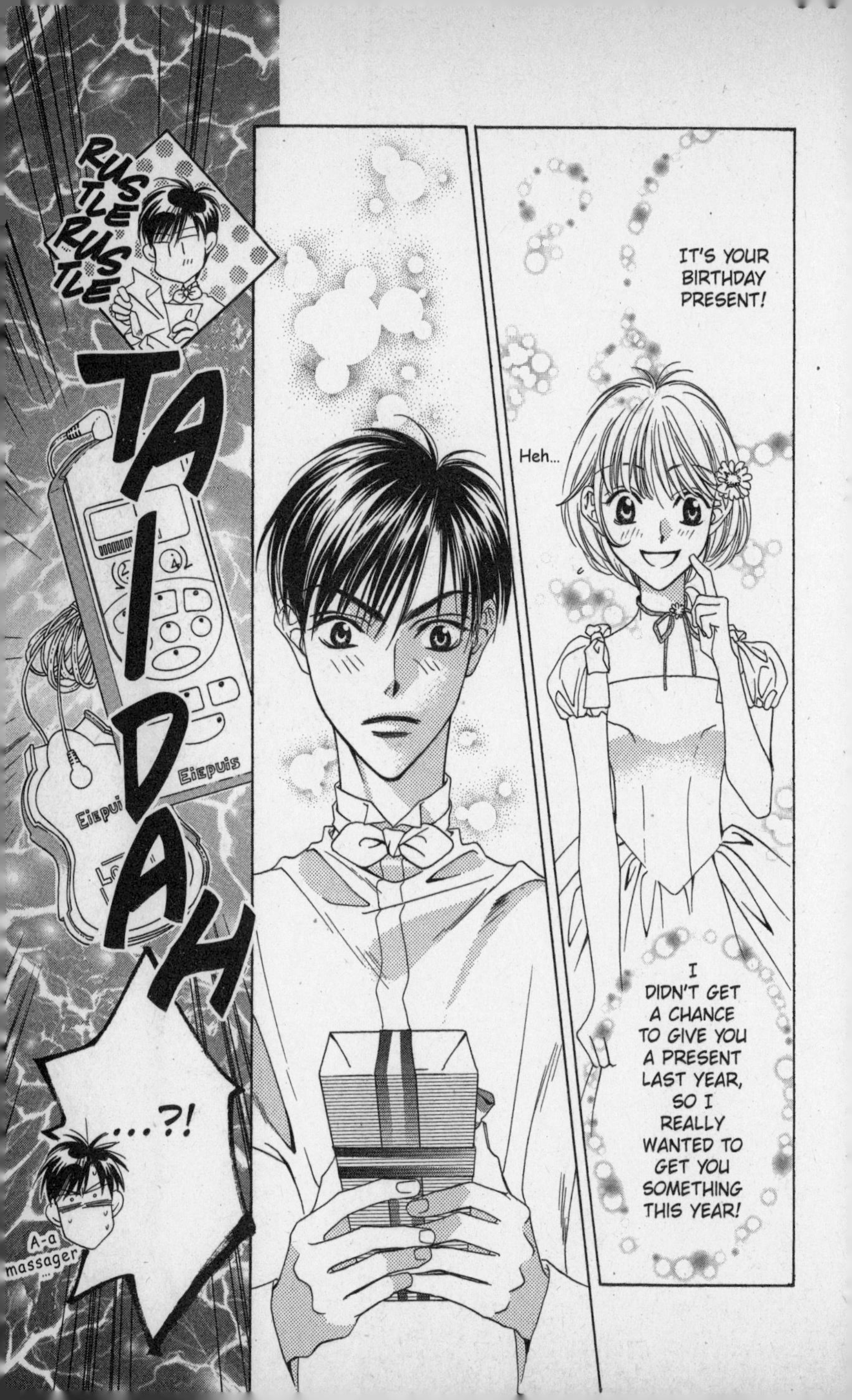
IT'S YOUR BIRTHDAY PRESENT!
Heh...
I DIDN'T GET A CHANCE TO GIVE YOU A PRESENT LAST YEAR, SO I REALLY WANTED TO GET YOU SOMETHING THIS YEAR!
RUSTLE RUSTLE
TA-DAH
Eiepuis
Eiepui
...?!
A-a massager...

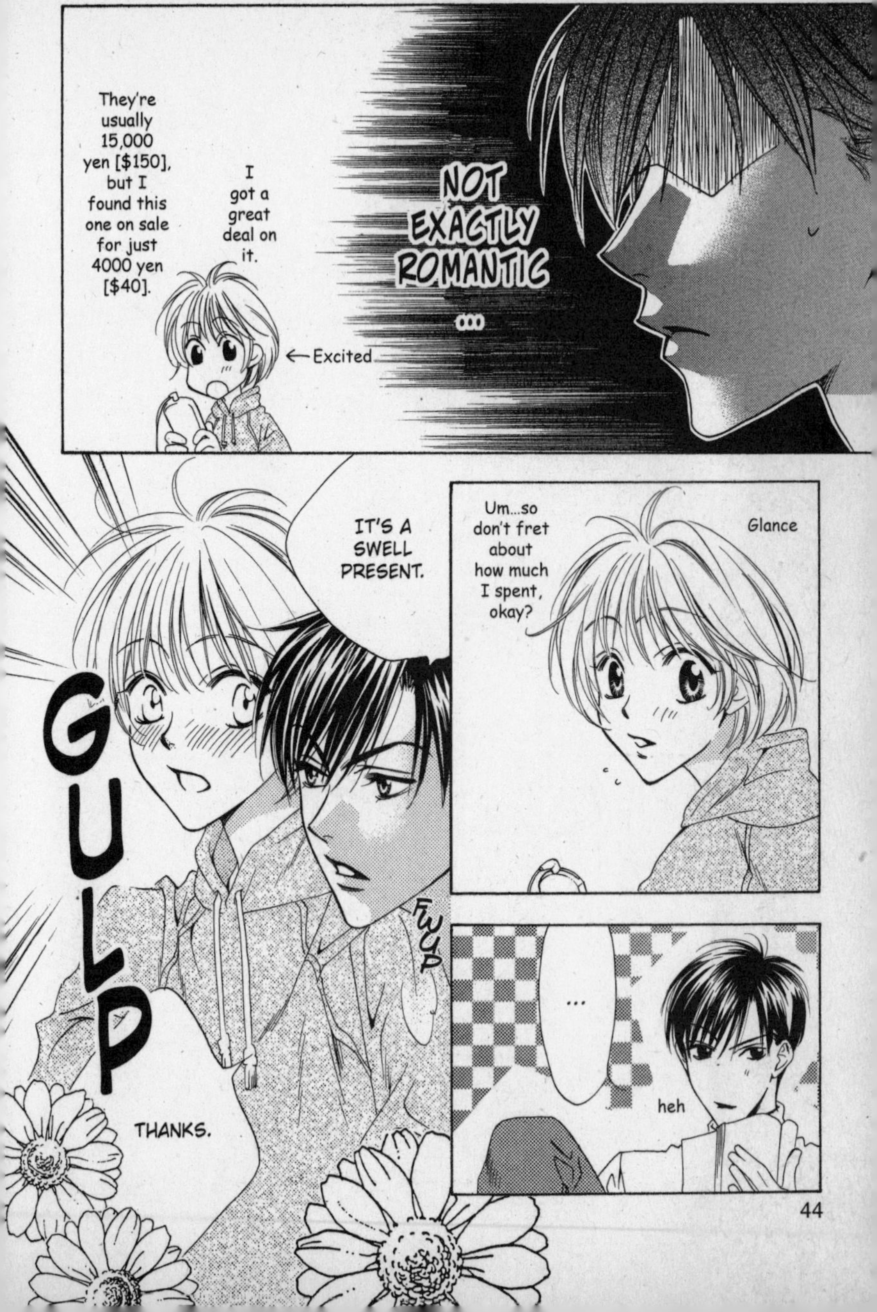
NOT EXACTLY ROMANTIC...
I got a great deal on it.
They're usually 15,000 yen [$150], but I found this one on sale for just 4000 yen [$40].
←Excited
Glance
Um...so don't fret about how much I spent, okay?
...
heh
IT'S A SWELL PRESENT.
FWUP
GULP
THANKS.

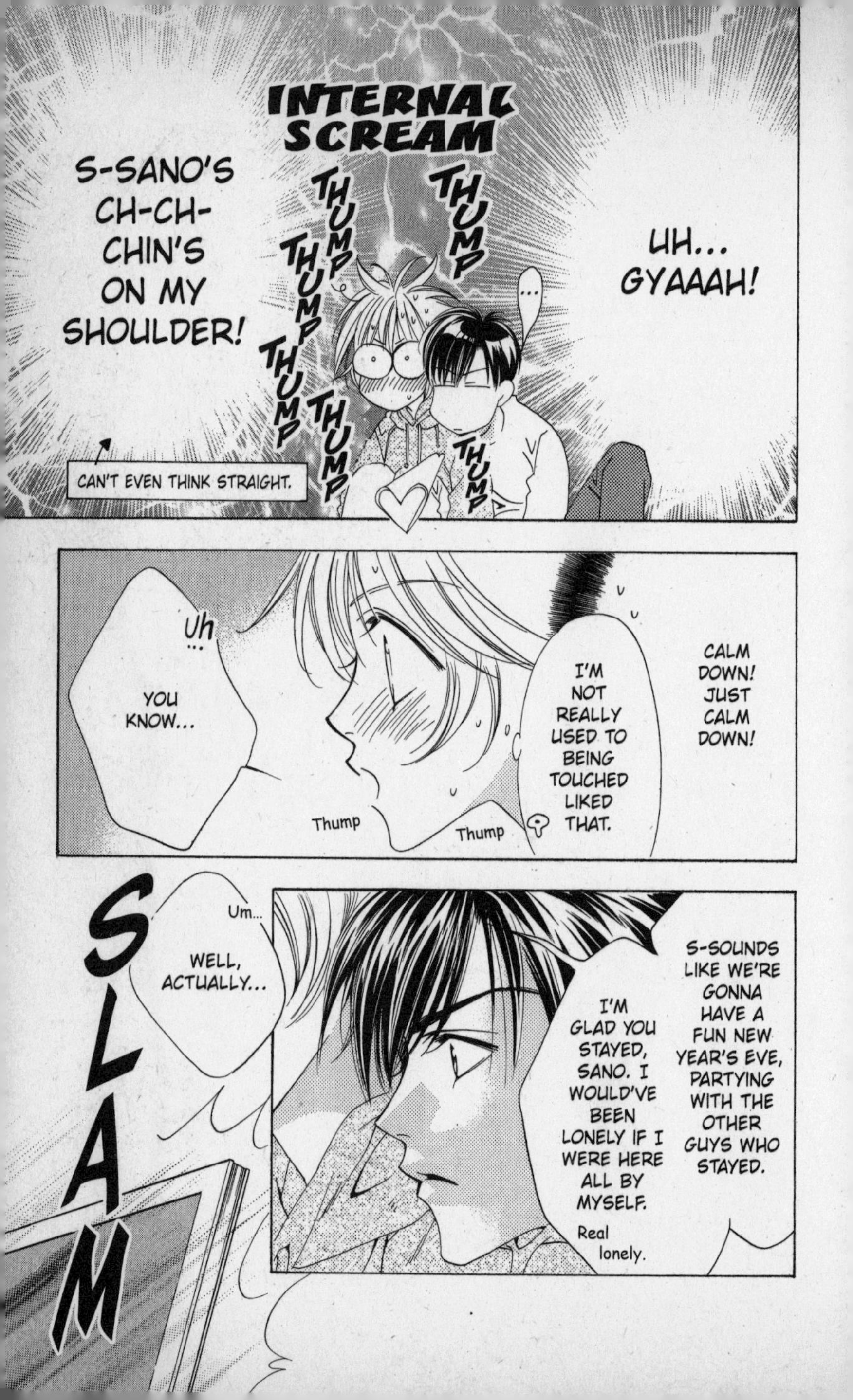
UH... GYAAAH!
INTERNAL SCREAM
THUMP
THUMP
THUMP
THUMP
THUMP
...
THUMP
S-SANO'S CH-CH-CHIN'S ON MY SHOULDER!
CAN'T EVEN THINK STRAIGHT.
CALM DOWN! JUST CALM DOWN!
I'M NOT REALLY USED TO BEING TOUCHED LIKED THAT.
Thump
Thump
Uh... YOU KNOW...
S-SOUNDS LIKE WE'RE GONNA HAVE A FUN NEW YEAR'S EVE, PARTYING WITH THE OTHER GUYS WHO STAYED.
I'M GLAD YOU STAYED, SANO. I WOULD'VE BEEN LONELY IF I WERE HERE ALL BY MYSELF.
Real lonely.
Um... WELL, ACTUALLY...
SLAM

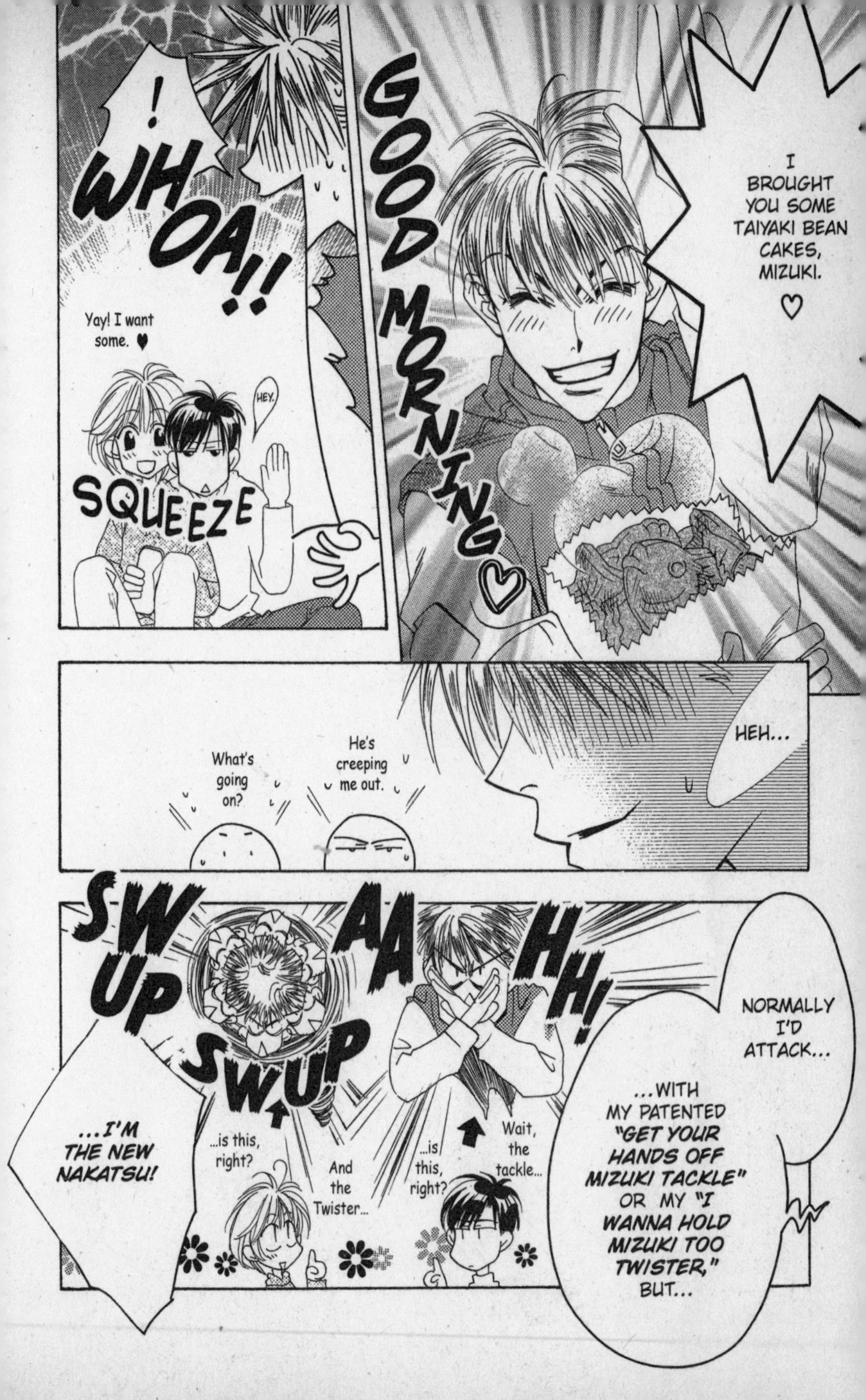
I BROUGHT YOU SOME TAIYAKI BEAN CAKES, MIZUKI. ♡
GOOD MORNING ♡
!
WHOA!!
Yay! I want some. ♥
HEY.
SQUEEZE
HEH...
He's creeping me out.
What's going on?
NORMALLY I'D ATTACK...
...WITH MY PATENTED "GET YOUR HANDS OFF MIZUKI TACKLE" OR MY "I WANNA HOLD MIZUKI TOO TWISTER," BUT...
AAHH!
Wait, the tackle...
...is this, right?
SW UP SWUP
And the Twister...
...is this, right?
...I'M THE NEW NAKATSU!

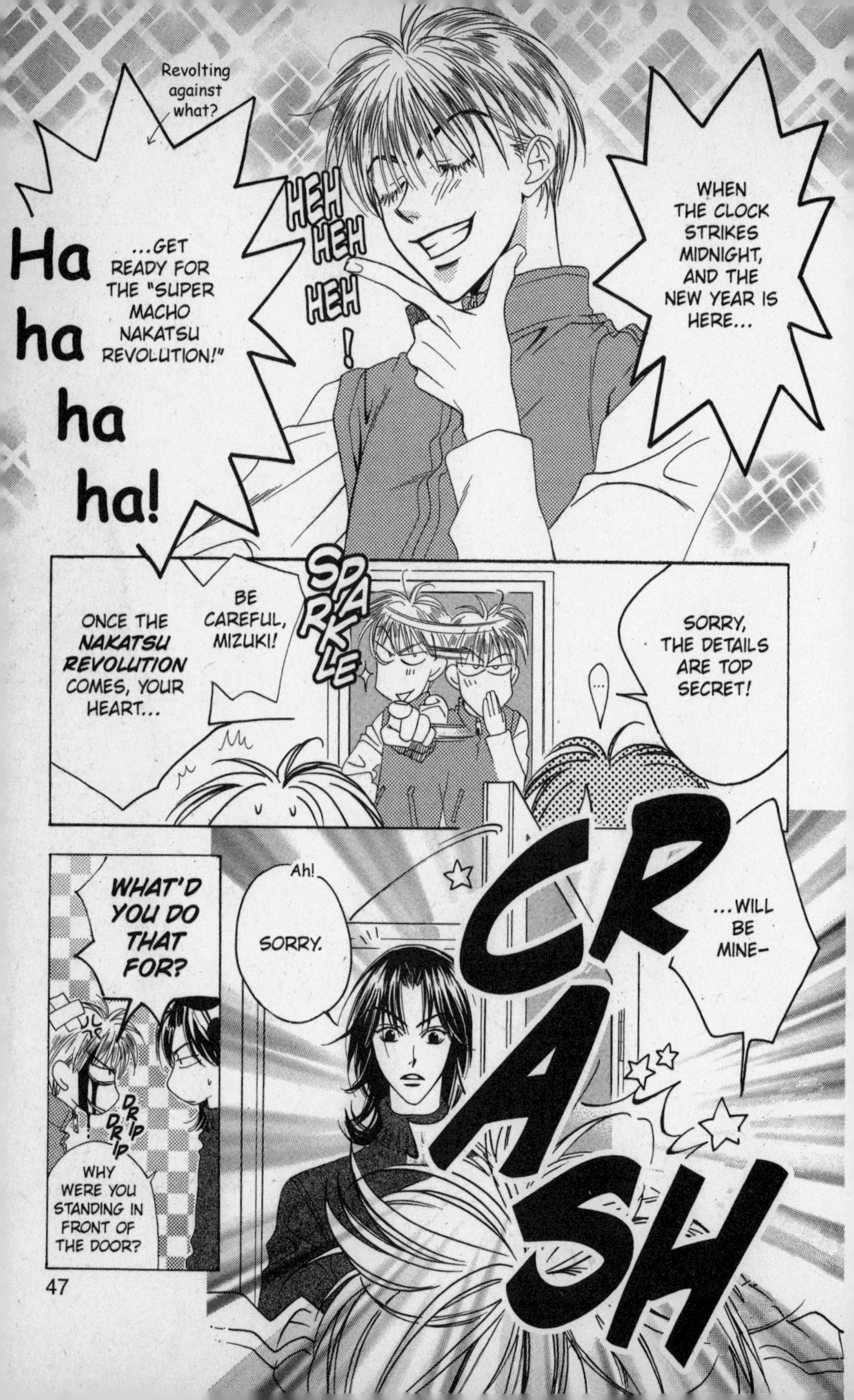
WHEN THE CLOCK STRIKES MIDNIGHT, AND THE NEW YEAR IS HERE...
HEH HEH HEH!
...GET READY FOR THE "SUPER MACHO NAKATSU REVOLUTION!"
Ha ha ha ha!
Revolting against what?
SORRY, THE DETAILS ARE TOP SECRET!
...
SPARKLE
BE CAREFUL, MIZUKI!
ONCE THE NAKATSU REVOLUTION COMES, YOUR HEART...
...WILL BE MINE-
CRASH
Ah!
SORRY.
WHAT'D YOU DO THAT FOR?
DRIP DRIP
WHY WERE YOU STANDING IN FRONT OF THE DOOR?

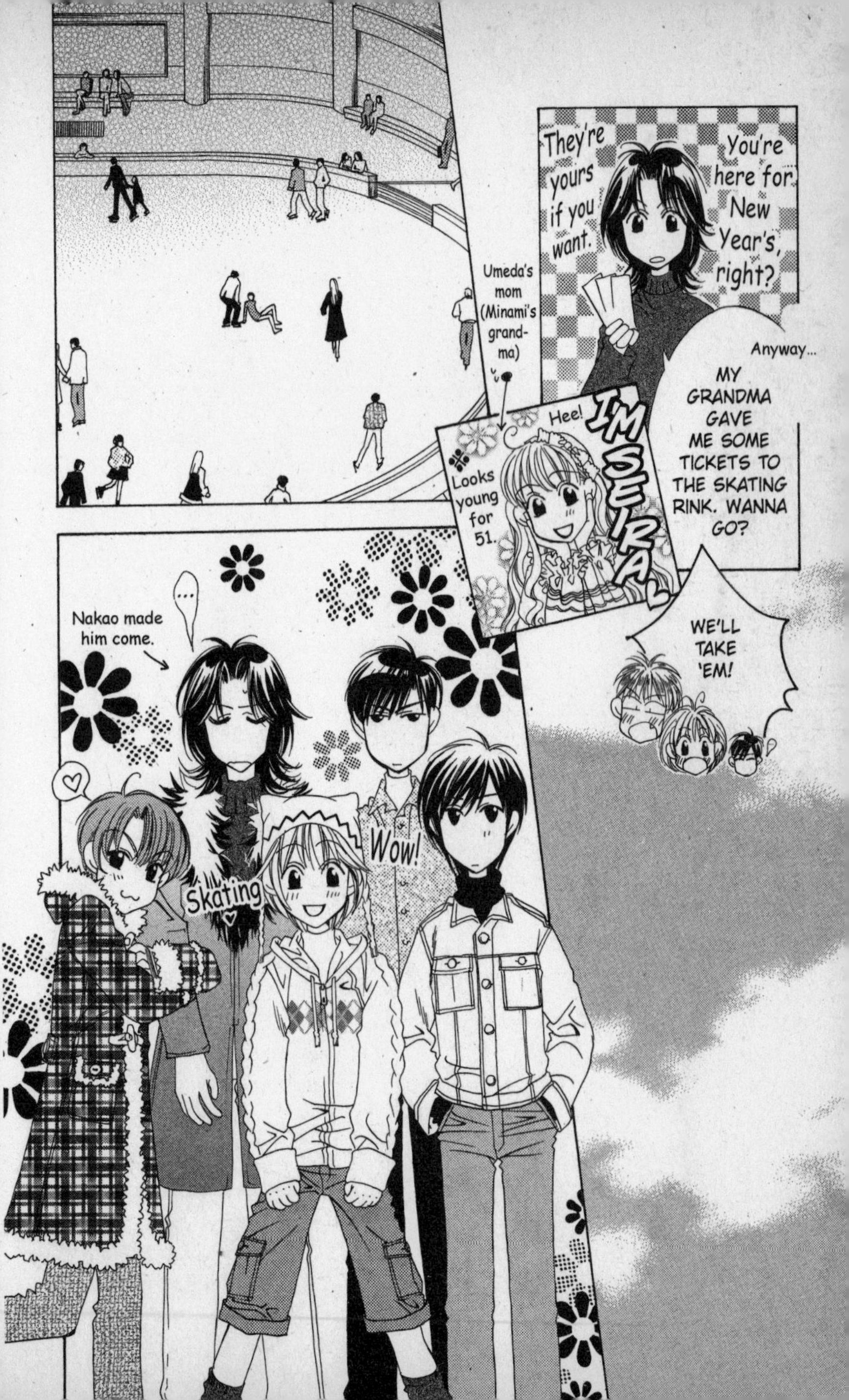
You're here for New Year's, right?
They're yours if you want.
Anyway...
MY GRANDMA GAVE ME SOME TICKETS TO THE SKATING RINK. WANNA GO?
Umeda's mom (Minami's grand-ma)
Hee!
I'M SEIRA
Looks young for 51.
WE'LL TAKE 'EM!
Wow!
Skating
...
Nakao made him come.

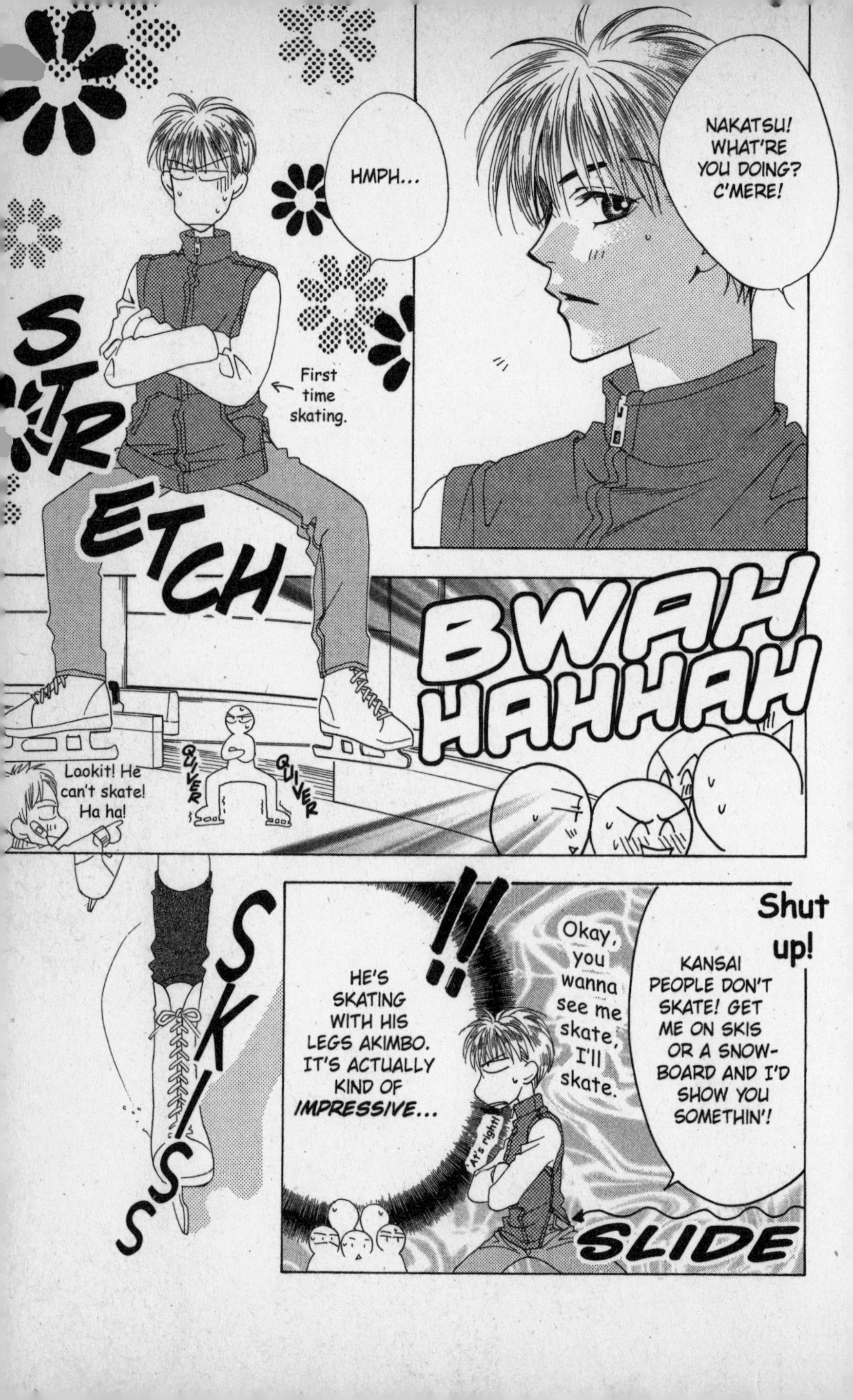
NAKATSU! WHAT'RE YOU DOING? C'MERE!
HMPH...
First time skating.
STRETCH
BWAH HAHHAH
Lookit! He can't skate! Ha ha!
QUIVER QUIVER
Shut up!
KANSAI PEOPLE DON'T SKATE! GET ME ON SKIS OR A SNOW-BOARD AND I'D SHOW YOU SOMETHIN'!
Okay, you wanna see me skate, I'll skate.
'At's right!
SLIDE
!!
HE'S SKATING WITH HIS LEGS AKIMBO. IT'S ACTUALLY KIND OF IMPRESSIVE...
SK/SS

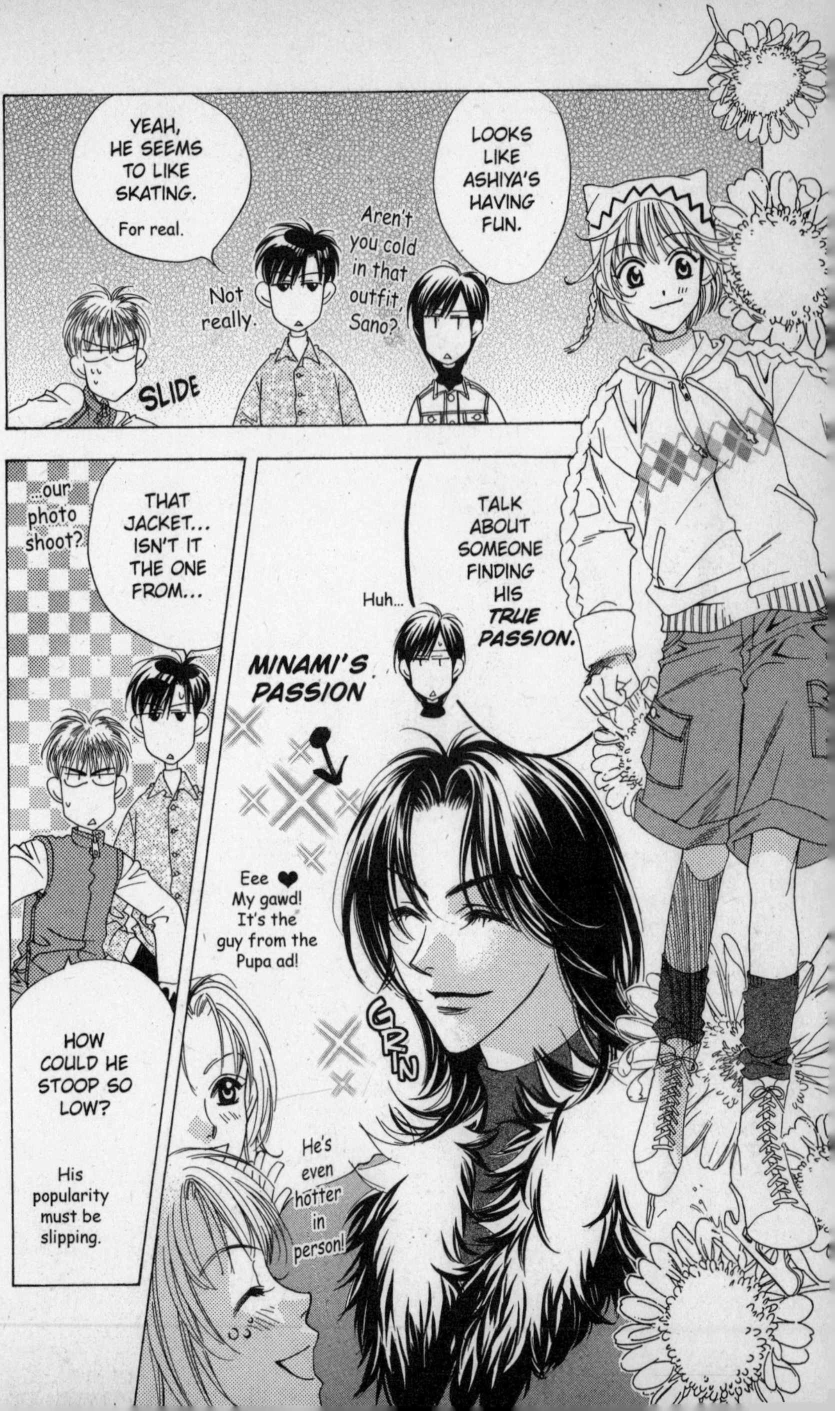
LOOKS LIKE ASHIYA'S HAVING FUN.
Aren't you cold in that outfit, Sano?
Not really.
YEAH, HE SEEMS TO LIKE SKATING.
For real.
SLIDE
TALK ABOUT SOMEONE FINDING HIS TRUE PASSION.
Huh...
MINAMI'S PASSION
Eee ❤ My gawd! It's the guy from the Pupa ad!
GRIN
He's even hotter in person!
THAT JACKET... ISN'T IT THE ONE FROM...
...our photo shoot?
HOW COULD HE STOOP SO LOW?
His popularity must be slipping.

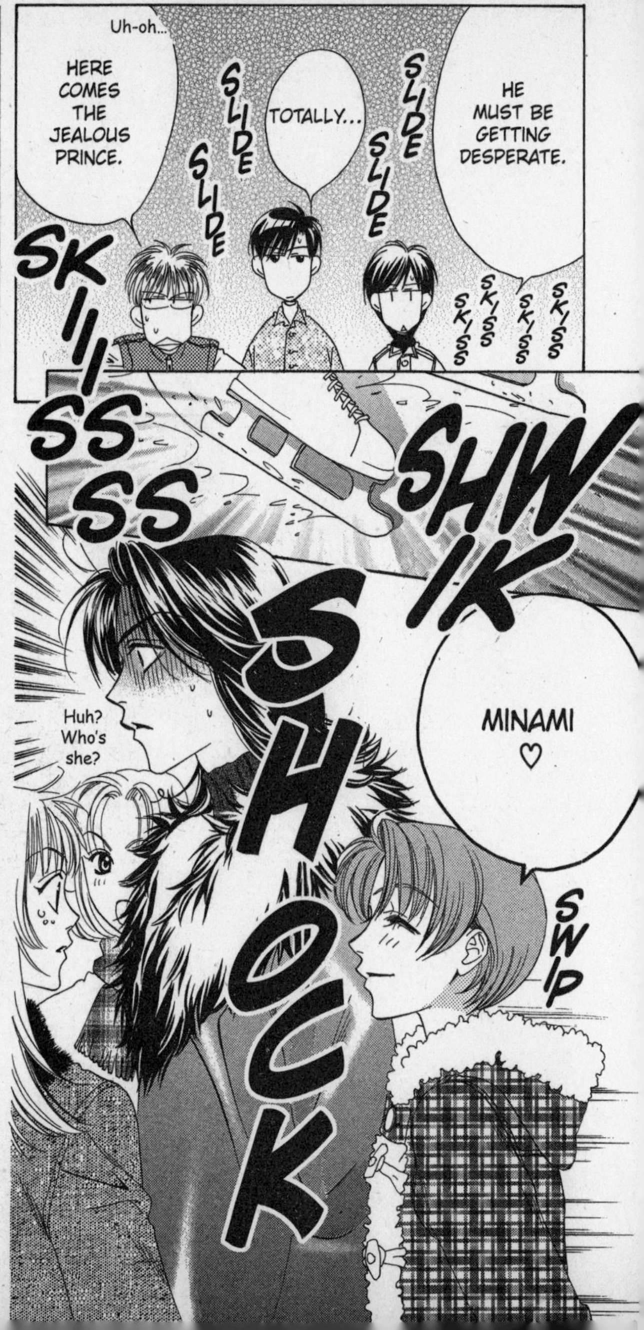
HE MUST BE GETTING DESPERATE.
SKISS SKISS SKISS SKISS
SLIDE SLIDE
TOTALLY...
SLIDE SLIDE
HERE COMES THE JEALOUS PRINCE.
Uh-oh...
SKIIIISSSSSS
SHWIK
MINAMI ♡
SWIP
SHOCK
Huh? Who's she?

Video Games

YEP...I'VE REALLY BEEN GETTING INTO GAMES ♥ LATELY. I USED TO THINK PLAYING GAMES WAS A WASTE OF TIME, BUT IT'S ACTUALLY A LOT OF FUN. TIME SURE FLIES WHEN YOU'RE AT IT! I STARTED OUT WITH FIGHTING GAMES, AND NOW I'M REALLY INTO RPGS. AAHHH! THEY'RE AWESOME! I'M NOT ALLOWED TO MENTION THE NAME HERE, BUT I REALLY LIKE THE ONE THAT HAS MULTIPLE CHARACTERS IN IT. I'M BECOMING A REAL GAMER. NEXT I WANNA TACKLE PC GAMES!

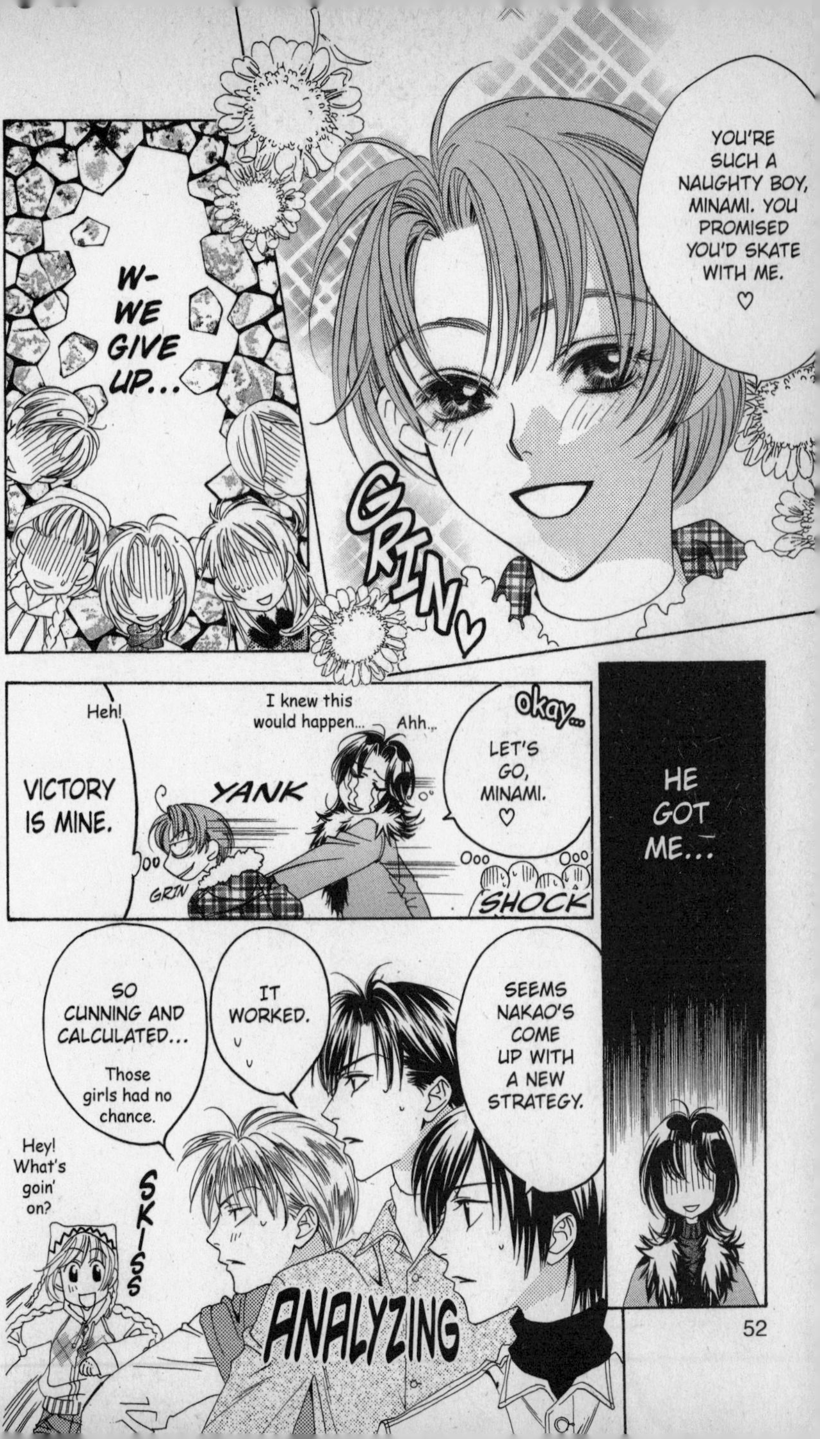
YOU'RE SUCH A NAUGHTY BOY, MINAMI. YOU PROMISED YOU'D SKATE WITH ME. ♡
GRIN ♡
W-WE GIVE UP...
HE GOT ME...
okay...
LET'S GO, MINAMI. ♡
Ahh...
I knew this would happen...
YANK
Heh!
VICTORY IS MINE.
GRIN
SHOCK
SEEMS NAKAO'S COME UP WITH A NEW STRATEGY.
IT WORKED.
SO CUNNING AND CALCULATED...
Those girls had no chance.
Hey! What's goin' on?
SKISS
ANALYZING

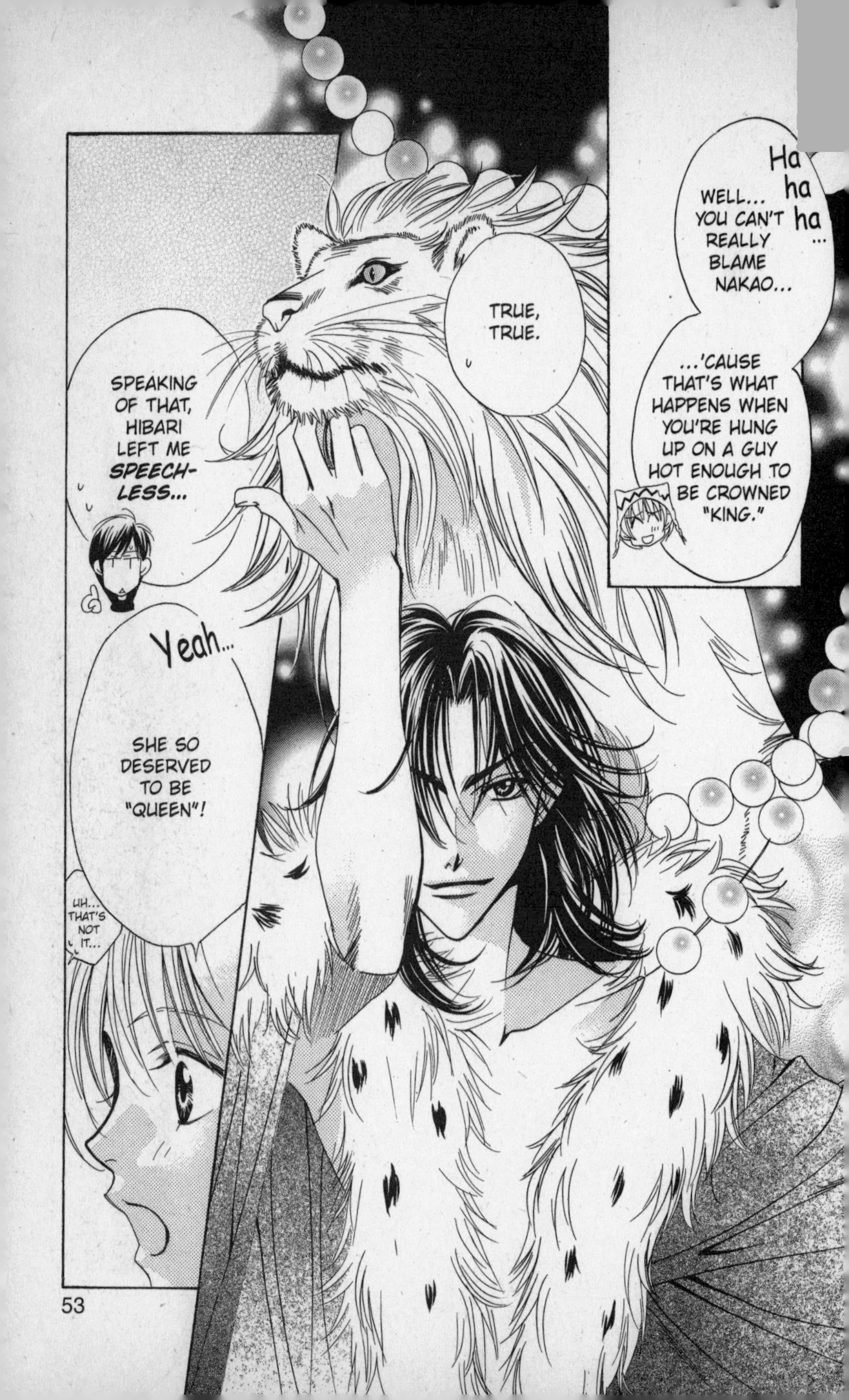
Ha ha ha...
WELL... YOU CAN'T REALLY BLAME NAKAO...
...'CAUSE THAT'S WHAT HAPPENS WHEN YOU'RE HUNG UP ON A GUY HOT ENOUGH TO BE CROWNED "KING."
TRUE, TRUE.
SPEAKING OF THAT, HIBARI LEFT ME SPEECH-LESS...
Yeah...
SHE SO DESERVED TO BE "QUEEN"!
UH... THAT'S NOT IT...

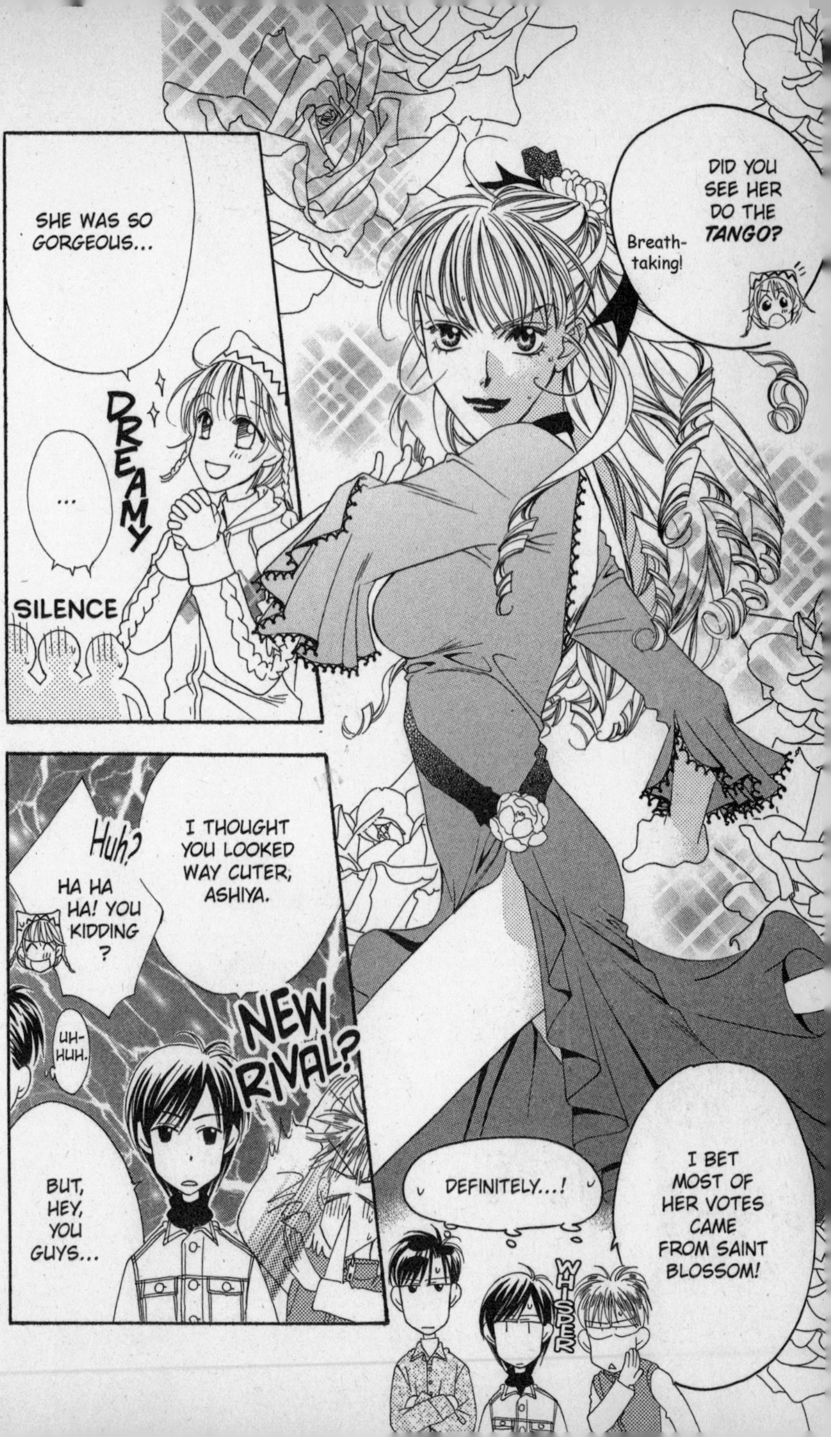
DID YOU SEE HER DO THE *TANGO?*
Breath-taking!
I BET MOST OF HER VOTES CAME FROM SAINT BLOSSOM!
WHISPER
DEFINITELY...!
SHE WAS SO GORGEOUS...
DREAMY
...
SILENCE
I THOUGHT YOU LOOKED WAY CUTER, ASHIYA.
Huh?
HA HA HA! YOU KIDDING ?
NEW RIVAL?
UH-HUH.
BUT, HEY, YOU GUYS...

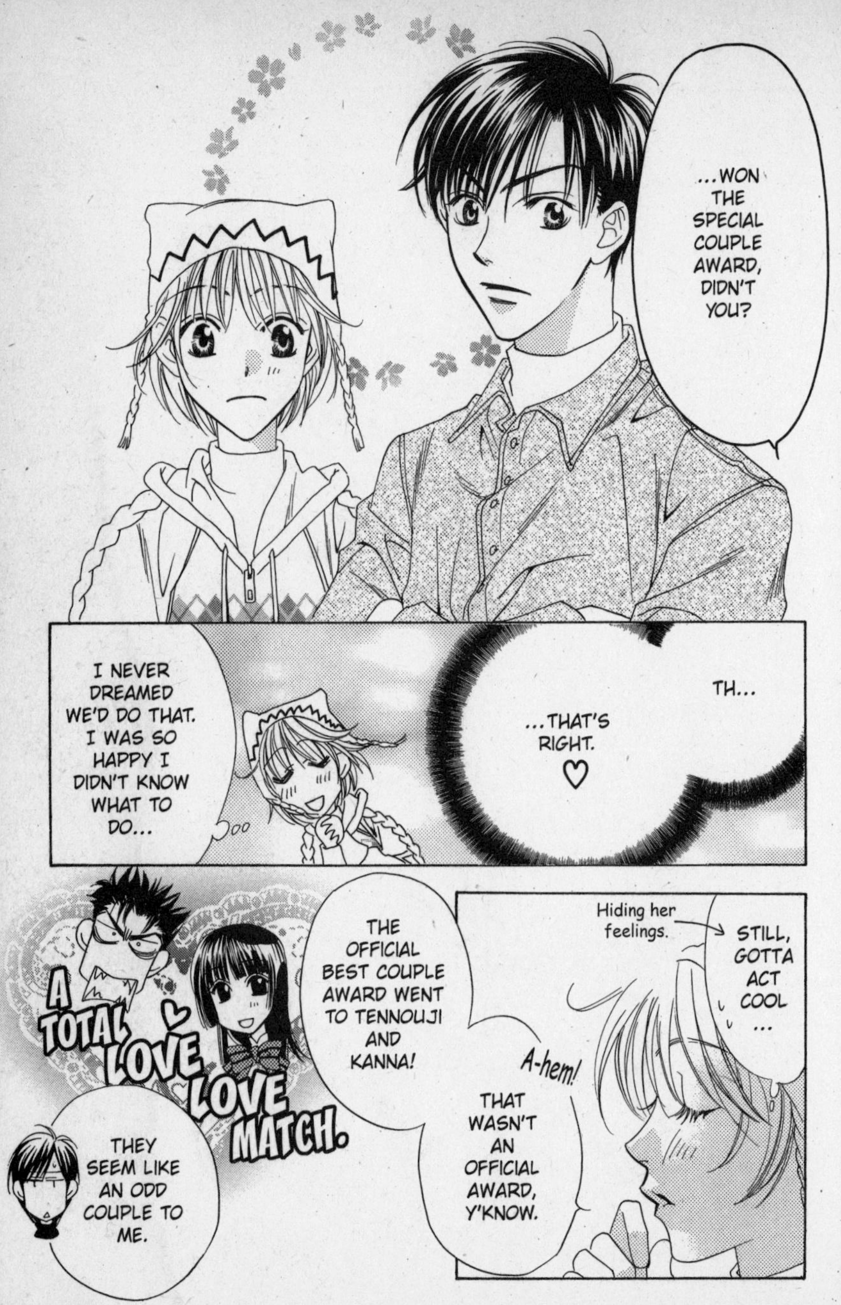
...WON THE SPECIAL COUPLE AWARD, DIDN'T YOU?
TH...
...THAT'S RIGHT. ♡
I NEVER DREAMED WE'D DO THAT. I WAS SO HAPPY I DIDN'T KNOW WHAT TO DO...
Hiding her feelings.
STILL, GOTTA ACT COOL...
A-hem!
THAT WASN'T AN OFFICIAL AWARD, Y'KNOW.
THE OFFICIAL BEST COUPLE AWARD WENT TO TENNOUJI AND KANNA!
A TOTAL ♡ LOVE LOVE MATCH.
THEY SEEM LIKE AN ODD COUPLE TO ME.

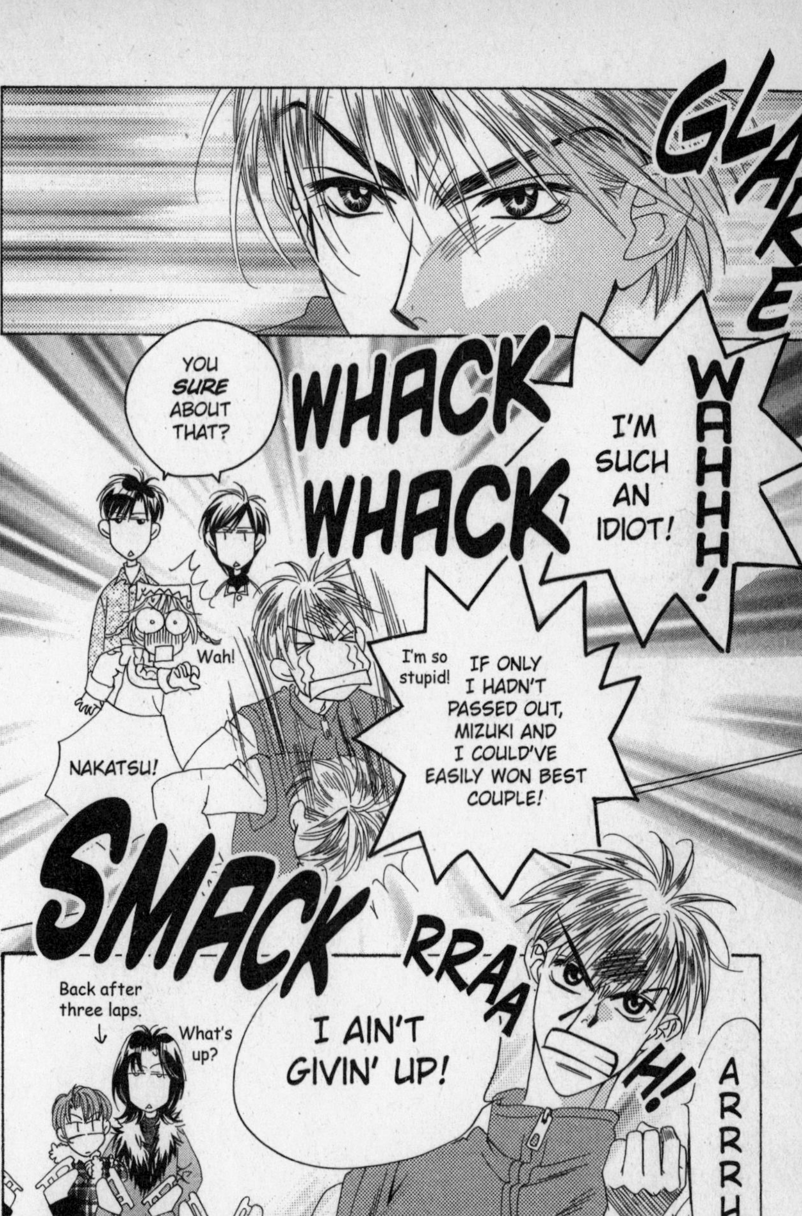
GLARE
WAHHH!
I'M SUCH AN IDIOT!
WHACK WHACK
YOU SURE ABOUT THAT?
IF ONLY I HADN'T PASSED OUT, MIZUKI AND I COULD'VE EASILY WON BEST COUPLE!
I'm so stupid!
Wah!
NAKATSU!
SMACK
RRAAH!
ARRRH!
I AIN'T GIVIN' UP!
What's up?
Back after three laps.

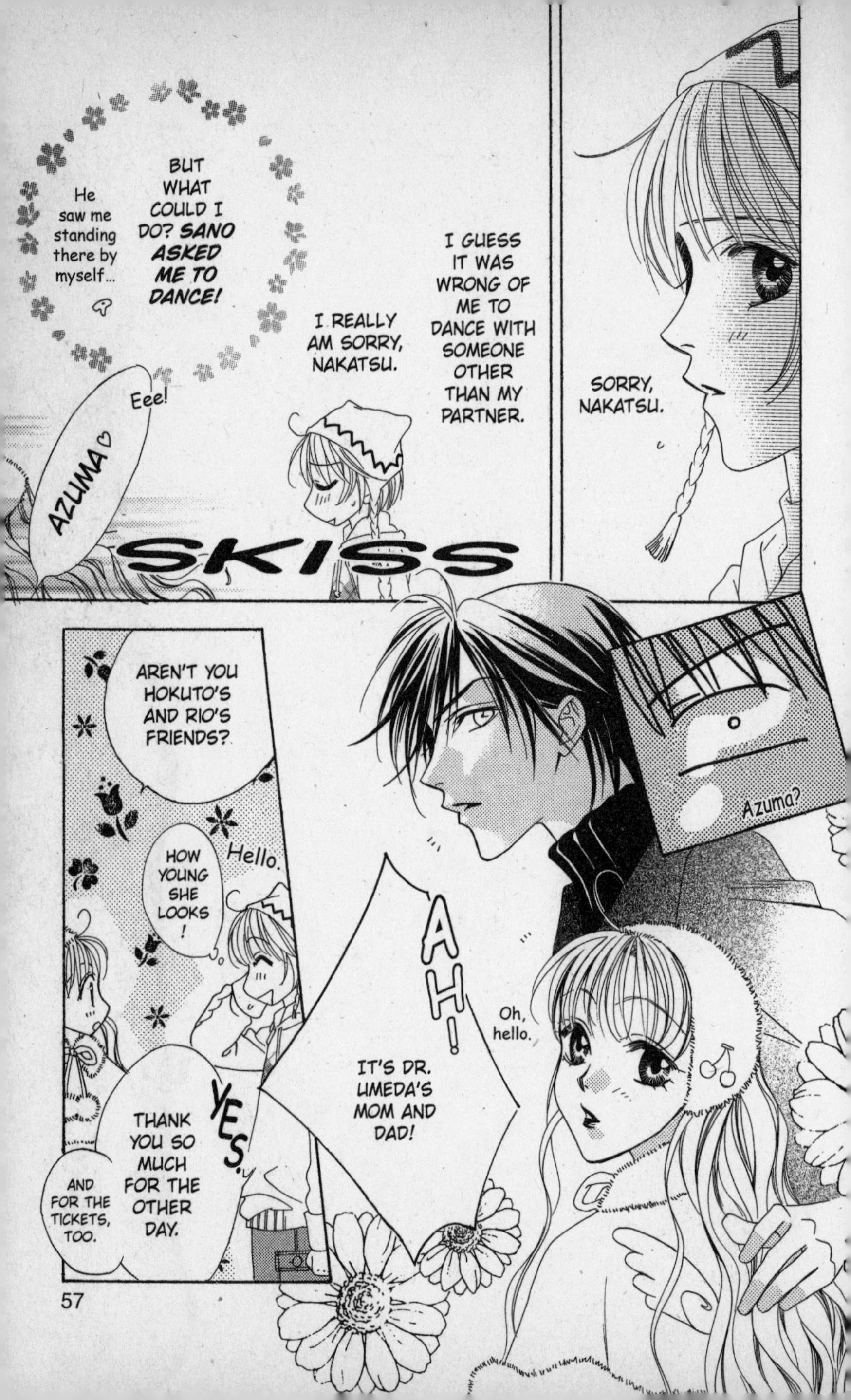
SORRY, NAKATSU.
I GUESS IT WAS WRONG OF ME TO DANCE WITH SOMEONE OTHER THAN MY PARTNER.
I REALLY AM SORRY, NAKATSU.
BUT WHAT COULD I DO? SANO ASKED ME TO DANCE!
He saw me standing there by myself...
Eee!
AZUMA♡
SKISS
Azuma?
AH!
Oh, hello.
IT'S DR. UMEDA'S MOM AND DAD!
AREN'T YOU HOKUTO'S AND RIO'S FRIENDS?
Hello.
HOW YOUNG SHE LOOKS!
YES.
THANK YOU SO MUCH FOR THE OTHER DAY.
AND FOR THE TICKETS, TOO.

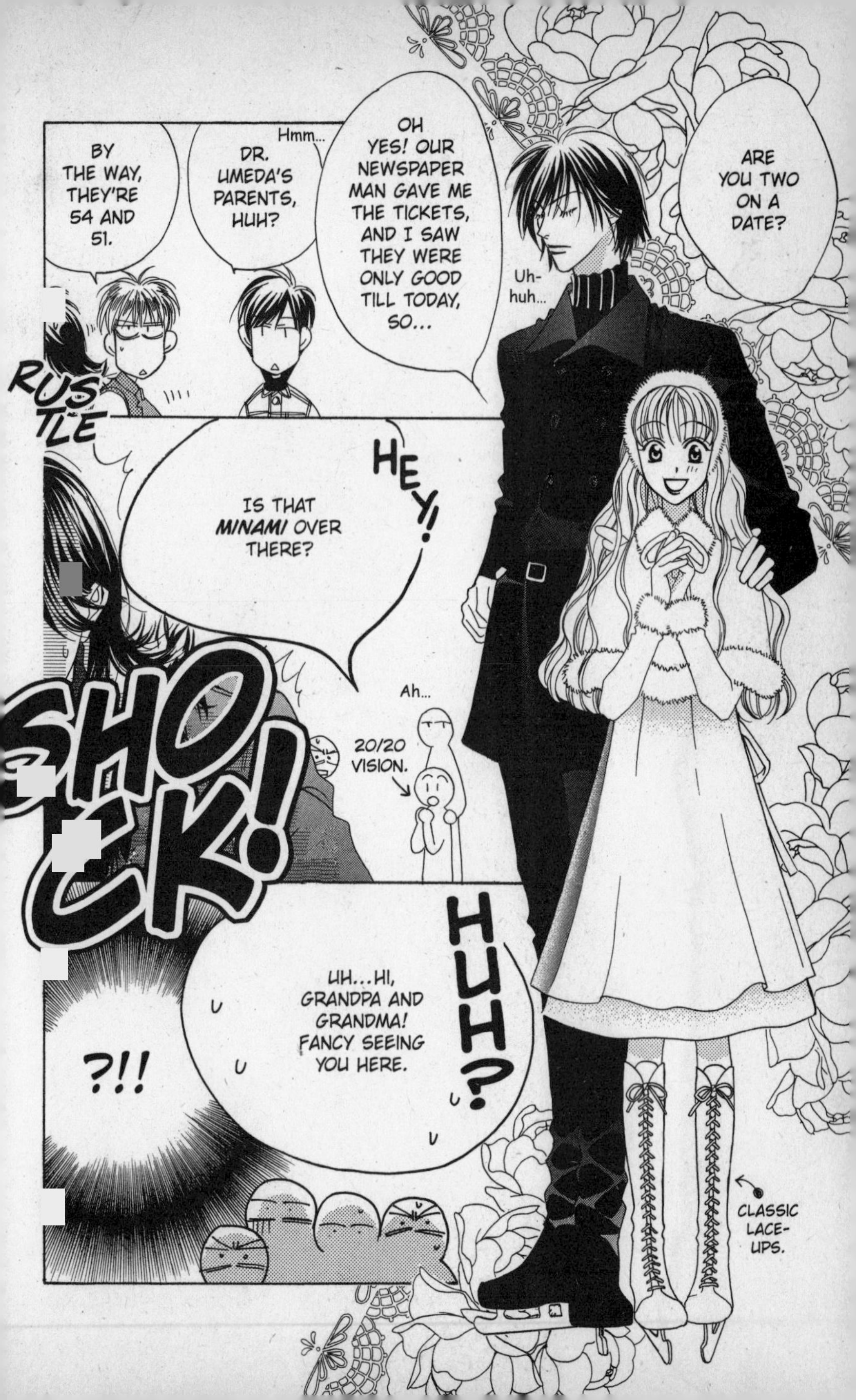
ARE YOU TWO ON A DATE?
Uh-huh...
OH YES! OUR NEWSPAPER MAN GAVE ME THE TICKETS, AND I SAW THEY WERE ONLY GOOD TILL TODAY, SO...
Hmm...
DR. UMEDA'S PARENTS, HUH?
BY THE WAY, THEY'RE 54 AND 51.
RUSTLE
HEY!
IS THAT MINAMI OVER THERE?
Ah...
20/20 VISION.
SHOCK!
HUH?
UH...HI, GRANDPA AND GRANDMA! FANCY SEEING YOU HERE.
?!!
CLASSIC LACE-UPS.

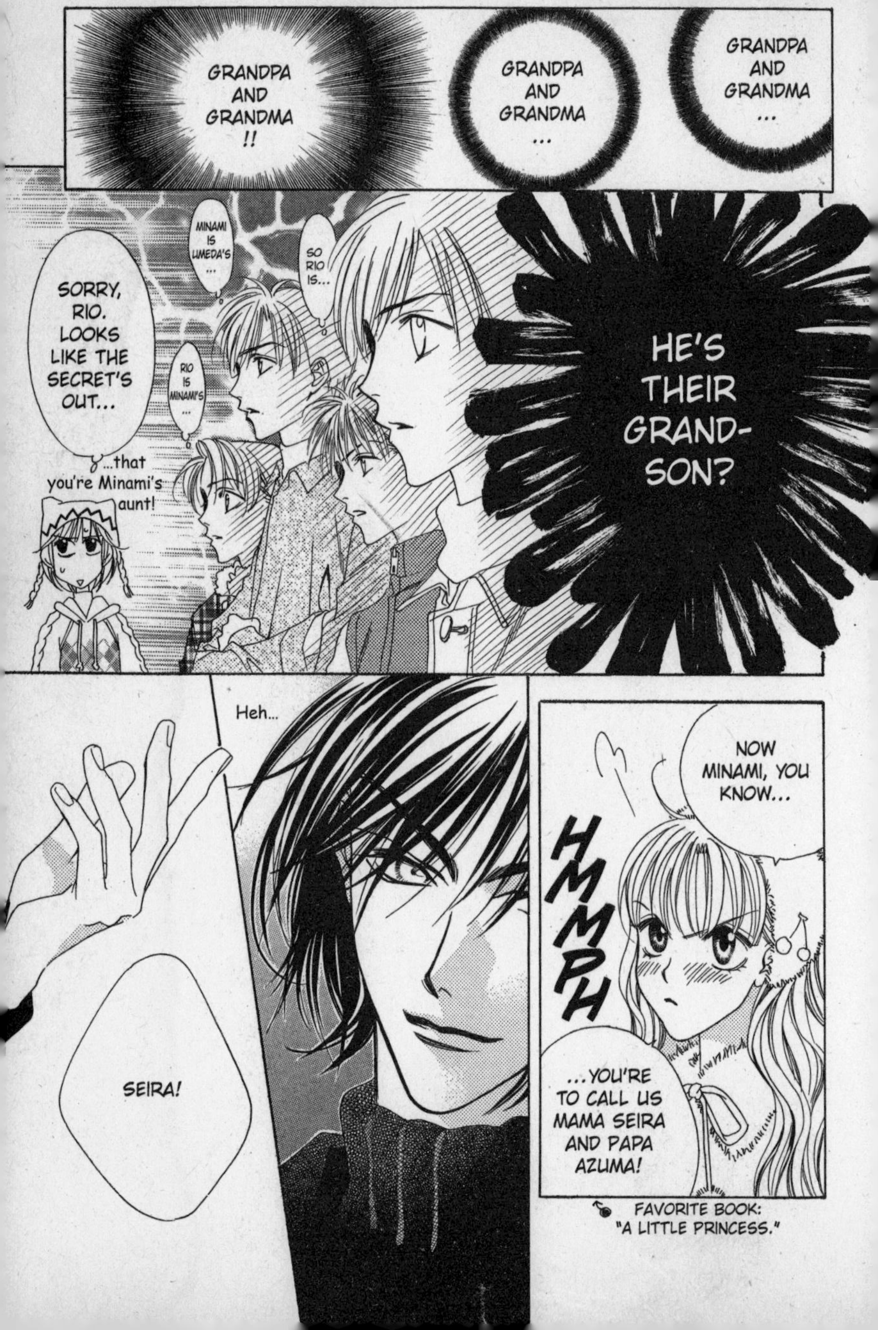
GRANDPA AND GRANDMA...
GRANDPA AND GRANDMA...
GRANDPA AND GRANDMA!!
HE'S THEIR GRAND-SON?
SO RIO IS...
MINAMI IS UMEDA'S...
RIO IS MINAMI'S...
SORRY, RIO. LOOKS LIKE THE SECRET'S OUT...
...that you're Minami's aunt!
NOW MINAMI, YOU KNOW...
HMMPH
...YOU'RE TO CALL US MAMA SEIRA AND PAPA AZUMA!
FAVORITE BOOK: "A LITTLE PRINCESS."
Heh...
SEIRA!

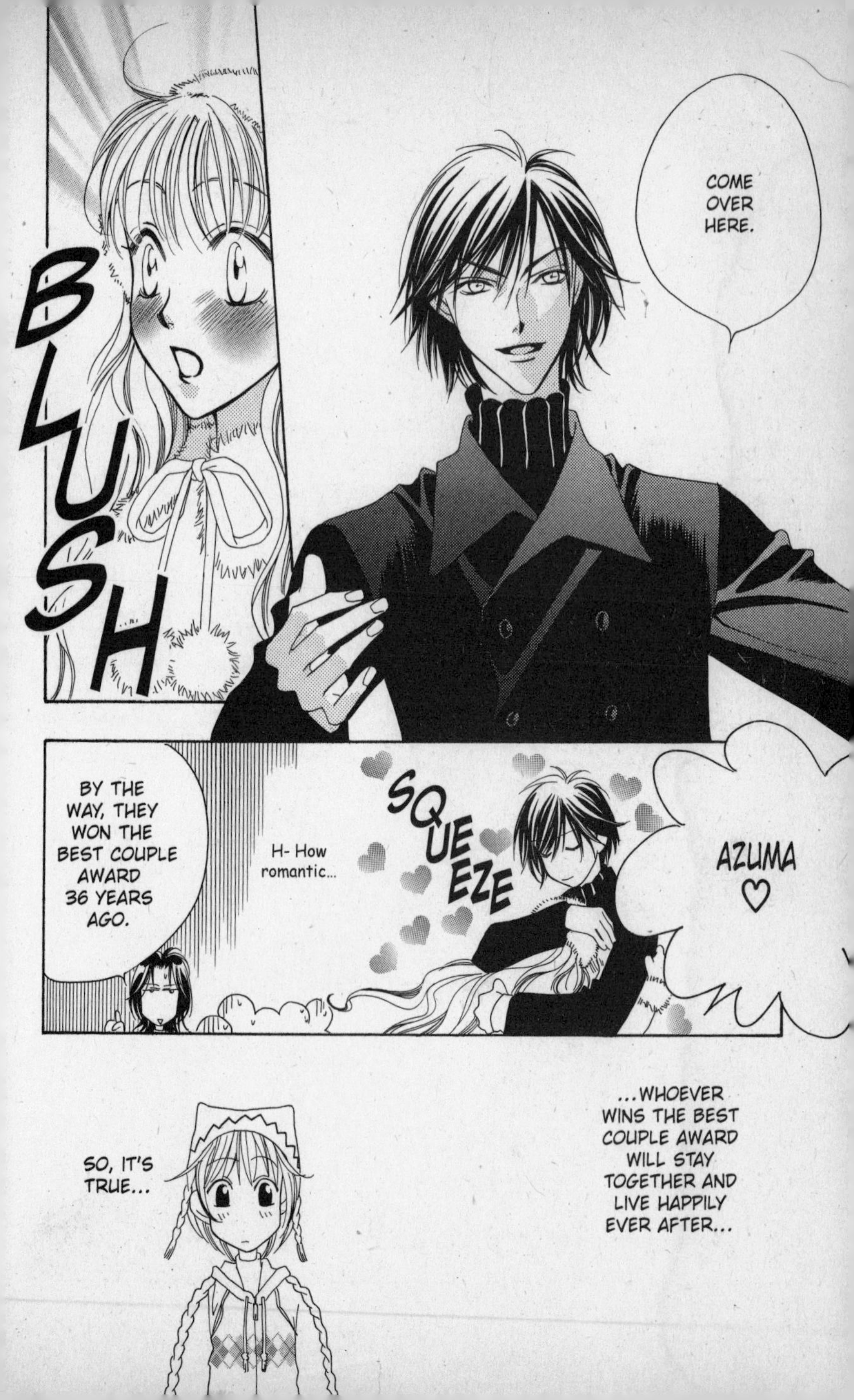
COME OVER HERE.
BLUSH
AZUMA ♡
SQUEEZE
H- How romantic...
BY THE WAY, THEY WON THE BEST COUPLE AWARD 36 YEARS AGO.
...WHOEVER WINS THE BEST COUPLE AWARD WILL STAY TOGETHER AND LIVE HAPPILY EVER AFTER...
SO, IT'S TRUE...

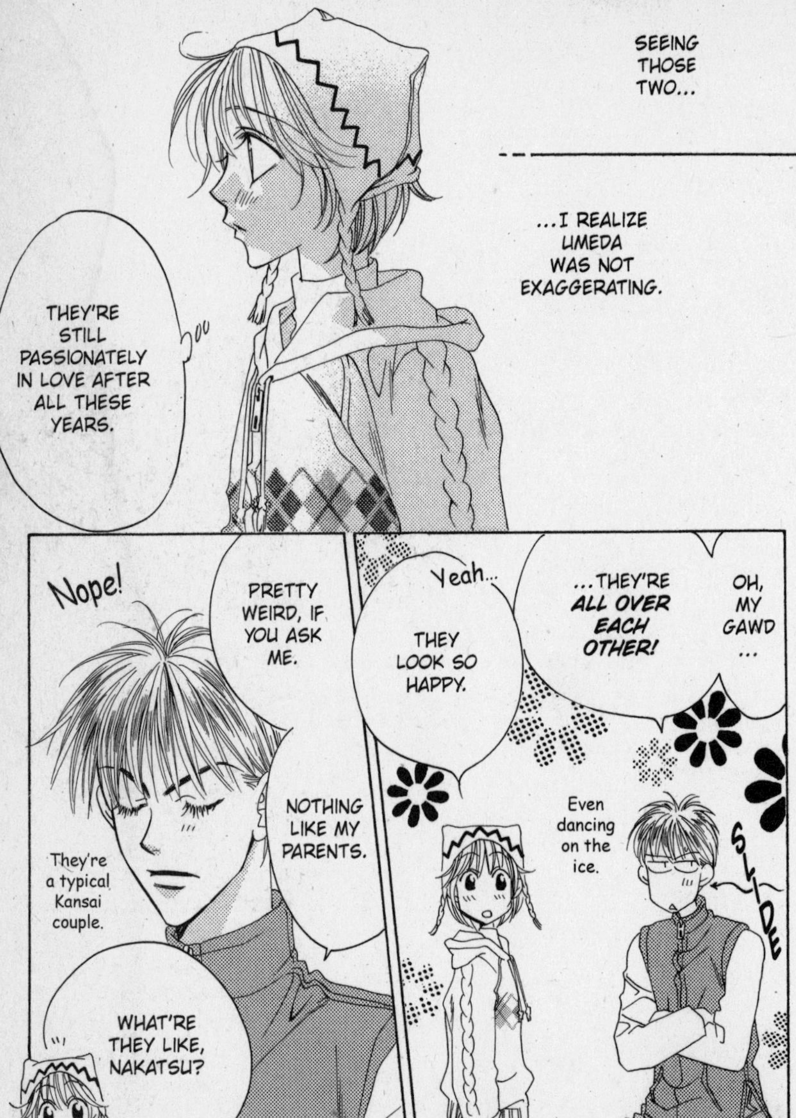
SEEING THOSE TWO...
...I REALIZE UMEDA WAS NOT EXAGGERATING.
THEY'RE STILL PASSIONATELY IN LOVE AFTER ALL THESE YEARS.
OH, MY GAWD ...
...THEY'RE ALL OVER EACH OTHER!
Yeah...
THEY LOOK SO HAPPY.
Even dancing on the ice.
SLIDE
PRETTY WEIRD, IF YOU ASK ME.
Nope!
NOTHING LIKE MY PARENTS.
They're a typical Kansai couple.
WHAT'RE THEY LIKE, NAKATSU?

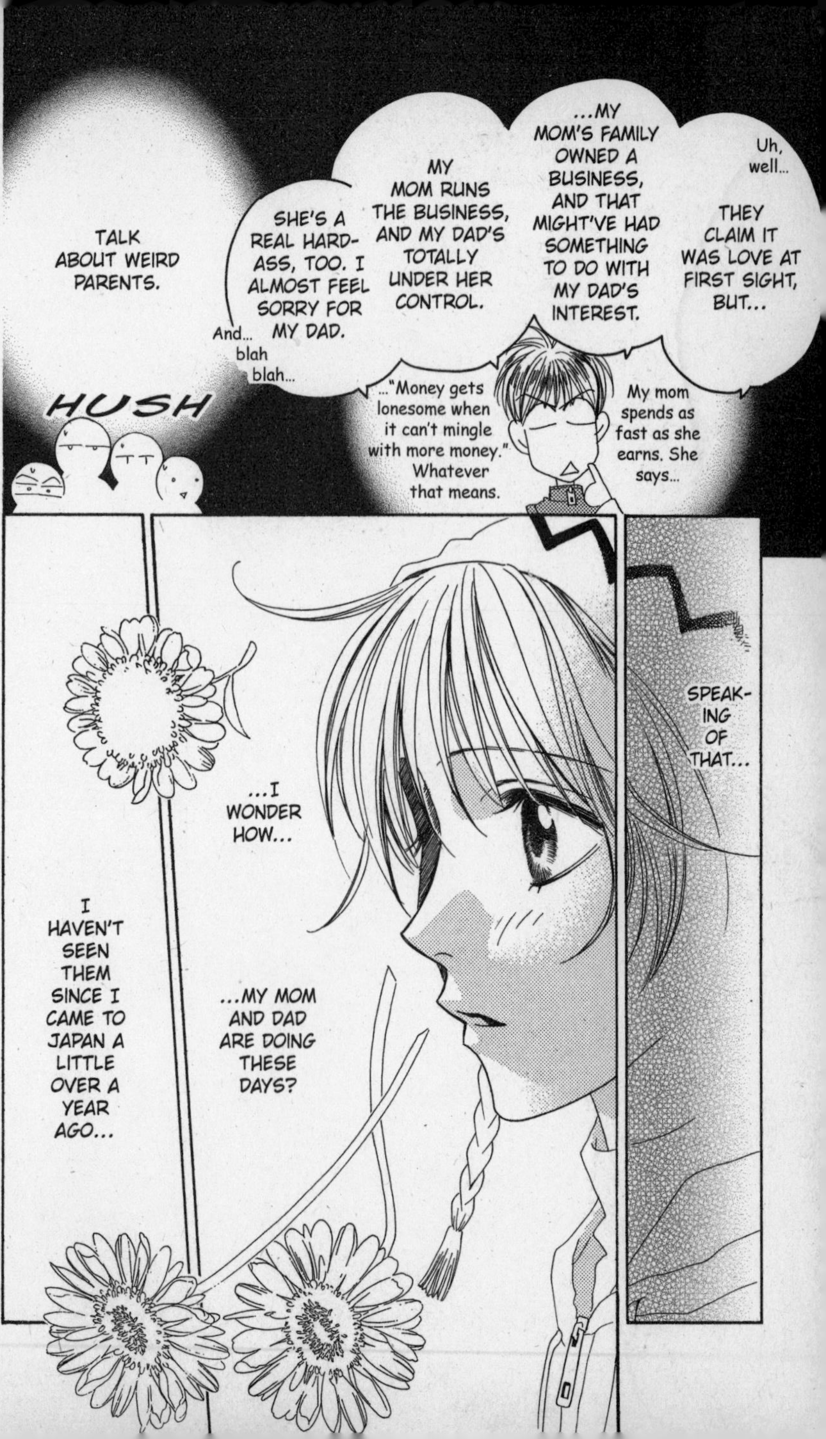
Uh, well...
THEY CLAIM IT WAS LOVE AT FIRST SIGHT, BUT...
...MY MOM'S FAMILY OWNED A BUSINESS, AND THAT MIGHT'VE HAD SOMETHING TO DO WITH MY DAD'S INTEREST.
MY MOM RUNS THE BUSINESS, AND MY DAD'S TOTALLY UNDER HER CONTROL.
SHE'S A REAL HARD-ASS, TOO. I ALMOST FEEL SORRY FOR MY DAD.
My mom spends as fast as she earns. She says...
..."Money gets lonesome when it can't mingle with more money." Whatever that means.
And... blah blah...
TALK ABOUT WEIRD PARENTS.
HUSH
SPEAK-ING OF THAT...
...I WONDER HOW...
...MY MOM AND DAD ARE DOING THESE DAYS?
I HAVEN'T SEEN THEM SINCE I CAME TO JAPAN A LITTLE OVER A YEAR AGO...

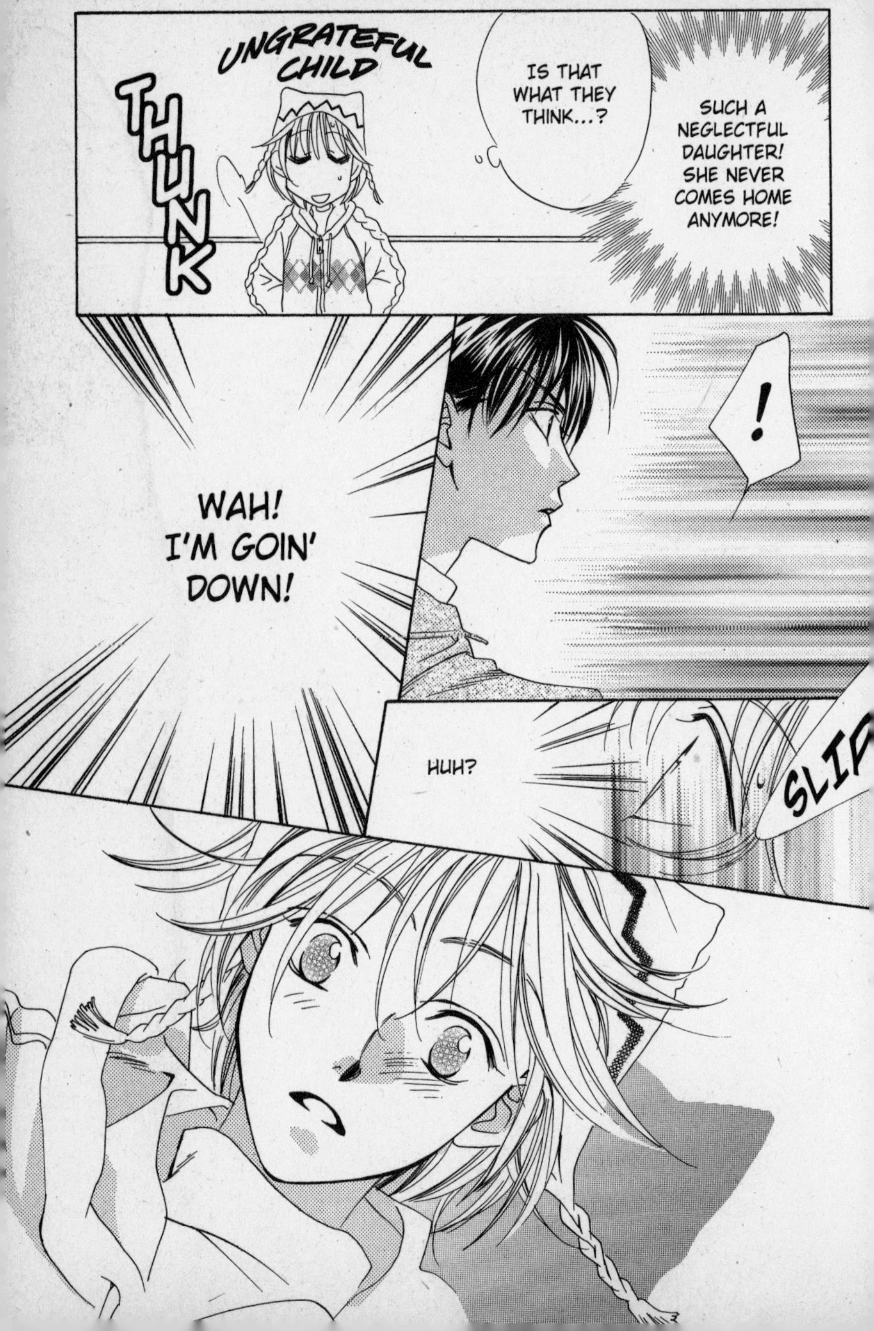
SUCH A NEGLECTFUL DAUGHTER! SHE NEVER COMES HOME ANYMORE!
IS THAT WHAT THEY THINK...?
UNGRATEFUL CHILD
THUNK
!
WAH! I'M GOIN' DOWN!
SLIP
HUH?

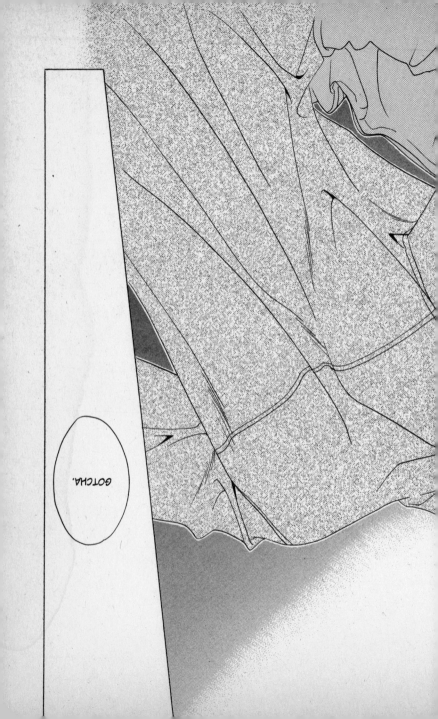

GOTCHA.

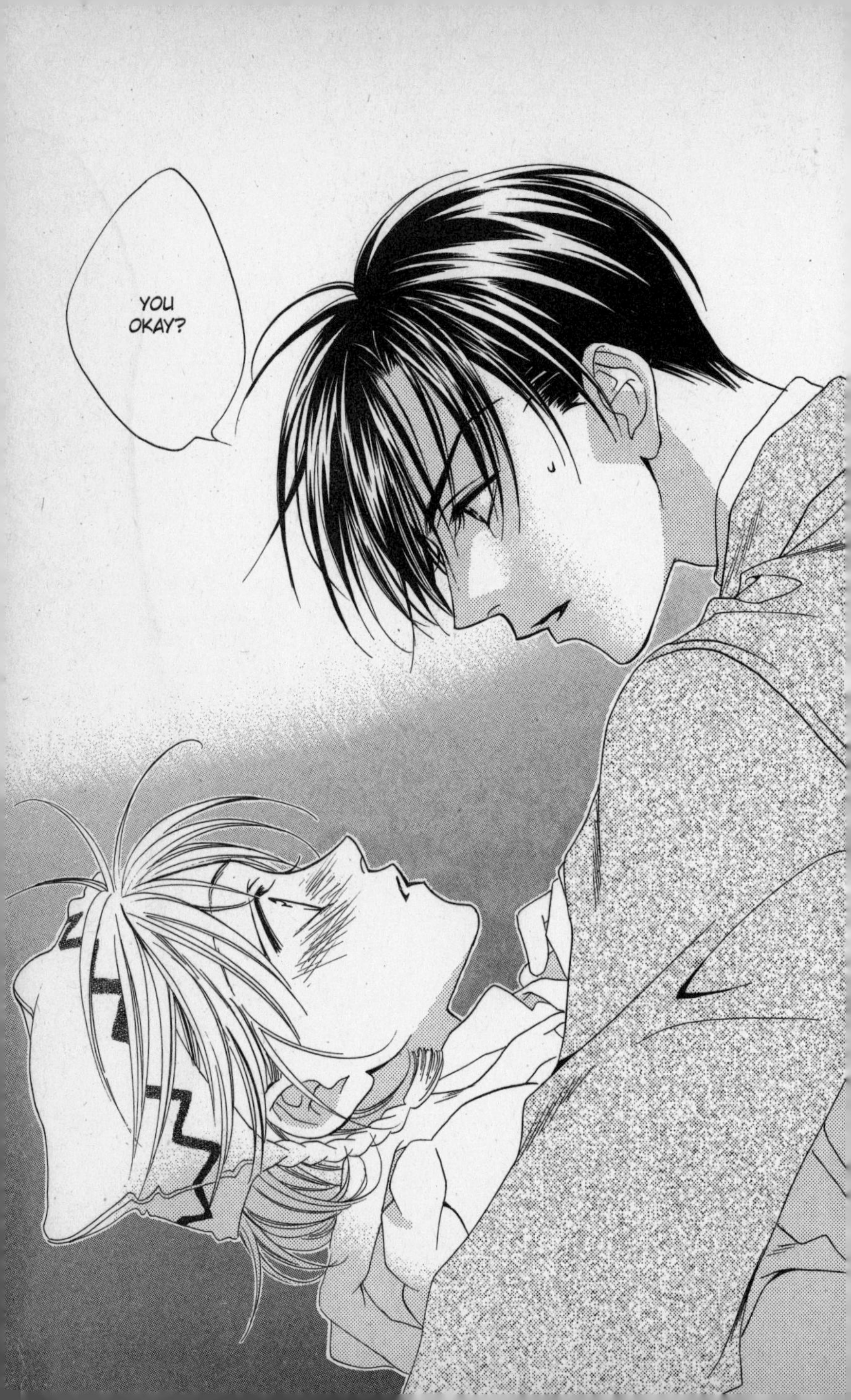
YOU OKAY?

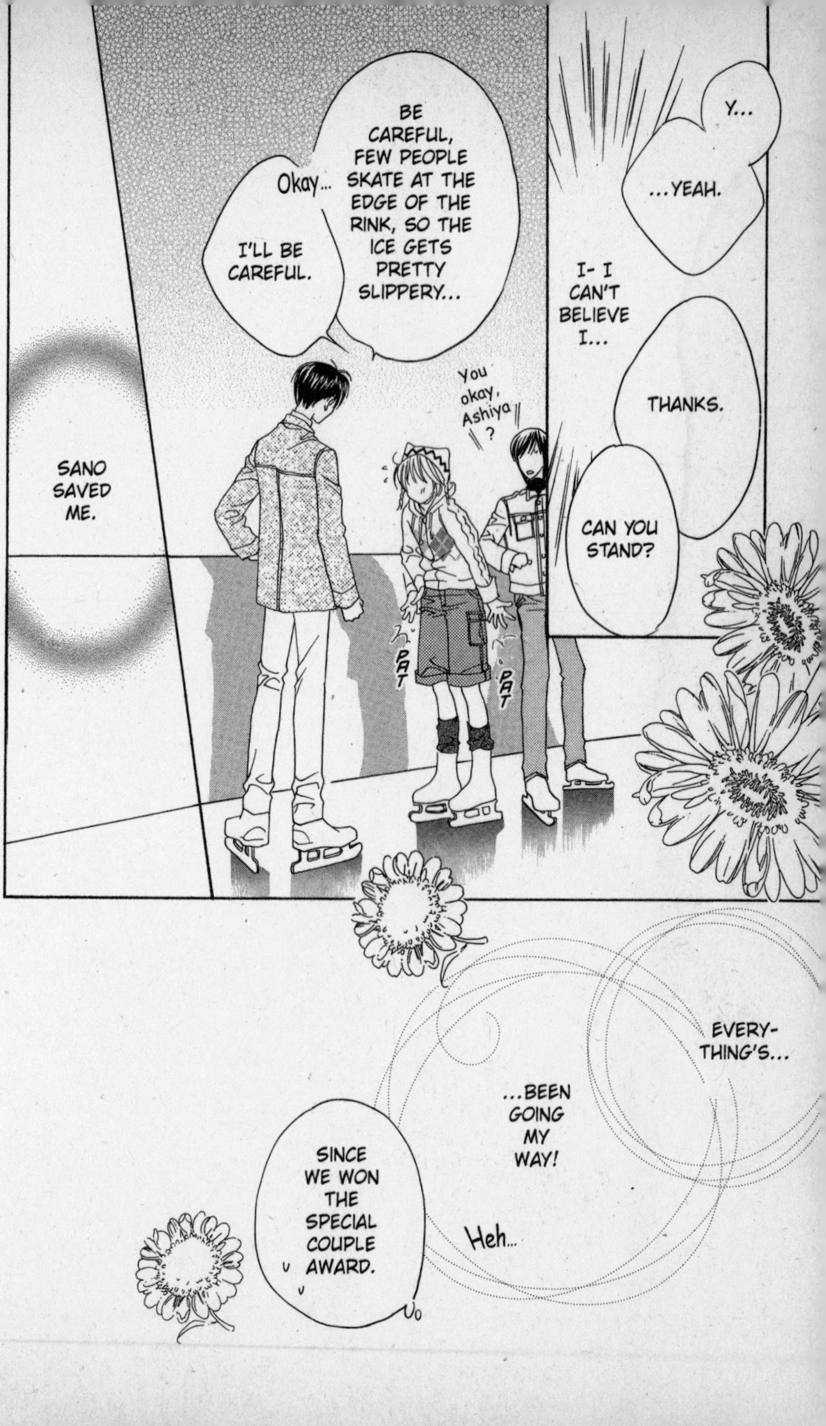
Y...
...YEAH.
I- I CAN'T BELIEVE I...
THANKS.
CAN YOU STAND?
BE CAREFUL, FEW PEOPLE SKATE AT THE EDGE OF THE RINK, SO THE ICE GETS PRETTY SLIPPERY...
Okay... I'LL BE CAREFUL.
You okay, Ashiya?
PAT
PAT
SANO SAVED ME.
EVERY-THING'S...
...BEEN GOING MY WAY!
Heh...
SINCE WE WON THE SPECIAL COUPLE AWARD.

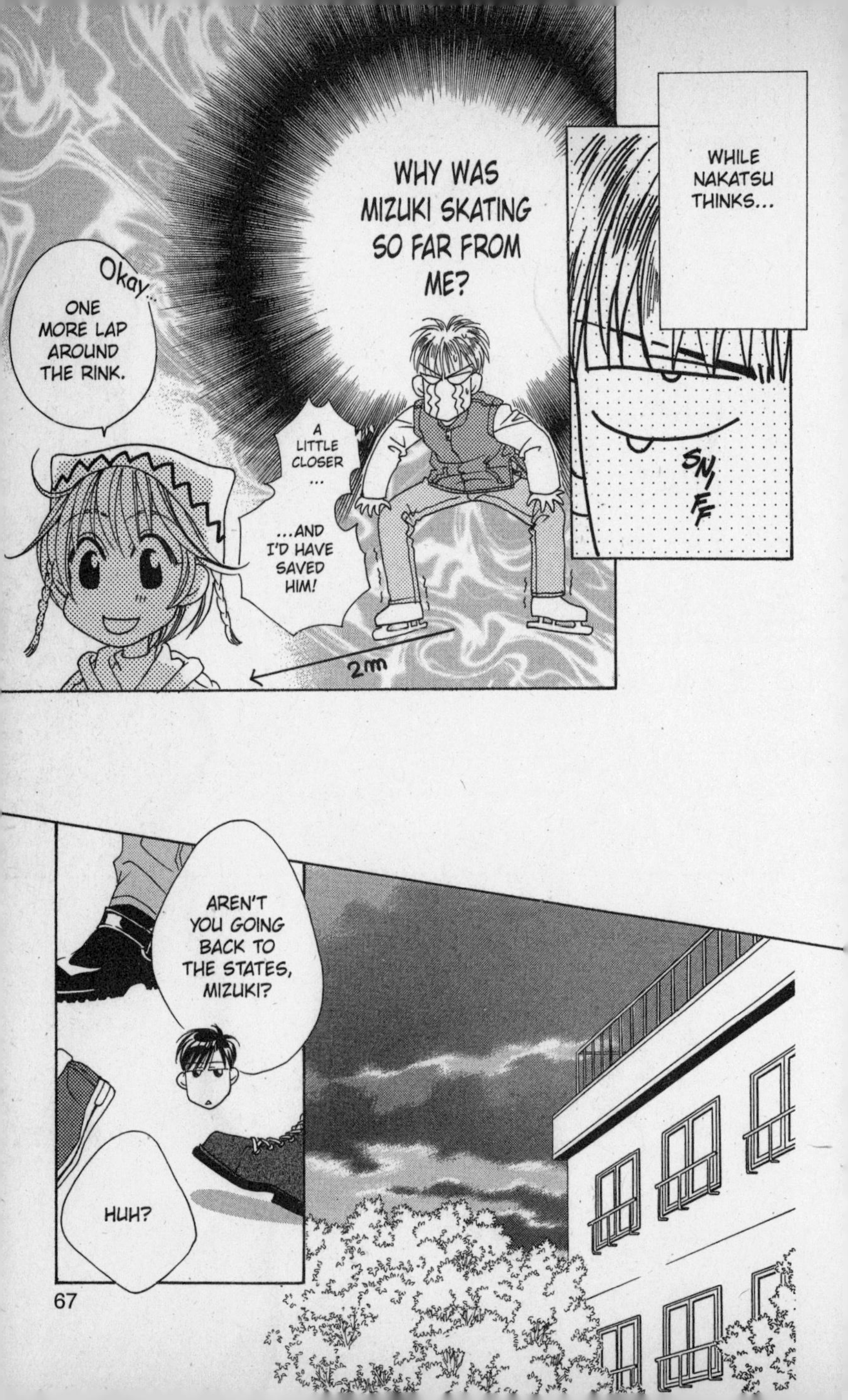
WHILE NAKATSU THINKS...
SNIFF
WHY WAS MIZUKI SKATING SO FAR FROM ME?
A LITTLE CLOSER ...
...AND I'D HAVE SAVED HIM!
2m
Okay...
ONE MORE LAP AROUND THE RINK.
AREN'T YOU GOING BACK TO THE STATES, MIZUKI?
HUH?

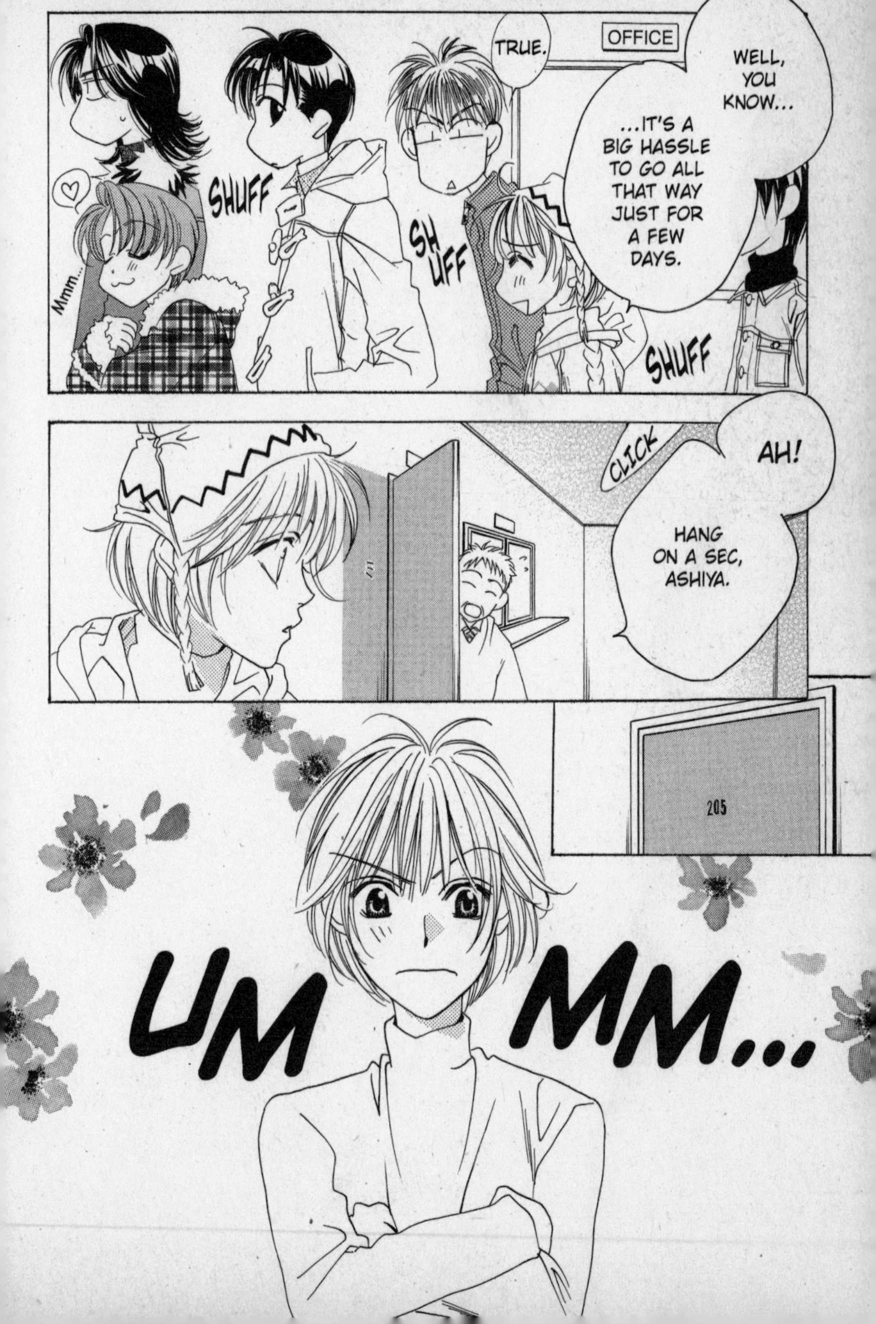
OFFICE
WELL, YOU KNOW...
...IT'S A BIG HASSLE TO GO ALL THAT WAY JUST FOR A FEW DAYS.
SHUFF
TRUE.
SH UFF
SHUFF
Mmm...
AH!
CLICK
HANG ON A SEC, ASHIYA.
205
UM MM...

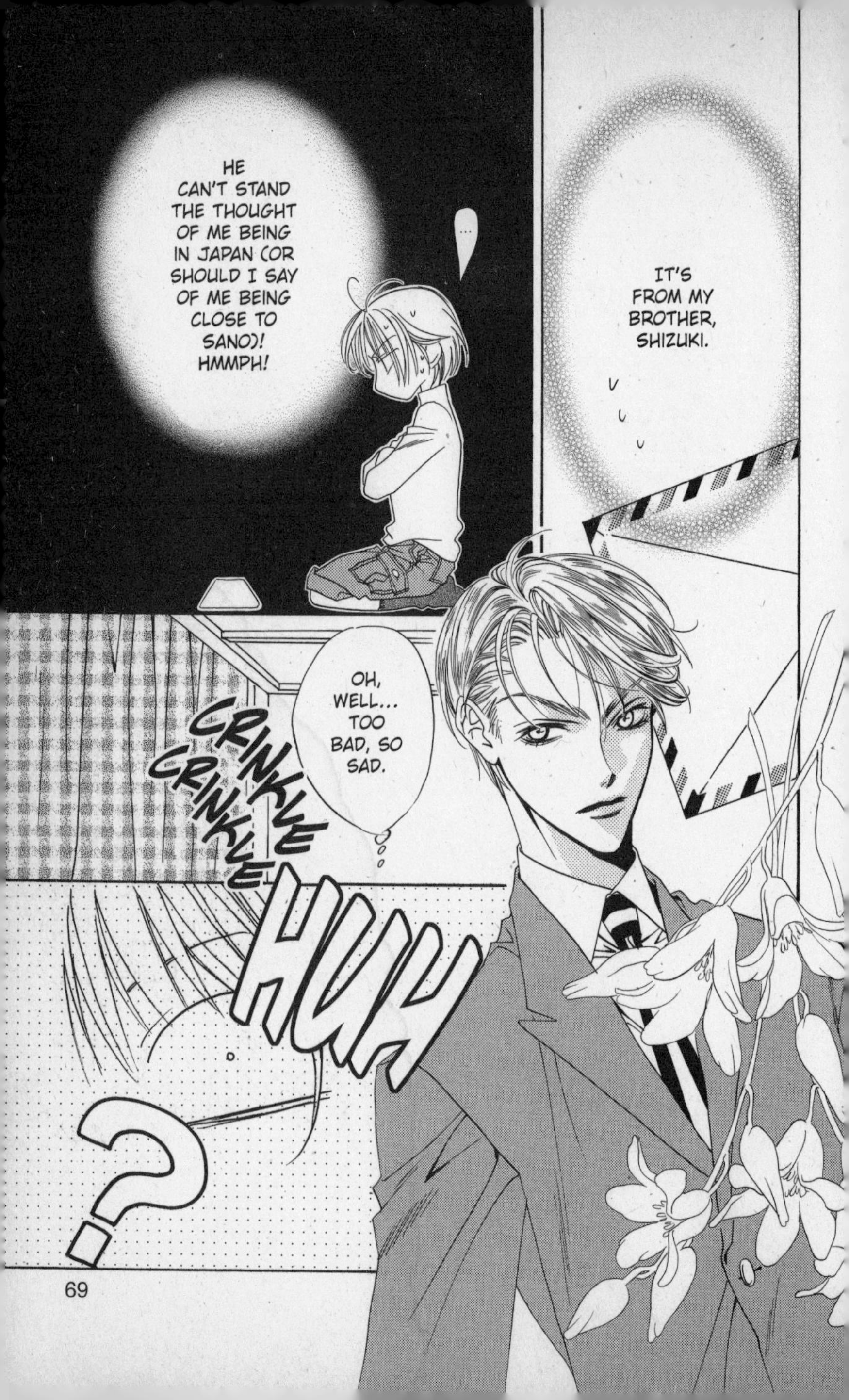
IT'S FROM MY BROTHER, SHIZUKI.
HE CAN'T STAND THE THOUGHT OF ME BEING IN JAPAN (OR SHOULD I SAY OF ME BEING CLOSE TO SANO)! HMMPH!
...
OH, WELL... TOO BAD, SO SAD.
CRINKLE CRINKLE
HUH
?

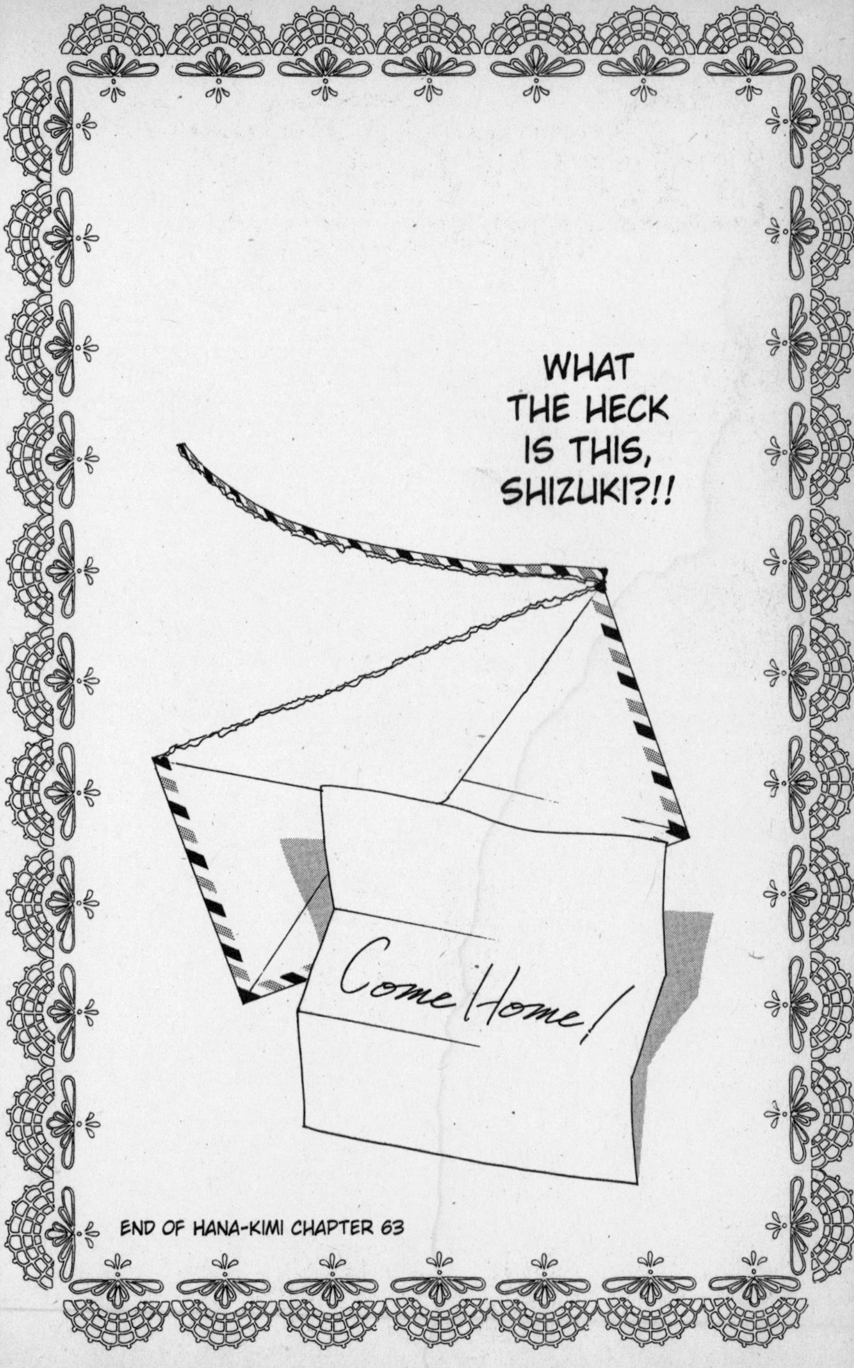
WHAT THE HECK IS THIS, SHIZUKI?!!
Come Home!
END OF HANA-KIMI CHAPTER 63

Hana-Kimi

For You in Full Blossom

CHAPTER 64

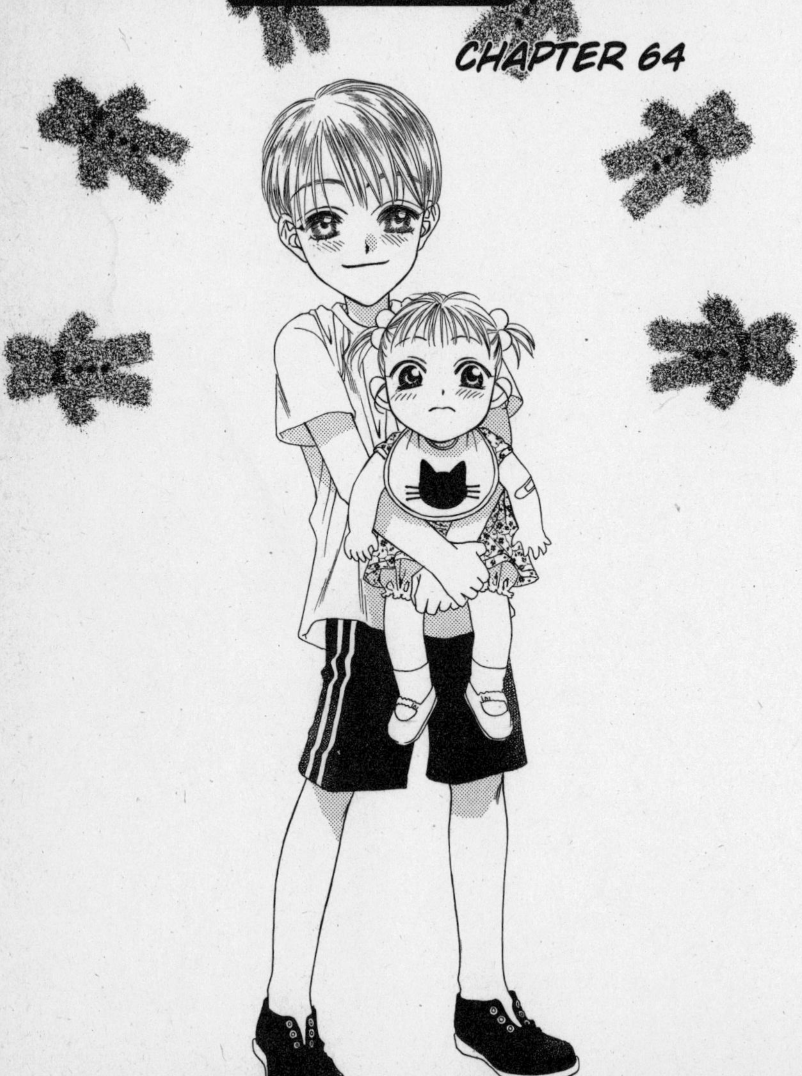

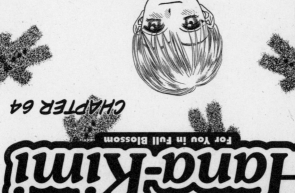

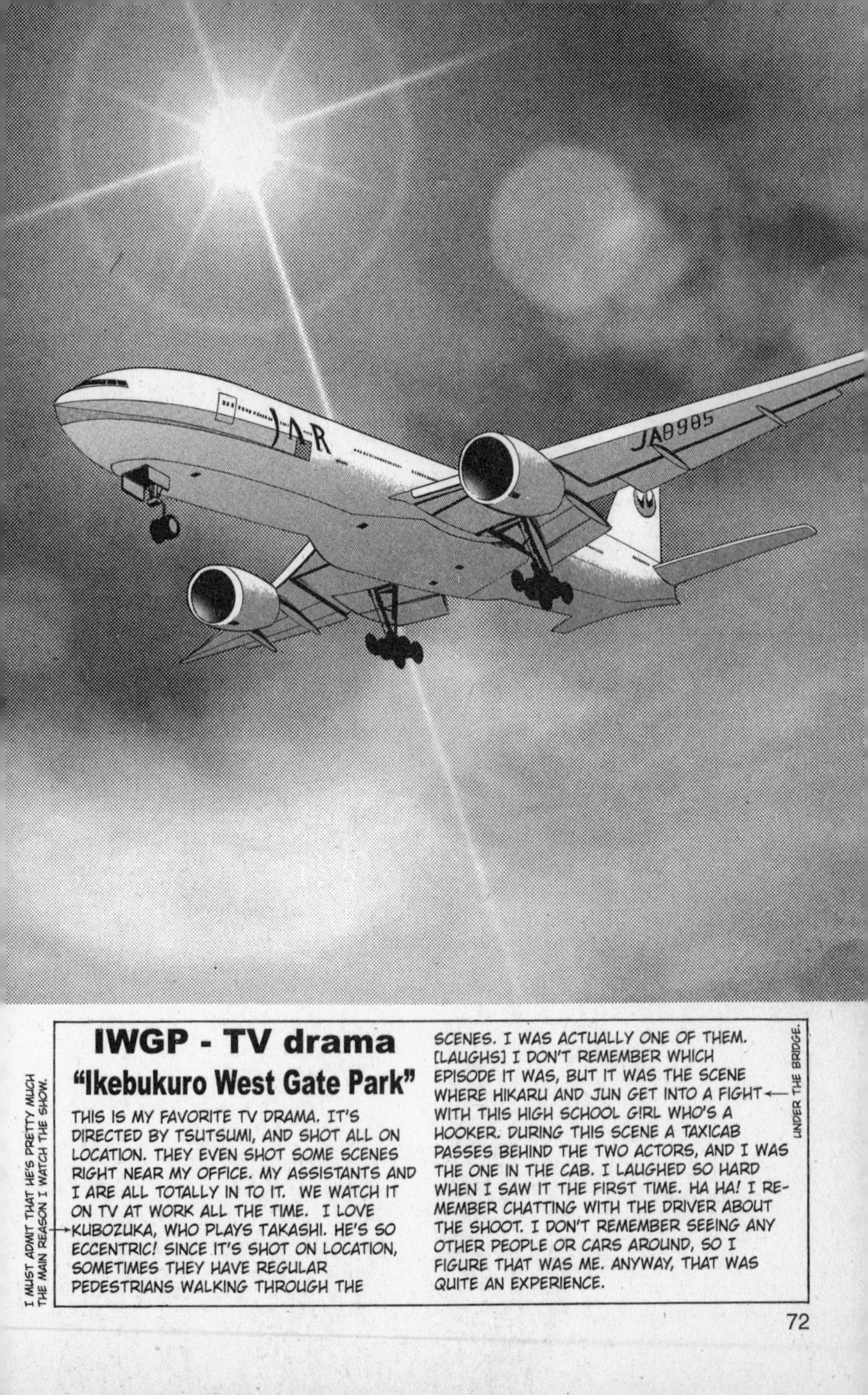
JAR
JA8985

IWGP - TV drama

"Ikebukuro West Gate Park"

THIS IS MY FAVORITE TV DRAMA. IT'S DIRECTED BY TSUTSUMI, AND SHOT ALL ON LOCATION. THEY EVEN SHOT SOME SCENES RIGHT NEAR MY OFFICE. MY ASSISTANTS AND I ARE ALL TOTALLY IN TO IT. WE WATCH IT ON TV AT WORK ALL THE TIME. I LOVE KUBOZUKA, WHO PLAYS TAKASHI. HE'S SO ECCENTRIC! SINCE IT'S SHOT ON LOCATION, SOMETIMES THEY HAVE REGULAR PEDESTRIANS WALKING THROUGH THE SCENES. I WAS ACTUALLY ONE OF THEM. [LAUGHS] I DON'T REMEMBER WHICH EPISODE IT WAS, BUT IT WAS THE SCENE WHERE HIKARU AND JUN GET INTO A FIGHT WITH THIS HIGH SCHOOL GIRL WHO'S A HOOKER. DURING THIS SCENE A TAXICAB PASSES BEHIND THE TWO ACTORS, AND I WAS THE ONE IN THE CAB. I LAUGHED SO HARD WHEN I SAW IT THE FIRST TIME. HA HA! I REMEMBER CHATTING WITH THE DRIVER ABOUT THE SHOOT. I DON'T REMEMBER SEEING ANY OTHER PEOPLE OR CARS AROUND, SO I FIGURE THAT WAS ME. ANYWAY, THAT WAS QUITE AN EXPERIENCE.

I MUST ADMIT THAT HE'S PRETTY MUCH THE MAIN REASON I WATCH THE SHOW.

UNDER THE BRIDGE.

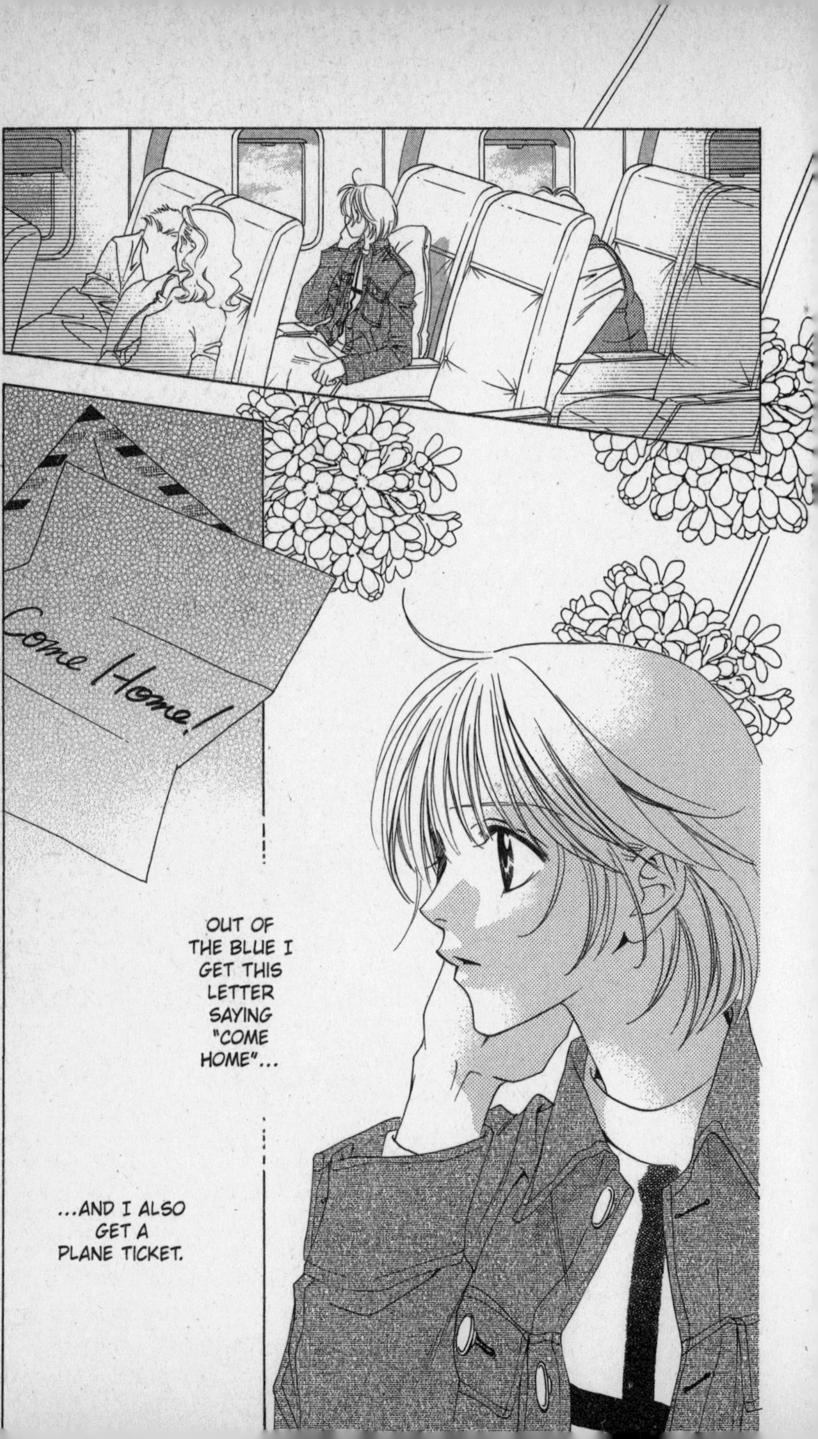
Come Home!
OUT OF THE BLUE I GET THIS LETTER SAYING "COME HOME"...
...AND I ALSO GET A PLANE TICKET.

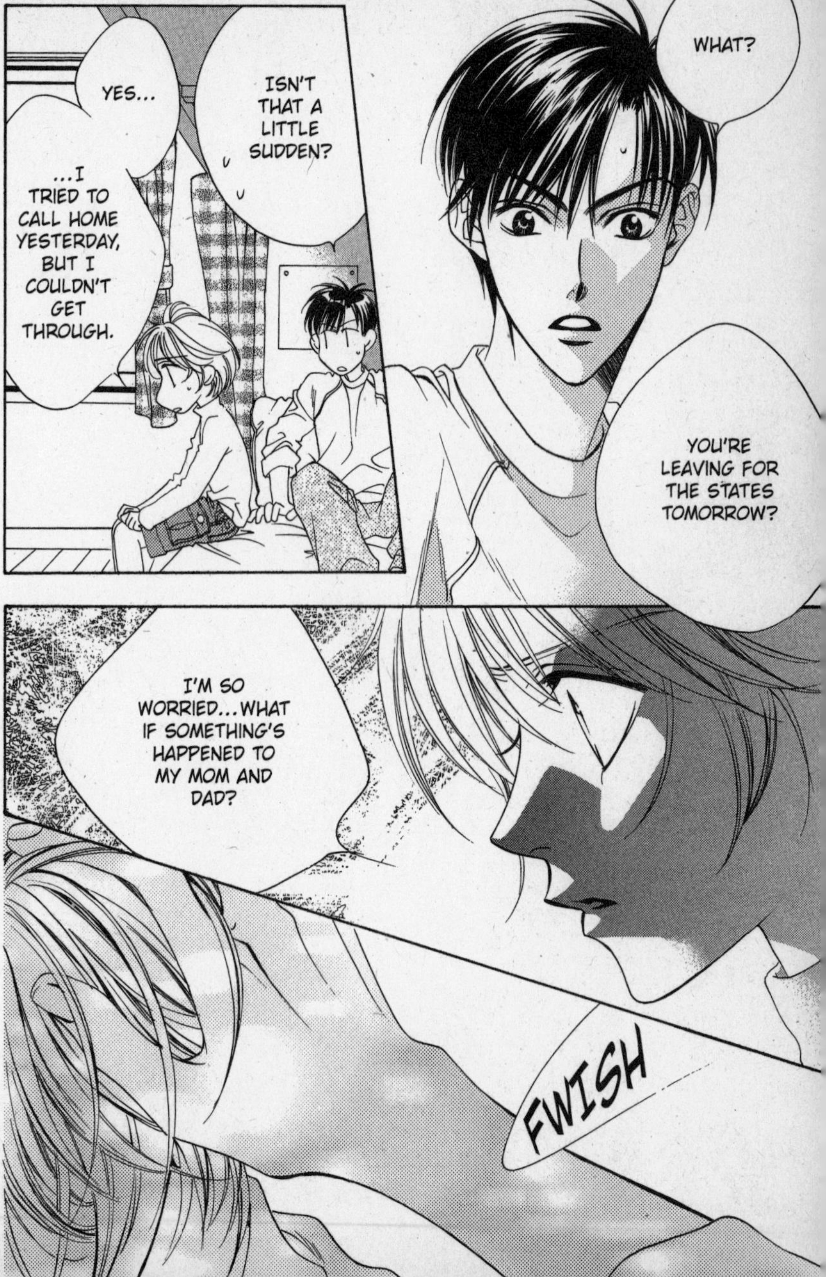
WHAT?
YOU'RE LEAVING FOR THE STATES TOMORROW?
ISN'T THAT A LITTLE SUDDEN?
YES...
...I TRIED TO CALL HOME YESTERDAY, BUT I COULDN'T GET THROUGH.
I'M SO WORRIED...WHAT IF SOMETHING'S HAPPENED TO MY MOM AND DAD?
FWISH

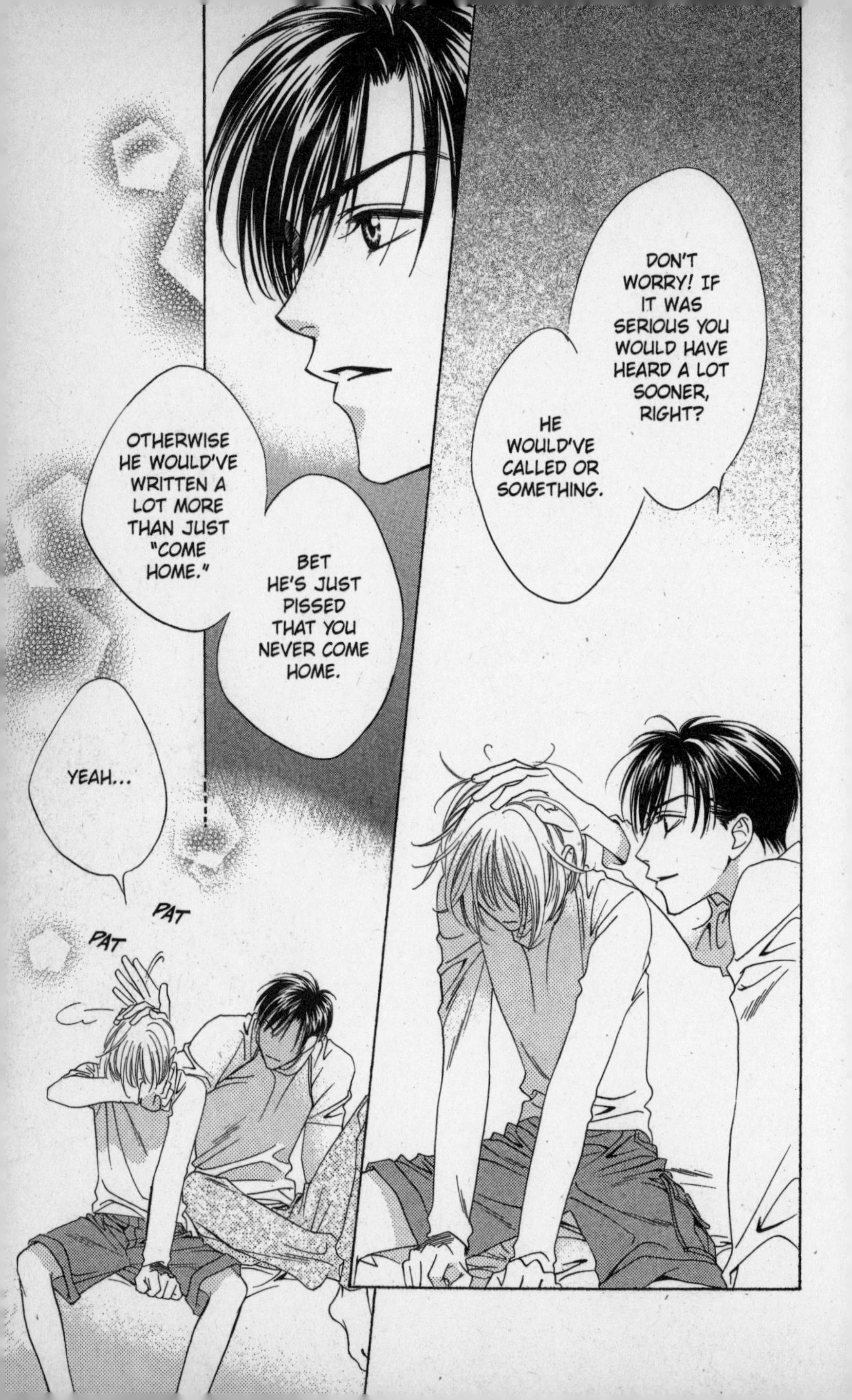
DON'T WORRY! IF IT WAS SERIOUS YOU WOULD HAVE HEARD A LOT SOONER, RIGHT?
HE WOULD'VE CALLED OR SOMETHING.
OTHERWISE HE WOULD'VE WRITTEN A LOT MORE THAN JUST "COME HOME."
BET HE'S JUST PISSED THAT YOU NEVER COME HOME.
YEAH...
PAT
PAT

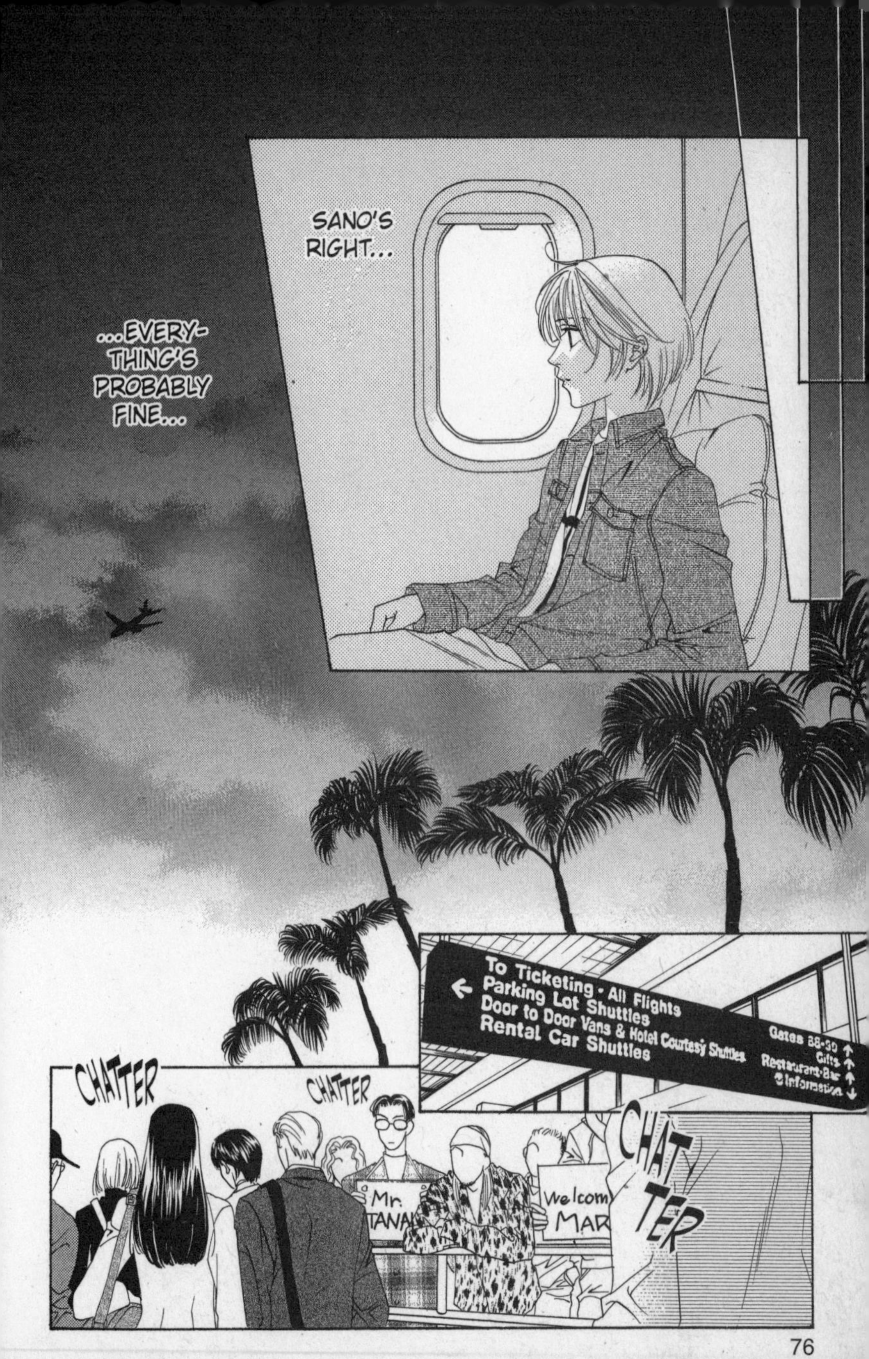
SANO'S RIGHT...
...EVERY-THING'S PROBABLY FINE...
To Ticketing · All Flights
Parking Lot Shuttles
Door to Door Vans & Hotel Courtesy Shuttles
Rental Car Shuttles
Gates 38-30
Gifts
Restaurant·Bar
Information
CHAT TER
Mr. TANA
Welcom MAR
CHATTER
CHATTER

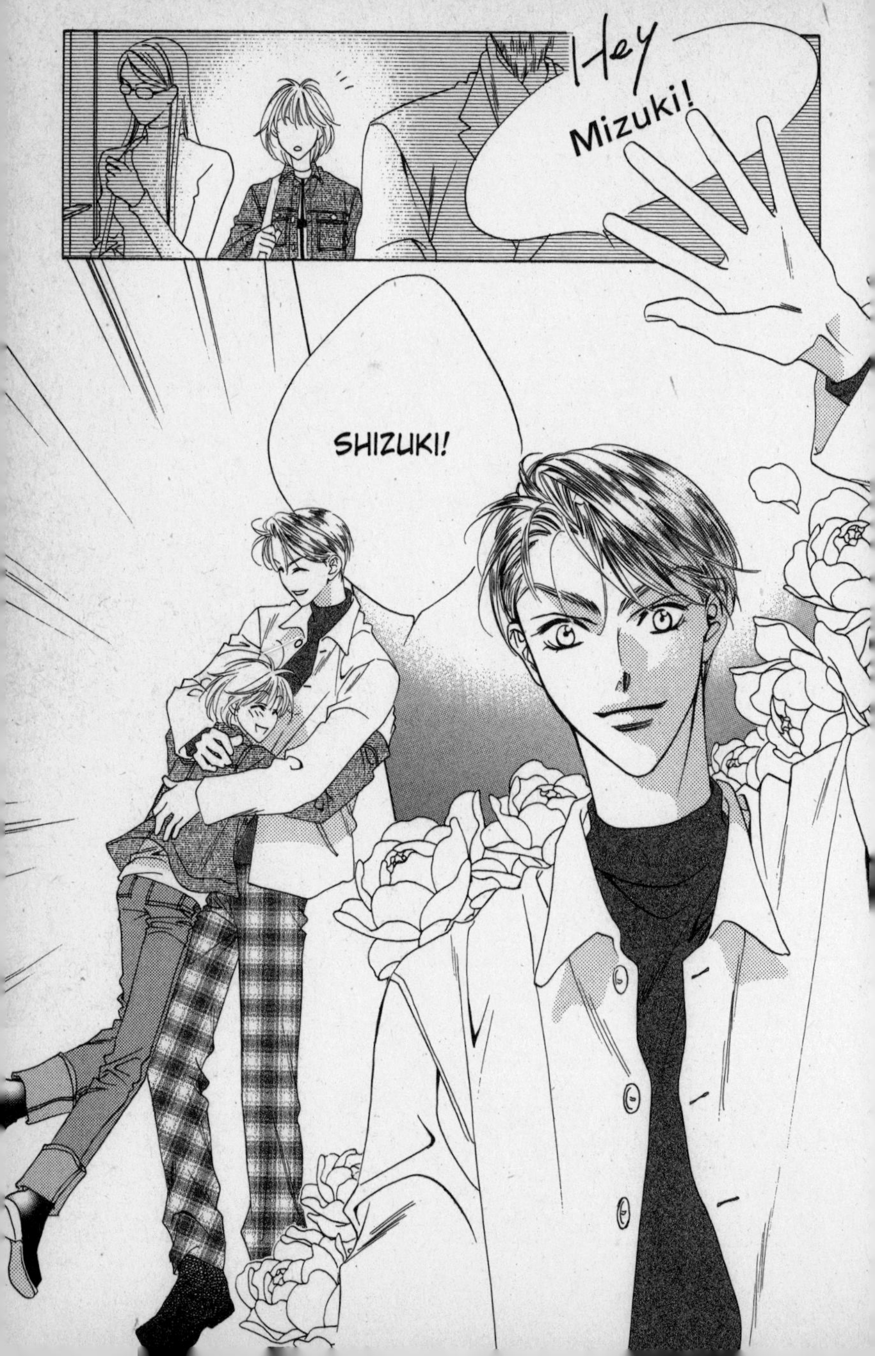
Hey
Mizuki!
SHIZUKI!

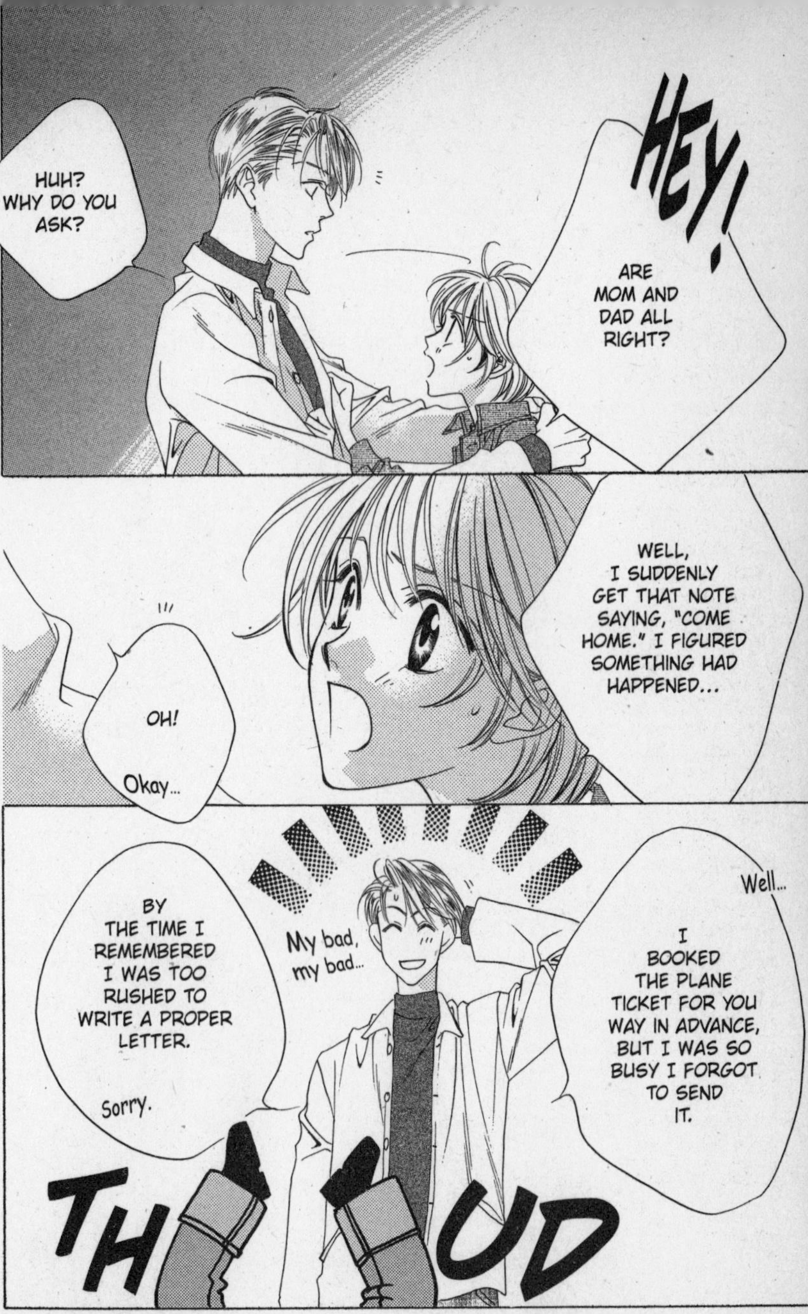
HEY!
ARE MOM AND DAD ALL RIGHT?
HUH? WHY DO YOU ASK?
WELL, I SUDDENLY GET THAT NOTE SAYING, "COME HOME." I FIGURED SOMETHING HAD HAPPENED...
OH!
Okay...
Well...
I BOOKED THE PLANE TICKET FOR YOU WAY IN ADVANCE, BUT I WAS SO BUSY I FORGOT TO SEND IT.
My bad, my bad...
BY THE TIME I REMEMBERED I WAS TOO RUSHED TO WRITE A PROPER LETTER.
Sorry.
THUD

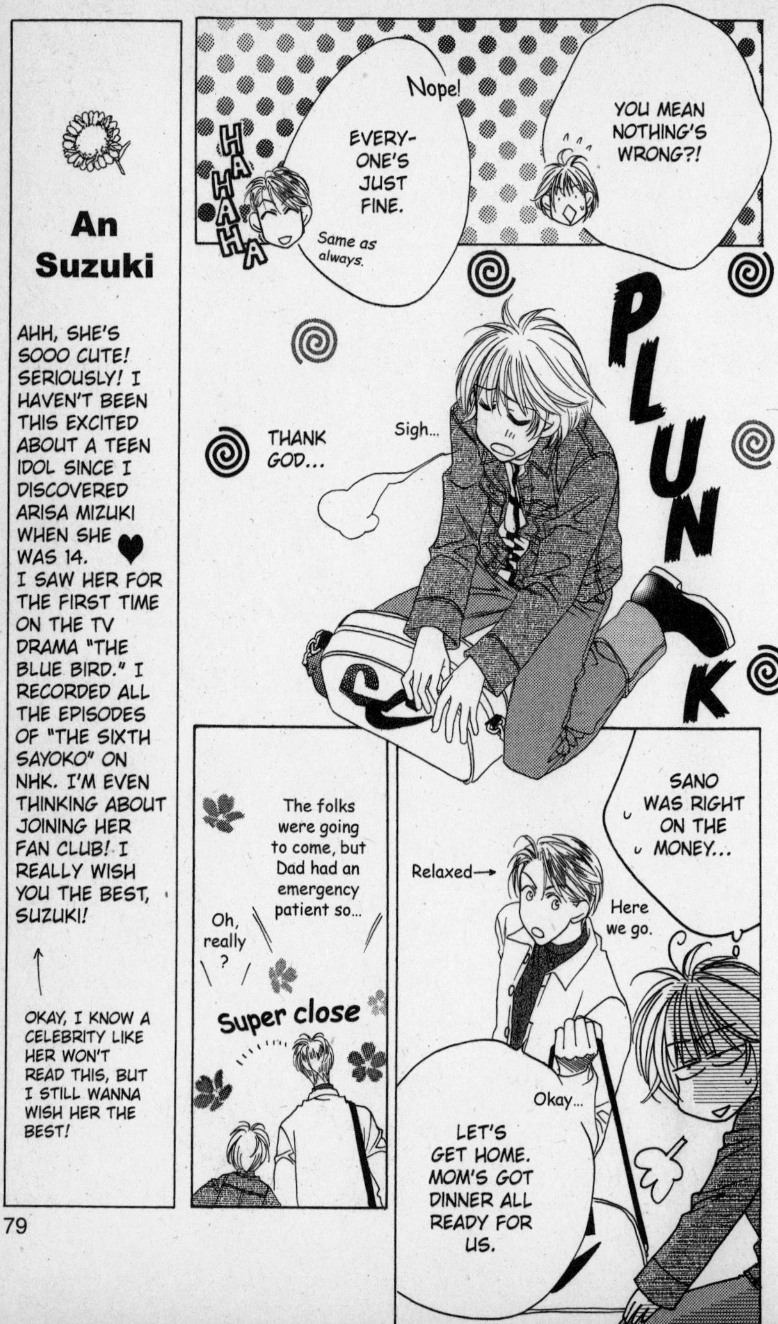
YOU MEAN NOTHING'S WRONG?!
Nope!
EVERY-ONE'S JUST FINE.
Same as always.
HAHAHAHA
PLUNK
Sigh...
THANK GOD...
SANO WAS RIGHT ON THE MONEY...
Here we go.
Relaxed
Okay...
LET'S GET HOME. MOM'S GOT DINNER ALL READY FOR US.
The folks were going to come, but Dad had an emergency patient so...
Oh, really?
Super close

An Suzuki

AHH, SHE'S SOOO CUTE! SERIOUSLY! I HAVEN'T BEEN THIS EXCITED ABOUT A TEEN IDOL SINCE I DISCOVERED ARISA MIZUKI WHEN SHE WAS 14. ♥ I SAW HER FOR THE FIRST TIME ON THE TV DRAMA "THE BLUE BIRD." I RECORDED ALL THE EPISODES OF "THE SIXTH SAYOKO" ON NHK. I'M EVEN THINKING ABOUT JOINING HER FAN CLUB! I REALLY WISH YOU THE BEST, SUZUKI!

↑

OKAY, I KNOW A CELEBRITY LIKE HER WON'T READ THIS, BUT I STILL WANNA WISH HER THE BEST!

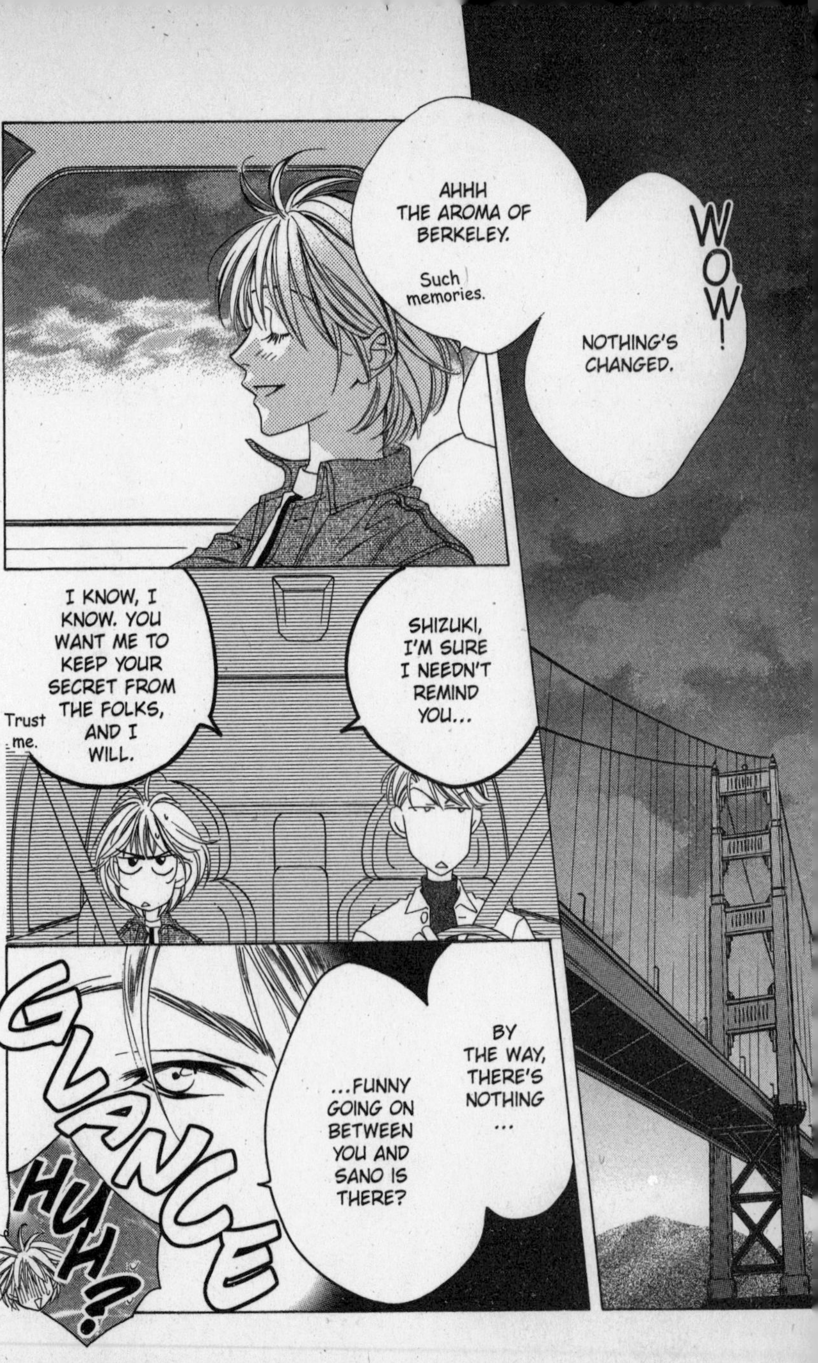
WOW!
NOTHING'S CHANGED.
AHHH THE AROMA OF BERKELEY.
Such memories.
SHIZUKI, I'M SURE I NEEDN'T REMIND YOU...
I KNOW, I KNOW. YOU WANT ME TO KEEP YOUR SECRET FROM THE FOLKS, AND I WILL.
Trust me.
BY THE WAY, THERE'S NOTHING ...
...FUNNY GOING ON BETWEEN YOU AND SANO IS THERE?
GLANCE
HUH?

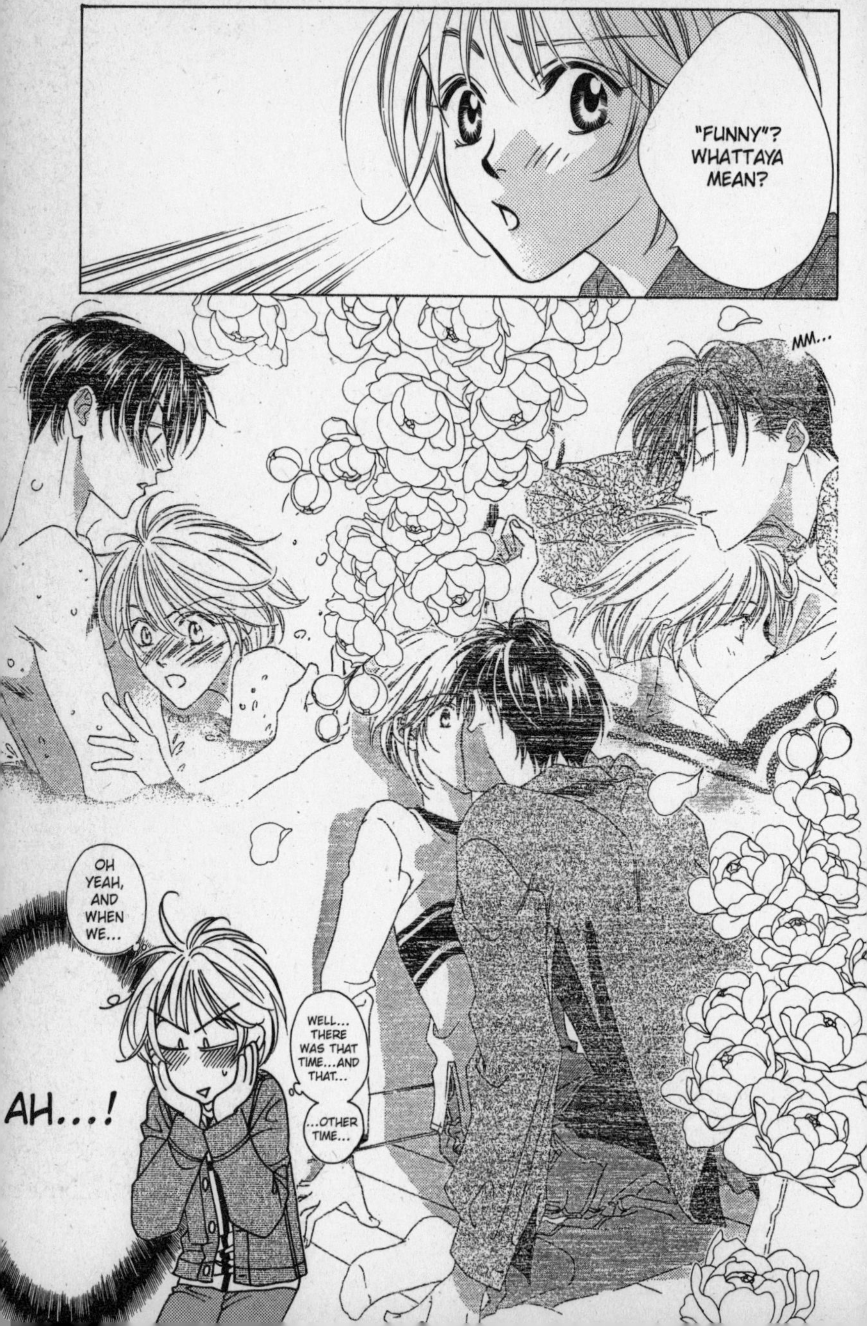
"FUNNY"? WHATTAYA MEAN?
MM...
OH YEAH, AND WHEN WE...
AH...!
WELL... THERE WAS THAT TIME...AND THAT...
...OTHER TIME...

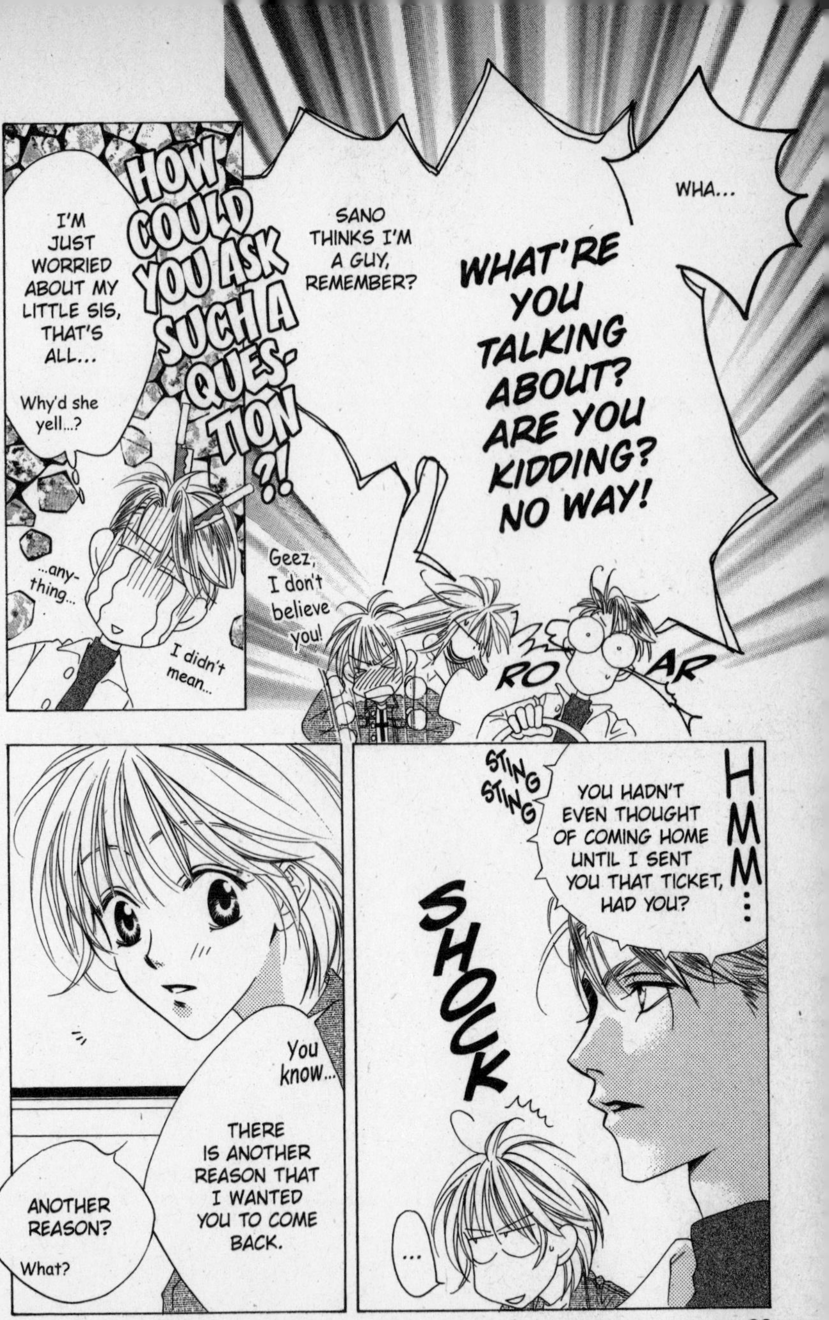
WHA...
WHAT'RE YOU TALKING ABOUT? ARE YOU KIDDING? NO WAY!
ROAR
SANO THINKS I'M A GUY, REMEMBER?
Geez, I don't believe you!
HOW COULD YOU ASK SUCH A QUES-TION?!
I'M JUST WORRIED ABOUT MY LITTLE SIS, THAT'S ALL...
Why'd she yell...?
...any-thing...
I didn't mean...
HMM...
YOU HADN'T EVEN THOUGHT OF COMING HOME UNTIL I SENT YOU THAT TICKET, HAD YOU?
STING STING
SHOUK
...
You know...
THERE IS ANOTHER REASON THAT I WANTED YOU TO COME BACK.
ANOTHER REASON?
What?

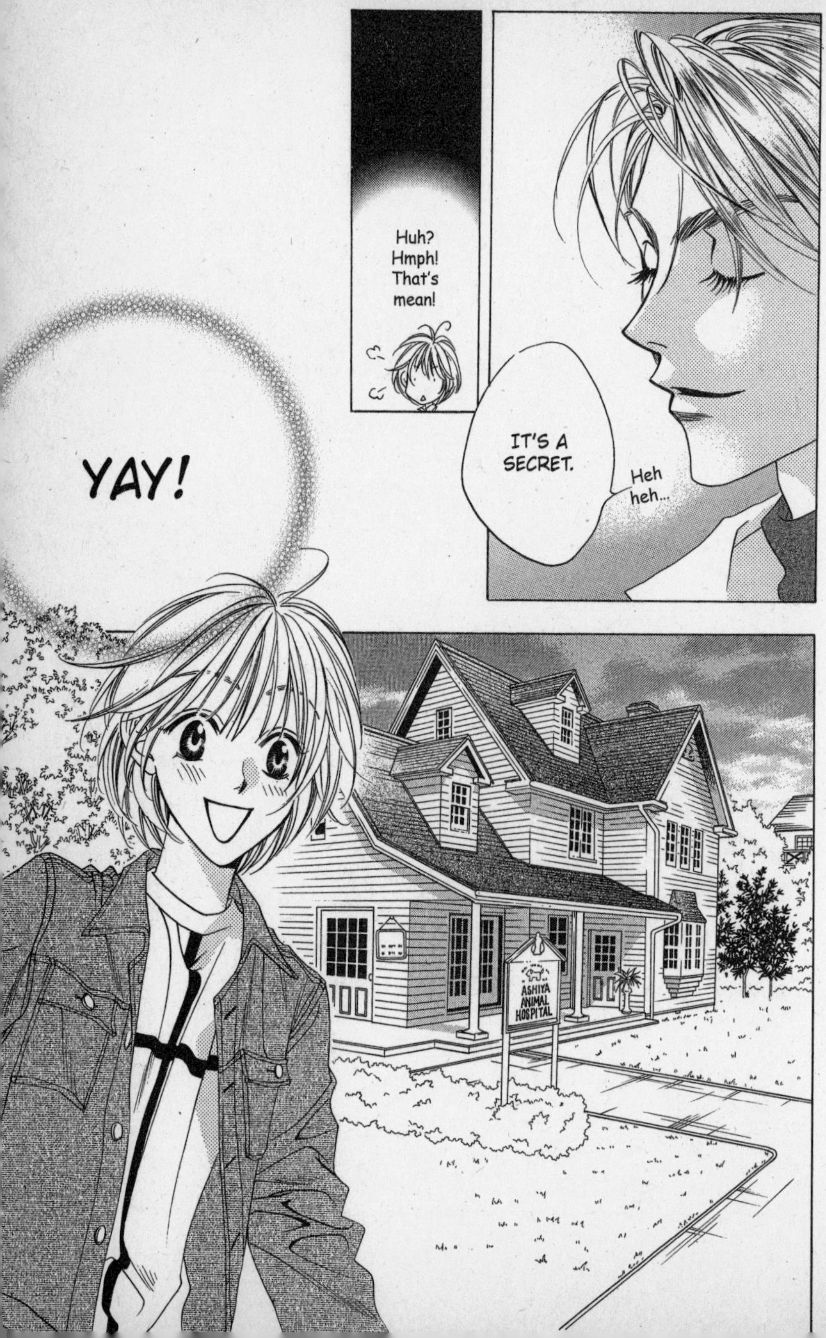
IT'S A SECRET.
Heh heh...
Huh? Hmph! That's mean!
YAY!
ASHIYA ANIMAL HOSPITAL

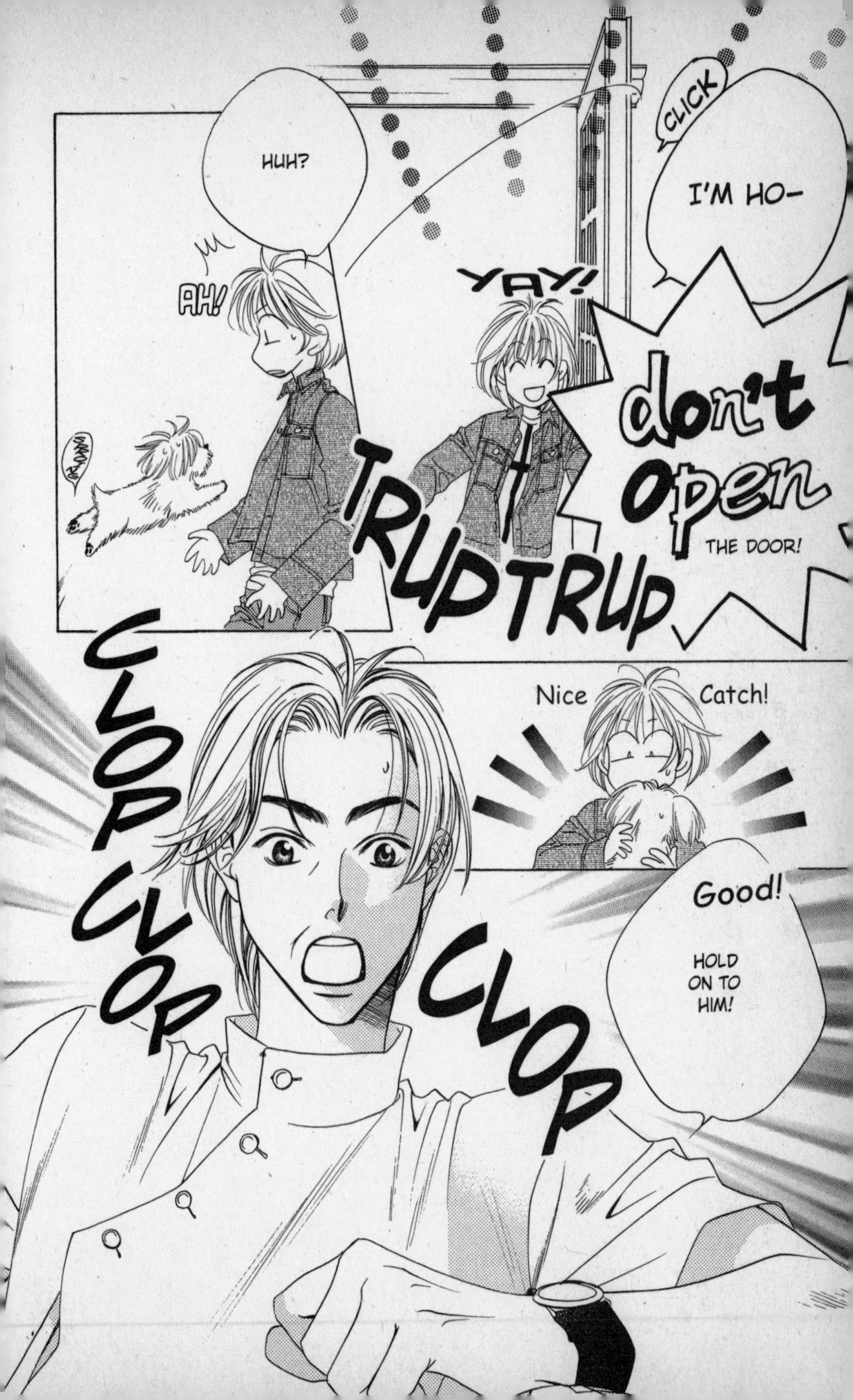
CLICK
I'M HO-
YAY!
don't open THE DOOR!
HUH?
AH!
TRUPTRUP
Nice Catch!
Good!
HOLD ON TO HIM!
CLOP CLOP CLOP

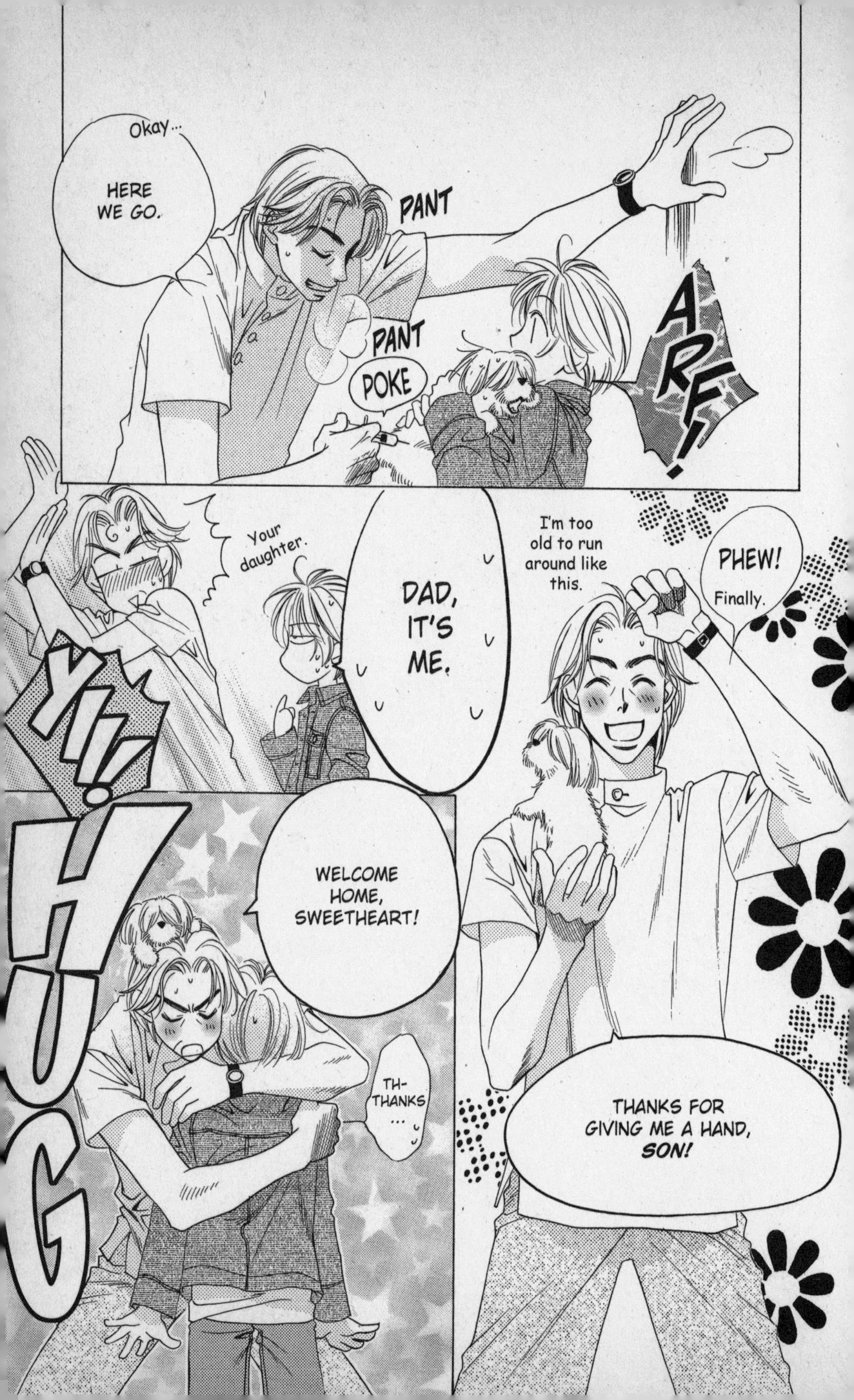
PANT
Okay...
HERE WE GO.
ARF!
PANT
POKE
PHEW!
Finally.
I'm too old to run around like this.
THANKS FOR GIVING ME A HAND, SON!
DAD, IT'S ME.
Your daughter.
YI!!
WELCOME HOME, SWEETHEART!
HUG
TH-THANKS ...

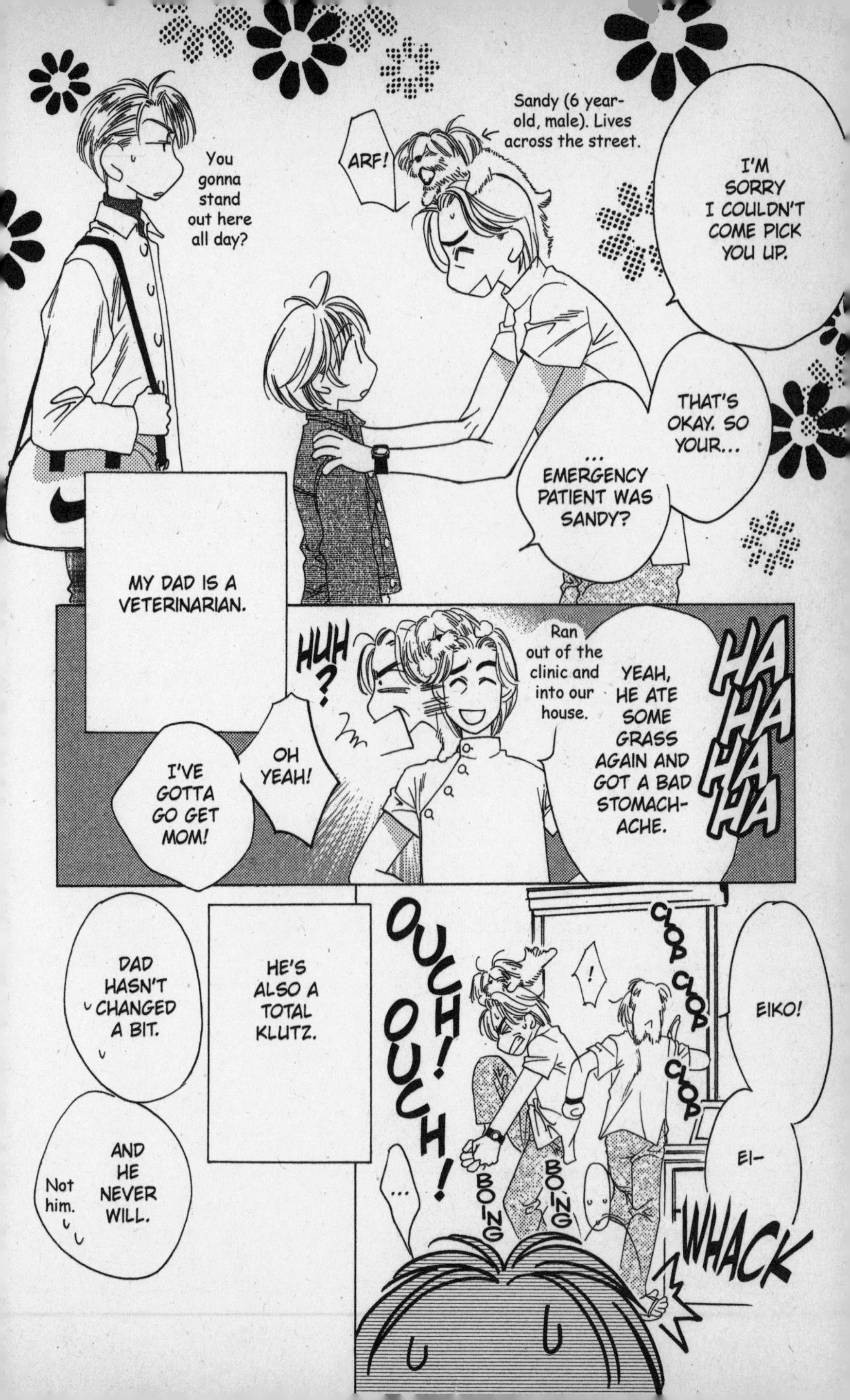
I'M SORRY I COULDN'T COME PICK YOU UP.
Sandy (6 year-old, male). Lives across the street.
ARF!
THAT'S OKAY. SO YOUR...
... EMERGENCY PATIENT WAS SANDY?
You gonna stand out here all day?
MY DAD IS A VETERINARIAN.
HAHAHAHA
YEAH, HE ATE SOME GRASS AGAIN AND GOT A BAD STOMACH-ACHE.
Ran out of the clinic and into our house.
HUH?
OH YEAH!
I'VE GOTTA GO GET MOM!
EIKO!
CLOP CLOP CLOP
!
EI-
WHACK
BOING BOING
OUCH! OUCH! OUCH!
...
HE'S ALSO A TOTAL KLUTZ.
DAD HASN'T CHANGED A BIT.
AND HE NEVER WILL.
Not him.

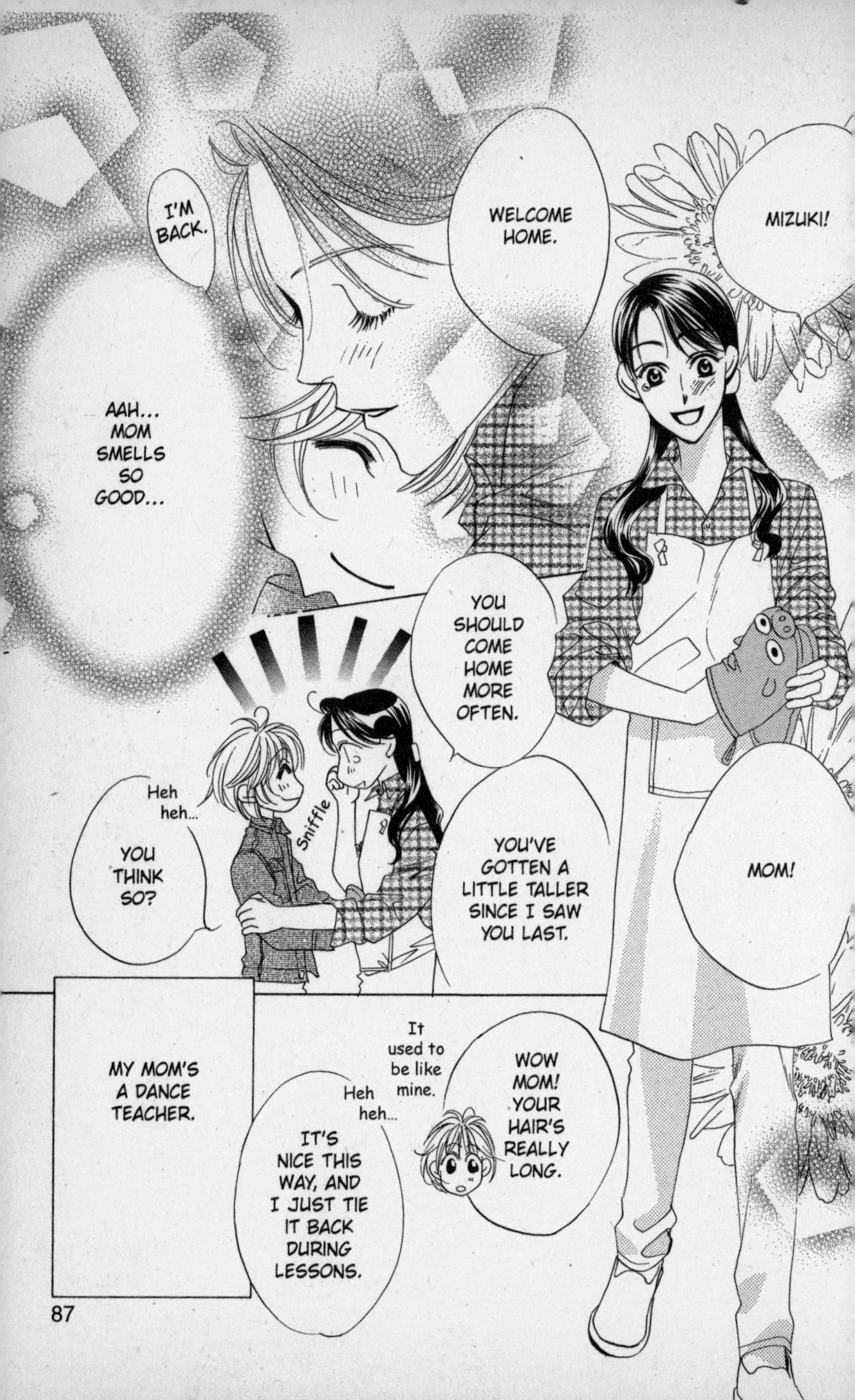
MIZUKI!
WELCOME HOME.
I'M BACK.
AAH... MOM SMELLS SO GOOD...
YOU SHOULD COME HOME MORE OFTEN.
MOM!
YOU'VE GOTTEN A LITTLE TALLER SINCE I SAW YOU LAST.
Sniffle
Heh heh...
YOU THINK SO?
WOW MOM! YOUR HAIR'S REALLY LONG.
It used to be like mine.
IT'S NICE THIS WAY, AND I JUST TIE IT BACK DURING LESSONS.
Heh heh...
MY MOM'S A DANCE TEACHER.

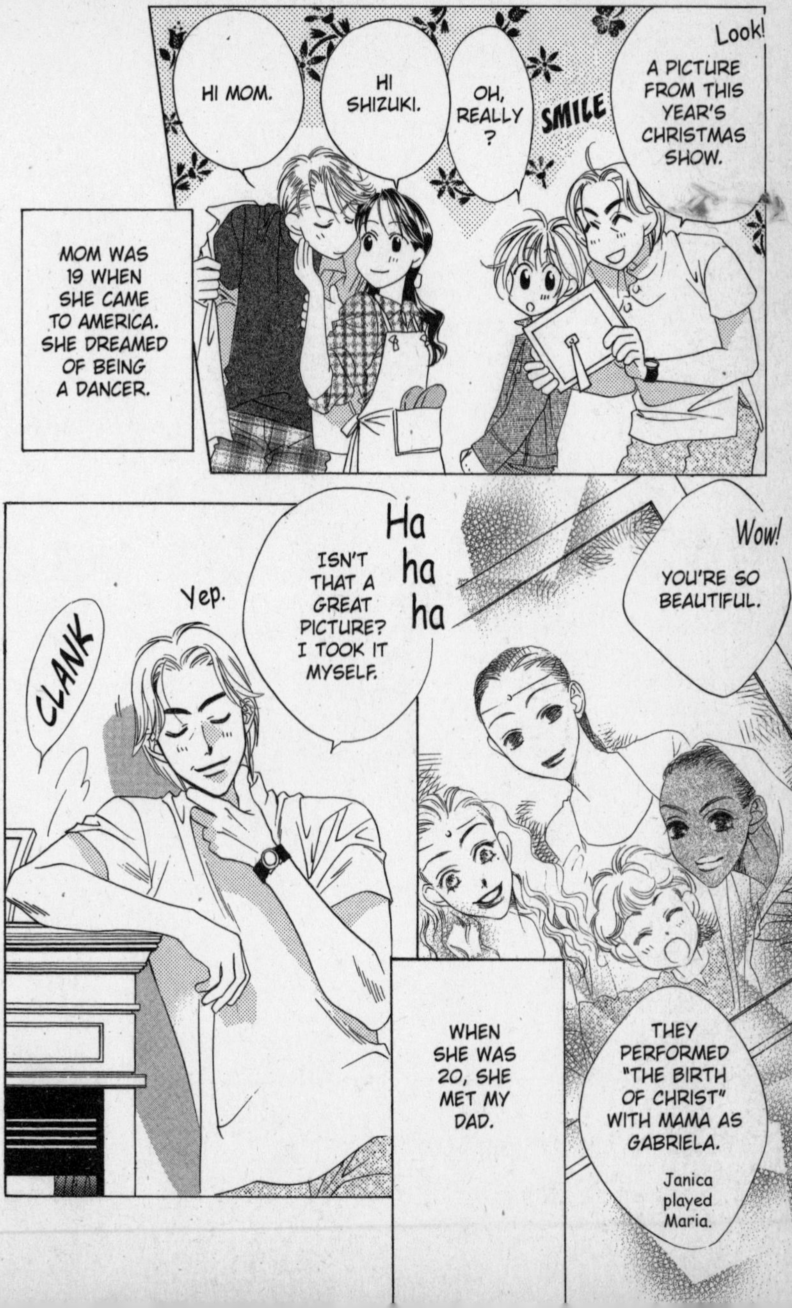
Look!
A PICTURE FROM THIS YEAR'S CHRISTMAS SHOW.
SMILE
OH, REALLY?
HI SHIZUKI.
HI MOM.
MOM WAS 19 WHEN SHE CAME TO AMERICA. SHE DREAMED OF BEING A DANCER.
Wow!
YOU'RE SO BEAUTIFUL.
Ha ha ha
ISN'T THAT A GREAT PICTURE? I TOOK IT MYSELF.
Yep.
CLANK
THEY PERFORMED "THE BIRTH OF CHRIST" WITH MAMA AS GABRIELA.
Janica played Maria.
WHEN SHE WAS 20, SHE MET MY DAD.

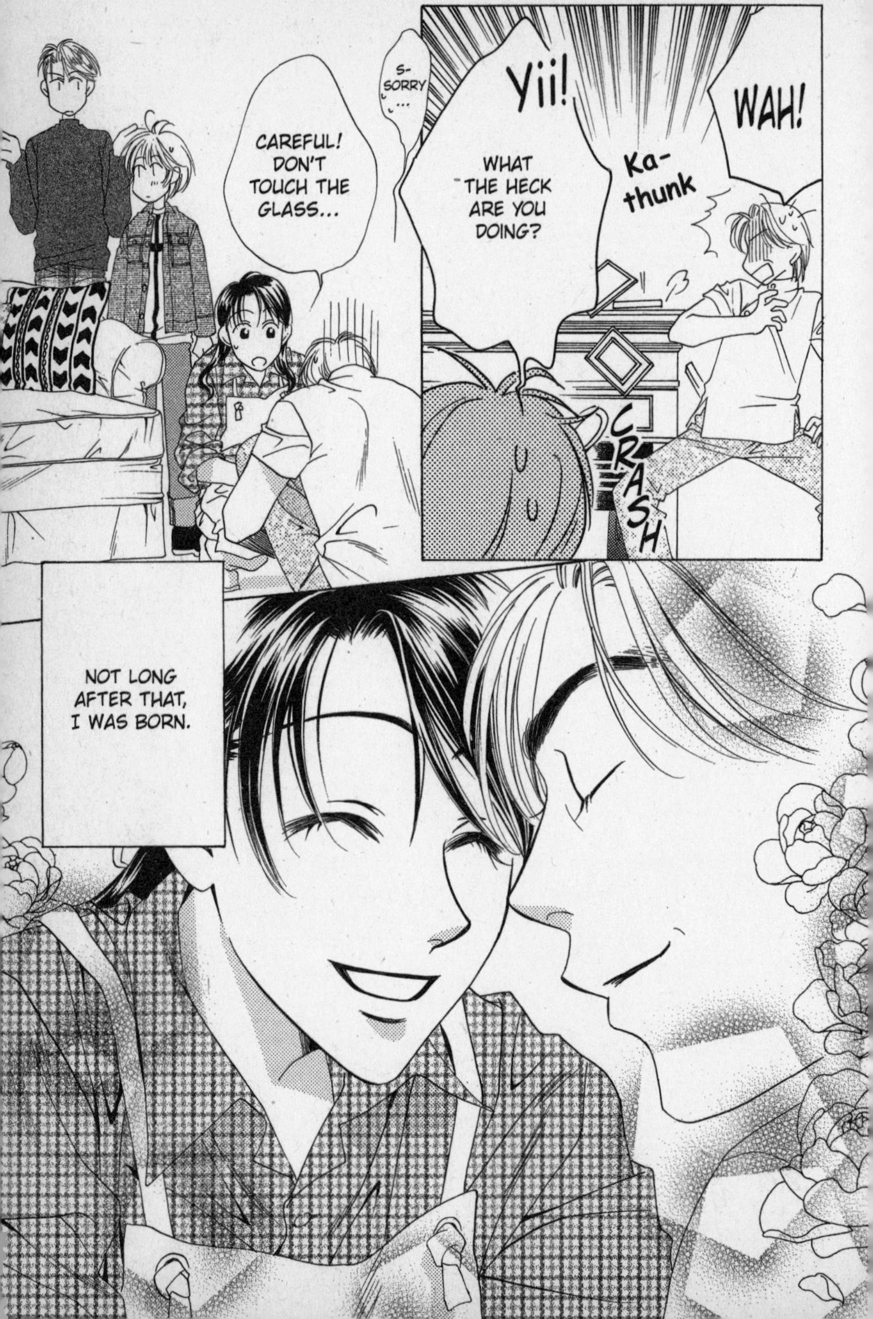
WAH!
Ka-thunk
Yii!
WHAT THE HECK ARE YOU DOING?
CRASH
S-SORRY...
CAREFUL! DON'T TOUCH THE GLASS...
NOT LONG AFTER THAT, I WAS BORN.

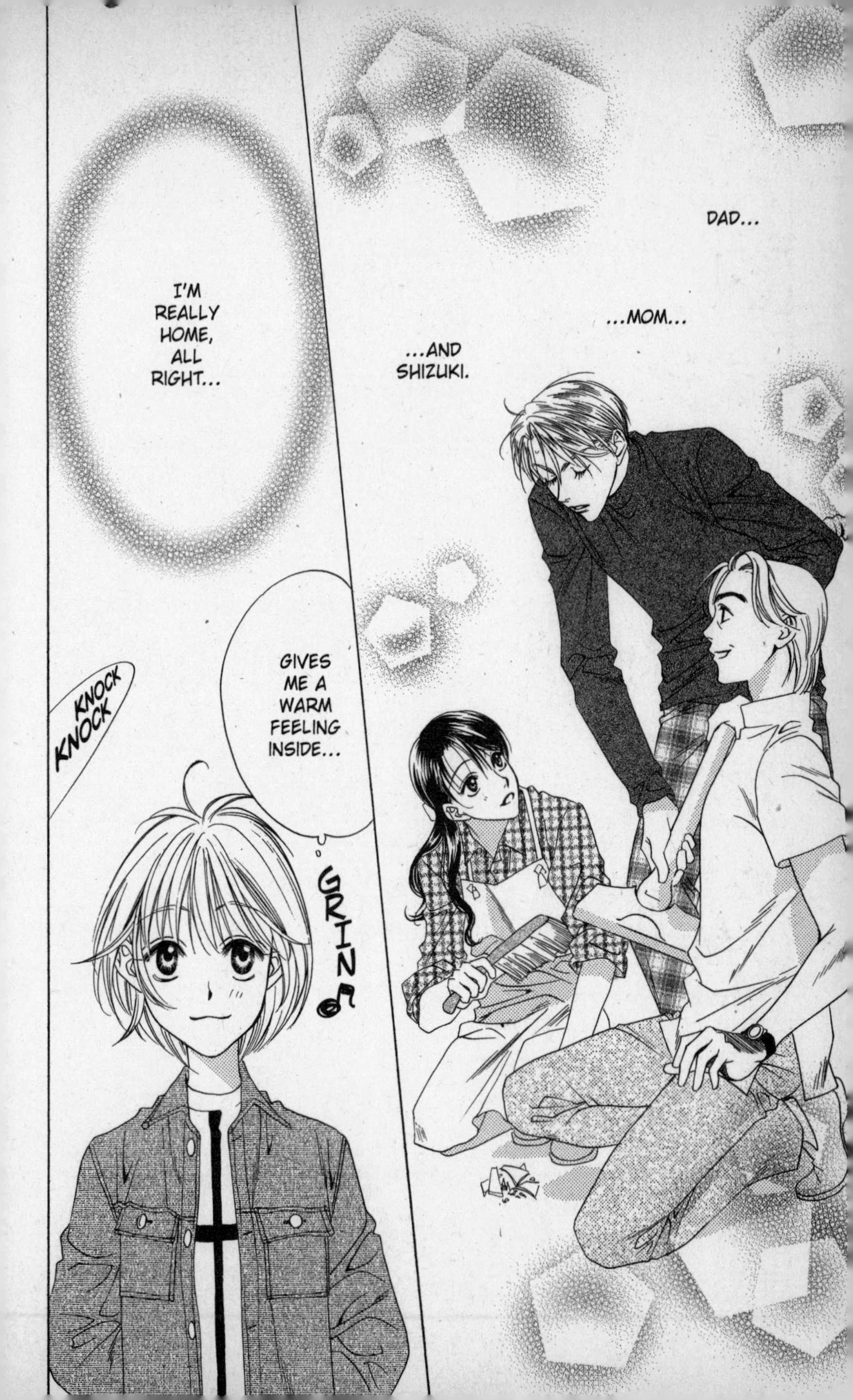
DAD...
...MOM...
...AND SHIZUKI.
I'M REALLY HOME, ALL RIGHT...
GIVES ME A WARM FEELING INSIDE...
GRIN
KNOCK KNOCK

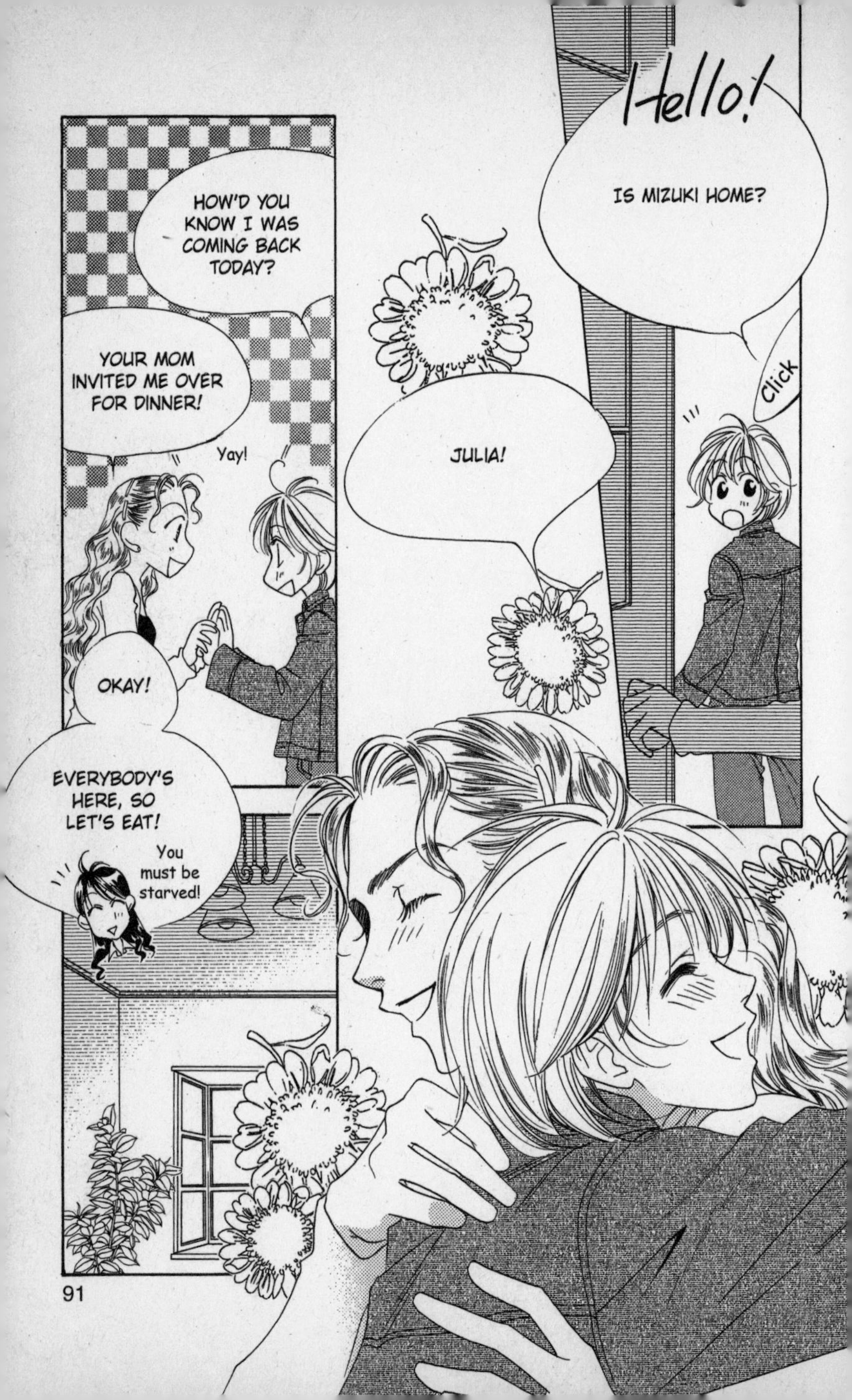
Hello!
IS MIZUKI HOME?
Click
JULIA!
HOW'D YOU KNOW I WAS COMING BACK TODAY?
YOUR MOM INVITED ME OVER FOR DINNER!
Yay!
OKAY!
EVERYBODY'S HERE, SO LET'S EAT!
You must be starved!

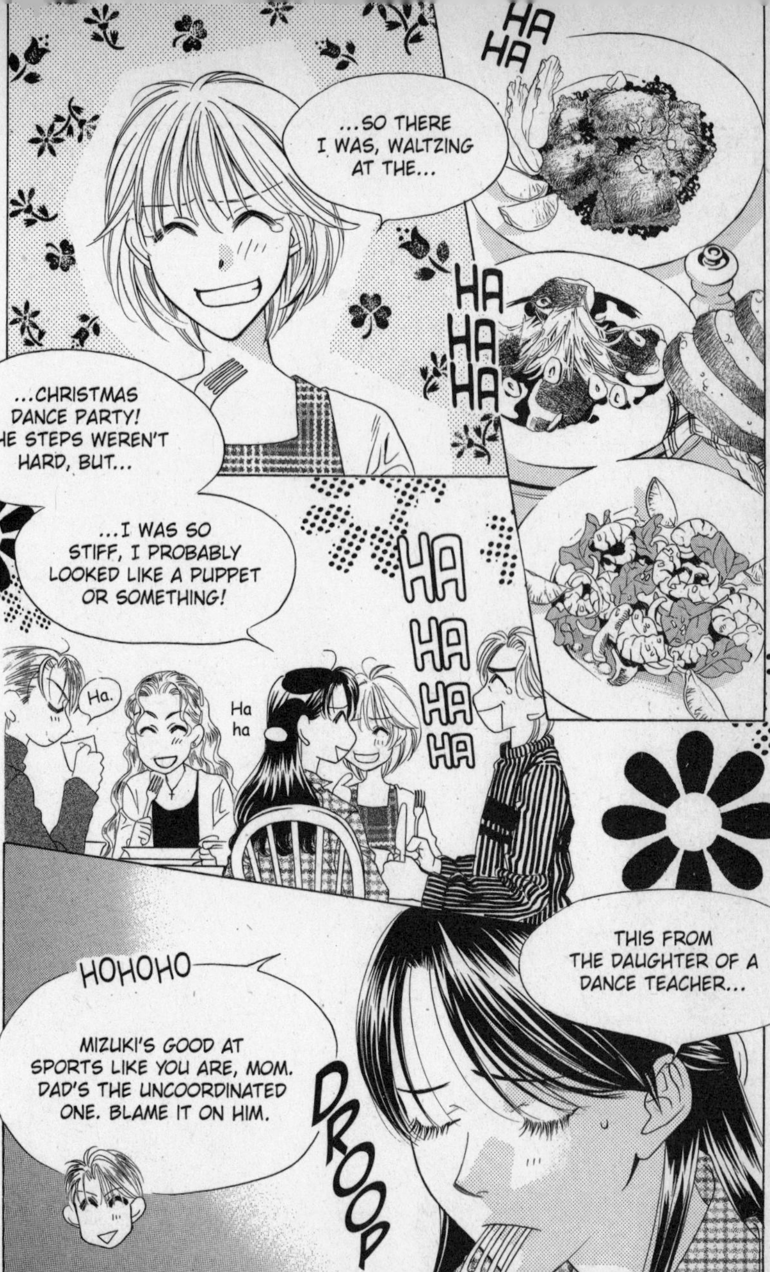
HA HA
HA HA HA
...SO THERE I WAS, WALTZING AT THE...
...CHRISTMAS DANCE PARTY! THE STEPS WEREN'T HARD, BUT...
...I WAS SO STIFF, I PROBABLY LOOKED LIKE A PUPPET OR SOMETHING!
HA HA HA HA
Ha ha
Ha.
THIS FROM THE DAUGHTER OF A DANCE TEACHER...
DROOP
HOHOHO
MIZUKI'S GOOD AT SPORTS LIKE YOU ARE, MOM. DAD'S THE UNCOORDINATED ONE. BLAME IT ON HIM.

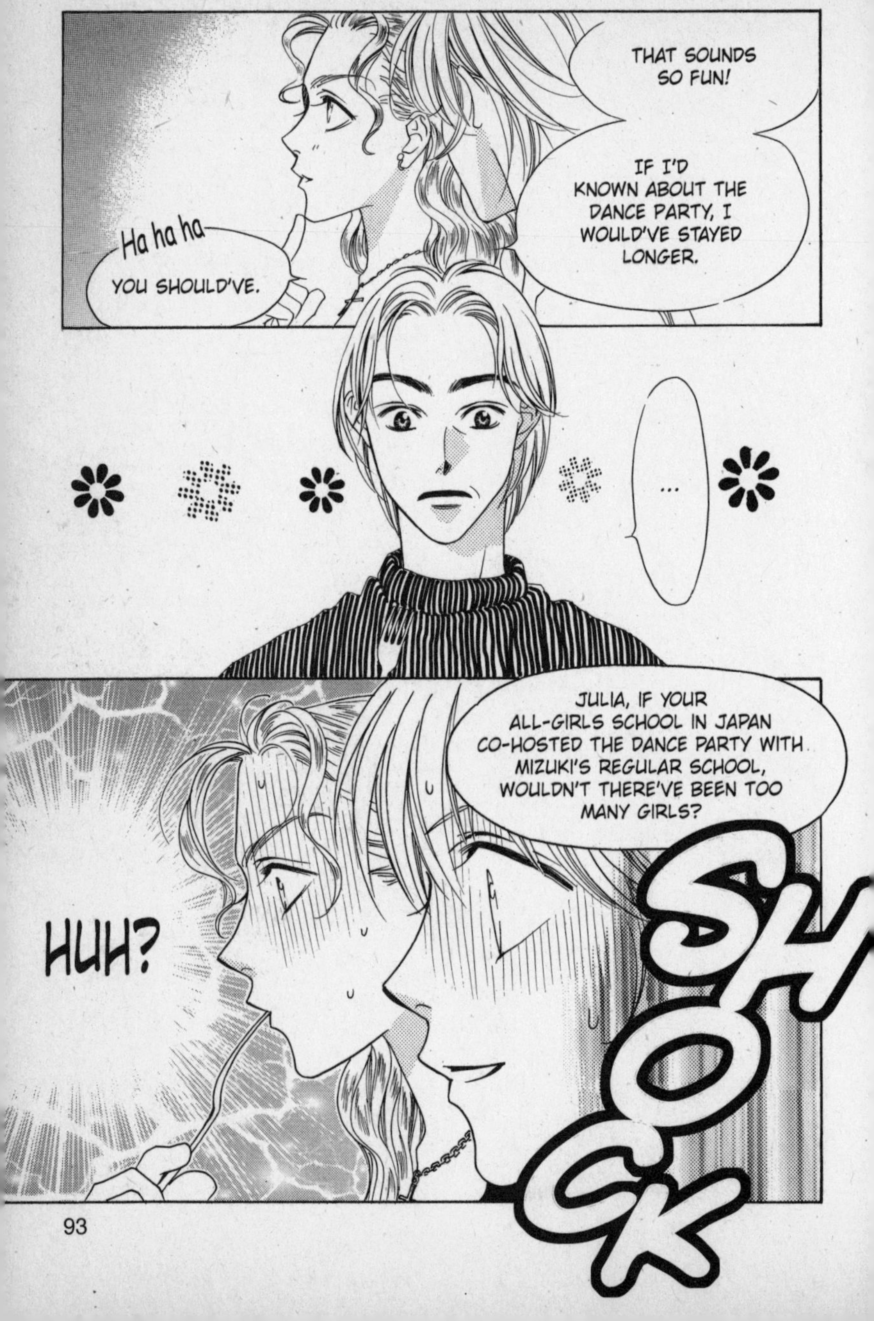
THAT SOUNDS SO FUN!
IF I'D KNOWN ABOUT THE DANCE PARTY, I WOULD'VE STAYED LONGER.
Ha ha ha
YOU SHOULD'VE.
...
JULIA, IF YOUR ALL-GIRLS SCHOOL IN JAPAN CO-HOSTED THE DANCE PARTY WITH MIZUKI'S REGULAR SCHOOL, WOULDN'T THERE'VE BEEN TOO MANY GIRLS?
SHOCK
HUH?

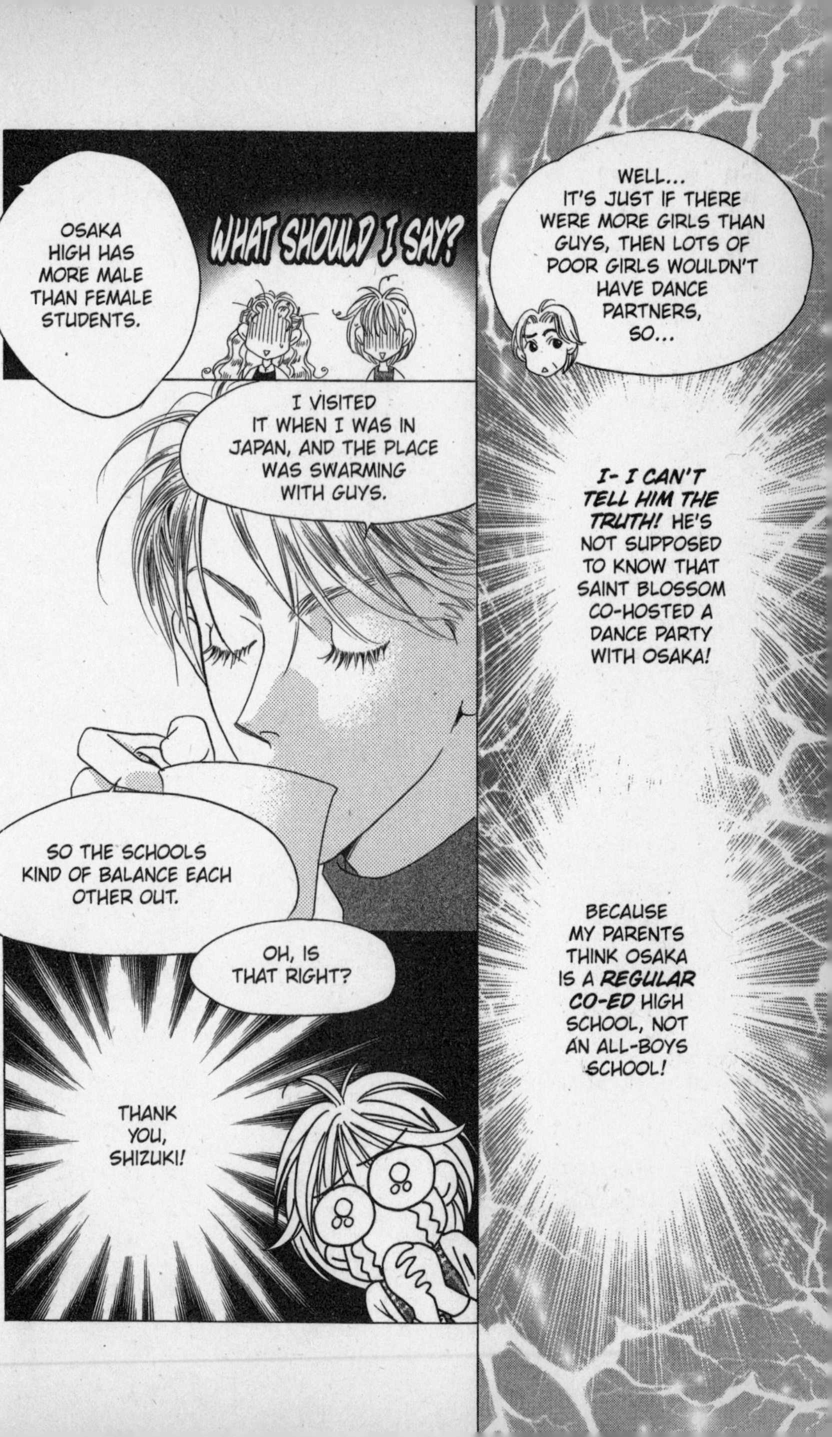
WELL... IT'S JUST IF THERE WERE MORE GIRLS THAN GUYS, THEN LOTS OF POOR GIRLS WOULDN'T HAVE DANCE PARTNERS, SO...
I- I CAN'T TELL HIM THE TRUTH! HE'S NOT SUPPOSED TO KNOW THAT SAINT BLOSSOM CO-HOSTED A DANCE PARTY WITH OSAKA!
BECAUSE MY PARENTS THINK OSAKA IS A *REGULAR CO-ED* HIGH SCHOOL, NOT AN ALL-BOYS SCHOOL!
OSAKA HIGH HAS MORE MALE THAN FEMALE STUDENTS.
WHAT SHOULD I SAY?
I VISITED IT WHEN I WAS IN JAPAN, AND THE PLACE WAS SWARMING WITH GUYS.
SO THE SCHOOLS KIND OF BALANCE EACH OTHER OUT.
OH, IS THAT RIGHT?
THANK YOU, SHIZUKI!

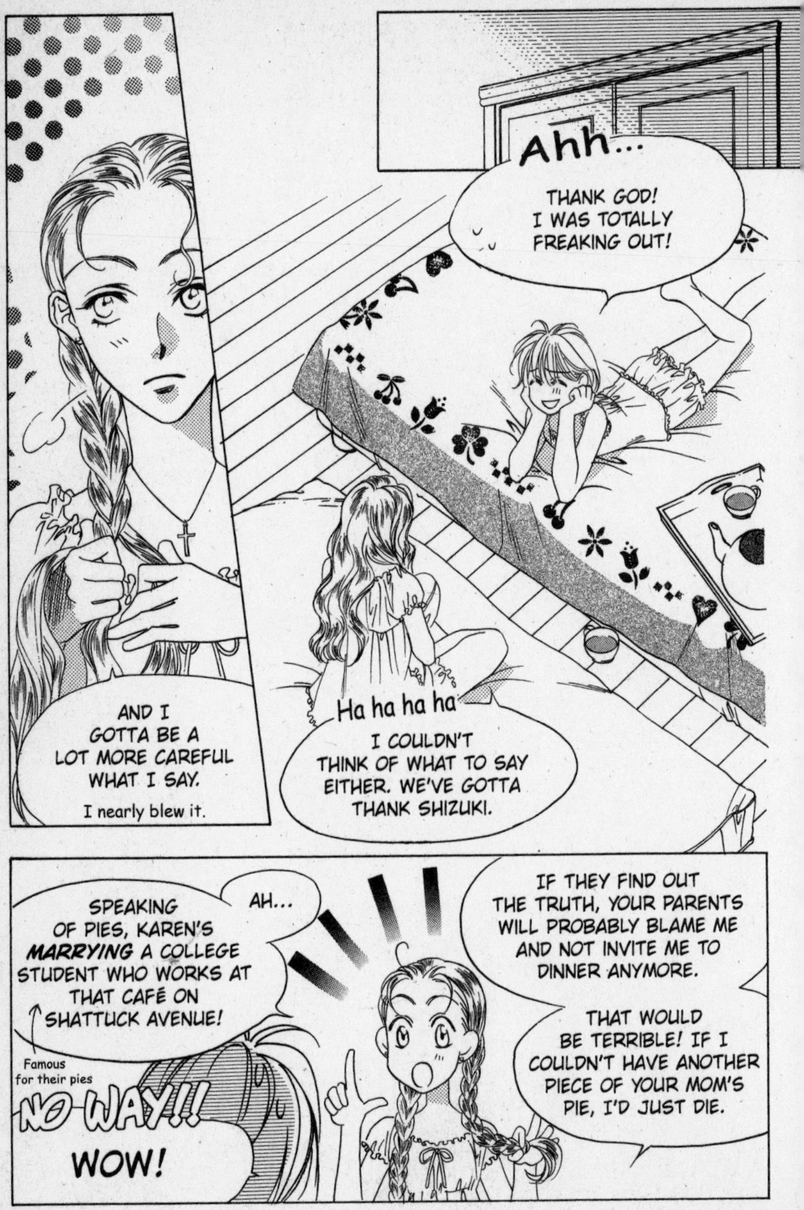
Ahh...
THANK GOD! I WAS TOTALLY FREAKING OUT!
Ha ha ha ha
I COULDN'T THINK OF WHAT TO SAY EITHER. WE'VE GOTTA THANK SHIZUKI.
AND I GOTTA BE A LOT MORE CAREFUL WHAT I SAY.
I nearly blew it.
IF THEY FIND OUT THE TRUTH, YOUR PARENTS WILL PROBABLY BLAME ME AND NOT INVITE ME TO DINNER ANYMORE.
THAT WOULD BE TERRIBLE! IF I COULDN'T HAVE ANOTHER PIECE OF YOUR MOM'S PIE, I'D JUST DIE.
AH...
SPEAKING OF PIES, KAREN'S MARRYING A COLLEGE STUDENT WHO WORKS AT THAT CAFÉ ON SHATTUCK AVENUE!
Famous for their pies
NO WAY!!
WOW!

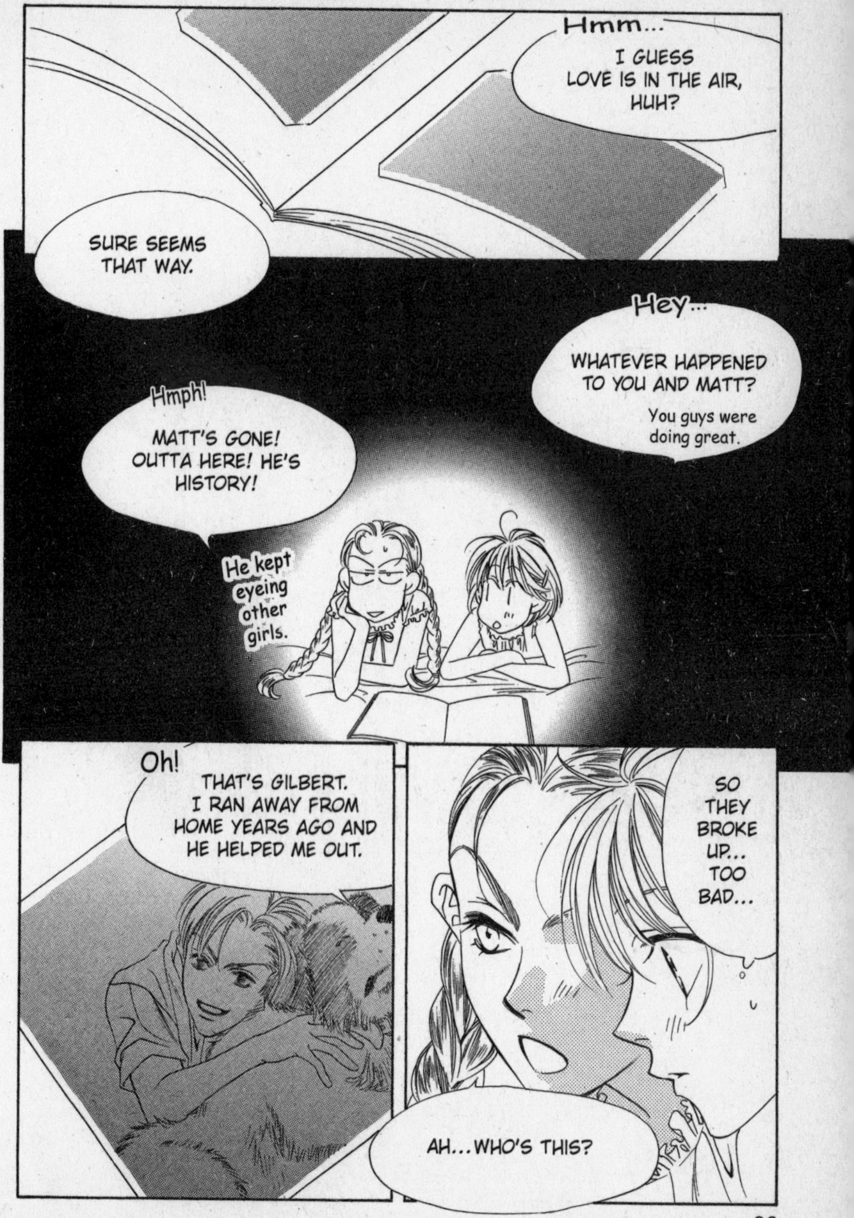
Hmm... I GUESS LOVE IS IN THE AIR, HUH?
SURE SEEMS THAT WAY.
Hey... WHATEVER HAPPENED TO YOU AND MATT?
You guys were doing great.
Hmph! MATT'S GONE! OUTTA HERE! HE'S HISTORY!
He kept eyeing other girls.
SO THEY BROKE UP... TOO BAD...
AH...WHO'S THIS?
Oh! THAT'S GILBERT. I RAN AWAY FROM HOME YEARS AGO AND HE HELPED ME OUT.

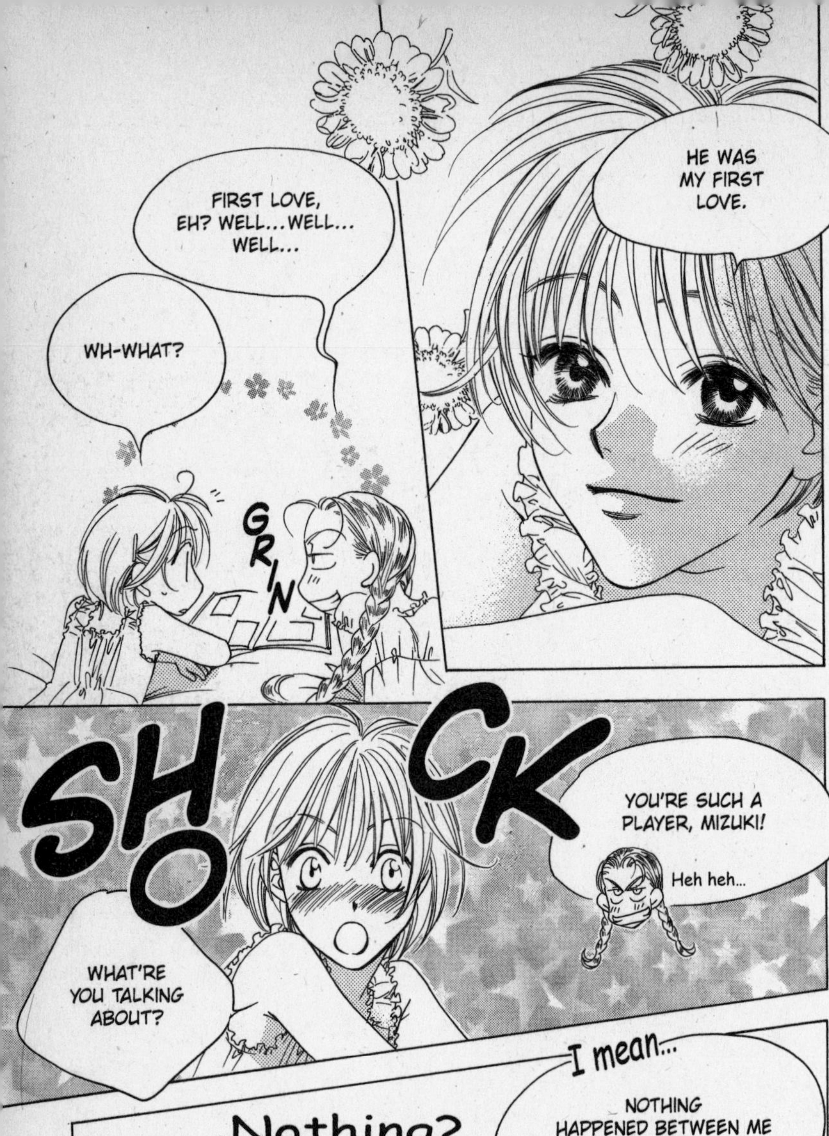
HE WAS MY FIRST LOVE.
FIRST LOVE, EH? WELL...WELL... WELL...
WH-WHAT?
GRIN
YOU'RE SUCH A PLAYER, MIZUKI!
Heh heh...
SHOCK
WHAT'RE YOU TALKING ABOUT?
I mean...
NOTHING HAPPENED BETWEEN ME AND GIL.
Nothing?
BUT YOU GOT CLOSE ENOUGH THAT SOMETHING *COULD'VE*, RIGHT?
UH...

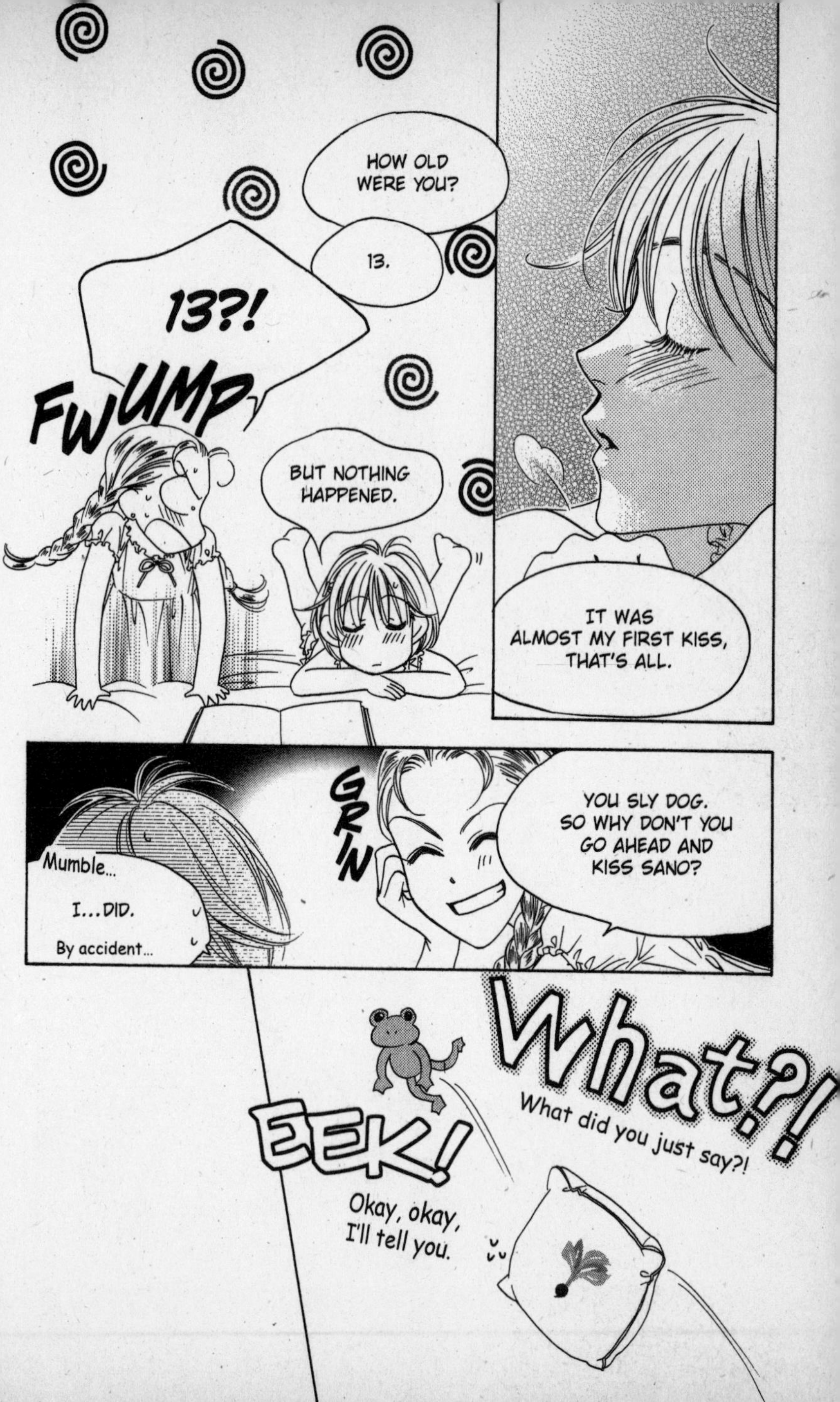
IT WAS ALMOST MY FIRST KISS, THAT'S ALL.
HOW OLD WERE YOU?
13.
13?!
FWUMP
BUT NOTHING HAPPENED.
YOU SLY DOG. SO WHY DON'T YOU GO AHEAD AND KISS SANO?
GRIN
Mumble...
I...DID.
By accident...
What?!
What did you just say?!
EEK!
Okay, okay, I'll tell you.

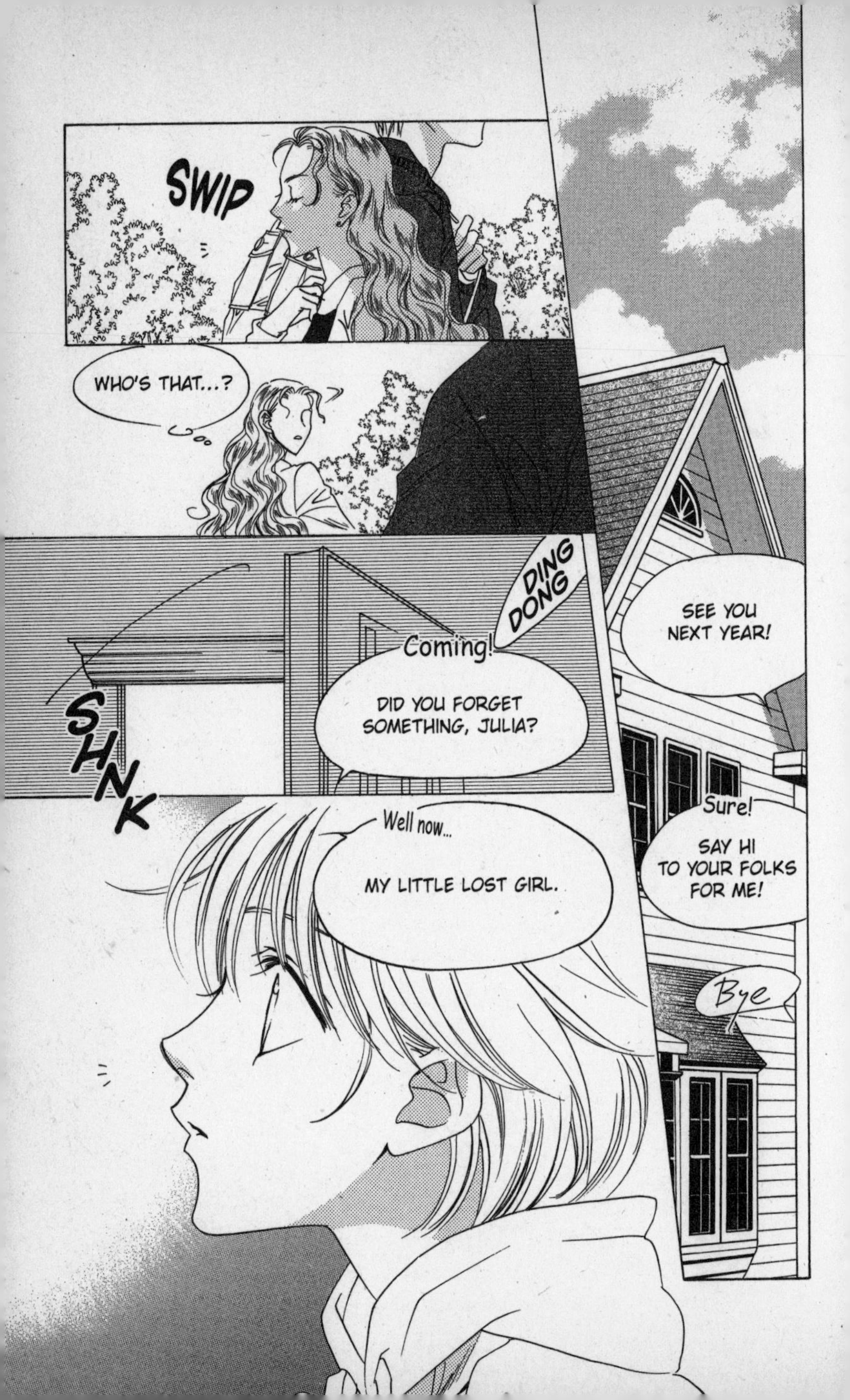
SEE YOU NEXT YEAR!
Sure!
SAY HI TO YOUR FOLKS FOR ME!
Bye
SWIP
WHO'S THAT...?
DING DONG
Coming!
DID YOU FORGET SOMETHING, JULIA?
SHNK
Well now...
MY LITTLE LOST GIRL.

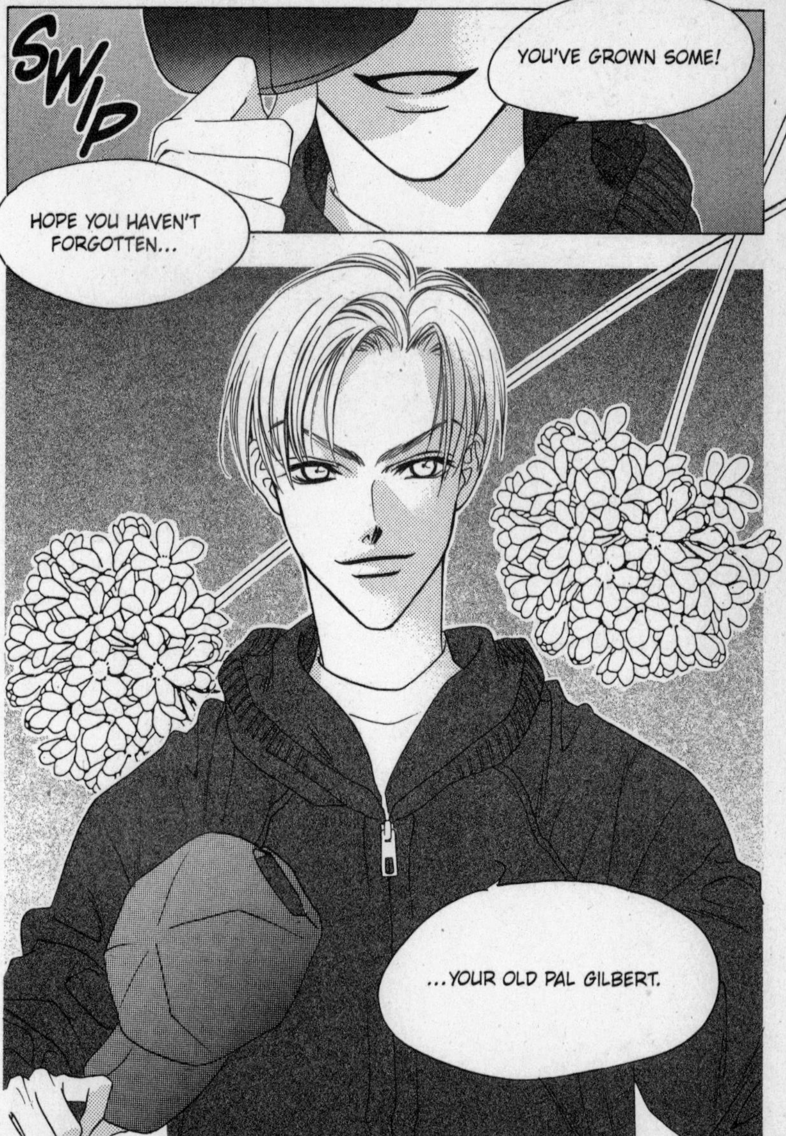
YOU'VE GROWN SOME!
SWIP
HOPE YOU HAVEN'T FORGOTTEN...
...YOUR OLD PAL GILBERT.

END OF HANA-KIMI CHAPTER 64

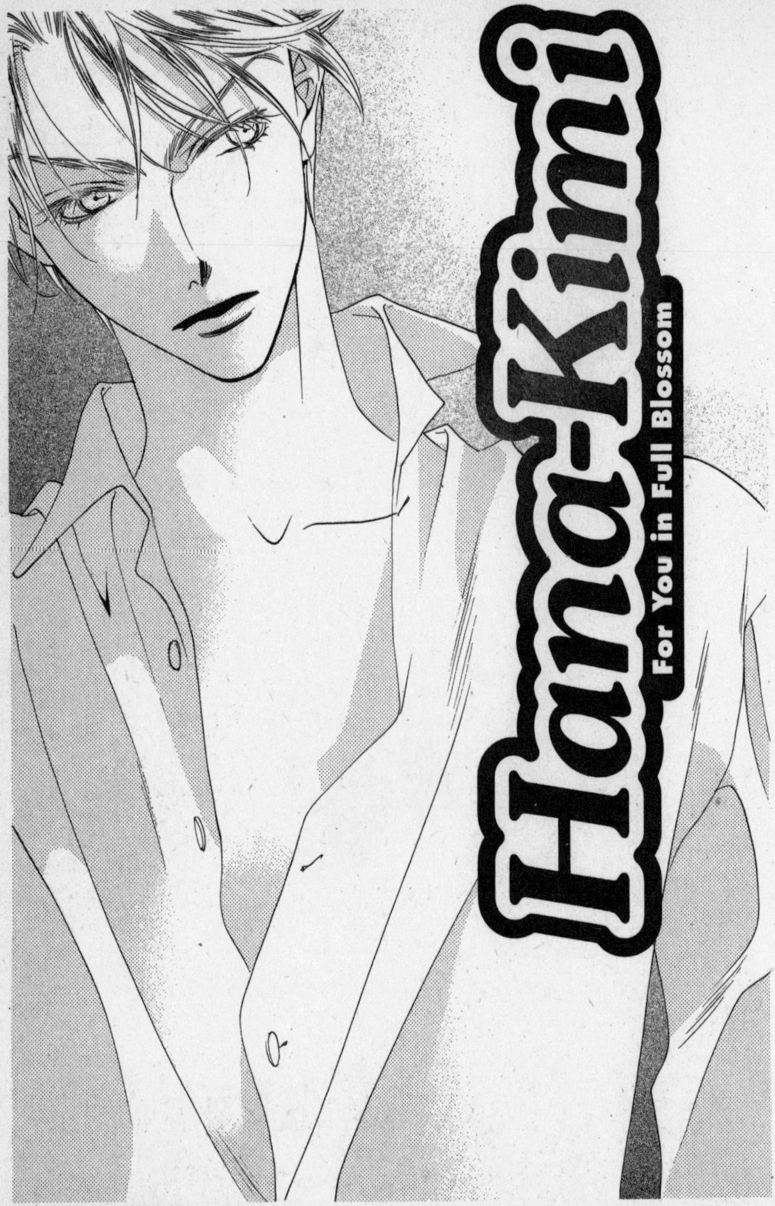
Hana-Kimi
For You in Full Blossom

CHAPTER 65

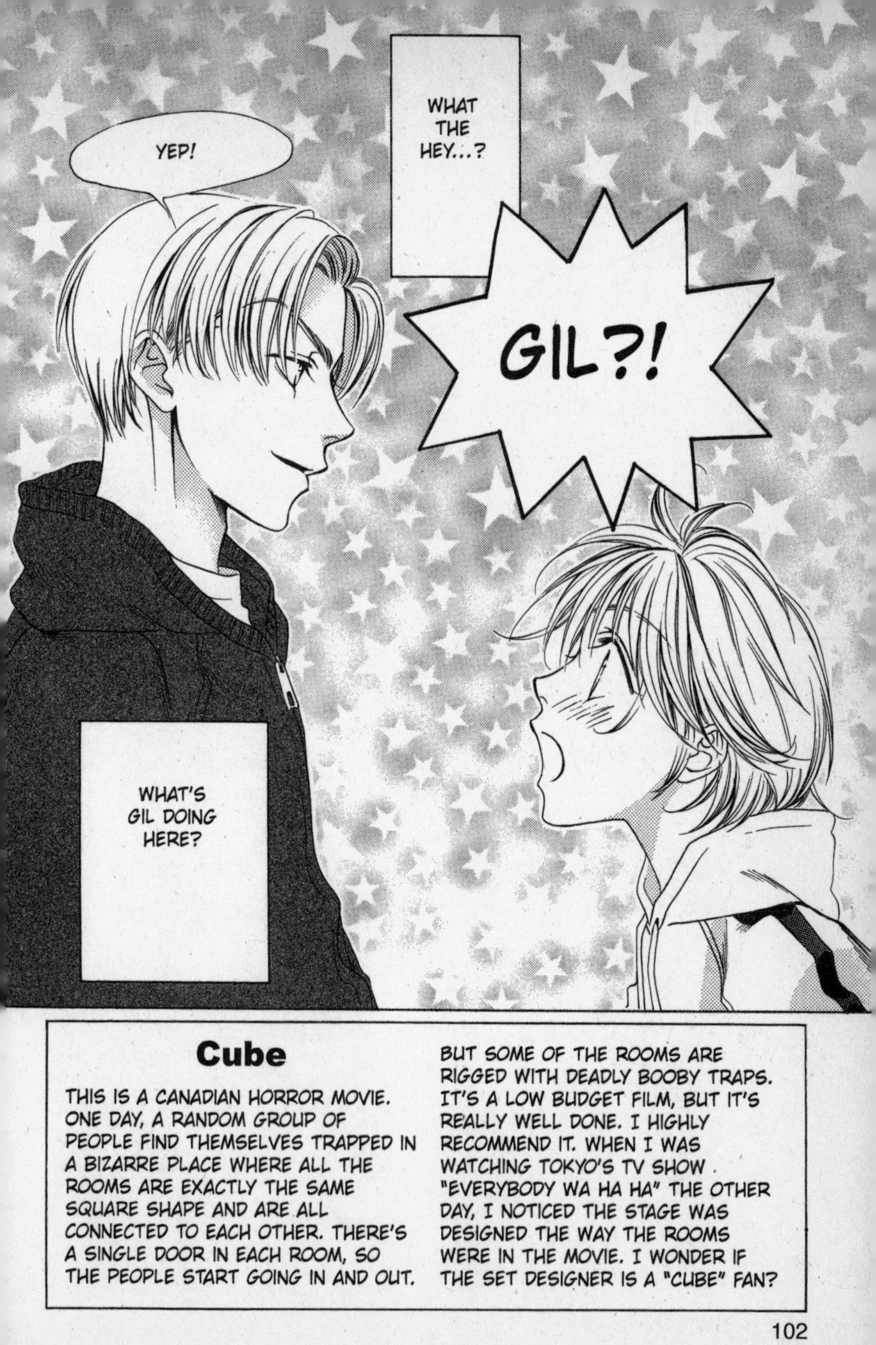
WHAT THE HEY...?
GIL?!
YEP!
WHAT'S GIL DOING HERE?

Cube

THIS IS A CANADIAN HORROR MOVIE. ONE DAY, A RANDOM GROUP OF PEOPLE FIND THEMSELVES TRAPPED IN A BIZARRE PLACE WHERE ALL THE ROOMS ARE EXACTLY THE SAME SQUARE SHAPE AND ARE ALL CONNECTED TO EACH OTHER. THERE'S A SINGLE DOOR IN EACH ROOM, SO THE PEOPLE START GOING IN AND OUT. BUT SOME OF THE ROOMS ARE RIGGED WITH DEADLY BOOBY TRAPS. IT'S A LOW BUDGET FILM, BUT IT'S REALLY WELL DONE. I HIGHLY RECOMMEND IT. WHEN I WAS WATCHING TOKYO'S TV SHOW "EVERYBODY WA HA HA" THE OTHER DAY, I NOTICED THE STAGE WAS DESIGNED THE WAY THE ROOMS WERE IN THE MOVIE. I WONDER IF THE SET DESIGNER IS A "CUBE" FAN?

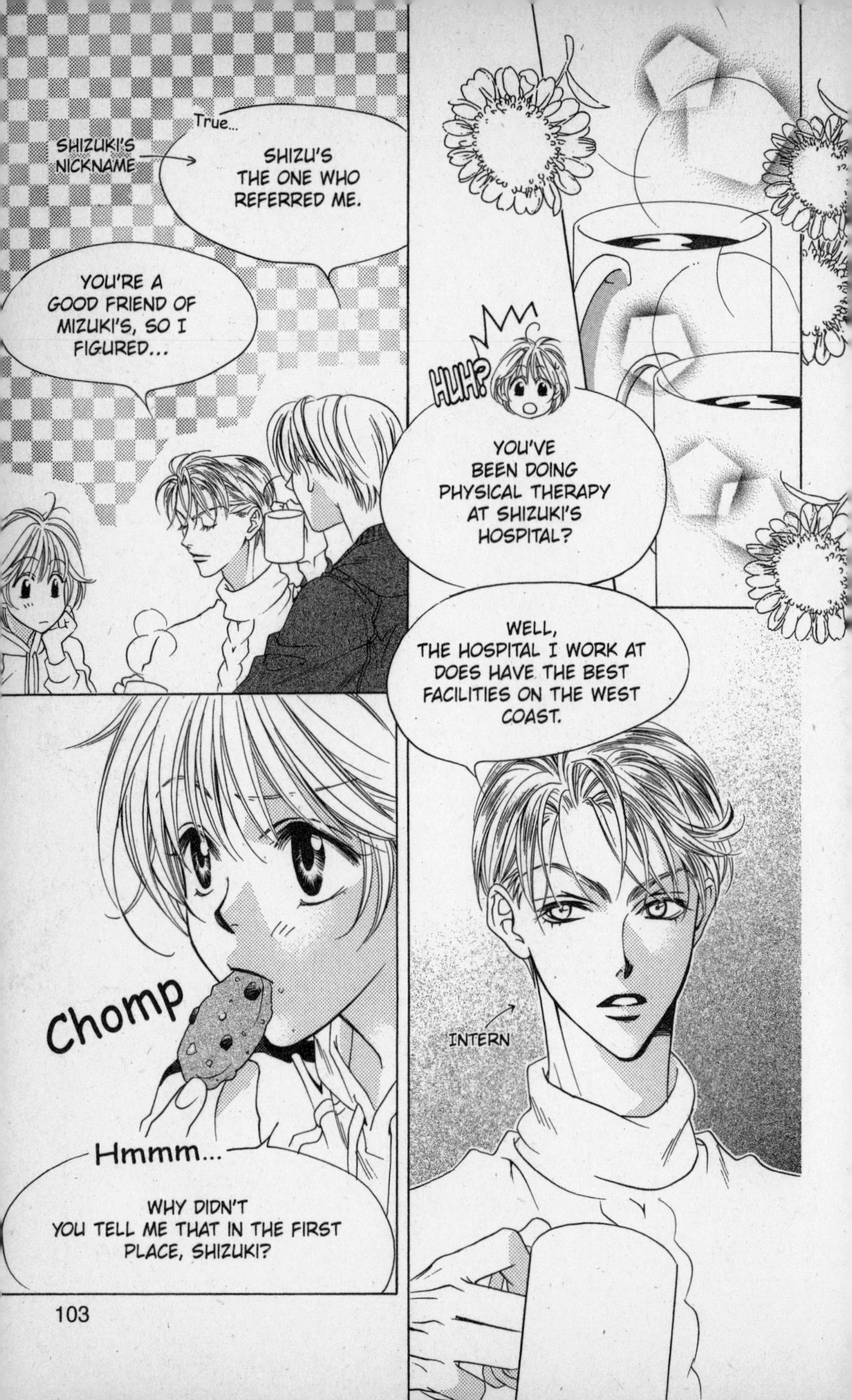
HUH?
YOU'VE BEEN DOING PHYSICAL THERAPY AT SHIZUKI'S HOSPITAL?
WELL, THE HOSPITAL I WORK AT DOES HAVE THE BEST FACILITIES ON THE WEST COAST.
INTERN
True...
SHIZU'S THE ONE WHO REFERRED ME.
SHIZUKI'S NICKNAME
YOU'RE A GOOD FRIEND OF MIZUKI'S, SO I FIGURED...
Chomp
Hmmm...
WHY DIDN'T YOU TELL ME THAT IN THE FIRST PLACE, SHIZUKI?

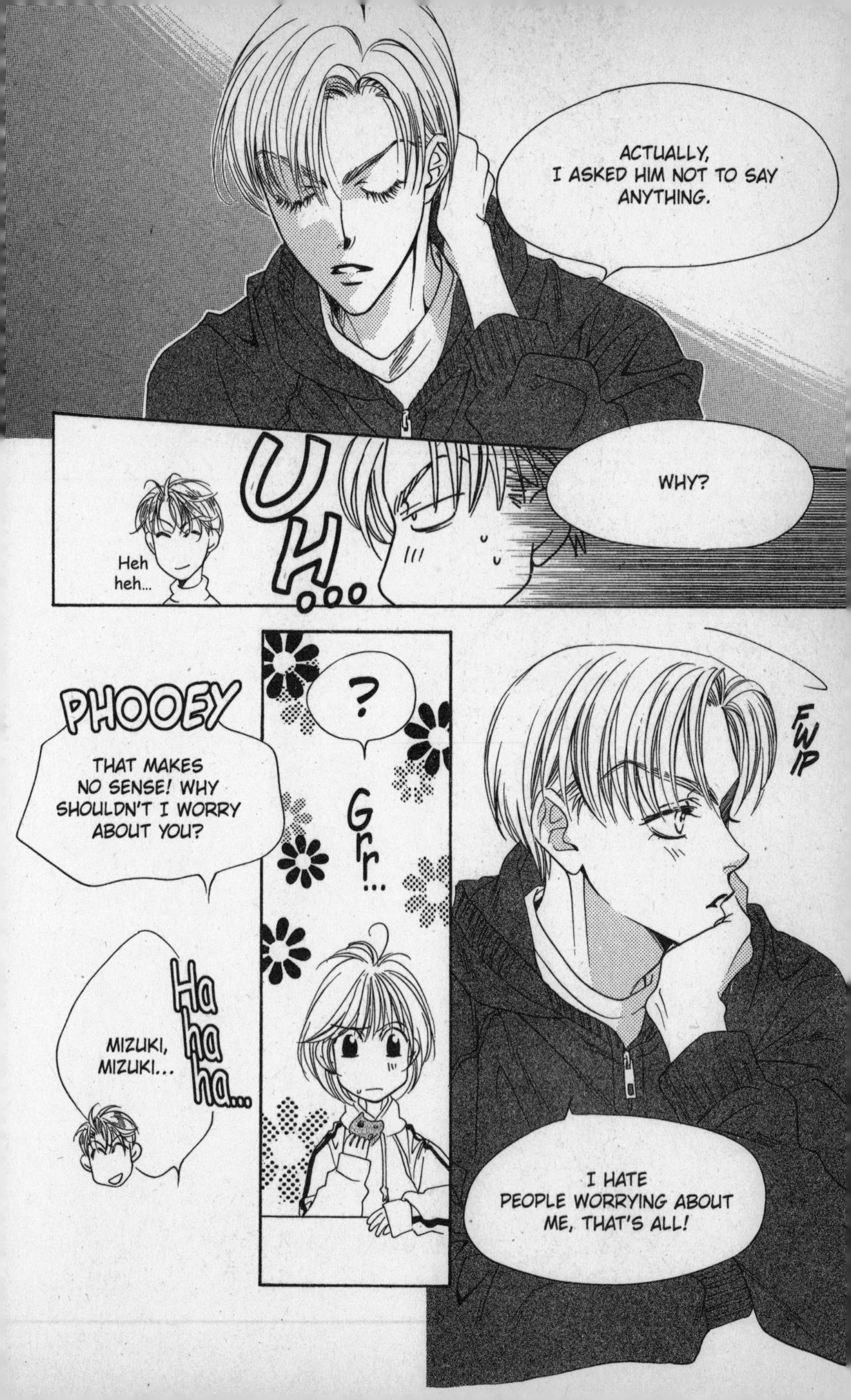
ACTUALLY, I ASKED HIM NOT TO SAY ANYTHING.
WHY?
UH...
Heh heh...
FWIP
I HATE PEOPLE WORRYING ABOUT ME, THAT'S ALL!
?
Grr...
PHOOEY
THAT MAKES NO SENSE! WHY SHOULDN'T I WORRY ABOUT YOU?
Ha ha ha...
MIZUKI, MIZUKI...

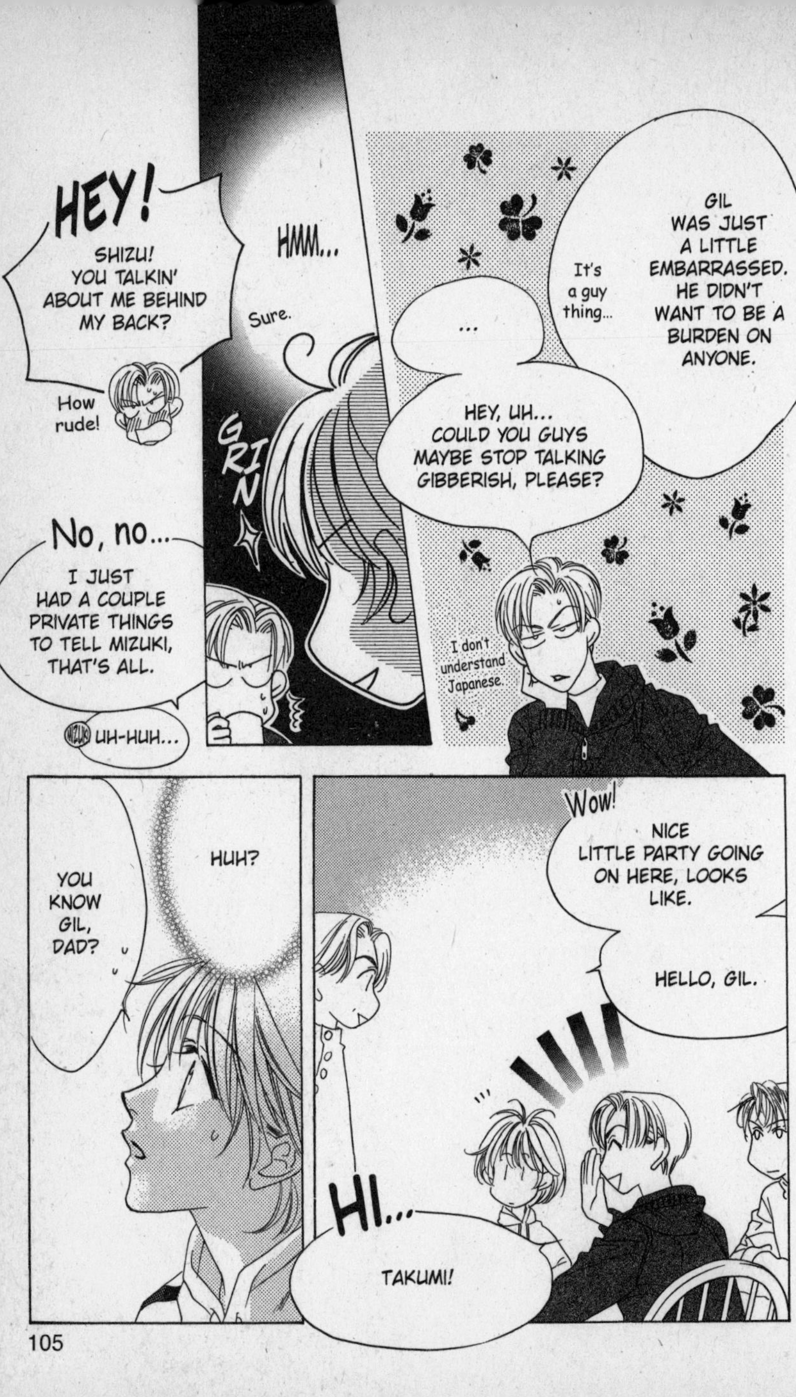
GIL WAS JUST A LITTLE EMBARRASSED. HE DIDN'T WANT TO BE A BURDEN ON ANYONE.
It's a guy thing...
...
HEY, UH... COULD YOU GUYS MAYBE STOP TALKING GIBBERISH, PLEASE?
I don't understand Japanese.
HMM...
Sure.
GRIN
HEY!
SHIZU! YOU TALKIN' ABOUT ME BEHIND MY BACK?
How rude!
No, no...
I JUST HAD A COUPLE PRIVATE THINGS TO TELL MIZUKI, THAT'S ALL.
MIZUKI
UH-HUH...
Wow!
NICE LITTLE PARTY GOING ON HERE, LOOKS LIKE.
HELLO, GIL.
HI...
TAKUMI!
HUH?
YOU KNOW GIL, DAD?

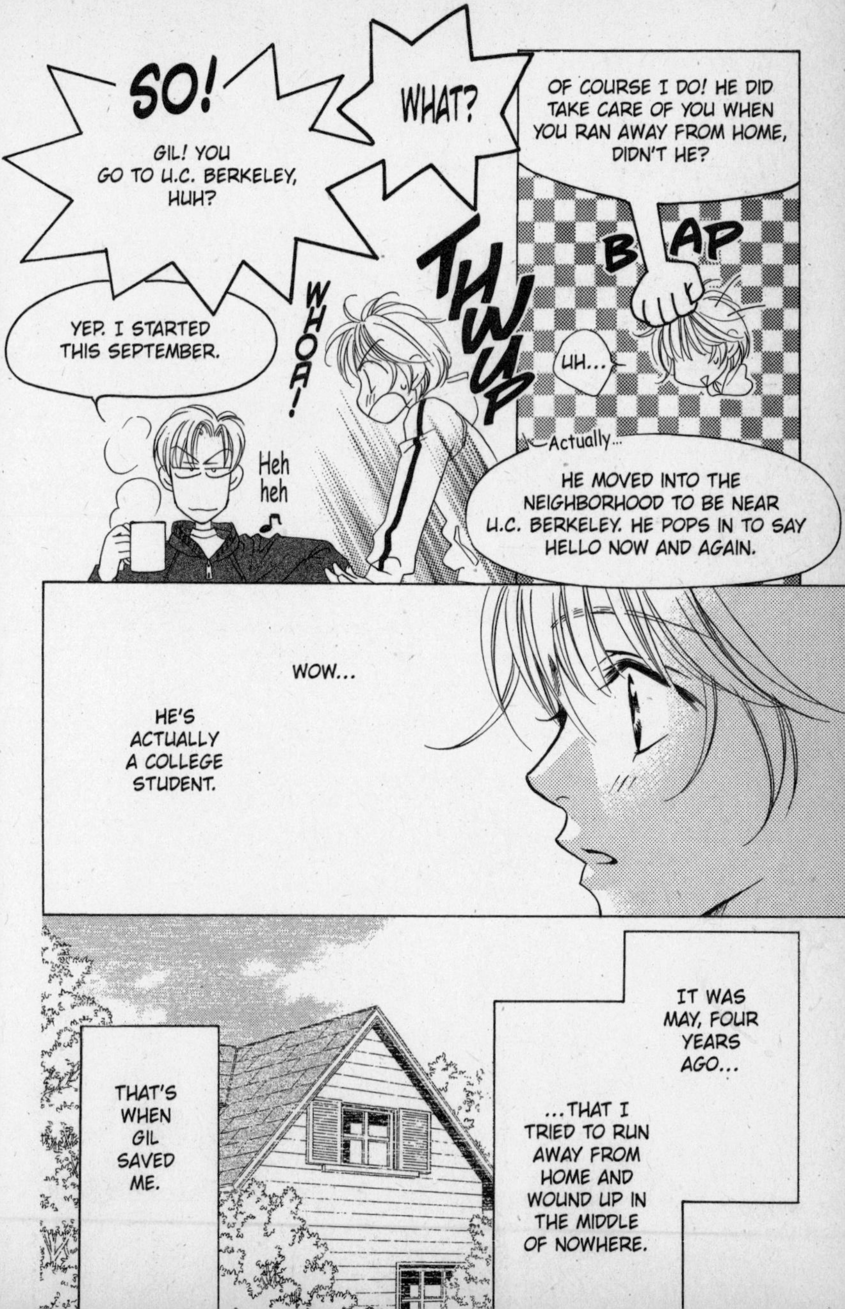
OF COURSE I DO! HE DID TAKE CARE OF YOU WHEN YOU RAN AWAY FROM HOME, DIDN'T HE?
BAP
UH...
Actually...
HE MOVED INTO THE NEIGHBORHOOD TO BE NEAR U.C. BERKELEY. HE POPS IN TO SAY HELLO NOW AND AGAIN.
WHAT?
SO!
GIL! YOU GO TO U.C. BERKELEY, HUH?
THWUP
WHOA!
YEP. I STARTED THIS SEPTEMBER.
Heh heh
WOW...
HE'S ACTUALLY A COLLEGE STUDENT.
IT WAS MAY, FOUR YEARS AGO...
...THAT I TRIED TO RUN AWAY FROM HOME AND WOUND UP IN THE MIDDLE OF NOWHERE.
THAT'S WHEN GIL SAVED ME.

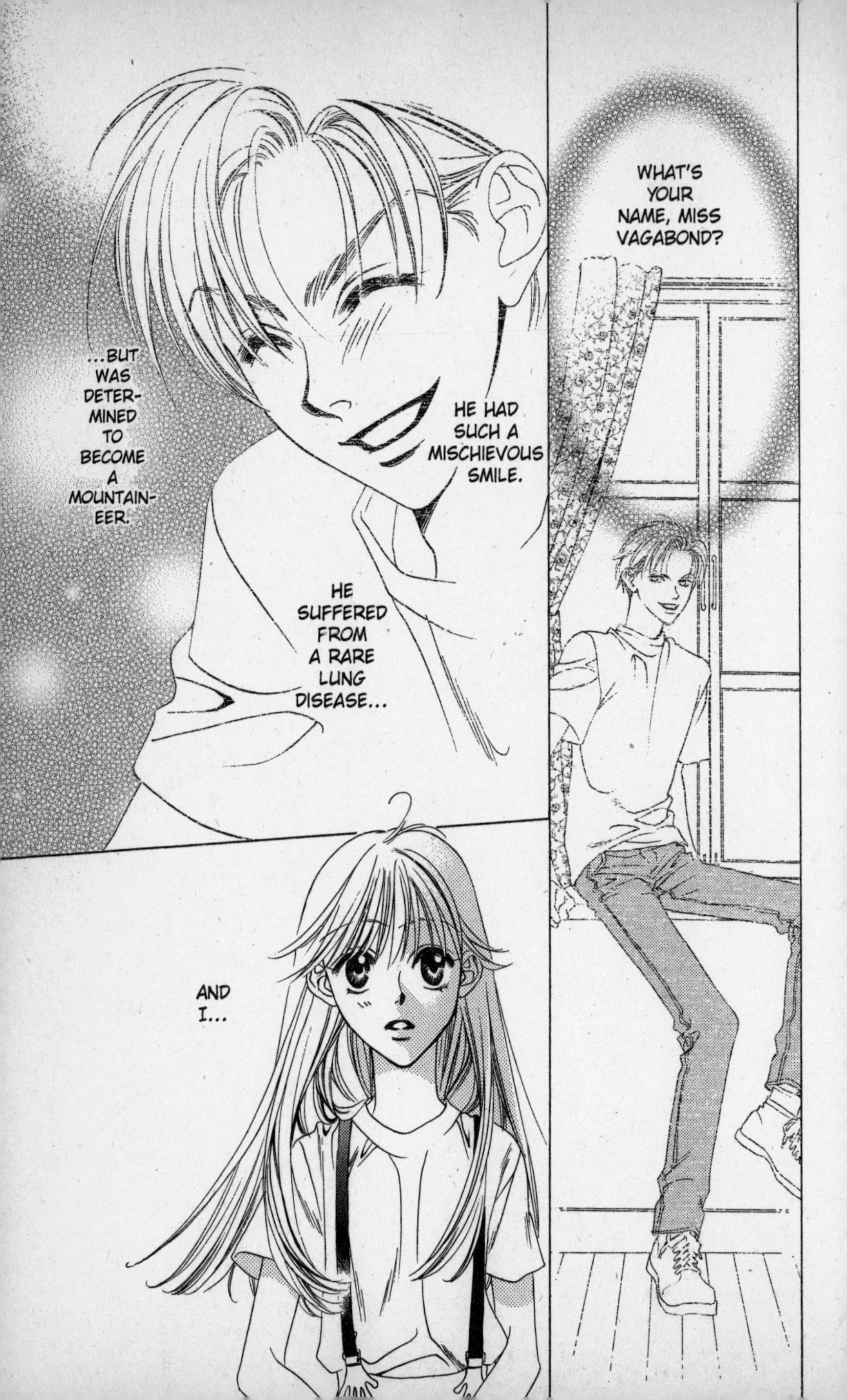
WHAT'S YOUR NAME, MISS VAGABOND?
HE HAD SUCH A MISCHIEVOUS SMILE.
HE SUFFERED FROM A RARE LUNG DISEASE...
...BUT WAS DETER-MINED TO BECOME A MOUNTAIN-EER.
AND I...

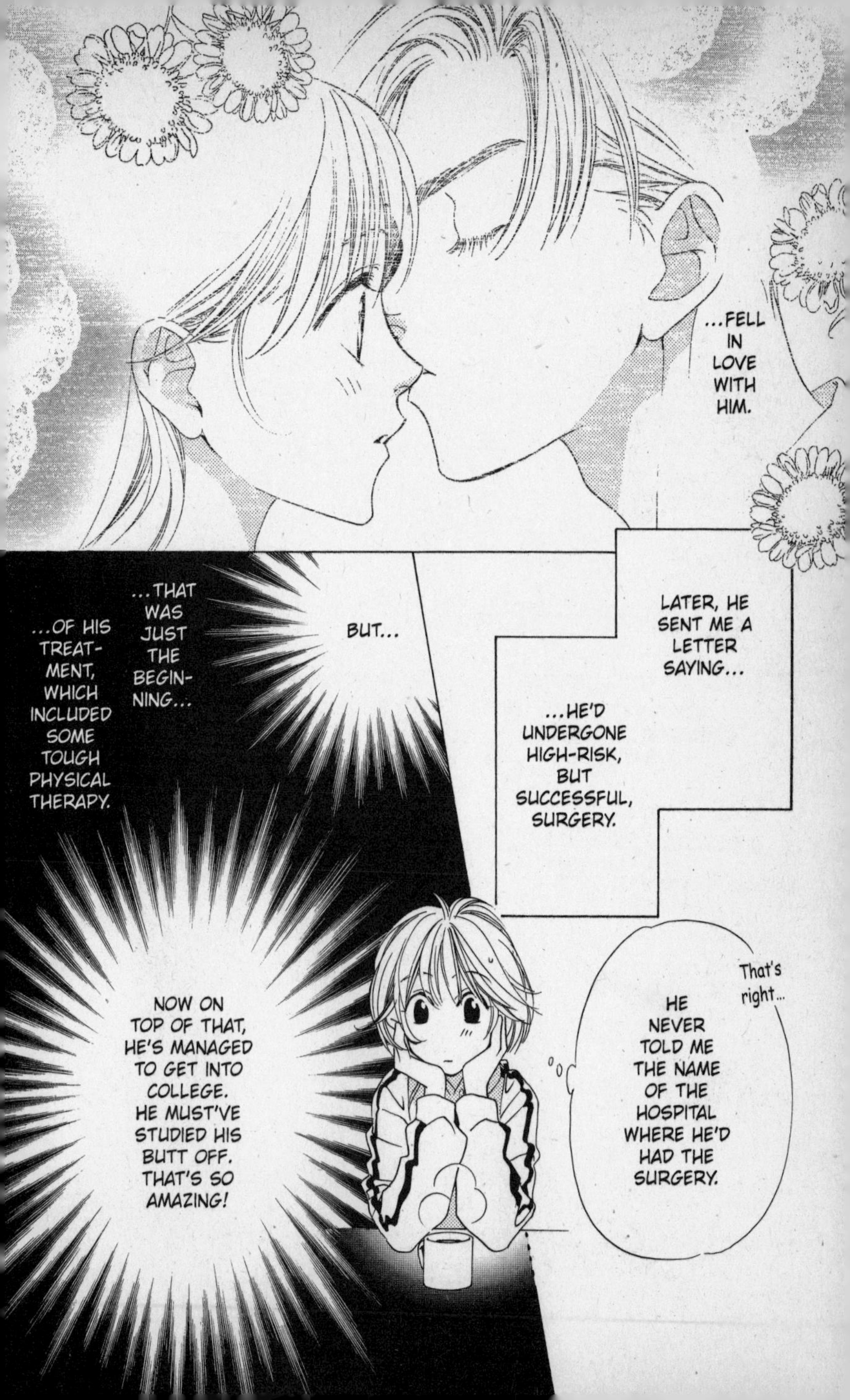
...FELL IN LOVE WITH HIM.
LATER, HE SENT ME A LETTER SAYING...
...HE'D UNDERGONE HIGH-RISK, BUT SUCCESSFUL, SURGERY.
BUT...
...THAT WAS JUST THE BEGIN-NING...
...OF HIS TREAT-MENT, WHICH INCLUDED SOME TOUGH PHYSICAL THERAPY.
That's right...
HE NEVER TOLD ME THE NAME OF THE HOSPITAL WHERE HE'D HAD THE SURGERY.
NOW ON TOP OF THAT, HE'S MANAGED TO GET INTO COLLEGE. HE MUST'VE STUDIED HIS BUTT OFF. THAT'S SO AMAZING!

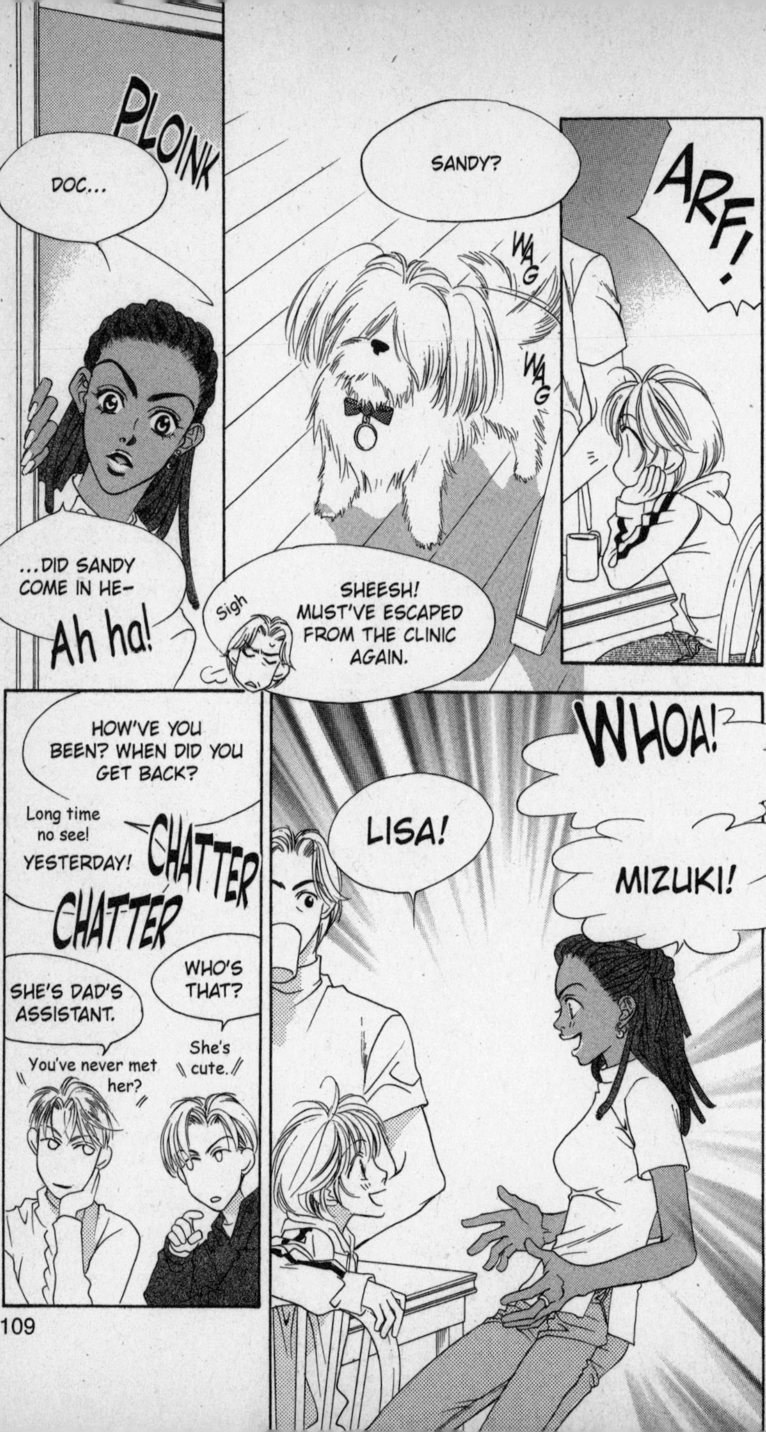
ARF!
SANDY?
WAG
WAG
SHEESH! MUST'VE ESCAPED FROM THE CLINIC AGAIN.
Sigh
PLOINK
DOC...
...DID SANDY COME IN HE-
Ah ha!
WHOA!
MIZUKI!
LISA!
HOW'VE YOU BEEN? WHEN DID YOU GET BACK?
Long time no see!
YESTERDAY!
CHATTER
CHATTER
WHO'S THAT?
SHE'S DAD'S ASSISTANT.
She's cute.
You've never met her?

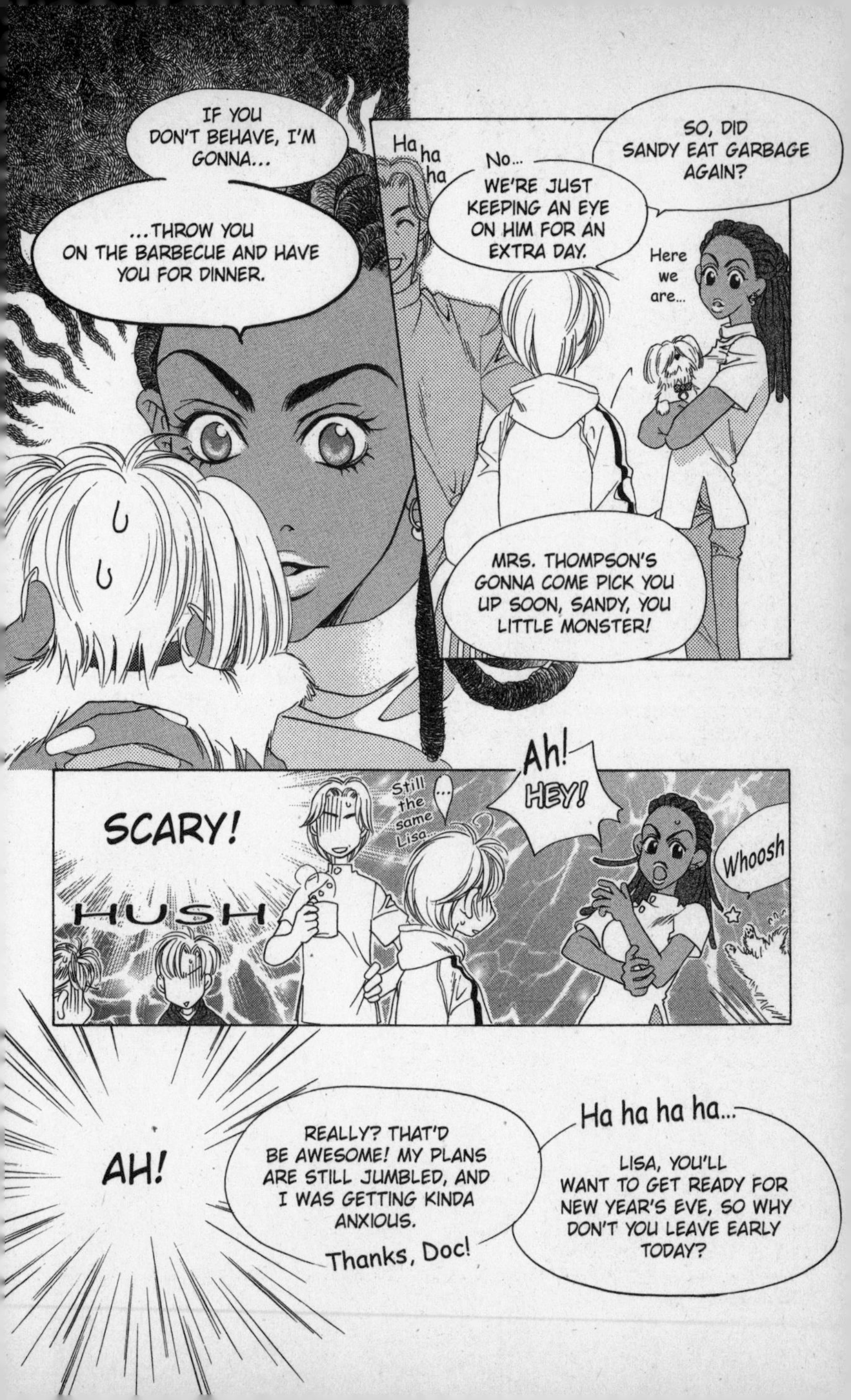
SO, DID SANDY EAT GARBAGE AGAIN?
Here we are...
No... WE'RE JUST KEEPING AN EYE ON HIM FOR AN EXTRA DAY.
Ha ha ha
MRS. THOMPSON'S GONNA COME PICK YOU UP SOON, SANDY, YOU LITTLE MONSTER!
IF YOU DON'T BEHAVE, I'M GONNA...
...THROW YOU ON THE BARBECUE AND HAVE YOU FOR DINNER.
Ah! HEY!
Whoosh
Still the same Lisa.
...
SCARY!
HUSH
Ha ha ha ha...
LISA, YOU'LL WANT TO GET READY FOR NEW YEAR'S EVE, SO WHY DON'T YOU LEAVE EARLY TODAY?
REALLY? THAT'D BE AWESOME! MY PLANS ARE STILL JUMBLED, AND I WAS GETTING KINDA ANXIOUS.
Thanks, Doc!
AH!

Glam Bands

EVER SINCE I MENTIONED MY FAVORITE BANDS, L'ARC-EN-CIEL AND LUNA SEA, I'VE BEEN GETTING TONS OF LETTERS FROM OTHER FANS OF THEIR MUSIC. I'M GLAD THERE'RE PEOPLE OUT THERE WHO ARE INTO THE SAME BANDS. SOMETIMES THEY EVEN SEND ME COSPLAY PHOTOS. IT'S SO COOL! ♪

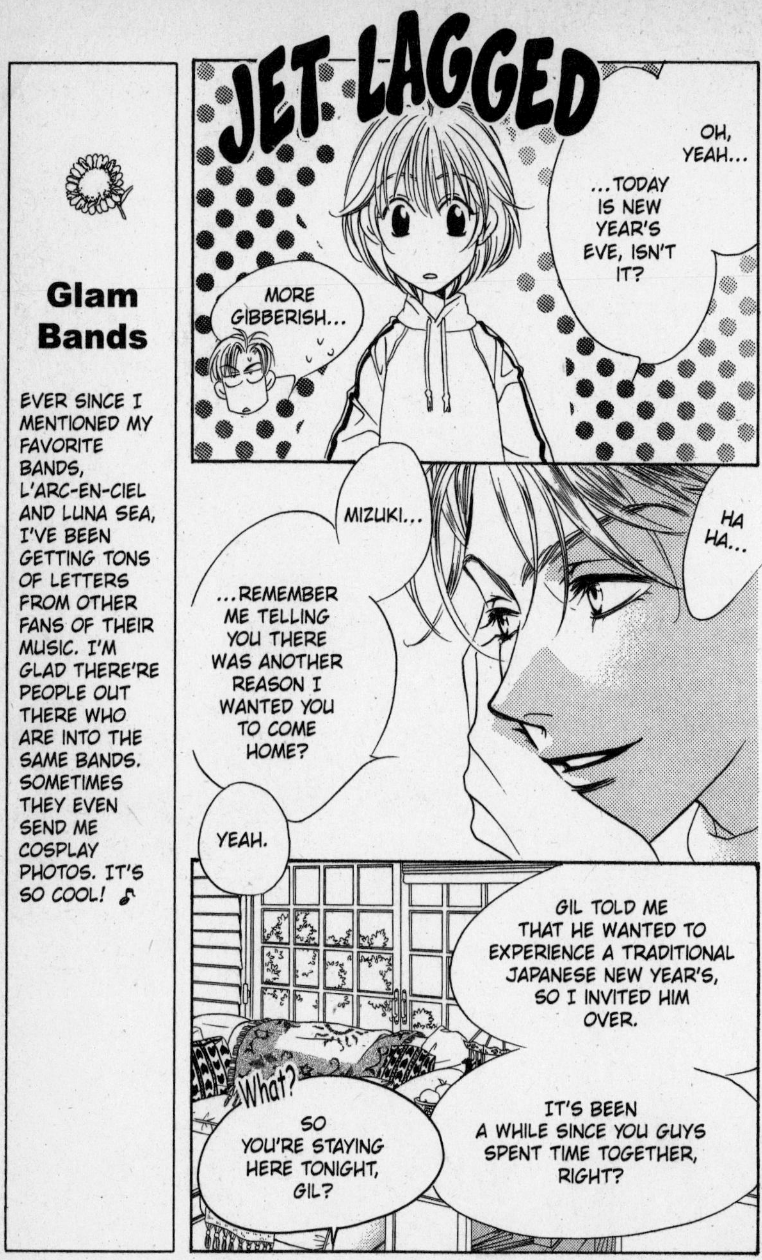
OH, YEAH...
...TODAY IS NEW YEAR'S EVE, ISN'T IT?
JET LAGGED
MORE GIBBERISH...
HA HA...
MIZUKI...
...REMEMBER ME TELLING YOU THERE WAS ANOTHER REASON I WANTED YOU TO COME HOME?
YEAH.
GIL TOLD ME THAT HE WANTED TO EXPERIENCE A TRADITIONAL JAPANESE NEW YEAR'S, SO I INVITED HIM OVER.
IT'S BEEN A WHILE SINCE YOU GUYS SPENT TIME TOGETHER, RIGHT?
What?
SO YOU'RE STAYING HERE TONIGHT, GIL?

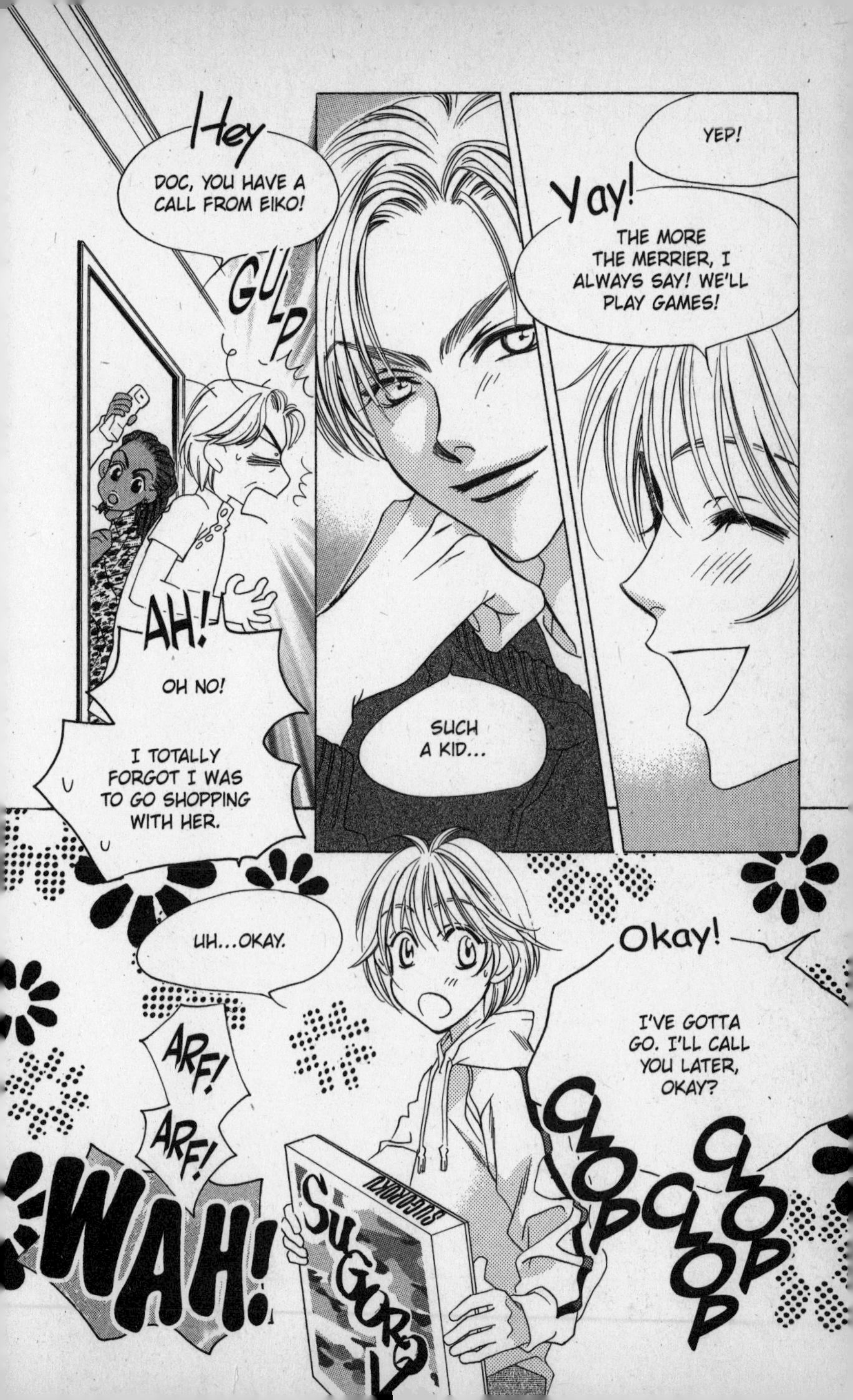
YEP!
Yay!
THE MORE THE MERRIER, I ALWAYS SAY! WE'LL PLAY GAMES!
SUCH A KID...
Hey
DOC, YOU HAVE A CALL FROM EIKO!
GULP
AH!
OH NO!
I TOTALLY FORGOT I WAS TO GO SHOPPING WITH HER.
Okay!
I'VE GOTTA GO. I'LL CALL YOU LATER, OKAY?
UH...OKAY.
ARF!
ARF!
WAH!
SUGOROKU

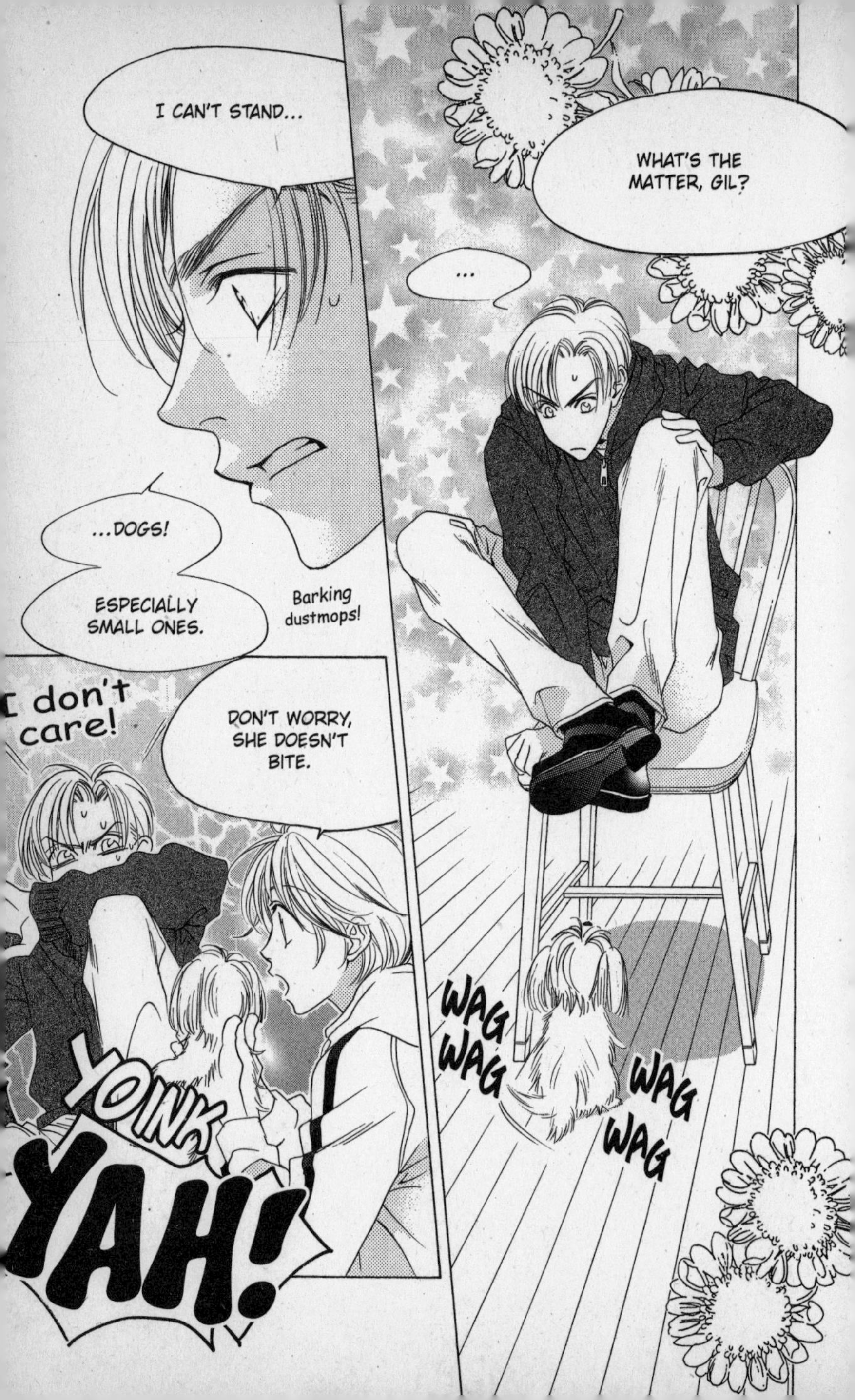
WHAT'S THE MATTER, GIL?
...
WAG WAG
WAG WAG
I CAN'T STAND...
...DOGS!
ESPECIALLY SMALL ONES.
Barking dustmops!
DON'T WORRY, SHE DOESN'T BITE.
I don't care!
YOINK
YAH!

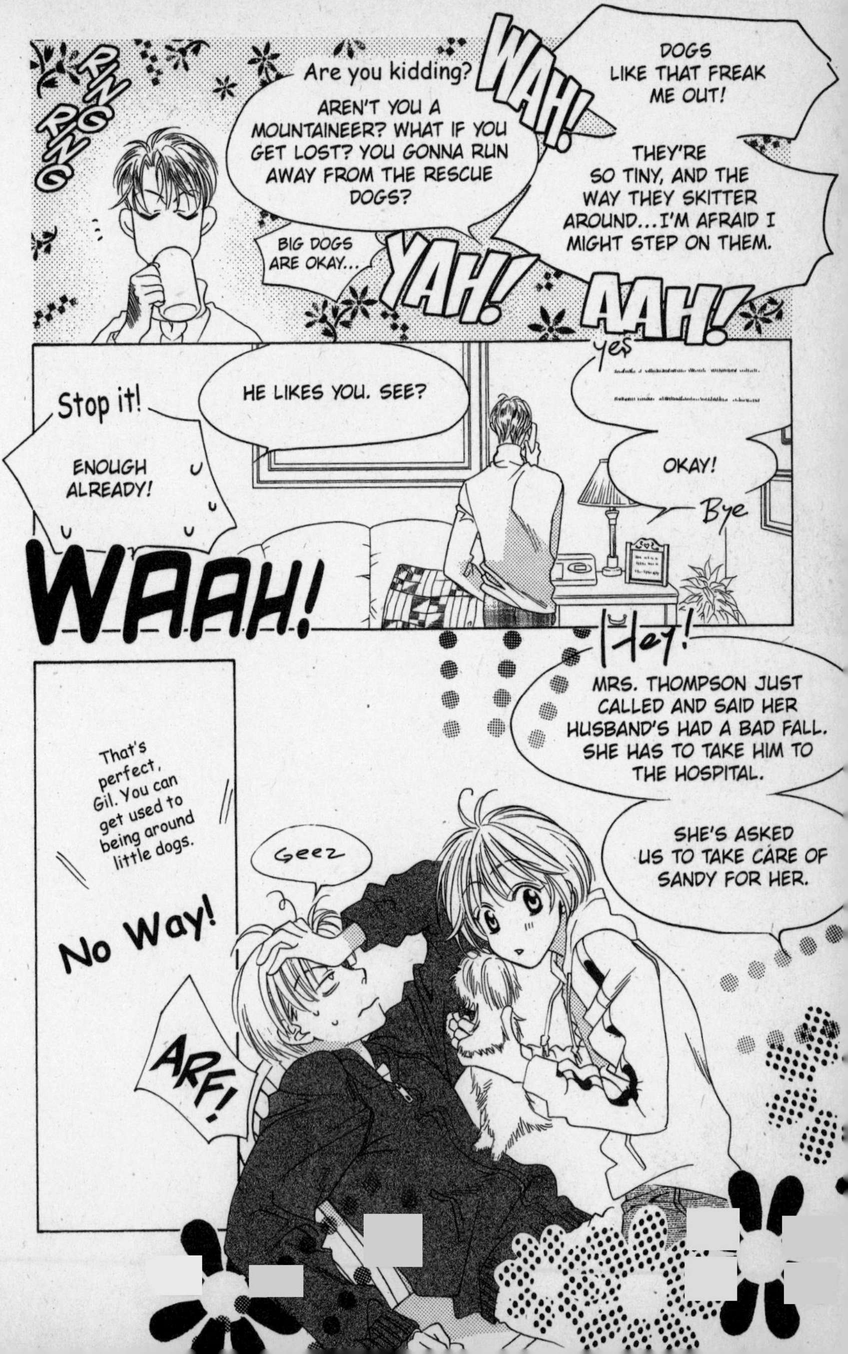
DOGS LIKE THAT FREAK ME OUT!
THEY'RE SO TINY, AND THE WAY THEY SKITTER AROUND...I'M AFRAID I MIGHT STEP ON THEM.
WAH!
Are you kidding?
AREN'T YOU A MOUNTAINEER? WHAT IF YOU GET LOST? YOU GONNA RUN AWAY FROM THE RESCUE DOGS?
RING RING
AAH!
YAH!
BIG DOGS ARE OKAY...
yes
OKAY!
Bye
HE LIKES YOU. SEE?
Stop it!
ENOUGH ALREADY!
WAAH!
Hey!
MRS. THOMPSON JUST CALLED AND SAID HER HUSBAND'S HAD A BAD FALL. SHE HAS TO TAKE HIM TO THE HOSPITAL.
SHE'S ASKED US TO TAKE CARE OF SANDY FOR HER.
Geez
That's perfect, Gil. You can get used to being around little dogs.
No Way!
ARF!

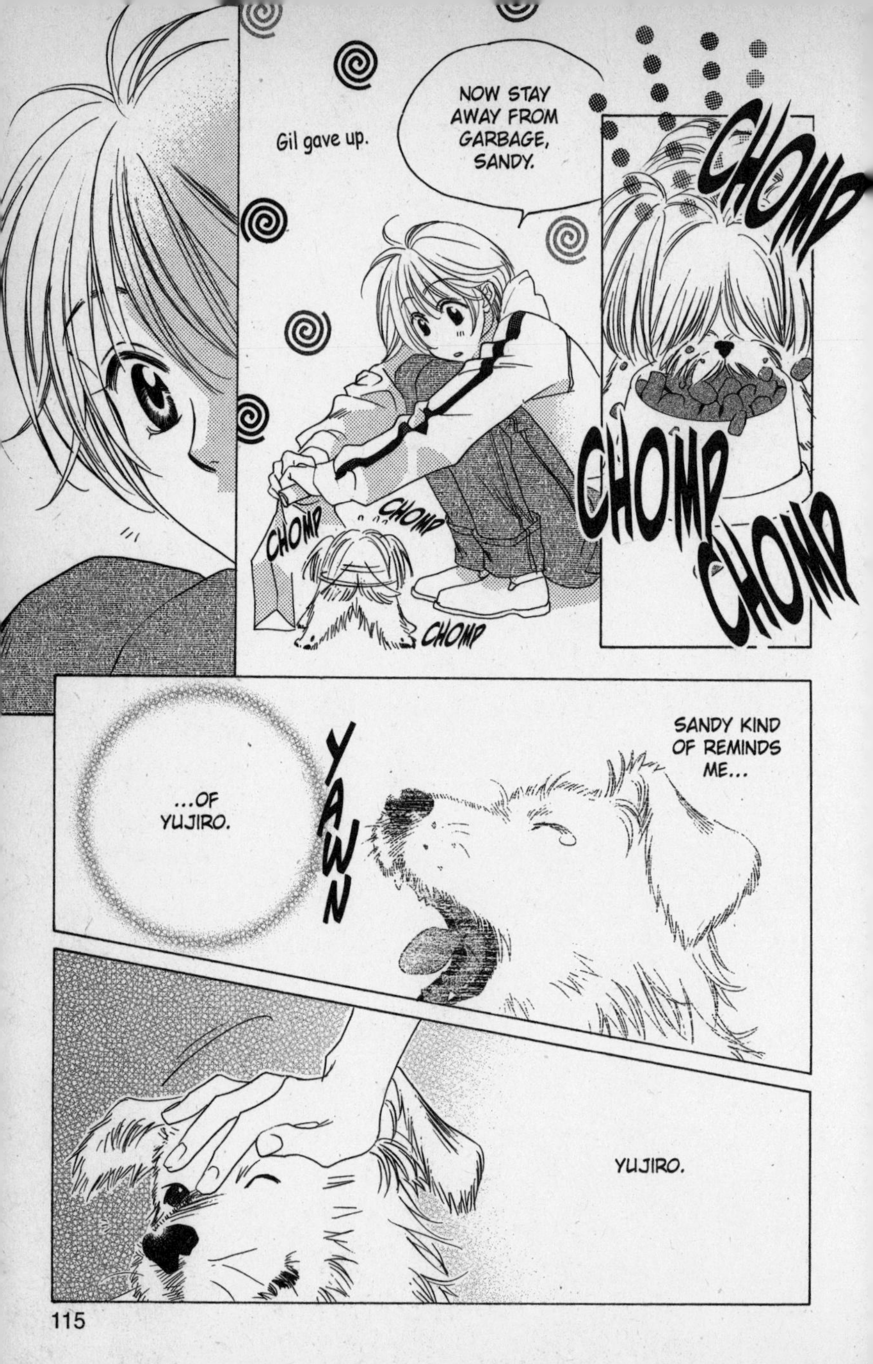
CHOMP
CHOMP
CHOMP
NOW STAY AWAY FROM GARBAGE, SANDY.
Gil gave up.
CHOMP
CHOMP
CHOMP
SANDY KIND OF REMINDS ME...
YAWN
...OF YUJIRO.
YUJIRO.

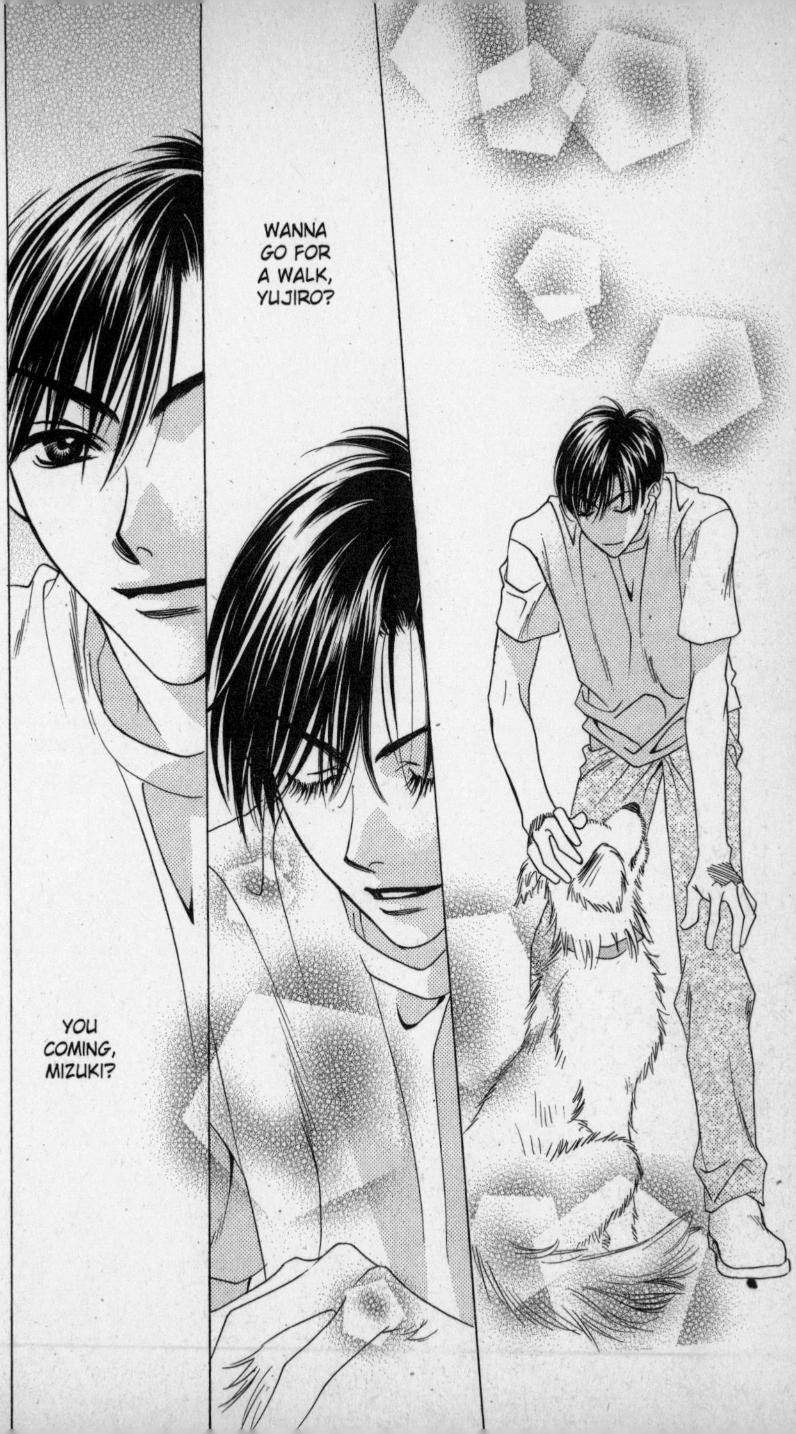
WANNA GO FOR A WALK, YUJIRO?
YOU COMING, MIZUKI?

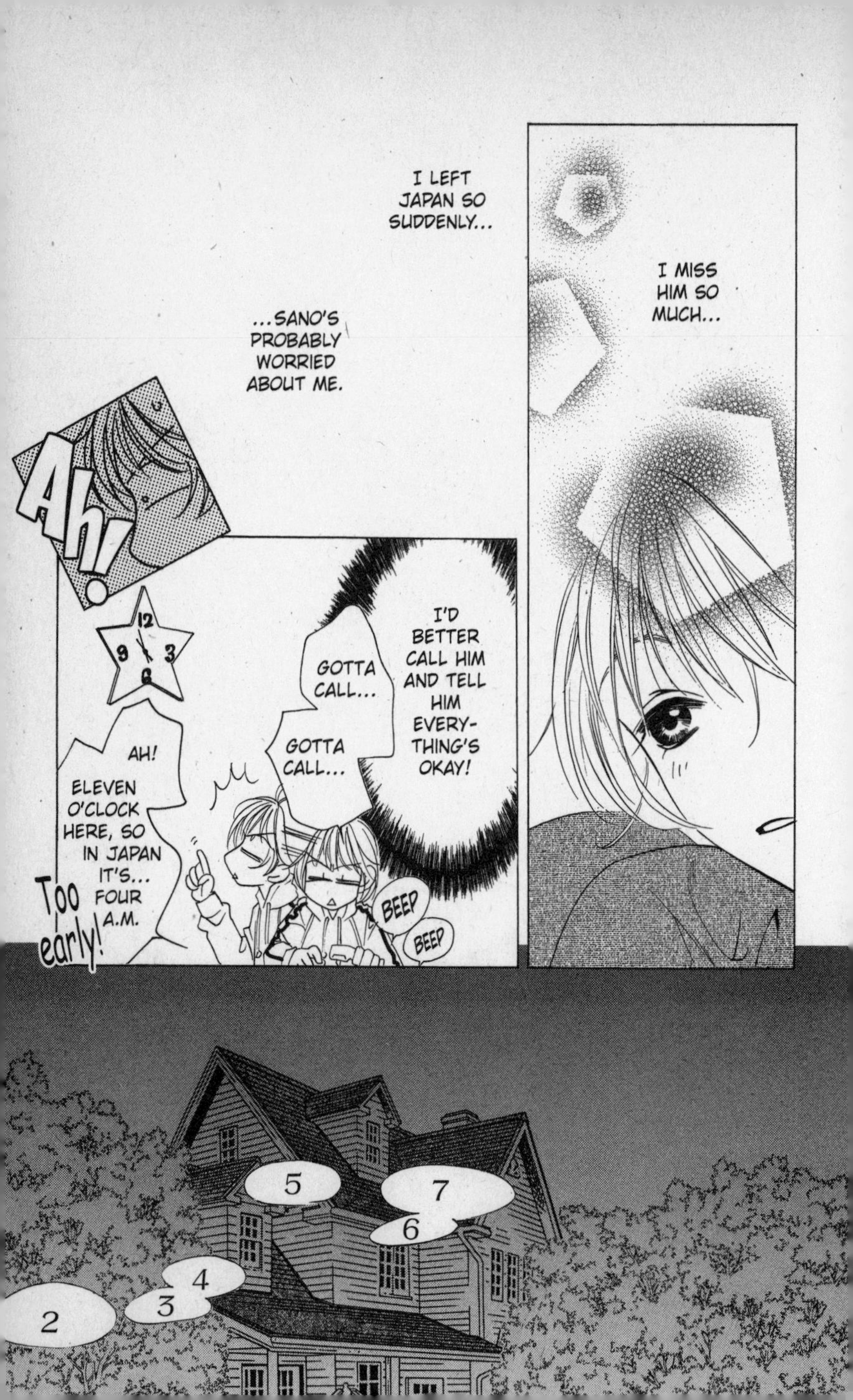
I MISS HIM SO MUCH...
I LEFT JAPAN SO SUDDENLY...
...SANO'S PROBABLY WORRIED ABOUT ME.
Ah!
I'D BETTER CALL HIM AND TELL HIM EVERY-THING'S OKAY!
GOTTA CALL...
GOTTA CALL...
12 3 6 9
AH!
ELEVEN O'CLOCK HERE, SO IN JAPAN IT'S... FOUR A.M.
Too early!
BEEP
BEEP
2
3
4
5
6
7

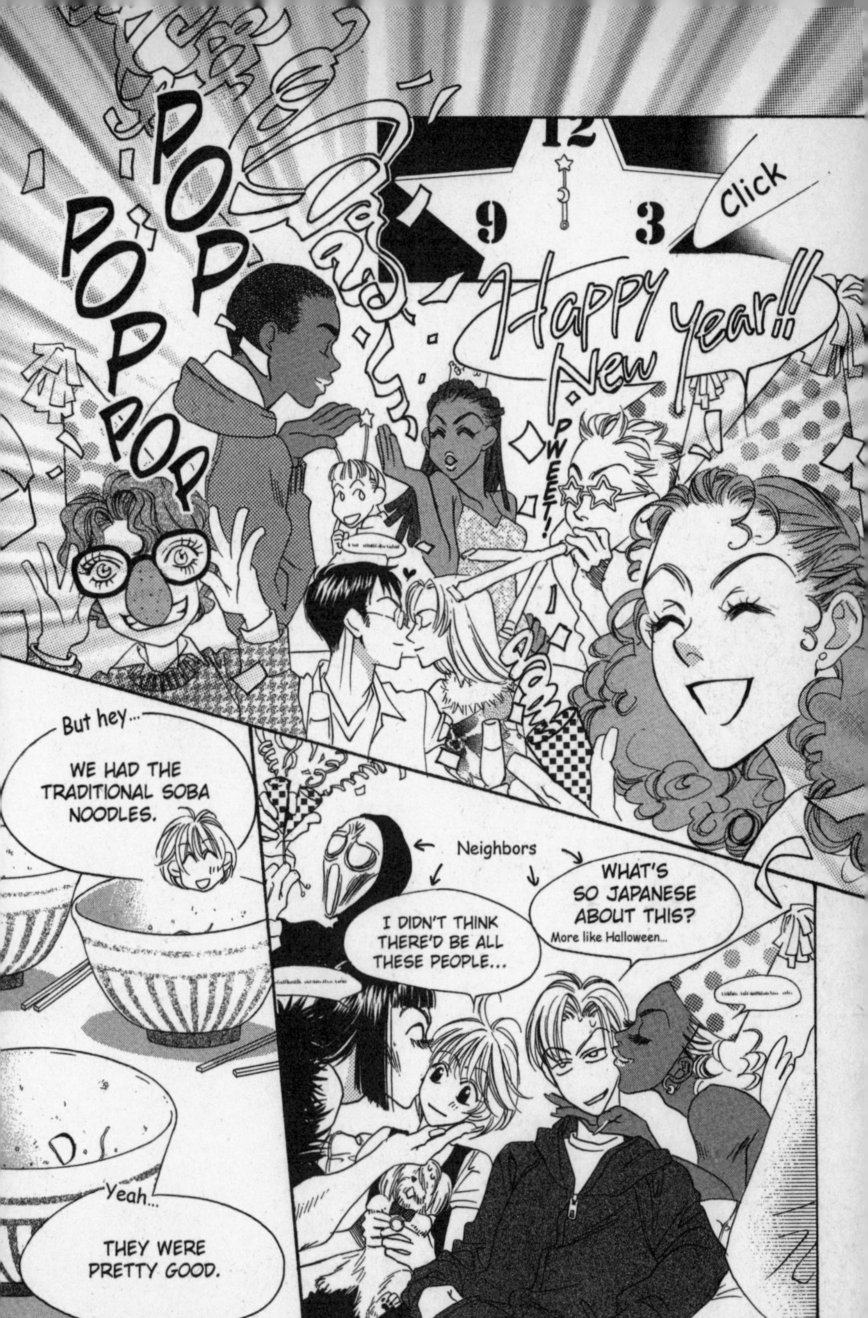

Click
Happy New year!!
PWEET!
POP POP POP POP
Neighbors
WHAT'S SO JAPANESE ABOUT THIS?
More like Halloween...
I DIDN'T THINK THERE'D BE ALL THESE PEOPLE...
But hey...
WE HAD THE TRADITIONAL SOBA NOODLES.
Yeah...
THEY WERE PRETTY GOOD.

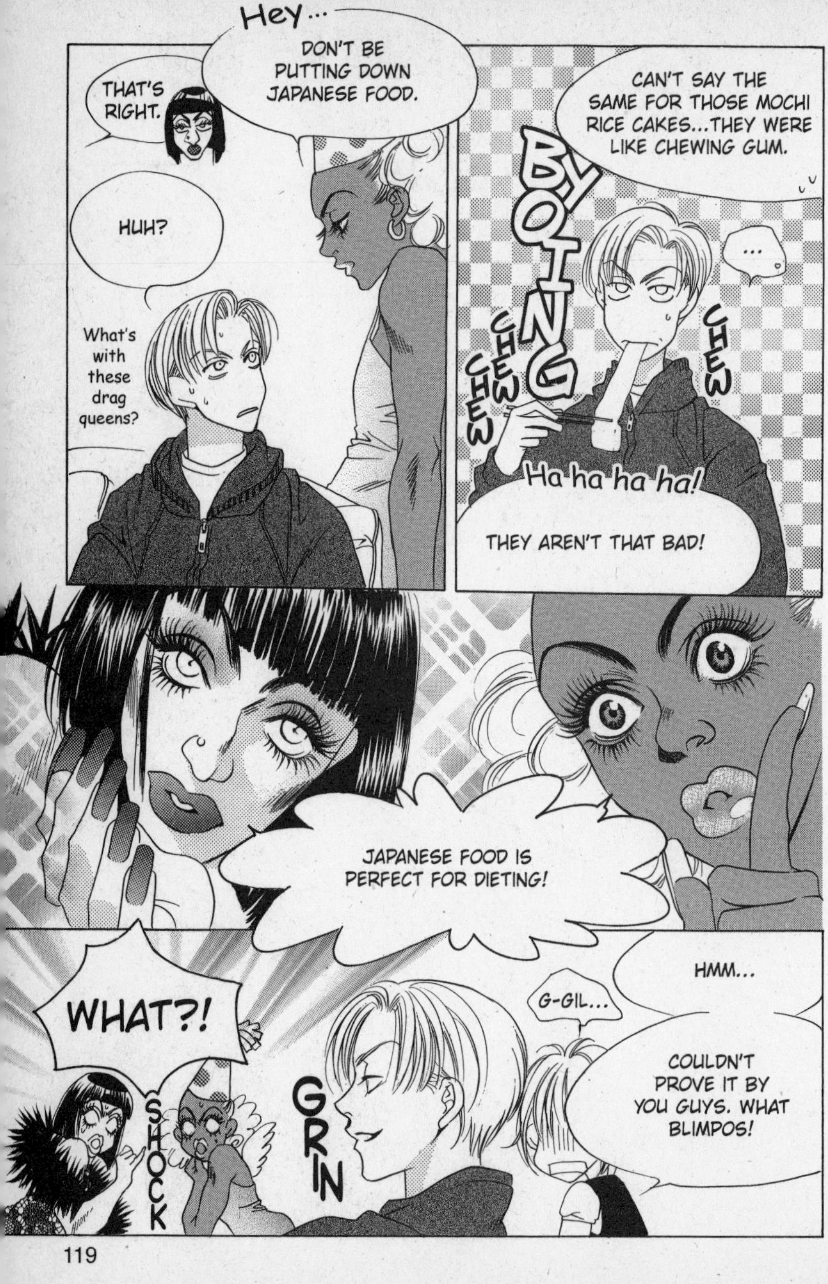
CAN'T SAY THE SAME FOR THOSE MOCHI RICE CAKES...THEY WERE LIKE CHEWING GUM.
BOING
CHEW
CHEW CHEW
...
Ha ha ha ha!
THEY AREN'T THAT BAD!
Hey...
DON'T BE PUTTING DOWN JAPANESE FOOD.
THAT'S RIGHT.
HUH?
What's with these drag queens?
JAPANESE FOOD IS PERFECT FOR DIETING!
HMM...
G-GIL...
COULDN'T PROVE IT BY YOU GUYS. WHAT BLIMPOS!
GRIN
WHAT?!
SHOCK

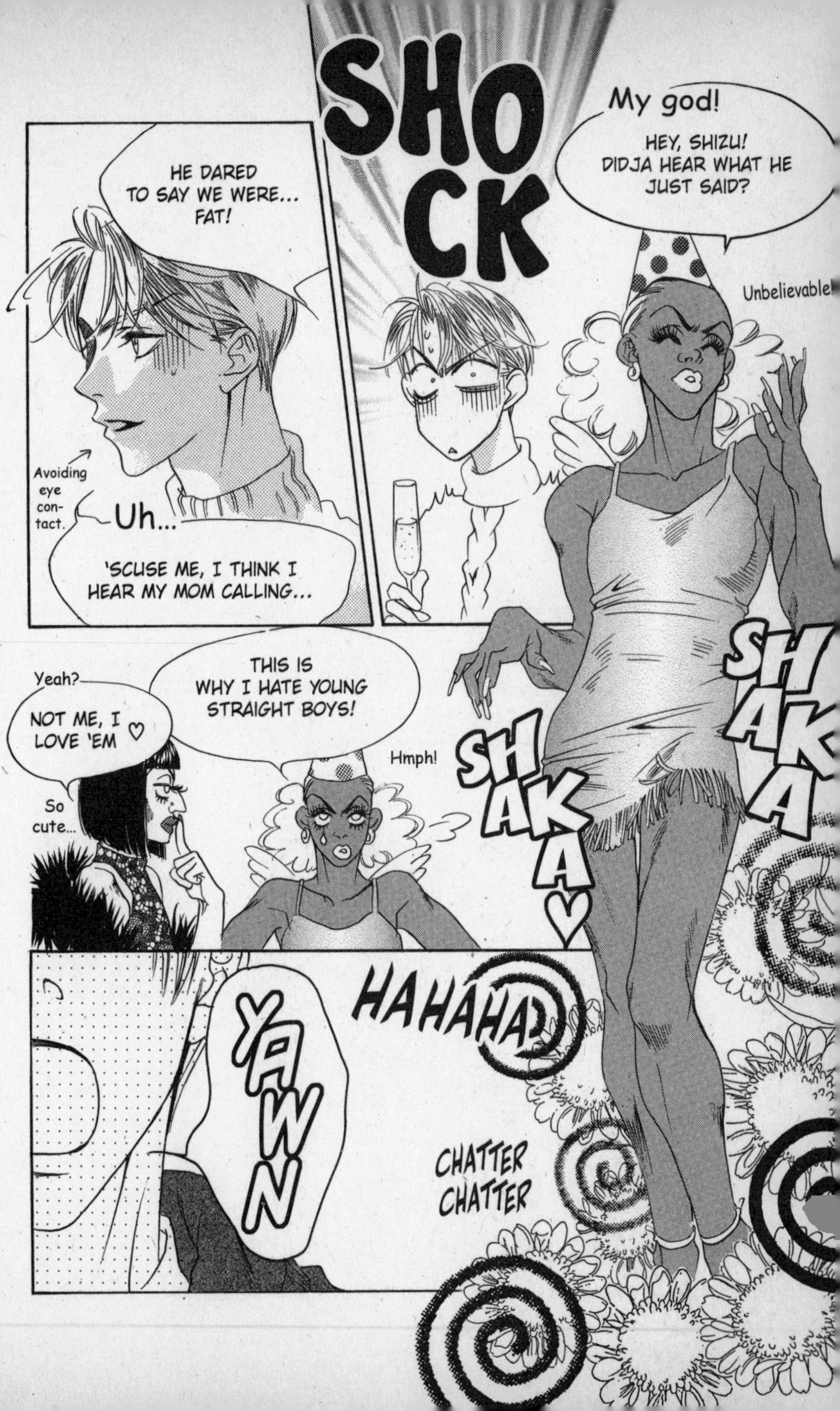
SHOCK
My god!
HEY, SHIZU! DIDJA HEAR WHAT HE JUST SAID?
Unbelievable!
HE DARED TO SAY WE WERE... FAT!
Avoiding eye con-tact.
Uh...
'SCUSE ME, I THINK I HEAR MY MOM CALLING...
SHAKA
SHAKA ♡
Hmph!
THIS IS WHY I HATE YOUNG STRAIGHT BOYS!
Yeah?
NOT ME, I LOVE 'EM ♡
So cute...
HAHAHA
YAWN
CHATTER CHATTER

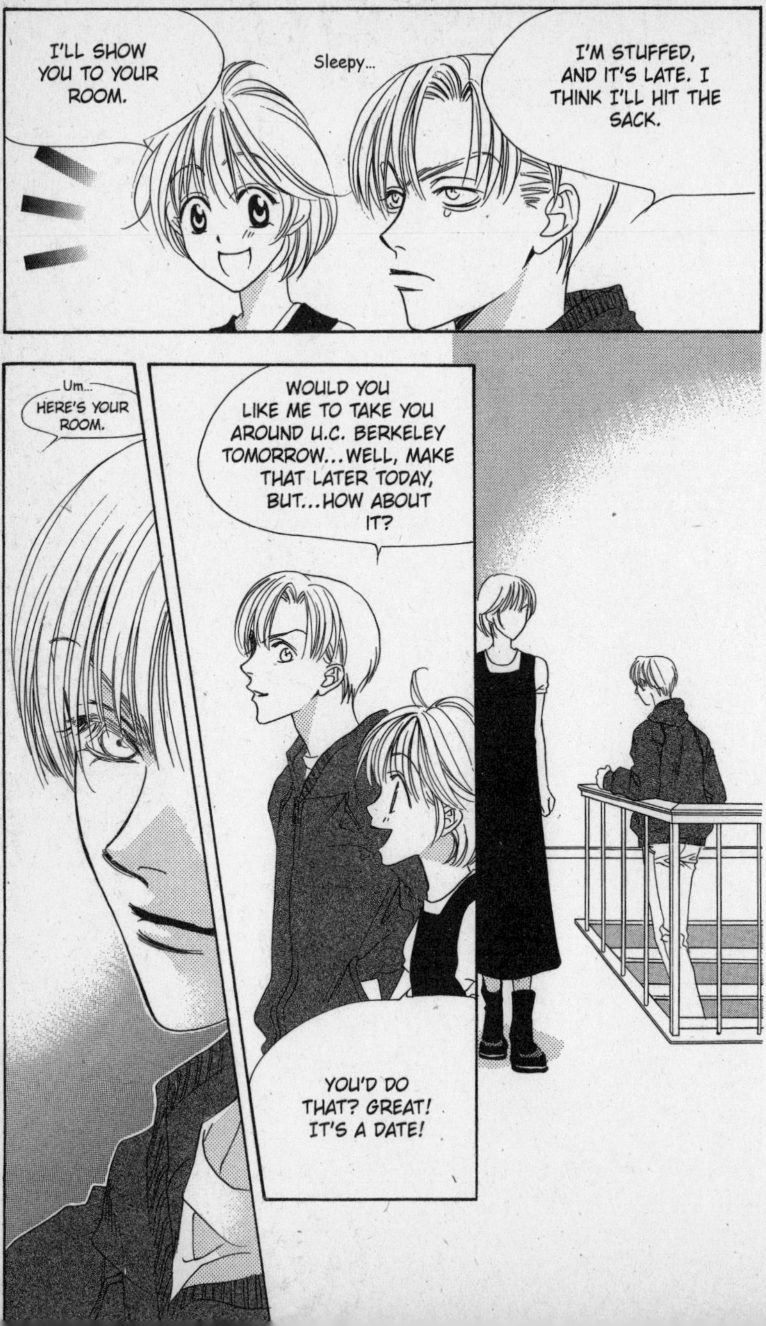
I'M STUFFED, AND IT'S LATE. I THINK I'LL HIT THE SACK.
Sleepy...
I'LL SHOW YOU TO YOUR ROOM.
WOULD YOU LIKE ME TO TAKE YOU AROUND U.C. BERKELEY TOMORROW...WELL, MAKE THAT LATER TODAY, BUT...HOW ABOUT IT?
YOU'D DO THAT? GREAT! IT'S A DATE!
Um... HERE'S YOUR ROOM.

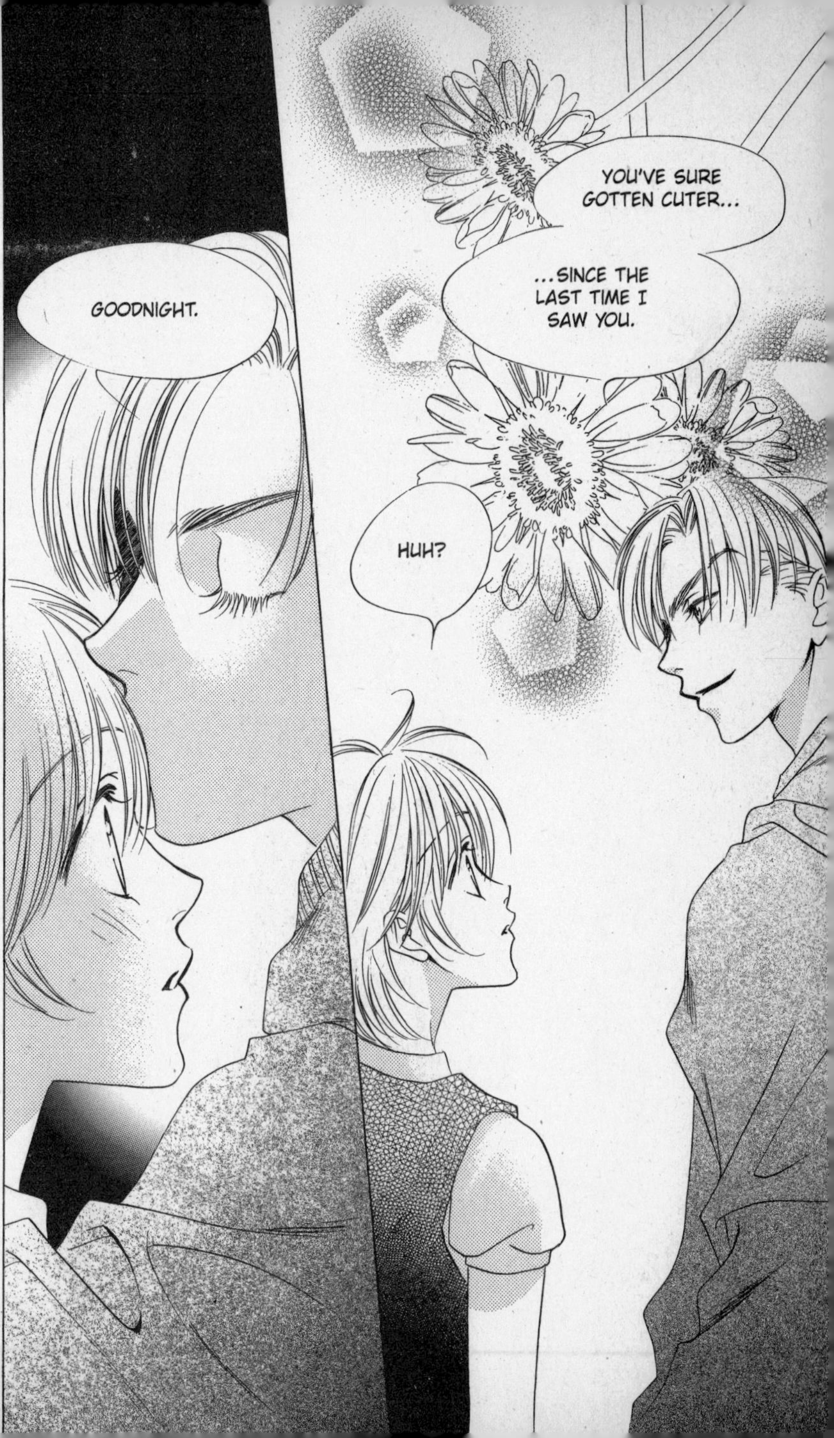
YOU'VE SURE GOTTEN CUTER...
...SINCE THE LAST TIME I SAW YOU.
HUH?
GOODNIGHT.

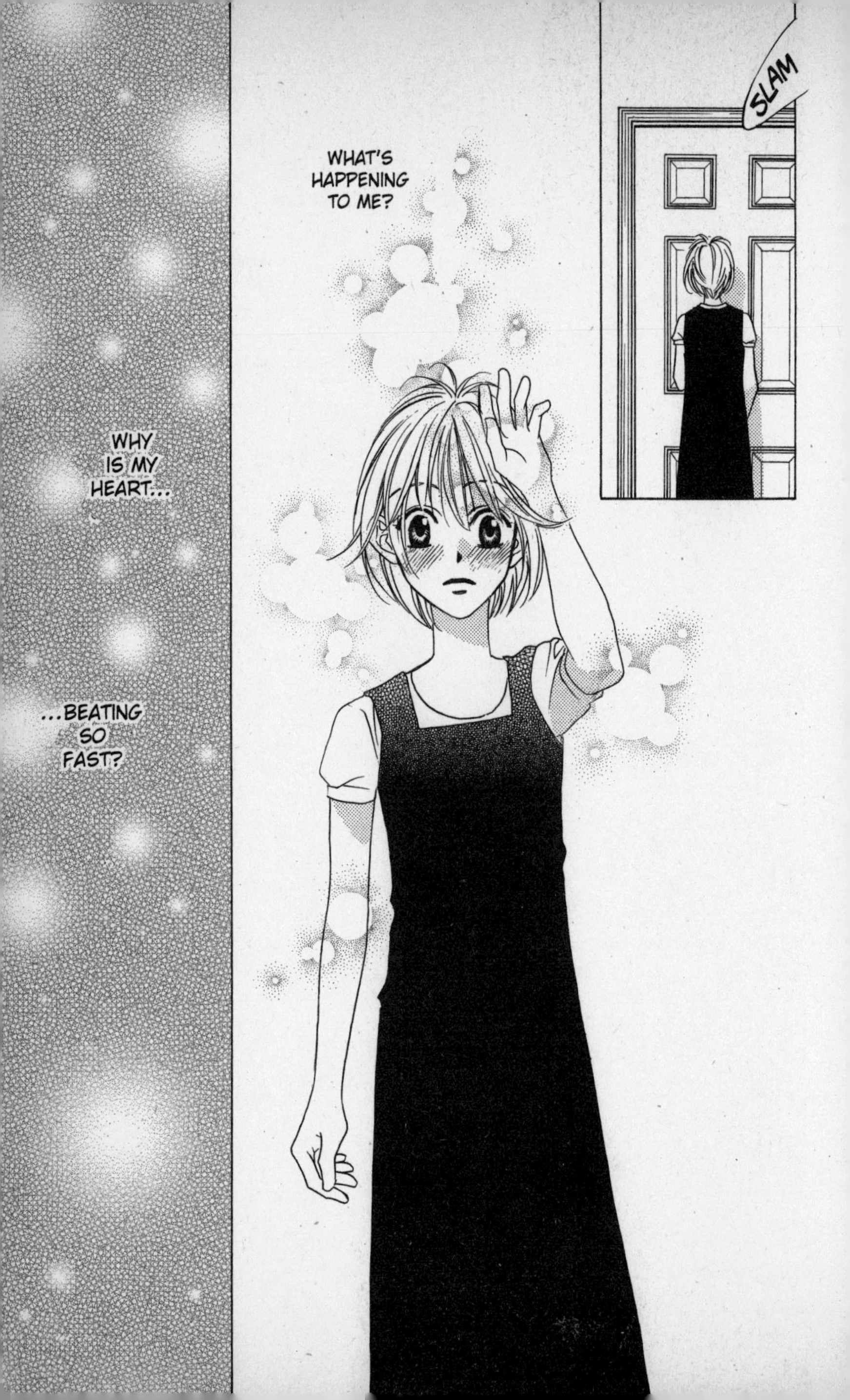
SLAM
WHAT'S HAPPENING TO ME?
WHY IS MY HEART...
...BEATING SO FAST?

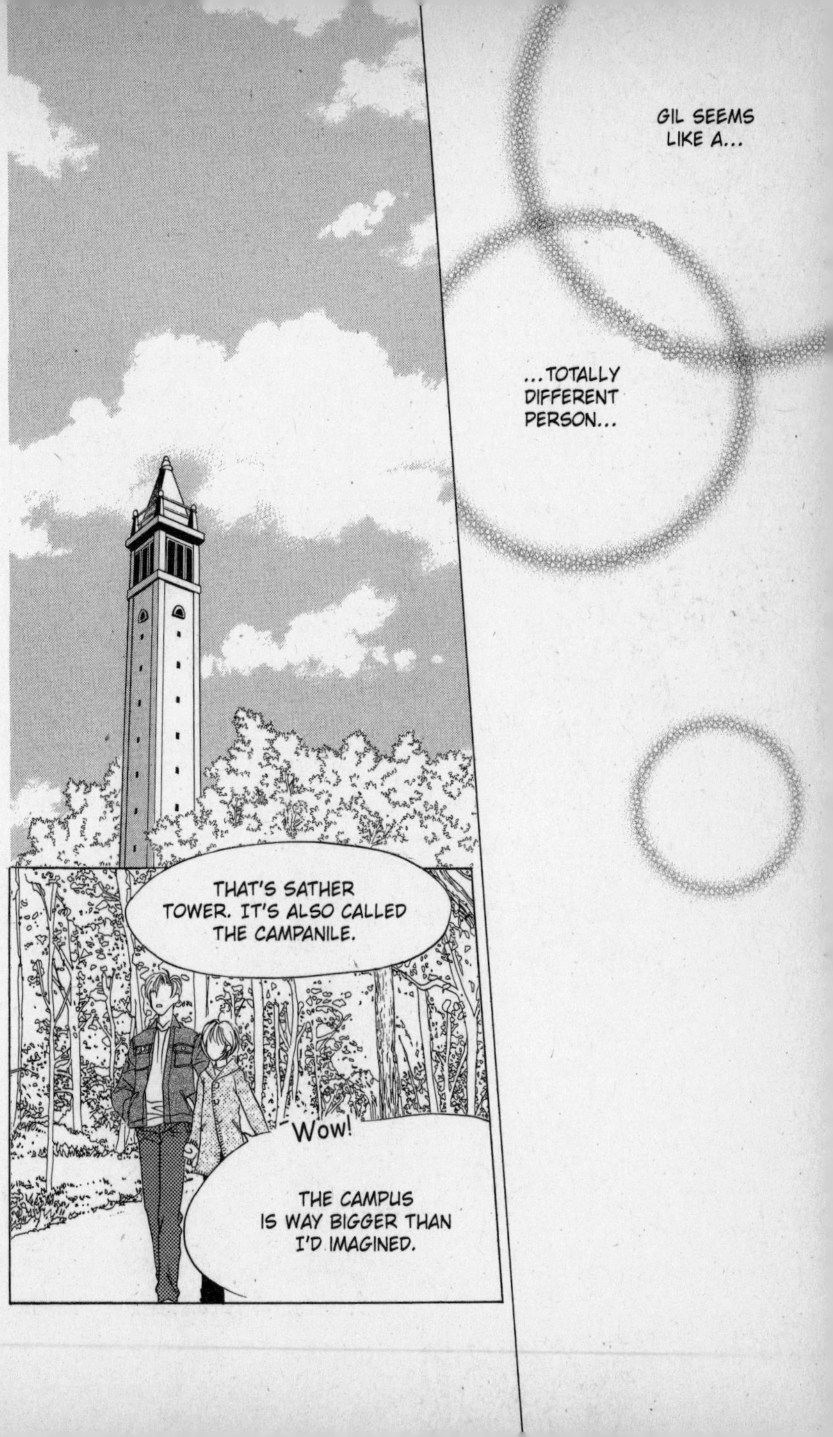
GIL SEEMS LIKE A...
...TOTALLY DIFFERENT PERSON...
THAT'S SATHER TOWER. IT'S ALSO CALLED THE CAMPANILE.
Wow!
THE CAMPUS IS WAY BIGGER THAN I'D IMAGINED.

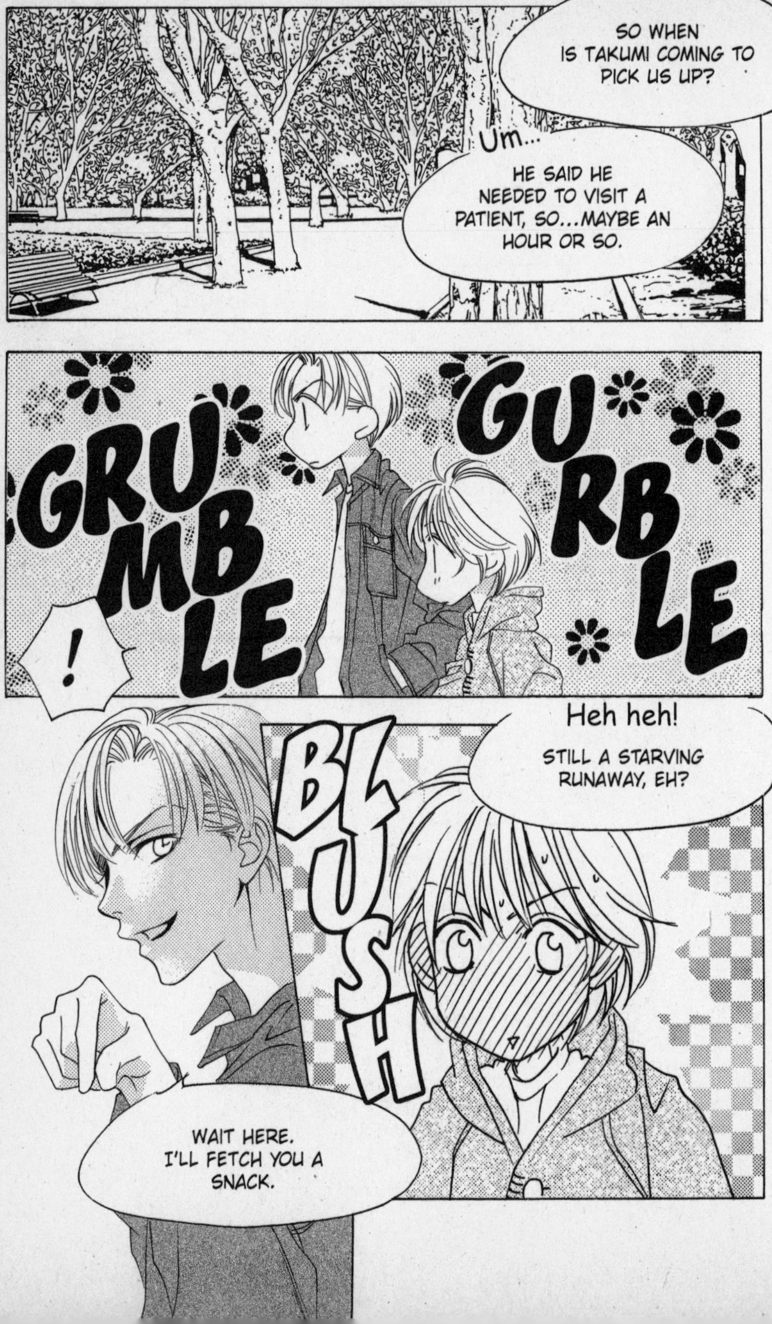
SO WHEN IS TAKUMI COMING TO PICK US UP?
Um...
HE SAID HE NEEDED TO VISIT A PATIENT, SO...MAYBE AN HOUR OR SO.
GURBLE
GRUMBLE
!
Heh heh!
STILL A STARVING RUNAWAY, EH?
BLUSH
WAIT HERE. I'LL FETCH YOU A SNACK.

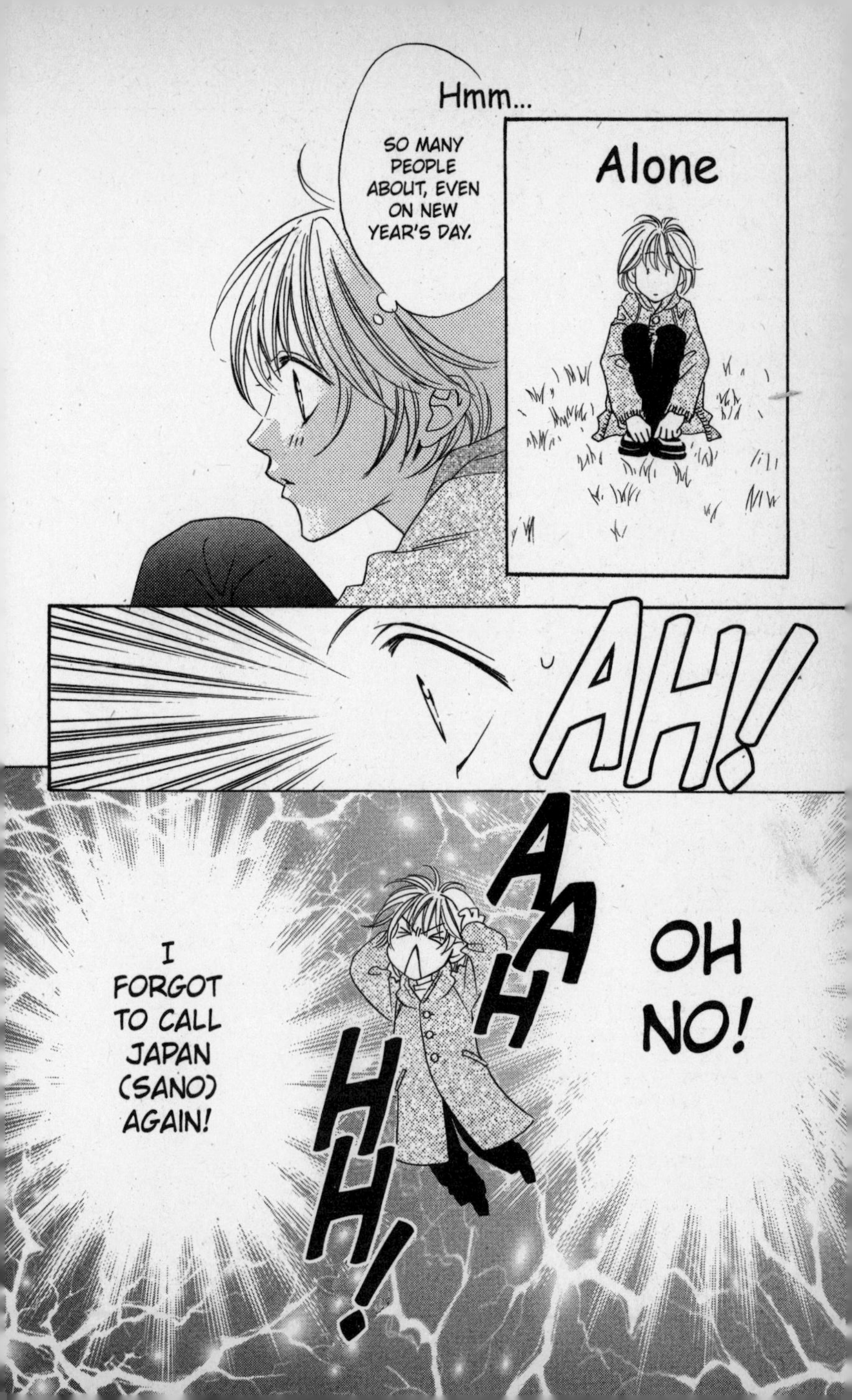
Alone
Hmm...
SO MANY PEOPLE ABOUT, EVEN ON NEW YEAR'S DAY.
AH!
OH NO!
AAAHHHH!!
I FORGOT TO CALL JAPAN (SANO) AGAIN!

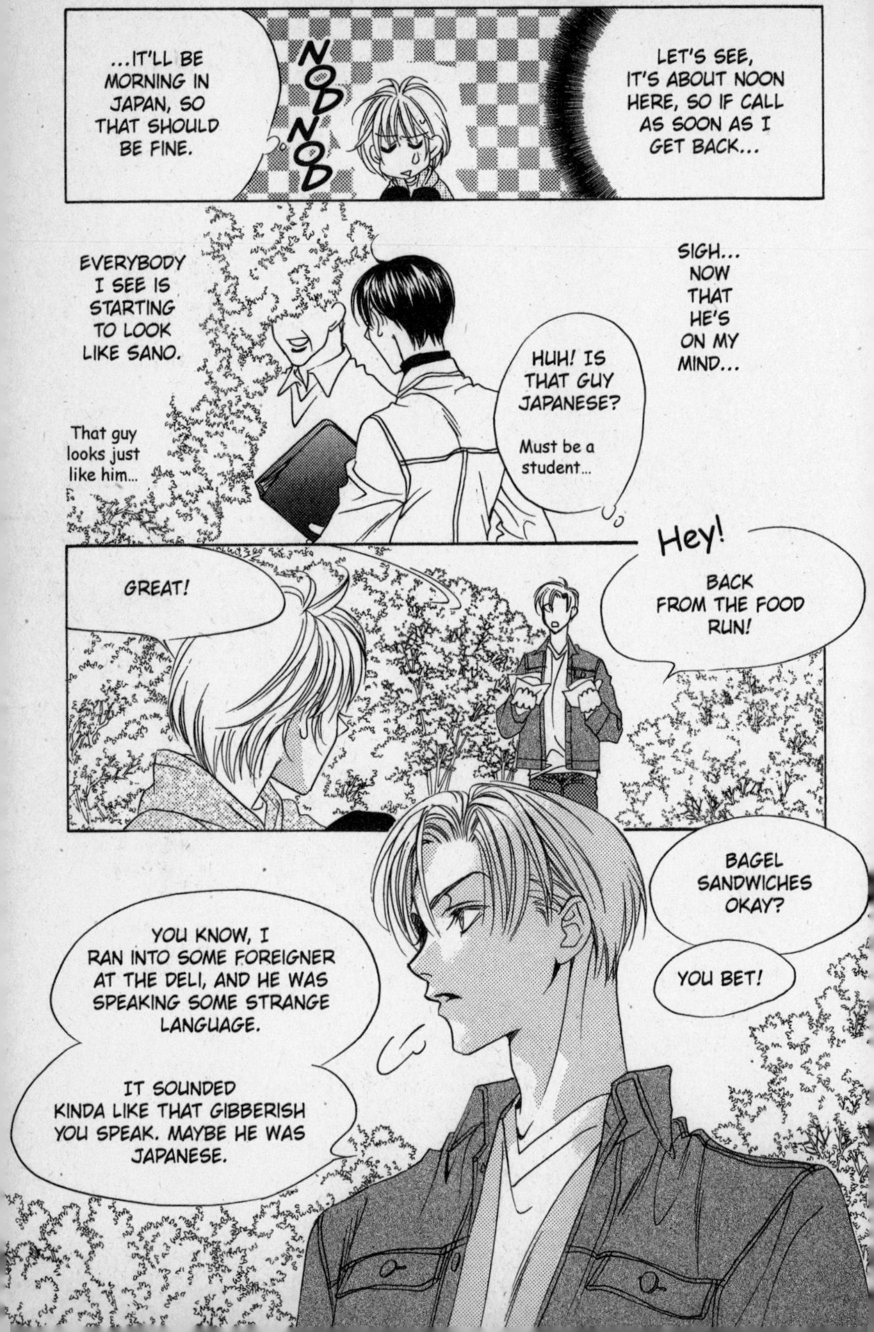
LET'S SEE, IT'S ABOUT NOON HERE, SO IF CALL AS SOON AS I GET BACK...
NOD NOD
...IT'LL BE MORNING IN JAPAN, SO THAT SHOULD BE FINE.
SIGH... NOW THAT HE'S ON MY MIND...
HUH! IS THAT GUY JAPANESE?
Must be a student...
EVERYBODY I SEE IS STARTING TO LOOK LIKE SANO.
That guy looks just like him...
Hey!
BACK FROM THE FOOD RUN!
GREAT!
BAGEL SANDWICHES OKAY?
YOU BET!
YOU KNOW, I RAN INTO SOME FOREIGNER AT THE DELI, AND HE WAS SPEAKING SOME STRANGE LANGUAGE.
IT SOUNDED KINDA LIKE THAT GIBBERISH YOU SPEAK. MAYBE HE WAS JAPANESE.

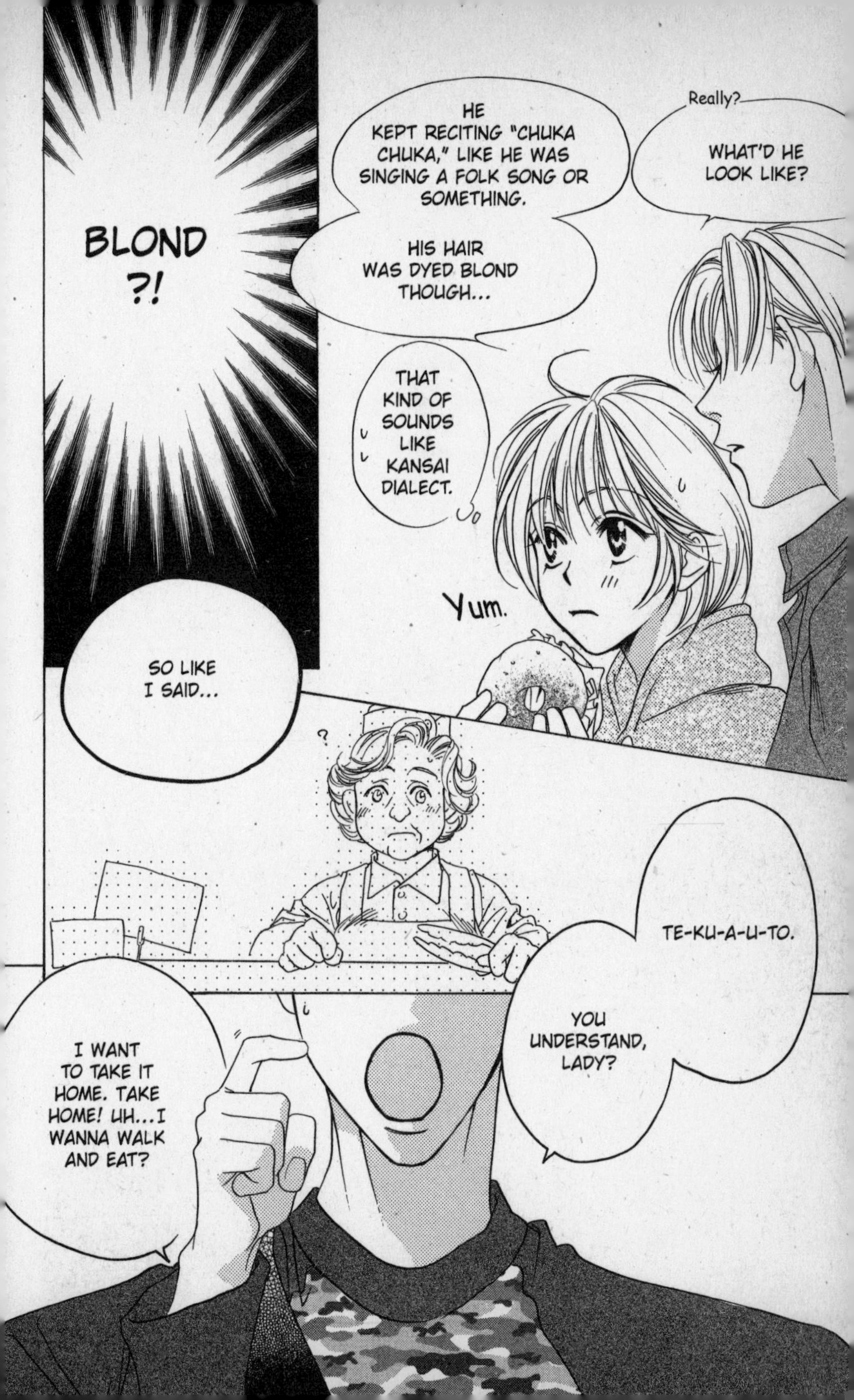
Really?
WHAT'D HE LOOK LIKE?
HE KEPT RECITING "CHUKA CHUKA," LIKE HE WAS SINGING A FOLK SONG OR SOMETHING.
HIS HAIR WAS DYED BLOND THOUGH...
THAT KIND OF SOUNDS LIKE KANSAI DIALECT.
Yum.
BLOND ?!
SO LIKE I SAID...
TE-KU-A-U-TO.
YOU UNDERSTAND, LADY?
I WANT TO TAKE IT HOME. TAKE HOME! UH...I WANNA WALK AND EAT?

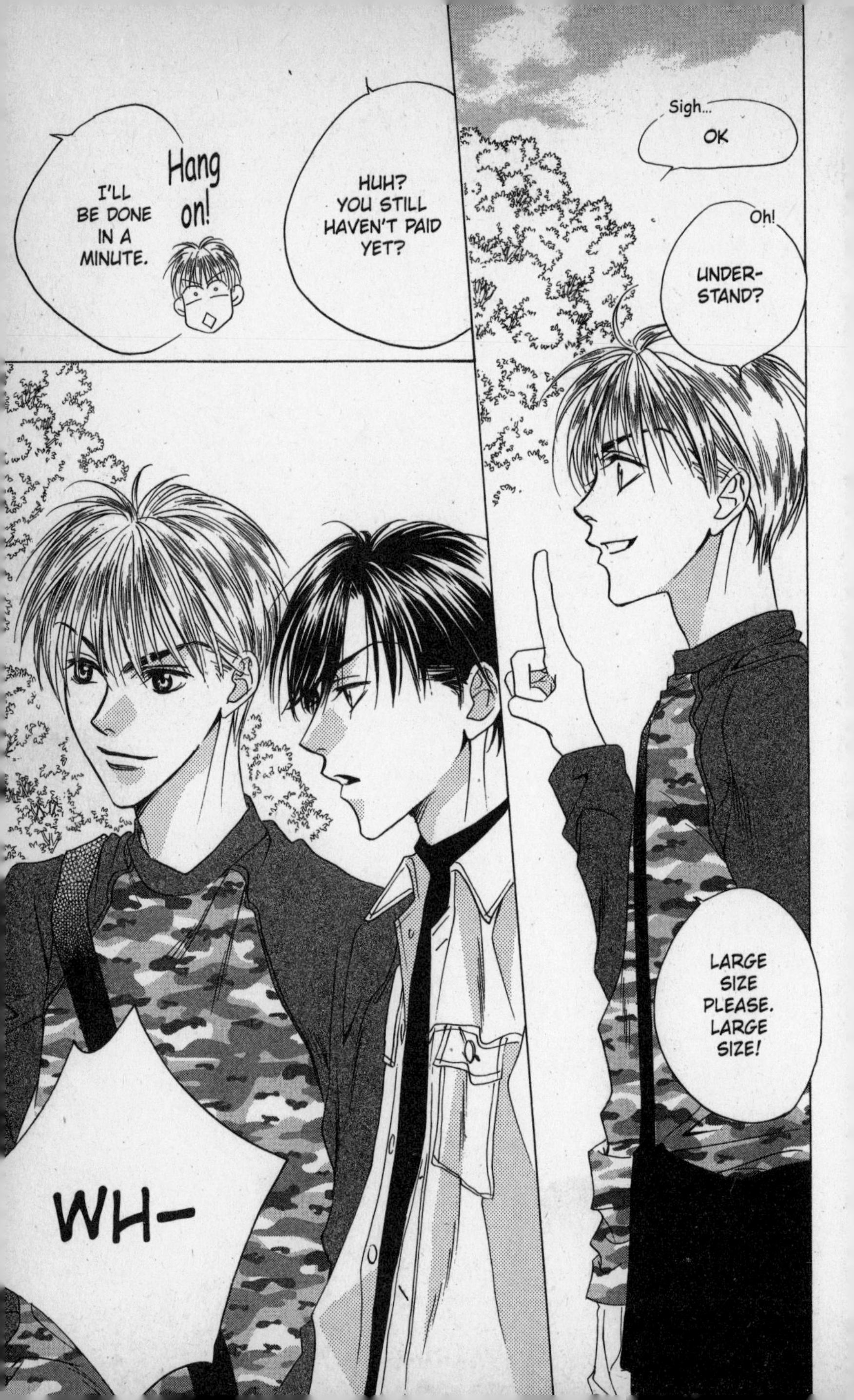
Sigh... OK
Oh!
UNDER-STAND?
LARGE SIZE PLEASE. LARGE SIZE!
HUH? YOU STILL HAVEN'T PAID YET?
Hang on!
I'LL BE DONE IN A MINUTE.
WH-

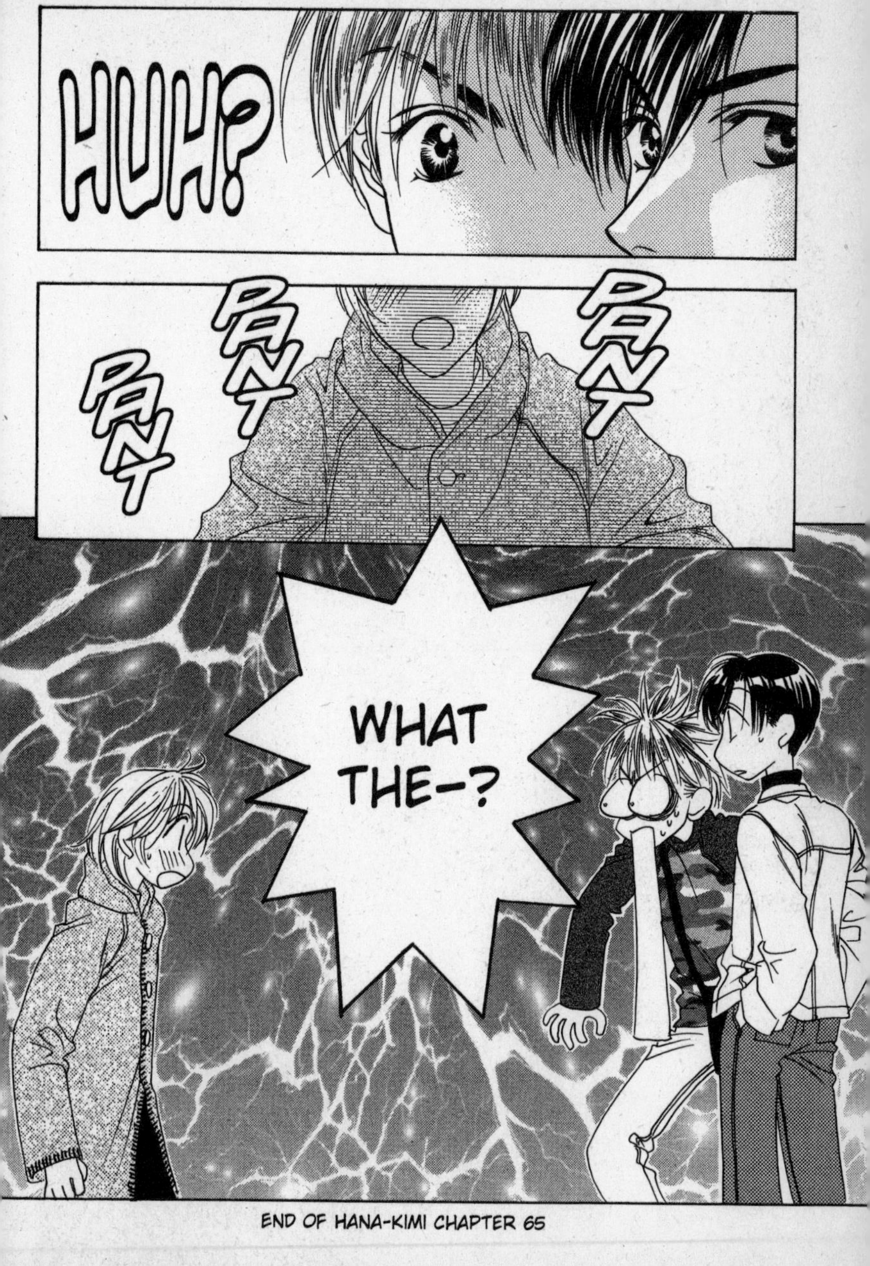
HUH?
PANT
PANT
WHAT THE-?

END OF HANA-KIMI CHAPTER 65

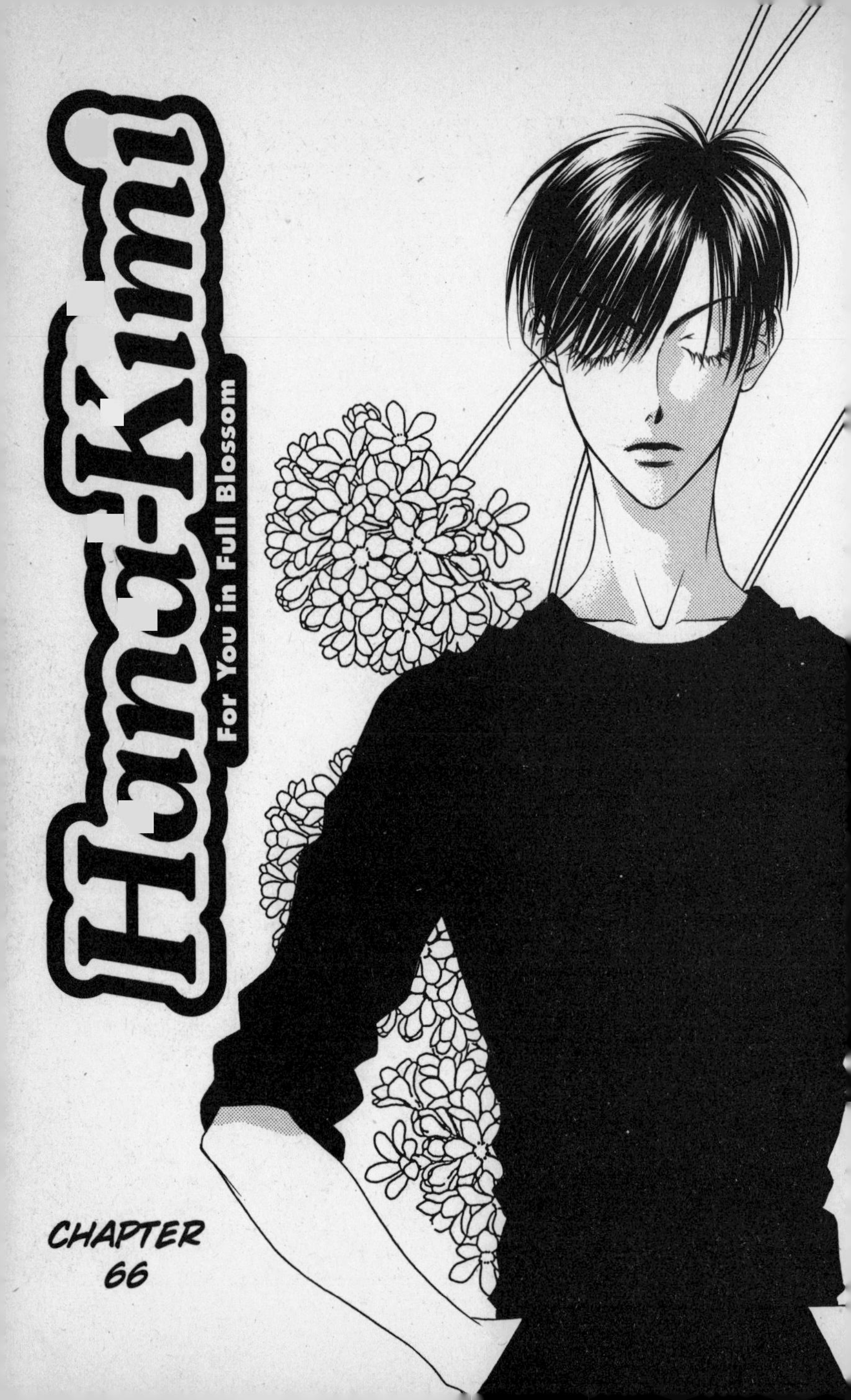
Hana-Kimi
For You in Full Blossom
CHAPTER
66

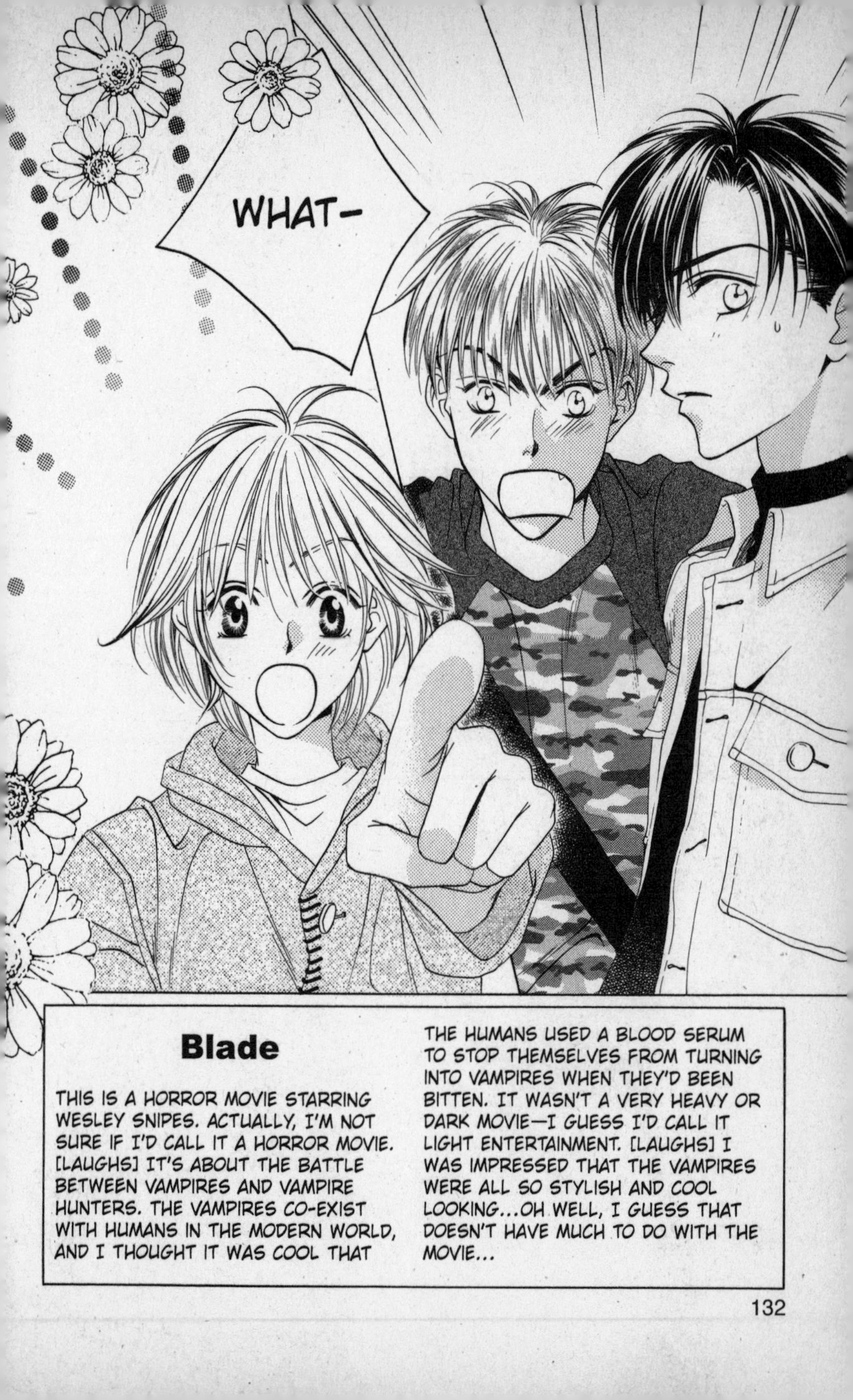
WHAT-

Blade

THIS IS A HORROR MOVIE STARRING WESLEY SNIPES. ACTUALLY, I'M NOT SURE IF I'D CALL IT A HORROR MOVIE. [LAUGHS] IT'S ABOUT THE BATTLE BETWEEN VAMPIRES AND VAMPIRE HUNTERS. THE VAMPIRES CO-EXIST WITH HUMANS IN THE MODERN WORLD, AND I THOUGHT IT WAS COOL THAT THE HUMANS USED A BLOOD SERUM TO STOP THEMSELVES FROM TURNING INTO VAMPIRES WHEN THEY'D BEEN BITTEN. IT WASN'T A VERY HEAVY OR DARK MOVIE—I GUESS I'D CALL IT LIGHT ENTERTAINMENT. [LAUGHS] I WAS IMPRESSED THAT THE VAMPIRES WERE ALL SO STYLISH AND COOL LOOKING...OH WELL, I GUESS THAT DOESN'T HAVE MUCH TO DO WITH THE MOVIE...

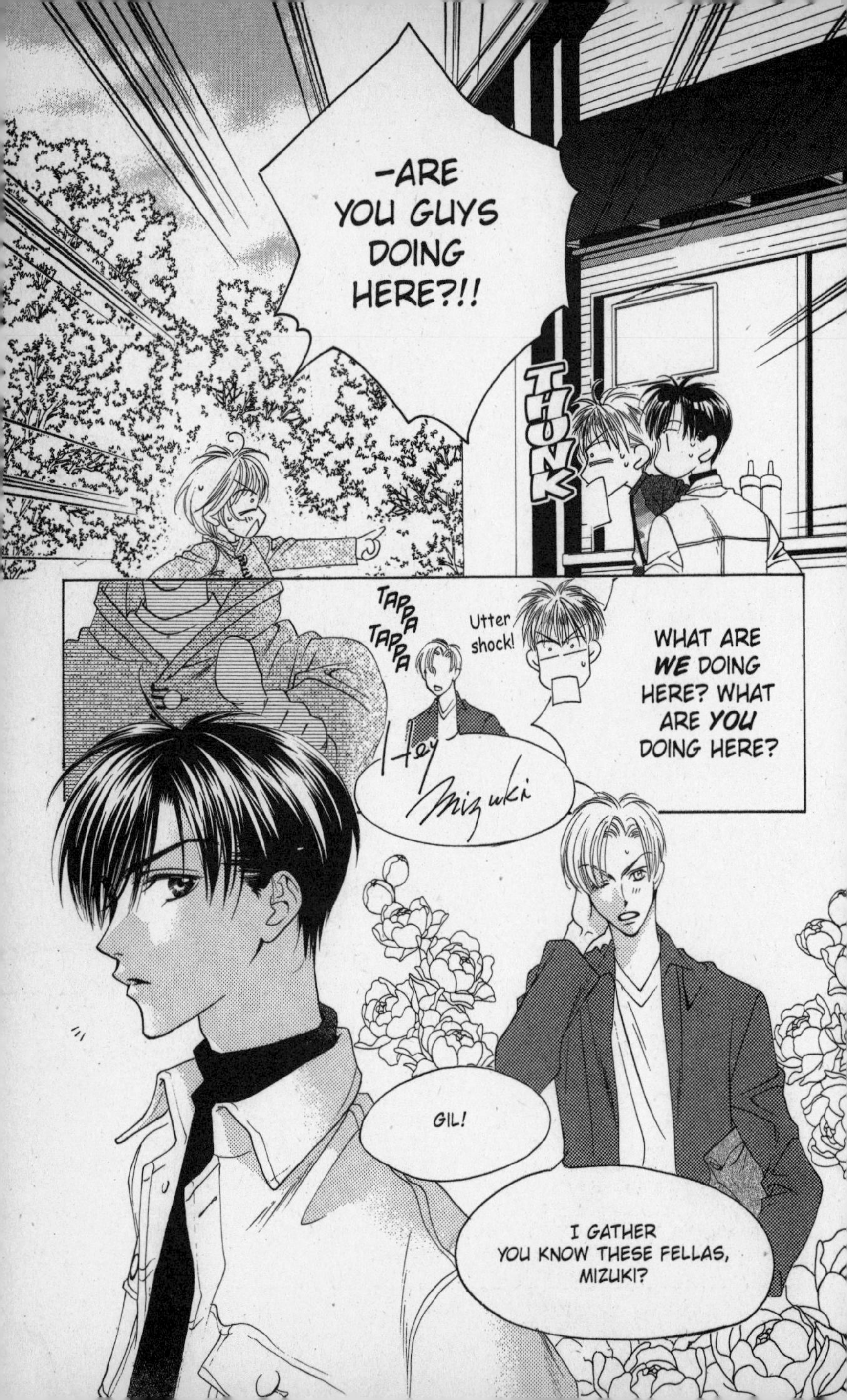
-ARE YOU GUYS DOING HERE?!!
THUNK
WHAT ARE WE DOING HERE? WHAT ARE YOU DOING HERE?
Utter shock!
TAPPA TAPPA
Hey Mizuki
GIL!
I GATHER YOU KNOW THESE FELLAS, MIZUKI?

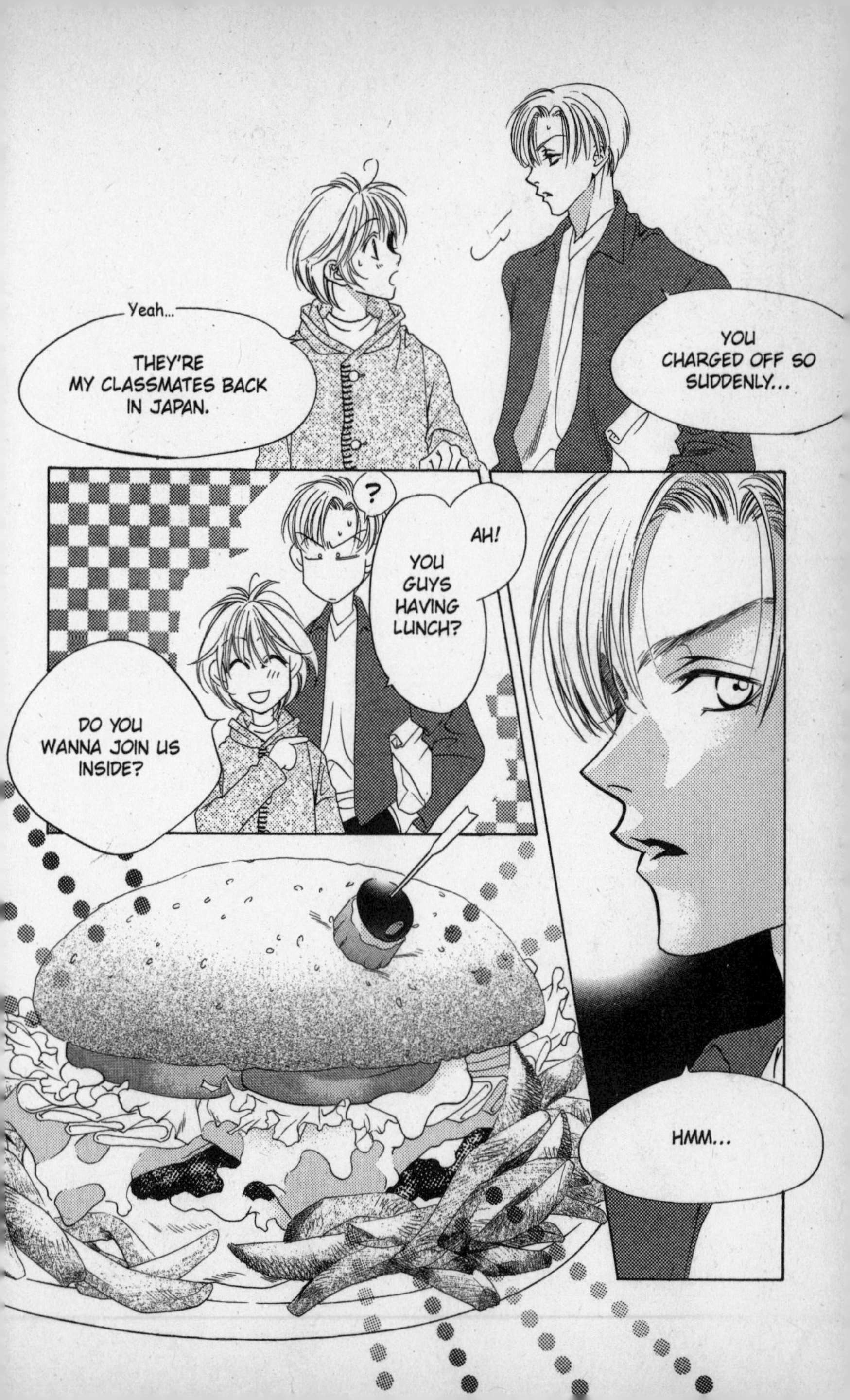
YOU CHARGED OFF SO SUDDENLY...
Yeah...
THEY'RE MY CLASSMATES BACK IN JAPAN.
?
AH!
YOU GUYS HAVING LUNCH?
DO YOU WANNA JOIN US INSIDE?
HMM...

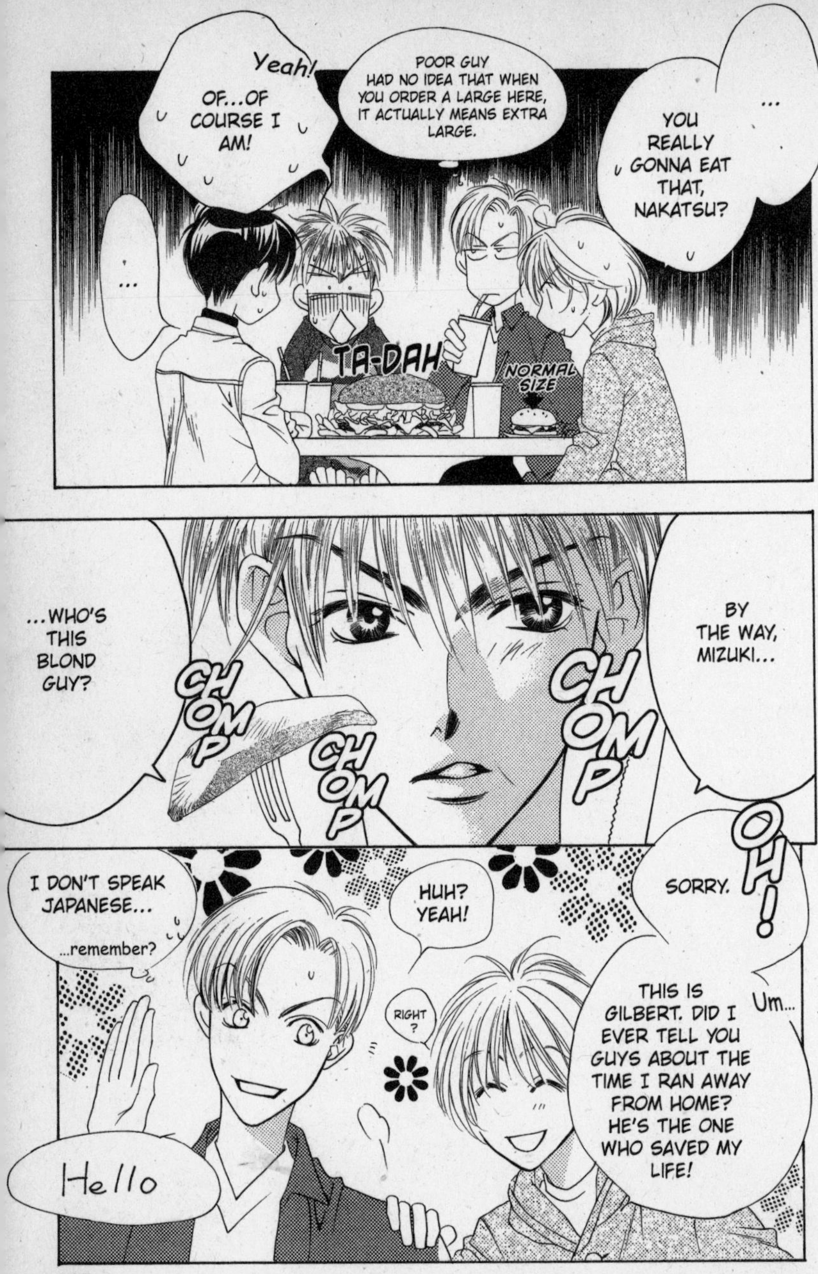
...
YOU REALLY GONNA EAT THAT, NAKATSU?
POOR GUY HAD NO IDEA THAT WHEN YOU ORDER A LARGE HERE, IT ACTUALLY MEANS EXTRA LARGE.
Yeah!
OF...OF COURSE I AM!
...
NORMAL SIZE
TA-DAH
BY THE WAY, MIZUKI...
CHOMP
CHOMP
CHOMP
...WHO'S THIS BLOND GUY?
OH!
SORRY.
Um...
THIS IS GILBERT. DID I EVER TELL YOU GUYS ABOUT THE TIME I RAN AWAY FROM HOME? HE'S THE ONE WHO SAVED MY LIFE!
RIGHT?
HUH? YEAH!
Hello
I DON'T SPEAK JAPANESE...
...remember?

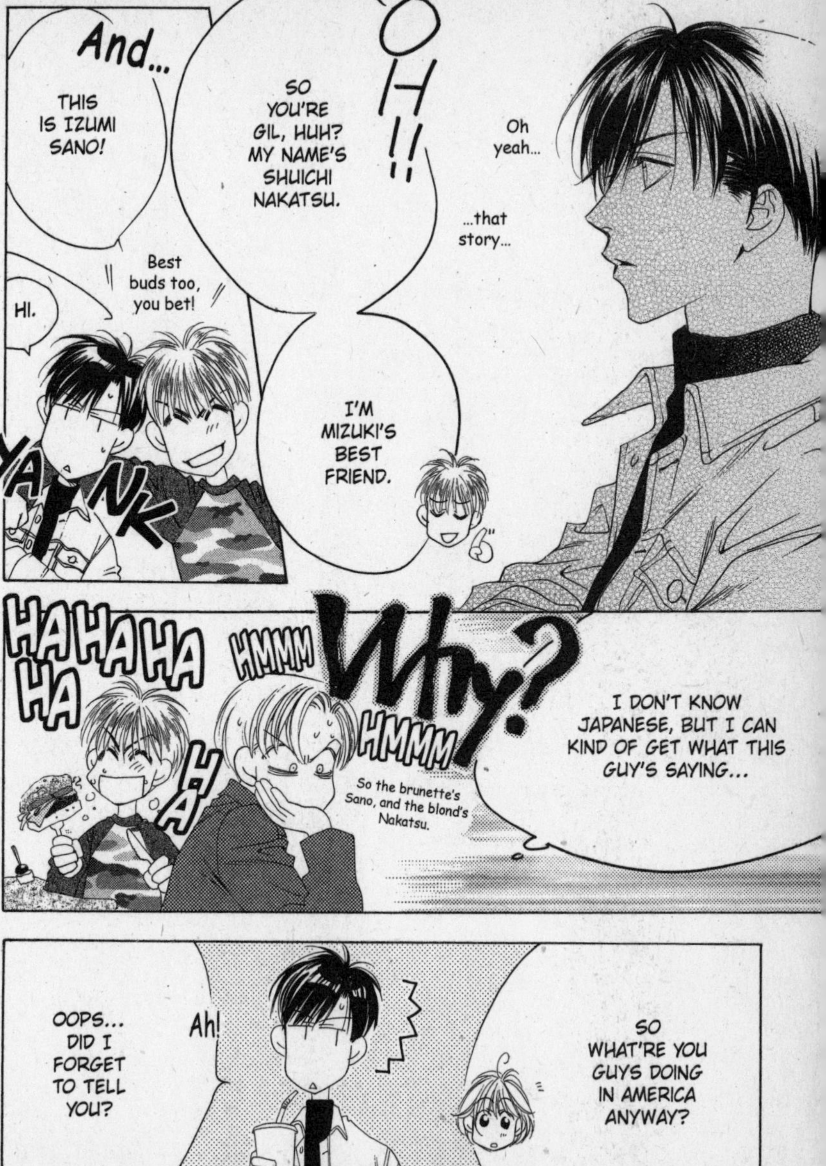
Oh yeah...
...that story...
OH!!
SO YOU'RE GIL, HUH? MY NAME'S SHUICHI NAKATSU.
I'M MIZUKI'S BEST FRIEND.
And...
THIS IS IZUMI SANO!
Best buds too, you bet!
HI.
YANK
I DON'T KNOW JAPANESE, BUT I CAN KIND OF GET WHAT THIS GUY'S SAYING...
Why?
So the brunette's Sano, and the blond's Nakatsu.
HMMM
HMMM
HA HA HA HA HA
HA
SO WHAT'RE YOU GUYS DOING IN AMERICA ANYWAY?
Ah!
OOPS... DID I FORGET TO TELL YOU?

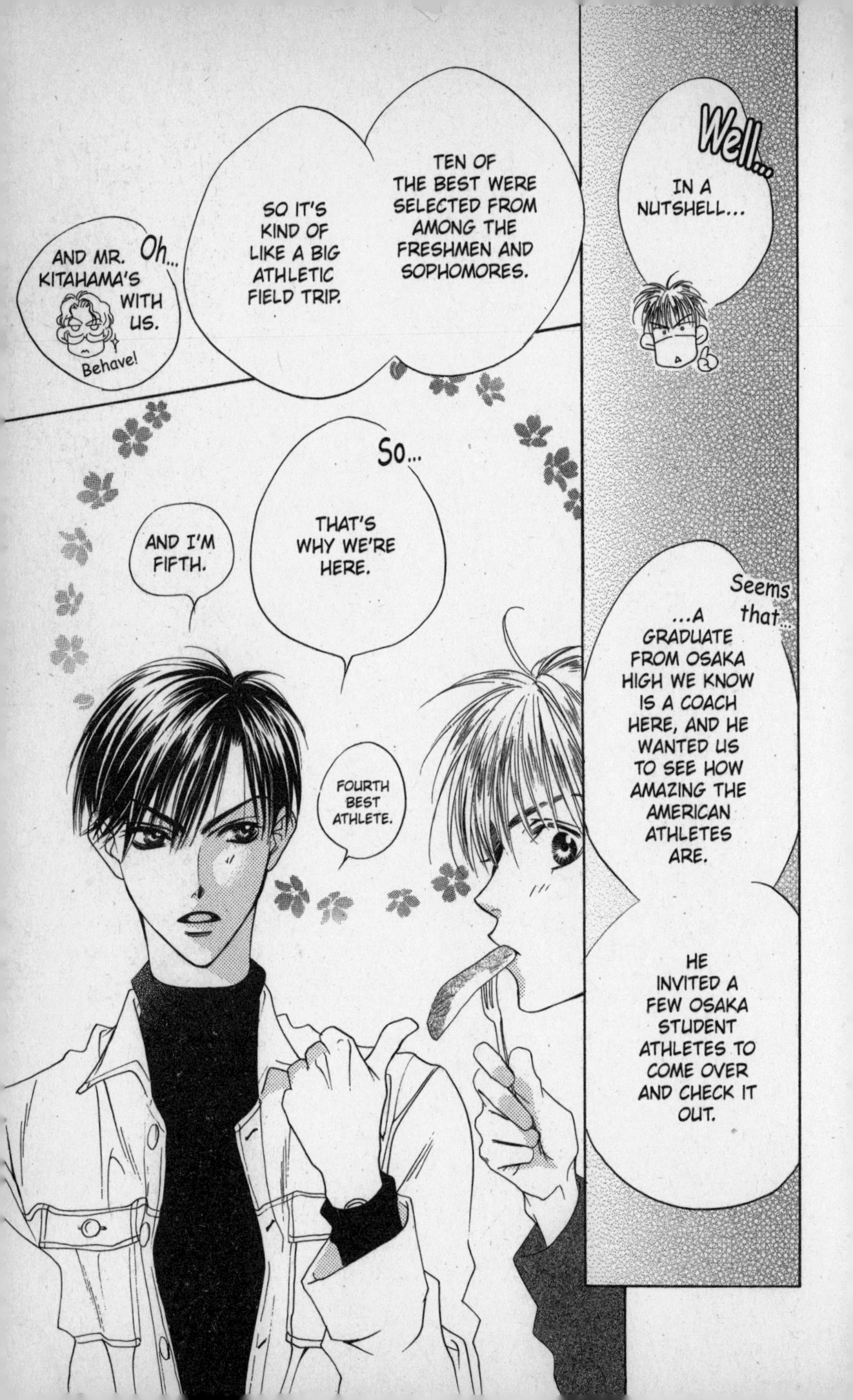
Well...
IN A NUTSHELL...
Seems that...
...A GRADUATE FROM OSAKA HIGH WE KNOW IS A COACH HERE, AND HE WANTED US TO SEE HOW AMAZING THE AMERICAN ATHLETES ARE.
HE INVITED A FEW OSAKA STUDENT ATHLETES TO COME OVER AND CHECK IT OUT.
TEN OF THE BEST WERE SELECTED FROM AMONG THE FRESHMEN AND SOPHOMORES.
SO IT'S KIND OF LIKE A BIG ATHLETIC FIELD TRIP.
Oh...
AND MR. KITAHAMA'S WITH US.
Behave!
So...
THAT'S WHY WE'RE HERE.
FOURTH BEST ATHLETE.
AND I'M FIFTH.

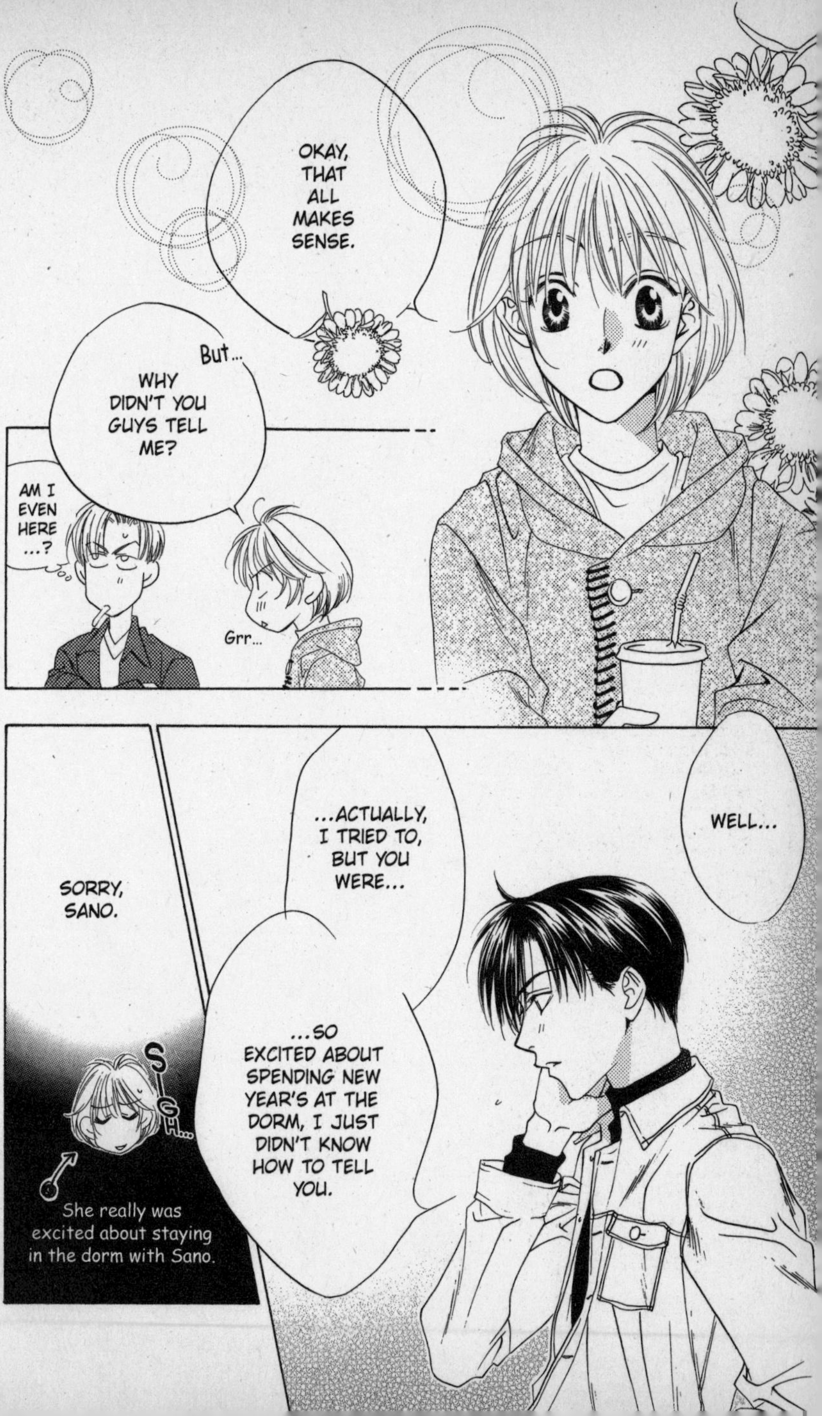
OKAY, THAT ALL MAKES SENSE.
But...
WHY DIDN'T YOU GUYS TELL ME?
AM I EVEN HERE ...?
Grr...
WELL...
...ACTUALLY, I TRIED TO, BUT YOU WERE...
...SO EXCITED ABOUT SPENDING NEW YEAR'S AT THE DORM, I JUST DIDN'T KNOW HOW TO TELL YOU.
SORRY, SANO.
SIGH...
She really was excited about staying in the dorm with Sano.

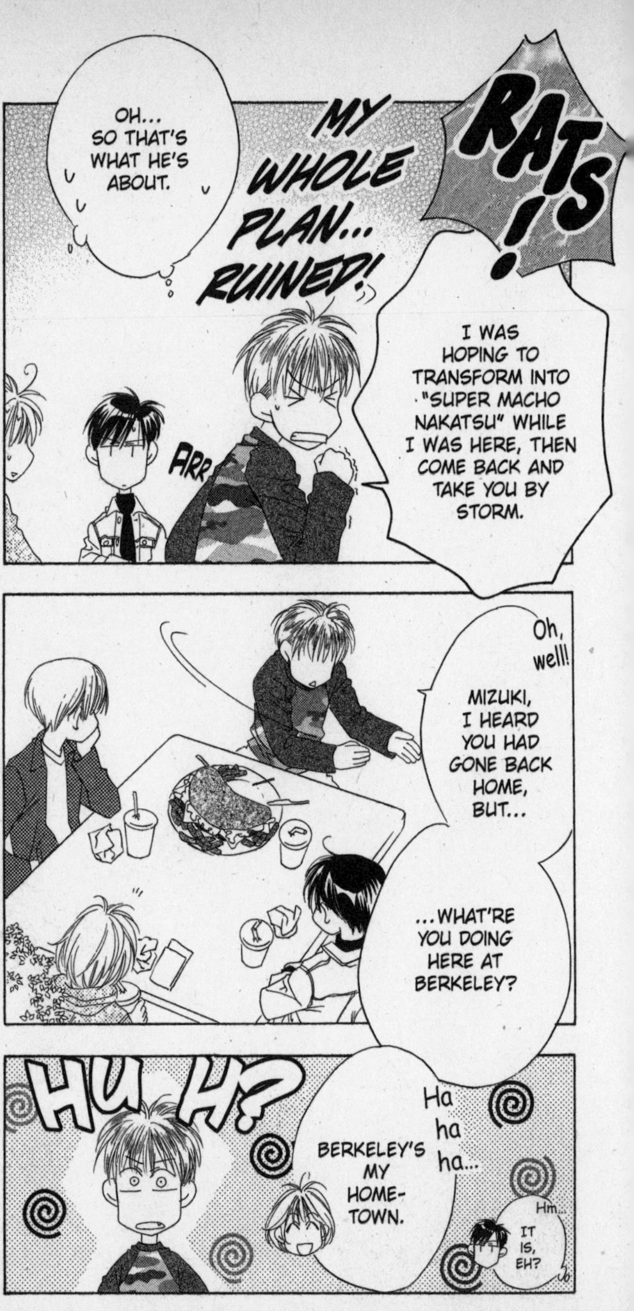
RATS!
MY WHOLE PLAN... RUINED!
OH... SO THAT'S WHAT HE'S ABOUT.
I WAS HOPING TO TRANSFORM INTO "SUPER MACHO NAKATSU" WHILE I WAS HERE, THEN COME BACK AND TAKE YOU BY STORM.
ARR
Oh, well!
MIZUKI, I HEARD YOU HAD GONE BACK HOME, BUT...
...WHAT'RE YOU DOING HERE AT BERKELEY?
HU H?
Ha ha ha...
BERKELEY'S MY HOME-TOWN.
Hm... IT IS, EH?

Zona

I'VE BEEN WATCHING THAT KIDS TV SHOW "OHAYO STUDIO" ALMOST EVERY DAY. I'M SUCH A HUGE FAN OF ZONA. [LAUGHS] ZONA'S SO COOL! I MASTERED THE ZONA DANCE AS WELL. (WHO'S GONNA DANCE WITH ME?) I ALREADY PRE-ORDERED THE CD, SO I SHOULD GET IT BY THE TIME THIS BOOK COMES OUT. I REALLY WANTED TO GET ALL THE "ZONA" MERCHANDISE, SO I ASKED MY EDITOR TO GO TO ITOXXXDO AND ORDER A BUNCH OF STUFF. APPARENTLY EVERYTHING WAS SOLD OUT. I CAN'T WAIT TO USE THE ZONA NOTEPAD!

THE MERCHANDISE IS ONLY AVAILABLE AT ITOXXXDO.

LATER I GOT A CALL FROM THE STORE, AND THEY TOLD ME THAT THEY HAD SOME OF THE STUFF SENT IN FROM THEIR OTHER STORES AROUND THE COUNTRY. THANKS SO MUCH!

APPARENTLY, MY EDITOR BECAME FAMOUS WITH THE ITOXXXDO EMPLOYEES. THEY ALL CALLED HIM "MR. ZONA"...SORRY

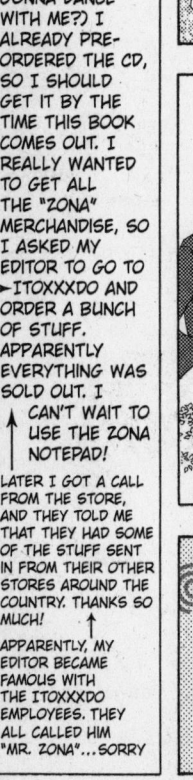

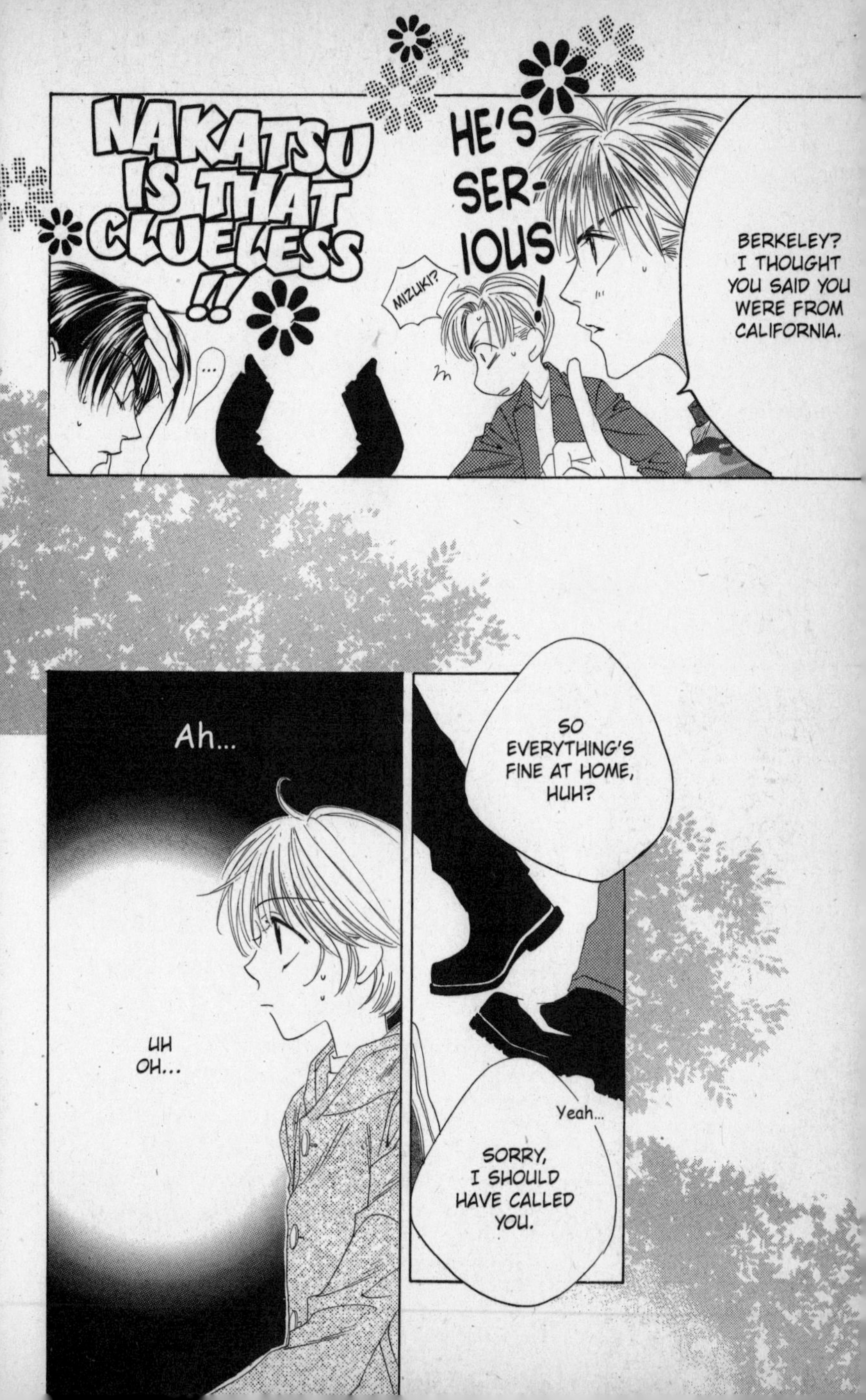
BERKELEY? I THOUGHT YOU SAID YOU WERE FROM CALIFORNIA.
HE'S SER-IOUS!
MIZUKI?
NAKATSU IS THAT CLUELESS!!
...
SO EVERYTHING'S FINE AT HOME, HUH?
Yeah...
SORRY, I SHOULD HAVE CALLED YOU.
Ah...
UH OH...

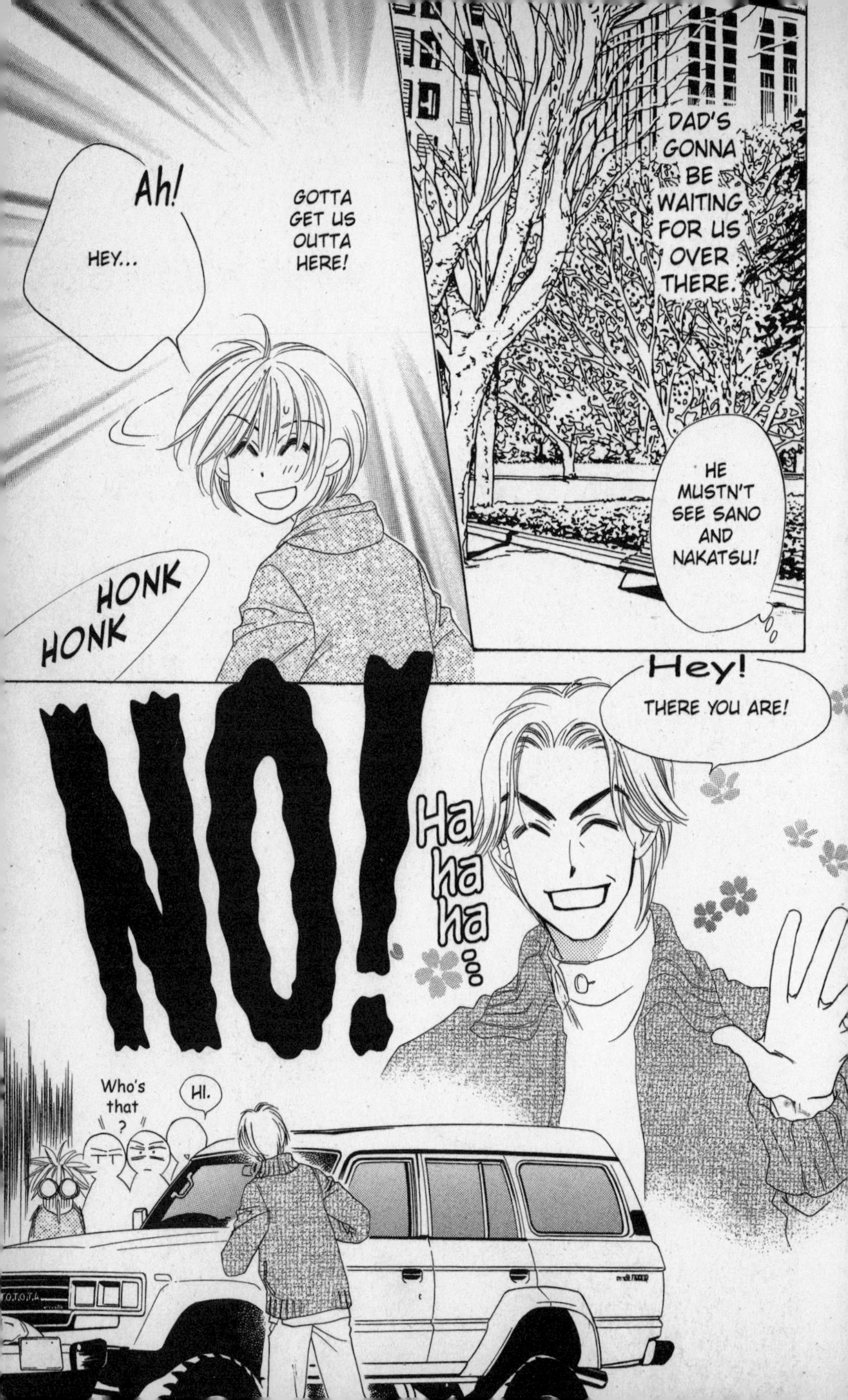
DAD'S GONNA BE WAITING FOR US OVER THERE.
HE MUSTN'T SEE SANO AND NAKATSU!
GOTTA GET US OUTTA HERE!
Ah! HEY...
HONK HONK
Hey! THERE YOU ARE!
Ha ha ha...
NO!
HI.
Who's that?

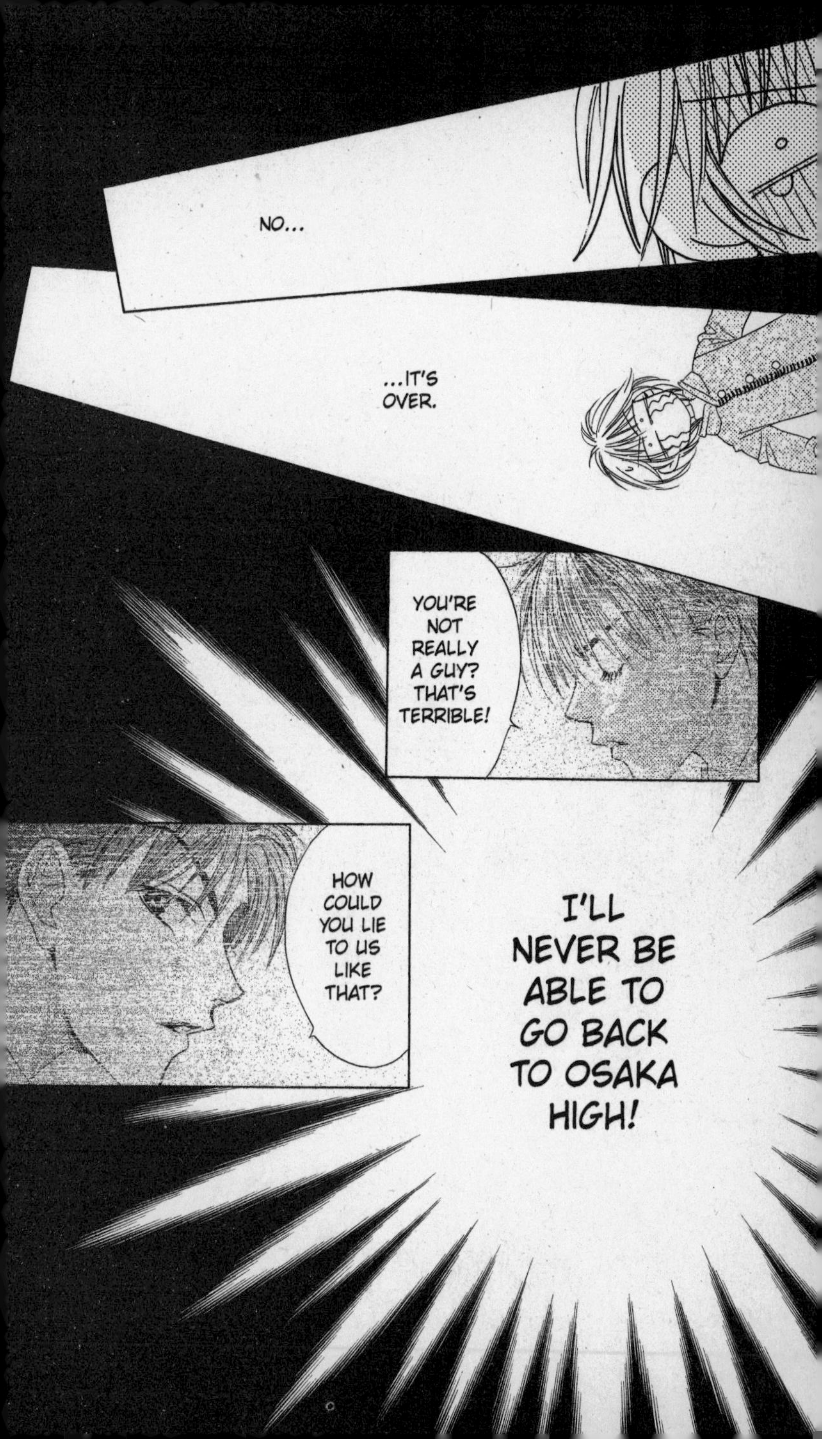
NO...
...IT'S OVER.
YOU'RE NOT REALLY A GUY? THAT'S TERRIBLE!
HOW COULD YOU LIE TO US LIKE THAT?
I'LL NEVER BE ABLE TO GO BACK TO OSAKA HIGH!

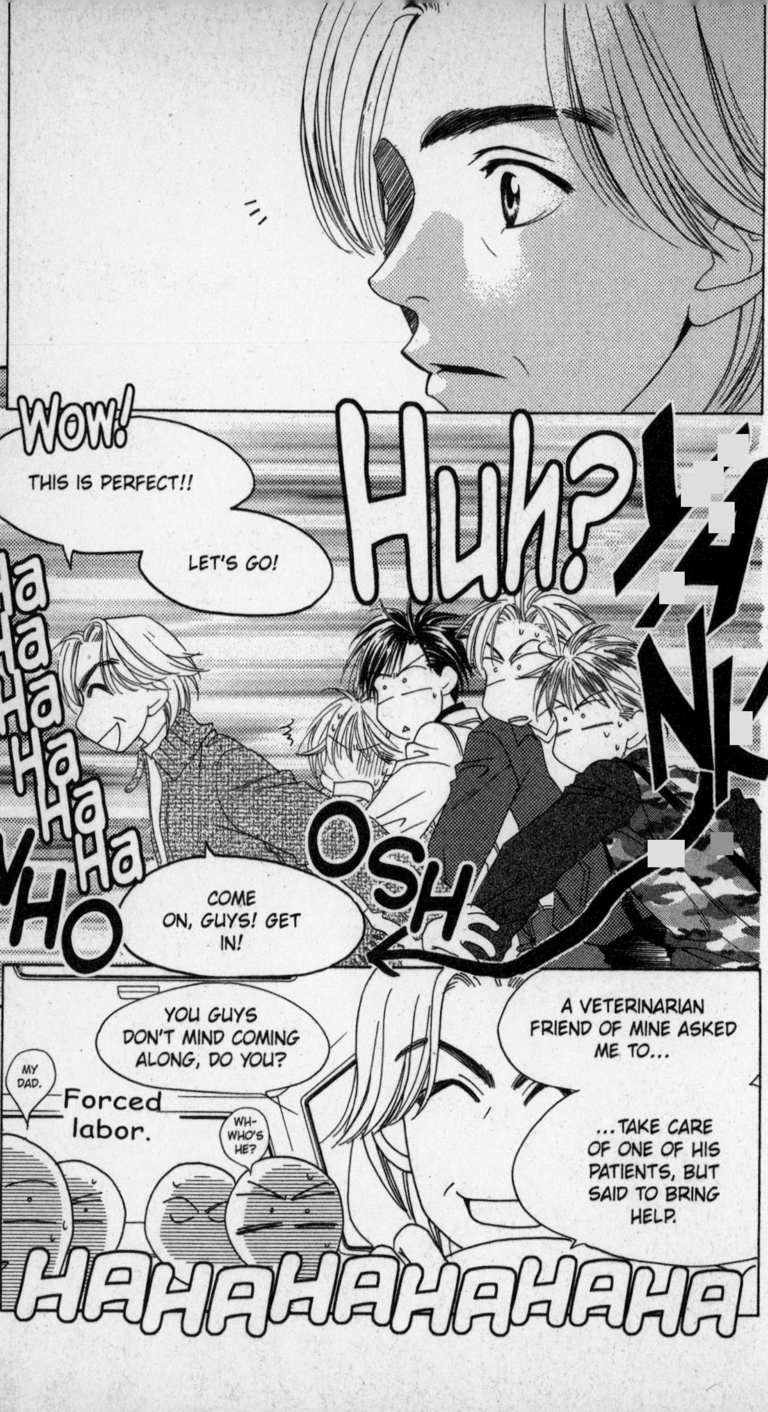
Huh?
Wow!
THIS IS PERFECT!!
LET'S GO!
WHOOSH
Ha Ha Ha Ha Ha Ha
COME ON, GUYS! GET IN!
A VETERINARIAN FRIEND OF MINE ASKED ME TO...
...TAKE CARE OF ONE OF HIS PATIENTS, BUT SAID TO BRING HELP.
YOU GUYS DON'T MIND COMING ALONG, DO YOU?
Forced labor.
MY DAD.
WH-WHO'S HE?
HAHAHAHAHAHAHA

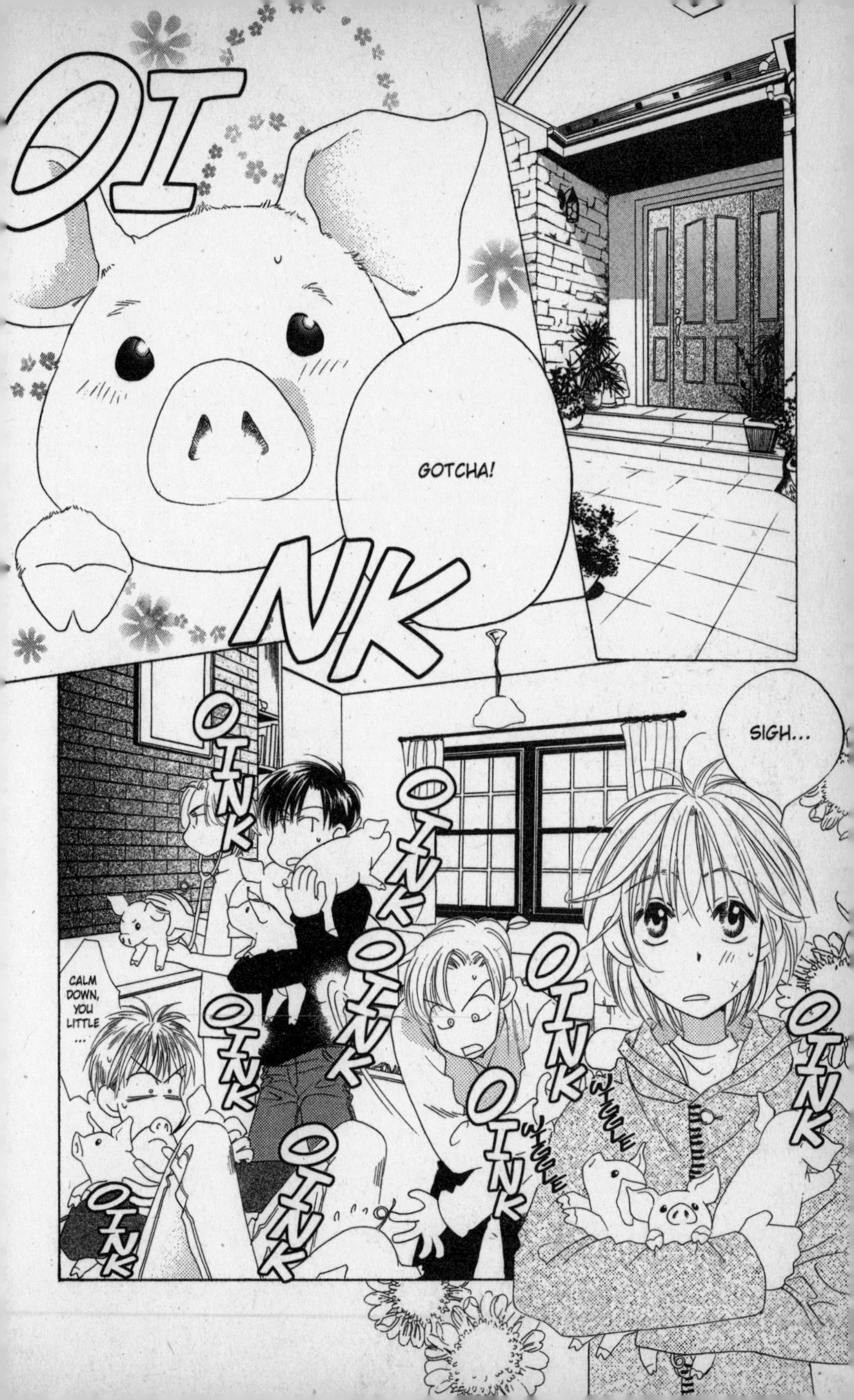
OINK
GOTCHA!
SIGH...
OINK
WIGGLE WIGGLE
OINK
OINK
OINK
OINK
OINK
OINK
CALM DOWN, YOU LITTLE ...
OINK
OINK

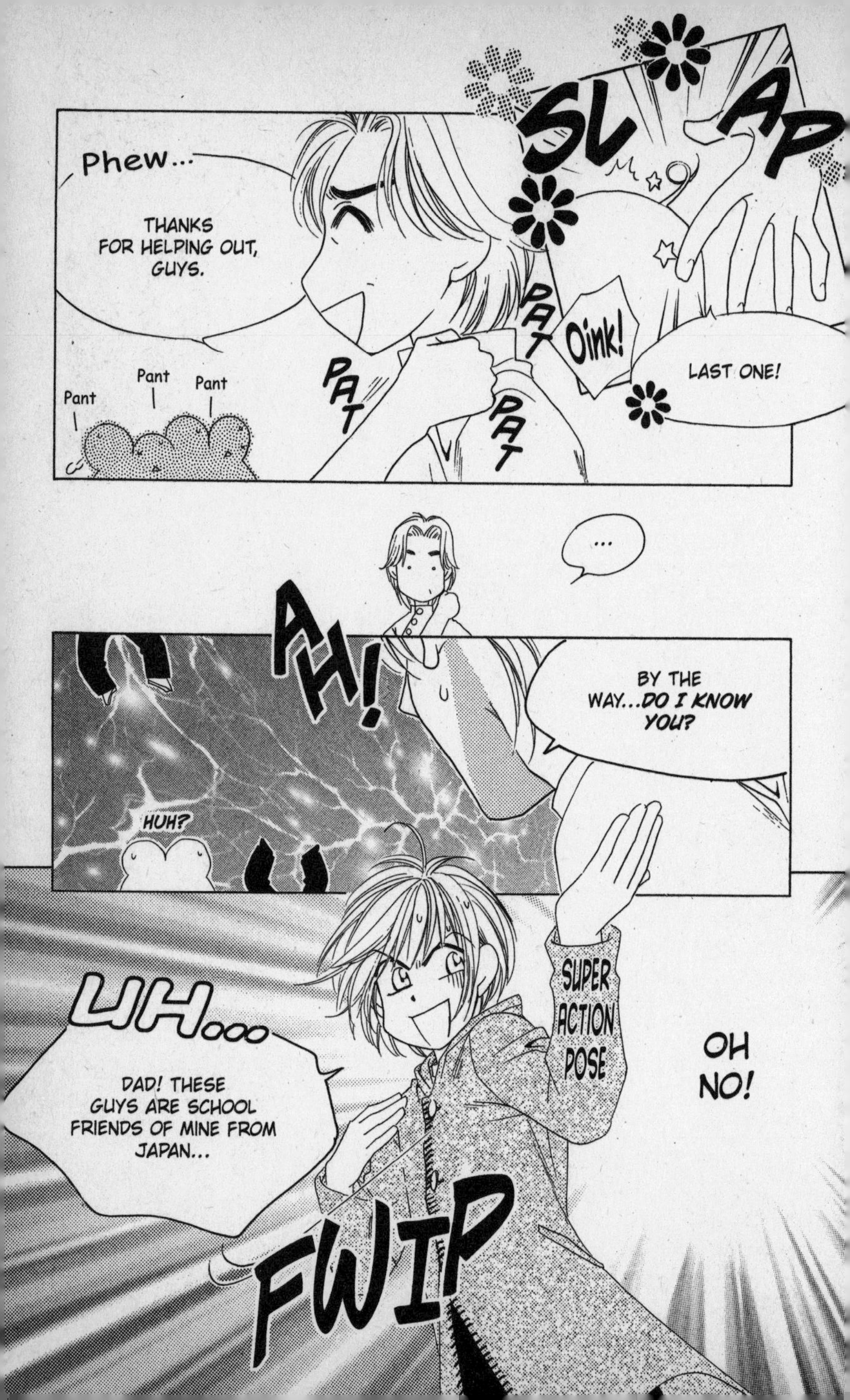
SLAP
LAST ONE!
Oink!
PAT PAT
PAT PAT
Phew...
THANKS FOR HELPING OUT, GUYS.
Pant
Pant
Pant
...
AH!
BY THE WAY...DO I KNOW YOU?
HUH?
OH NO!
SUPER ACTION POSE
UH...
DAD! THESE GUYS ARE SCHOOL FRIENDS OF MINE FROM JAPAN...
FWIP

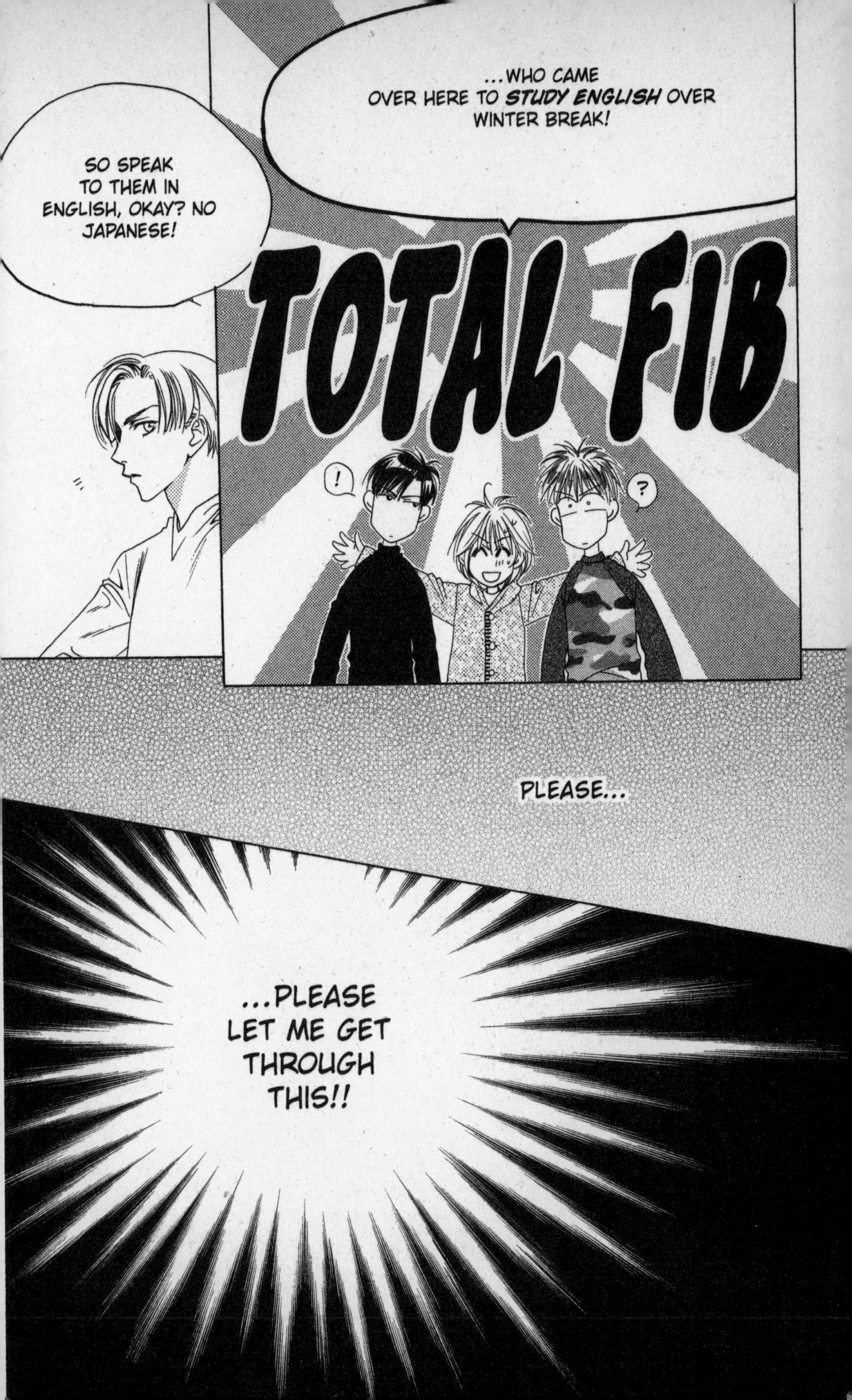
...WHO CAME OVER HERE TO ***STUDY ENGLISH*** OVER WINTER BREAK!
TOTAL FIB
!
?
SO SPEAK TO THEM IN ENGLISH, OKAY? NO JAPANESE!
PLEASE...
...PLEASE LET ME GET THROUGH THIS!!

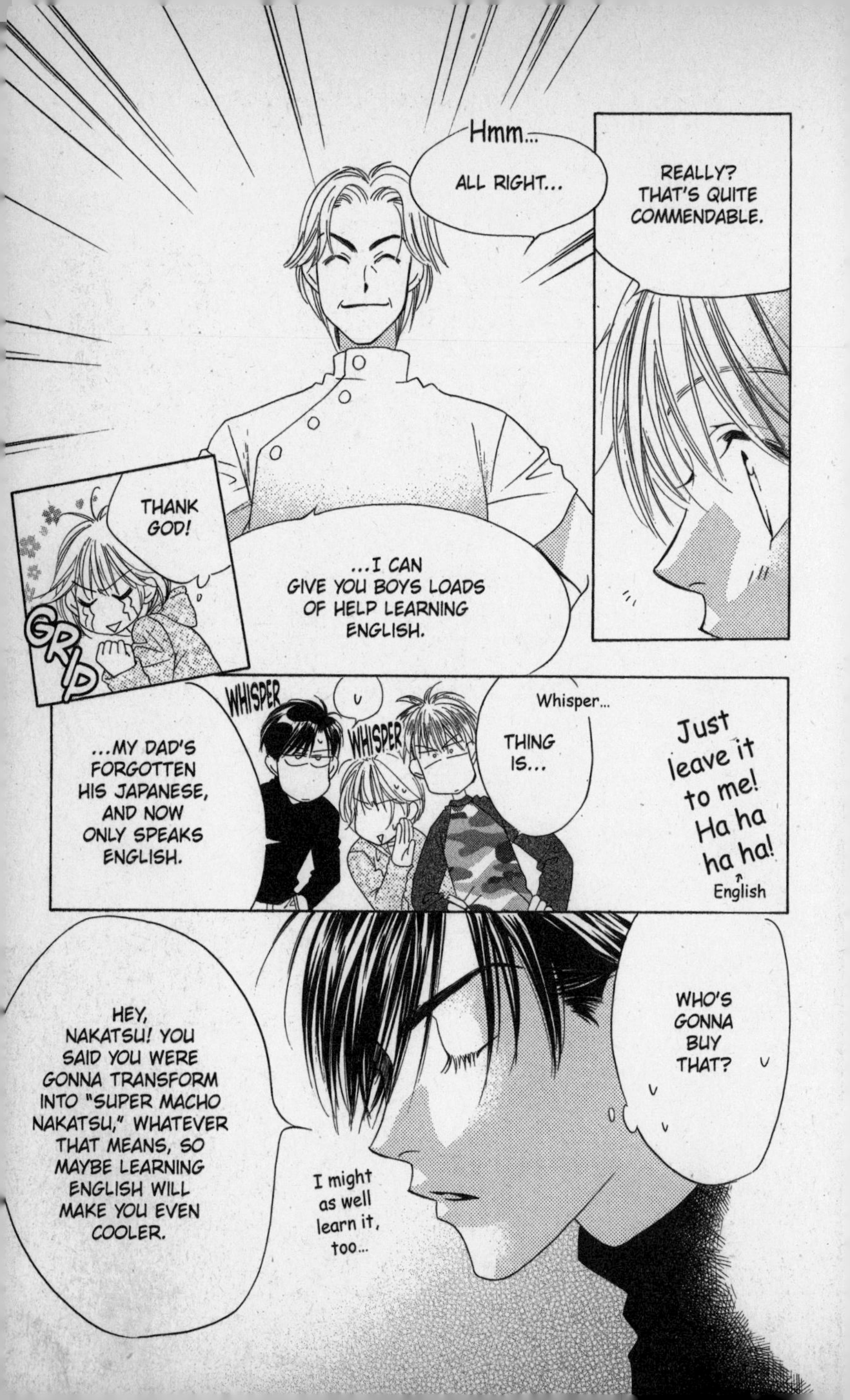
REALLY? THAT'S QUITE COMMENDABLE.
Hmm...
ALL RIGHT...
...I CAN GIVE YOU BOYS LOADS OF HELP LEARNING ENGLISH.
THANK GOD!
GRIP
Just leave it to me! Ha ha ha ha!
English
Whisper...
THING IS...
WHISPER
WHISPER
...MY DAD'S FORGOTTEN HIS JAPANESE, AND NOW ONLY SPEAKS ENGLISH.
WHO'S GONNA BUY THAT?
I might as well learn it, too...
HEY, NAKATSU! YOU SAID YOU WERE GONNA TRANSFORM INTO "SUPER MACHO NAKATSU," WHATEVER THAT MEANS, SO MAYBE LEARNING ENGLISH WILL MAKE YOU EVEN COOLER.

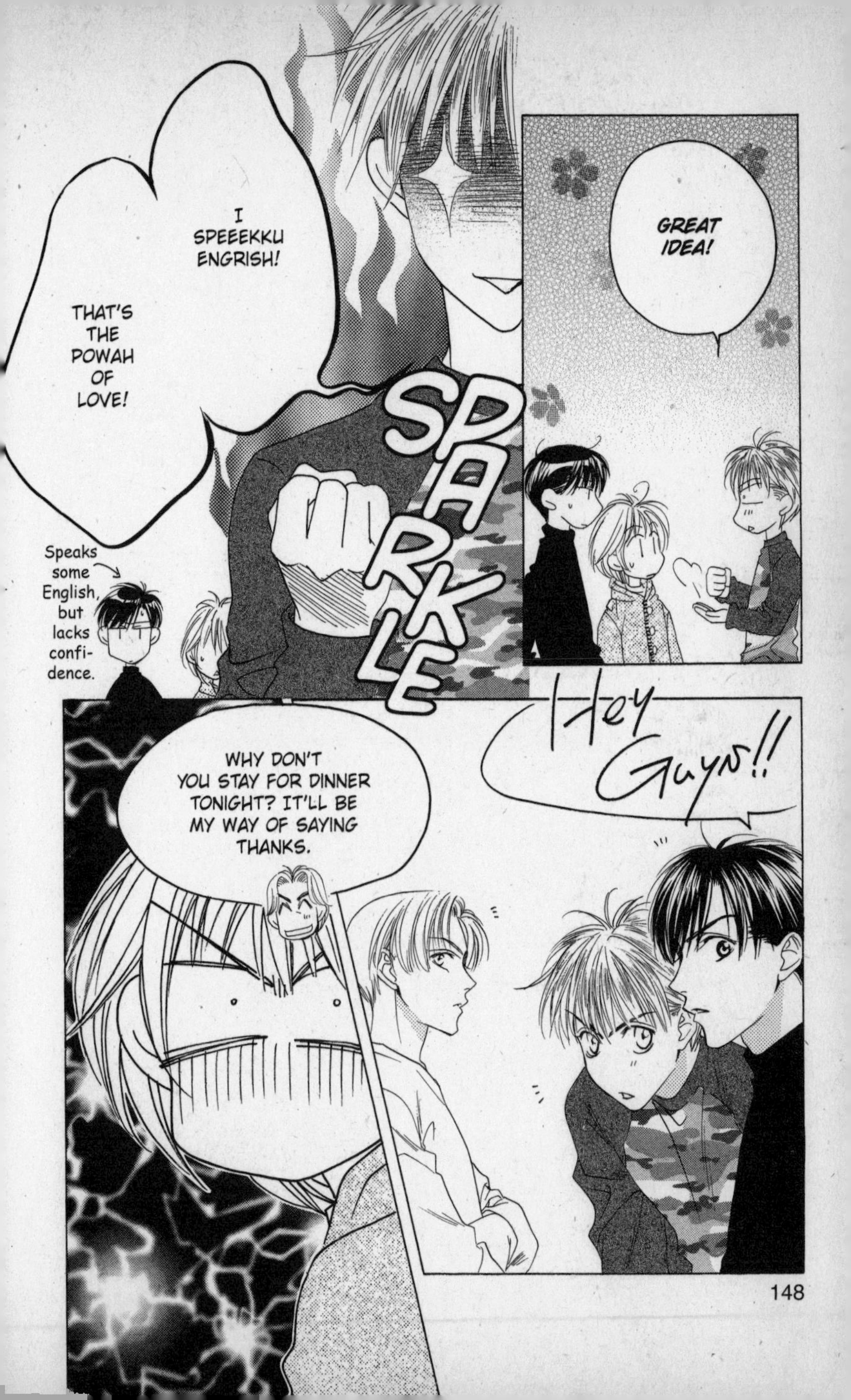
GREAT IDEA!
I SPEEEKKU ENGRISH!
THAT'S THE POWAH OF LOVE!
SPARKLE
Speaks some English, but lacks confi-dence.
Hey Guys!!
WHY DON'T YOU STAY FOR DINNER TONIGHT? IT'LL BE MY WAY OF SAYING THANKS.

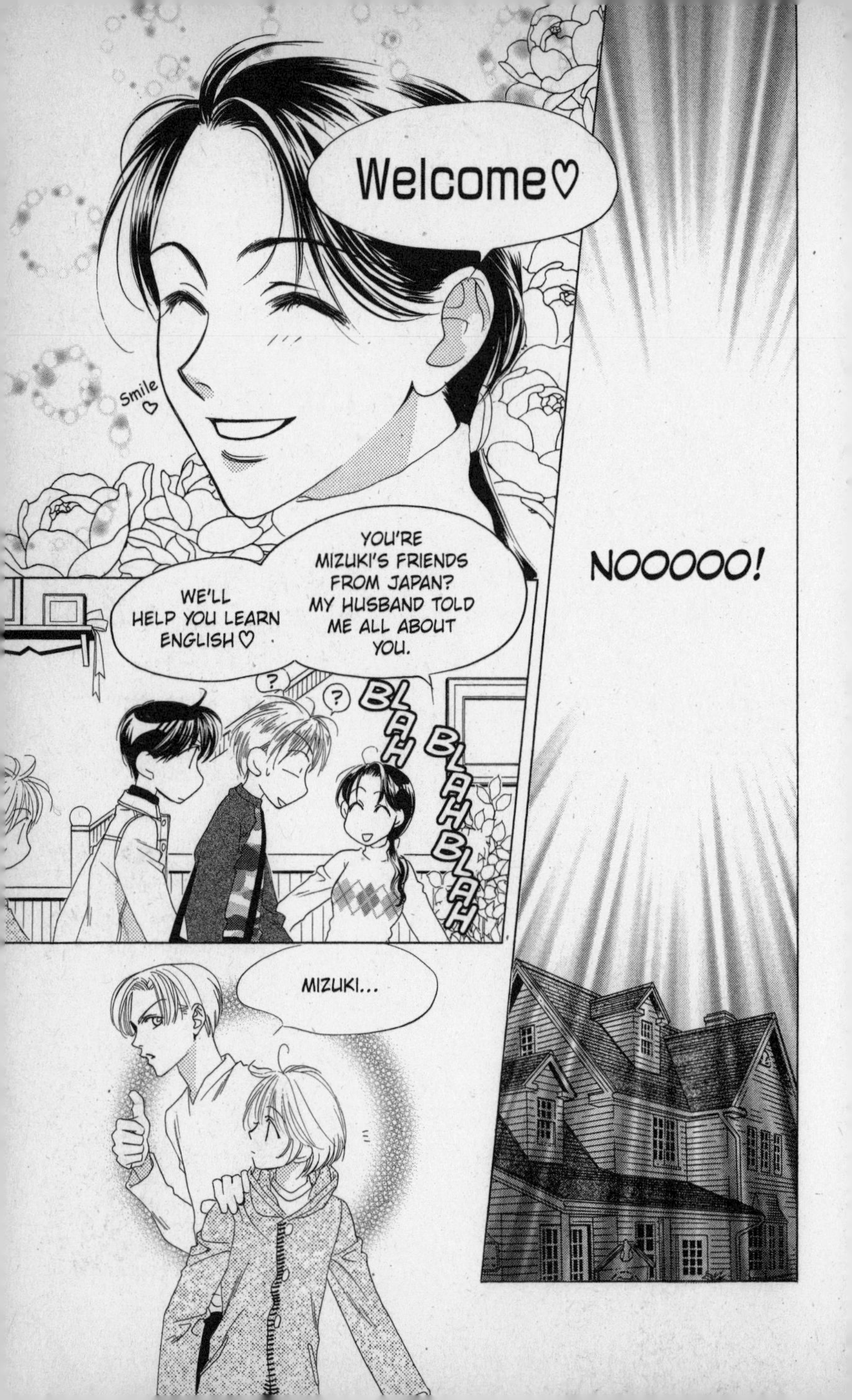
NOOOOO!
Welcome♡
Smile♡
YOU'RE MIZUKI'S FRIENDS FROM JAPAN? MY HUSBAND TOLD ME ALL ABOUT YOU.
WE'LL HELP YOU LEARN ENGLISH♡
?
?
BLAH BLAH BLAH BLAH
MIZUKI...

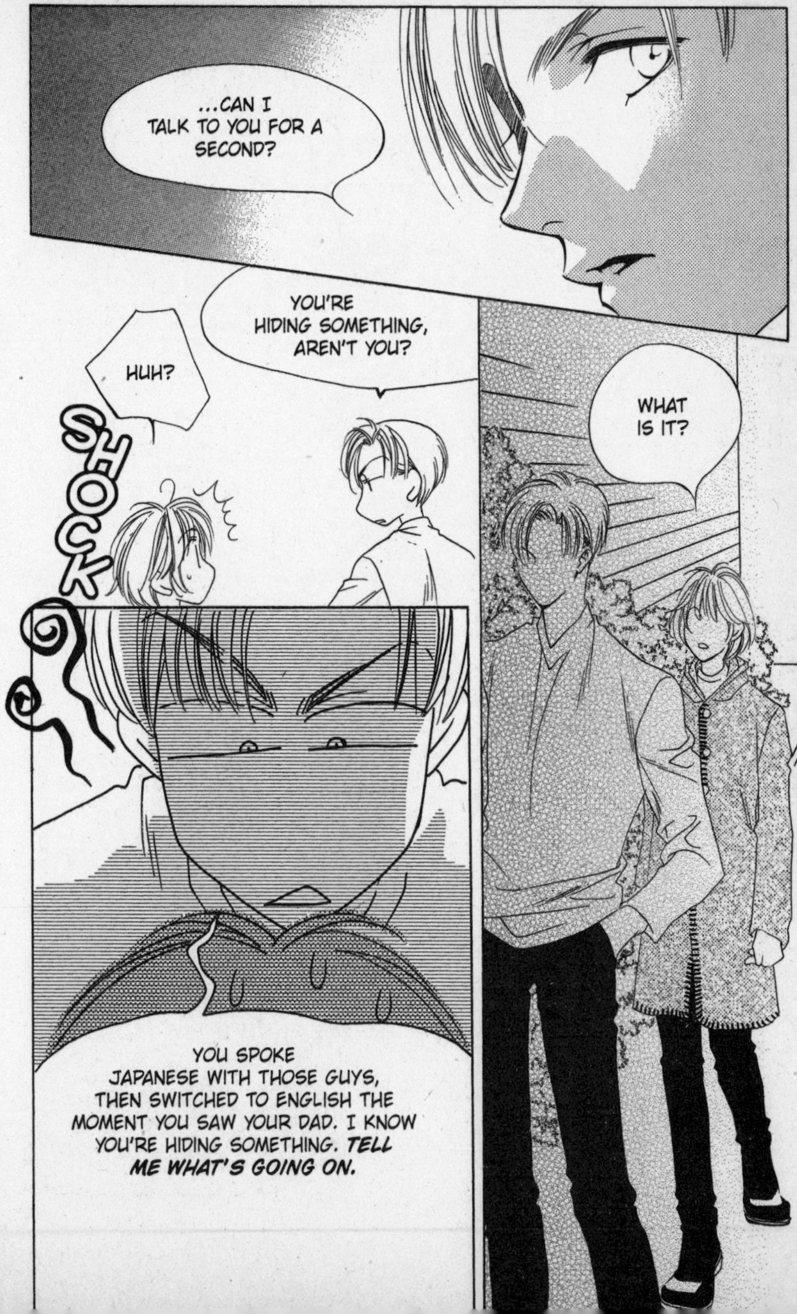
...CAN I TALK TO YOU FOR A SECOND?
WHAT IS IT?
YOU'RE HIDING SOMETHING, AREN'T YOU?
HUH?
SHOCK
YOU SPOKE JAPANESE WITH THOSE GUYS, THEN SWITCHED TO ENGLISH THE MOMENT YOU SAW YOUR DAD. I KNOW YOU'RE HIDING SOMETHING. TELL ME WHAT'S GOING ON.

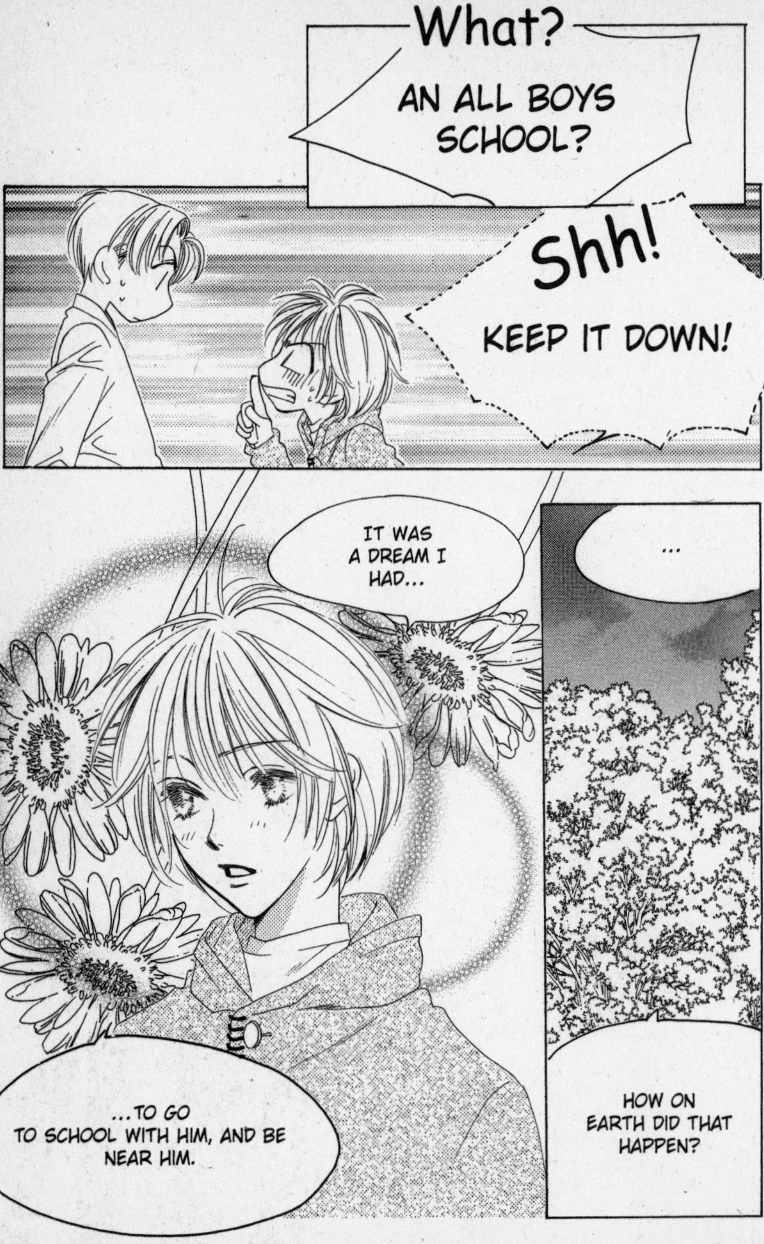
What?
AN ALL BOYS SCHOOL?
Shh!
KEEP IT DOWN!
...
HOW ON EARTH DID THAT HAPPEN?
IT WAS A DREAM I HAD...
...TO GO TO SCHOOL WITH HIM, AND BE NEAR HIM.

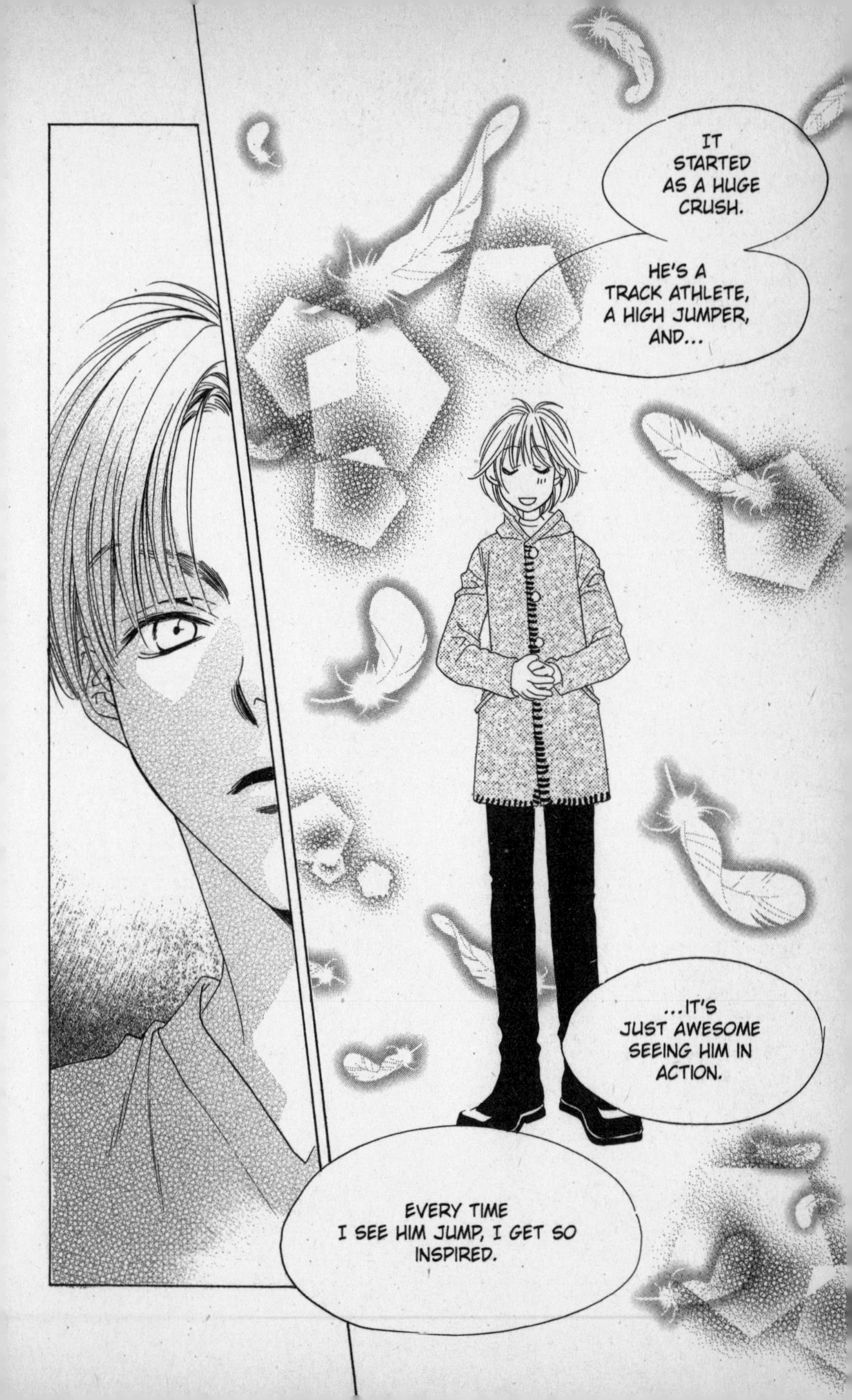
IT STARTED AS A HUGE CRUSH.
HE'S A TRACK ATHLETE, A HIGH JUMPER, AND...
...IT'S JUST AWESOME SEEING HIM IN ACTION.
EVERY TIME I SEE HIM JUMP, I GET SO INSPIRED.

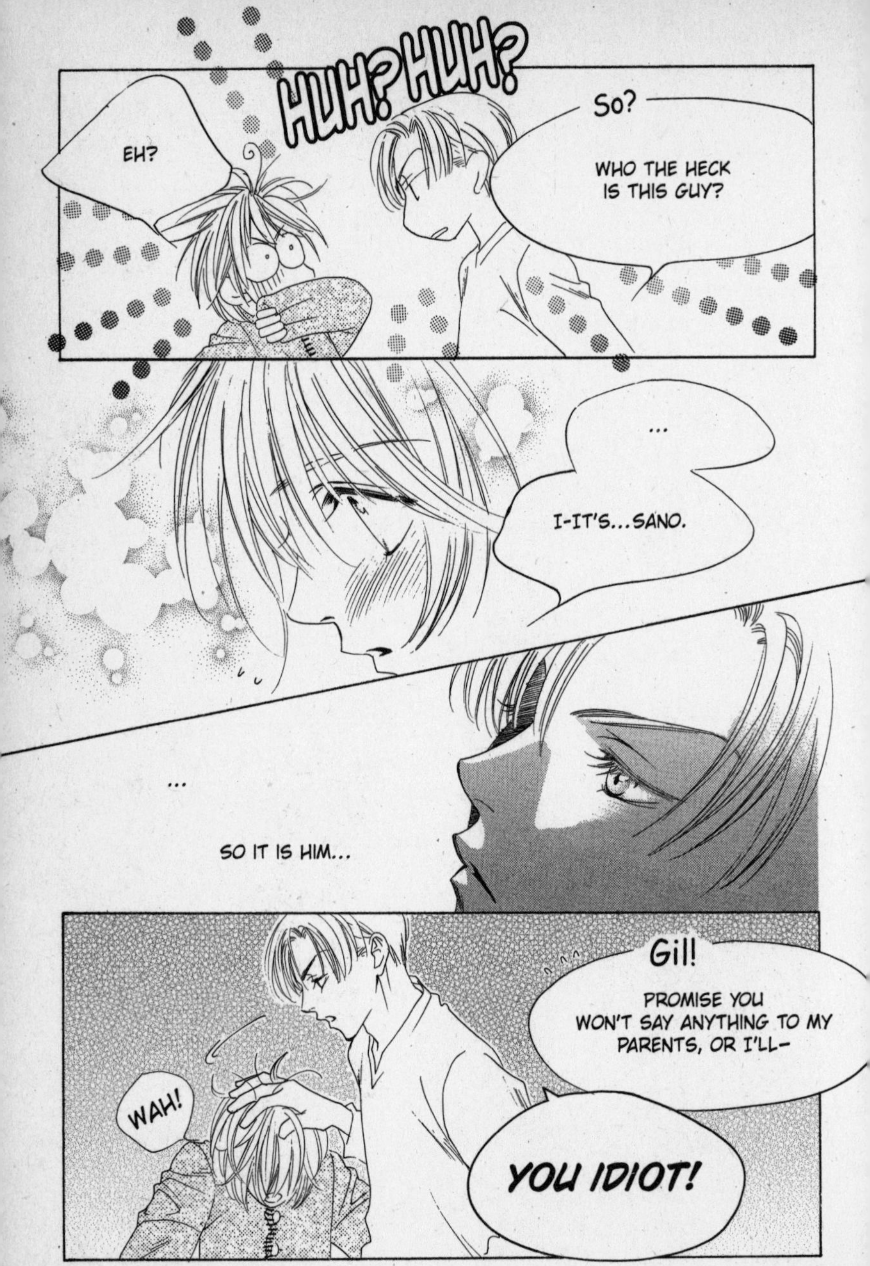
So?
WHO THE HECK IS THIS GUY?
HUH? HUH?
EH?
...
I-IT'S...SANO.
...
SO IT IS HIM...
Gil!
PROMISE YOU WON'T SAY ANYTHING TO MY PARENTS, OR I'LL-
YOU IDIOT!
WAH!

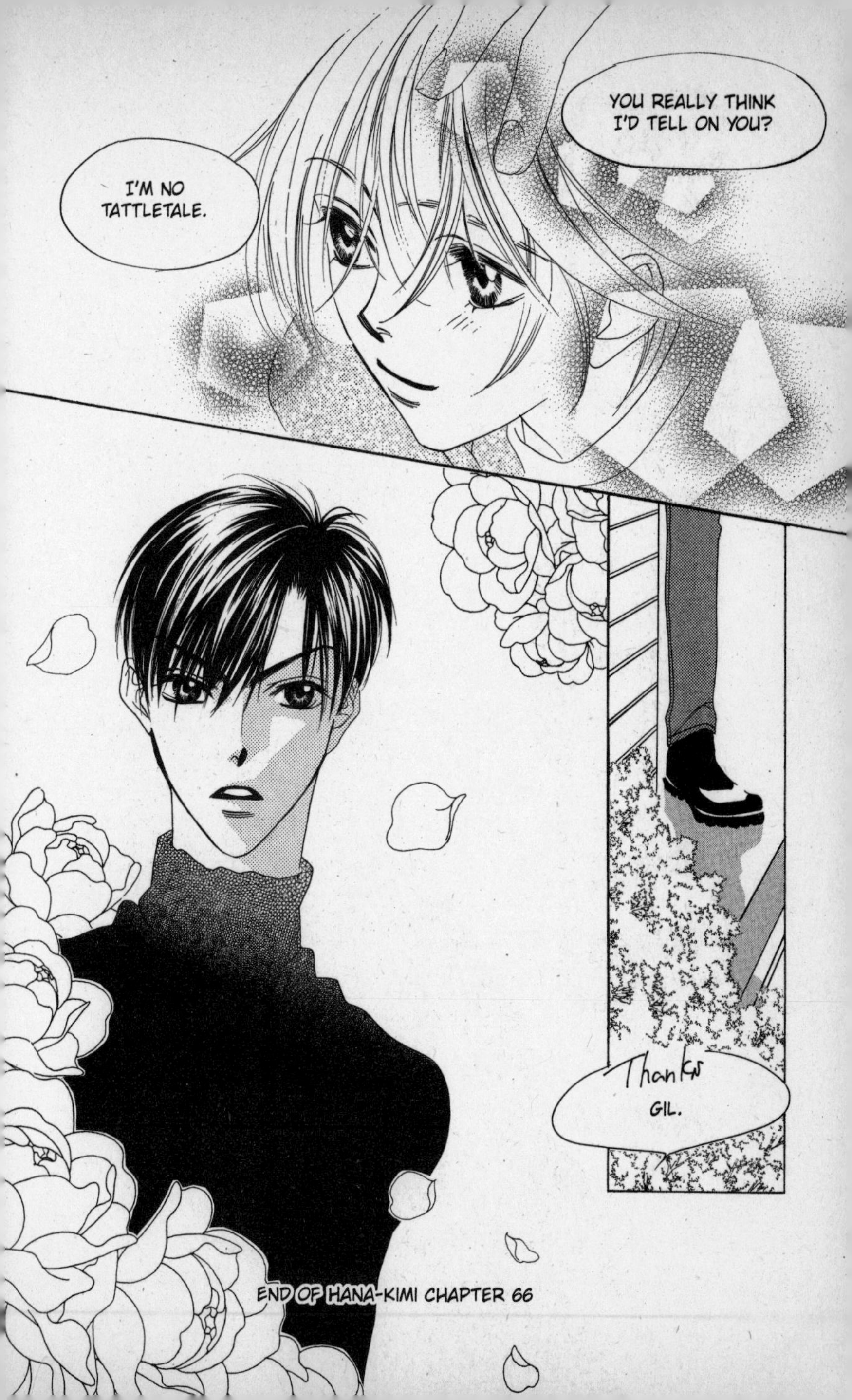
YOU REALLY THINK I'D TELL ON YOU?
I'M NO TATTLETALE.
Thanks
GIL.
END OF HANA-KIMI CHAPTER 66

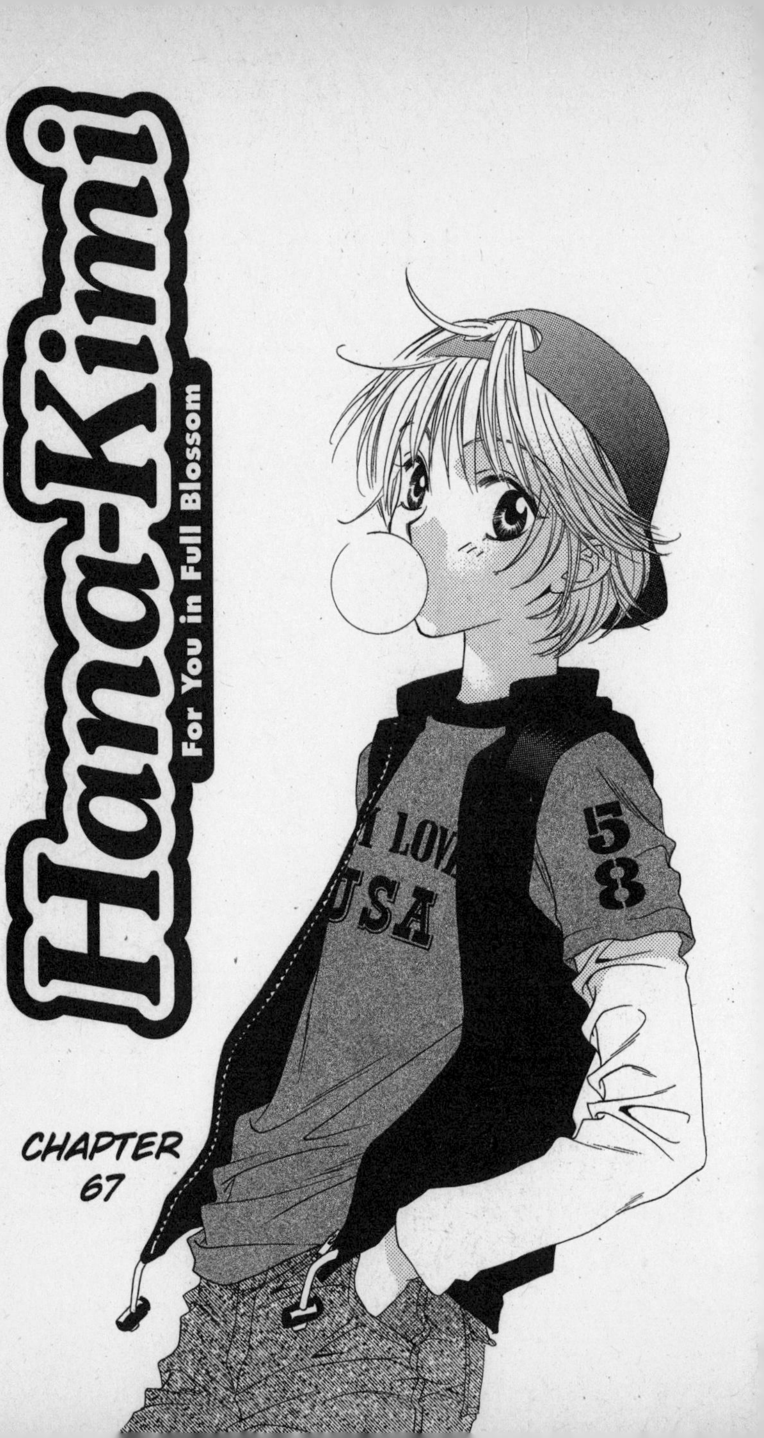
Hana-Kimi
For You in Full Blossom
I LOV
USA
58
CHAPTER
67

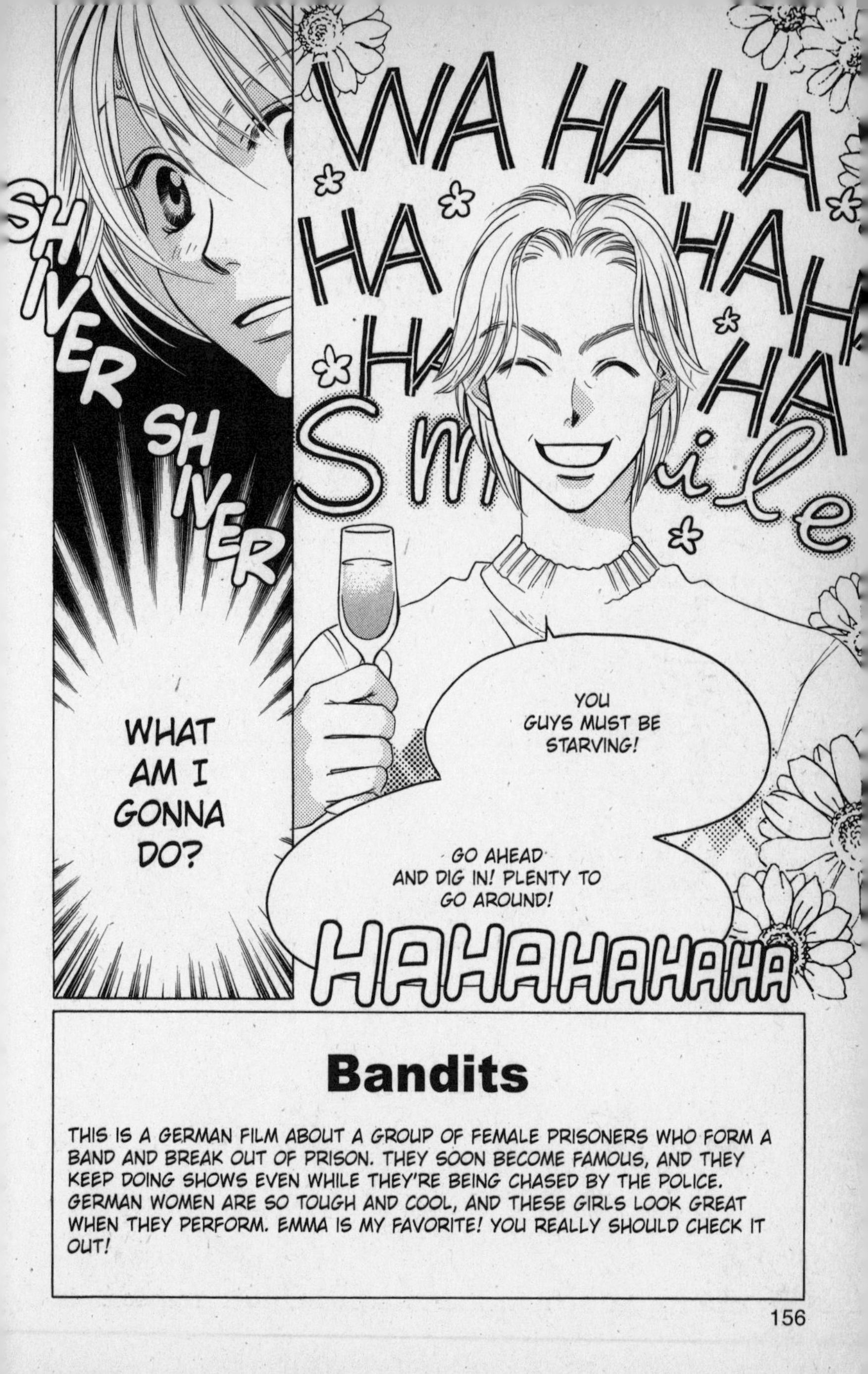
WA HA HA HA HA HA HA HA HA
Smile
YOU GUYS MUST BE STARVING!
GO AHEAD AND DIG IN! PLENTY TO GO AROUND!
HAHAHAHAHAHA
SHIVER SHIVER
WHAT AM I GONNA DO?

Bandits

THIS IS A GERMAN FILM ABOUT A GROUP OF FEMALE PRISONERS WHO FORM A BAND AND BREAK OUT OF PRISON. THEY SOON BECOME FAMOUS, AND THEY KEEP DOING SHOWS EVEN WHILE THEY'RE BEING CHASED BY THE POLICE. GERMAN WOMEN ARE SO TOUGH AND COOL, AND THESE GIRLS LOOK GREAT WHEN THEY PERFORM. EMMA IS MY FAVORITE! YOU REALLY SHOULD CHECK IT OUT!

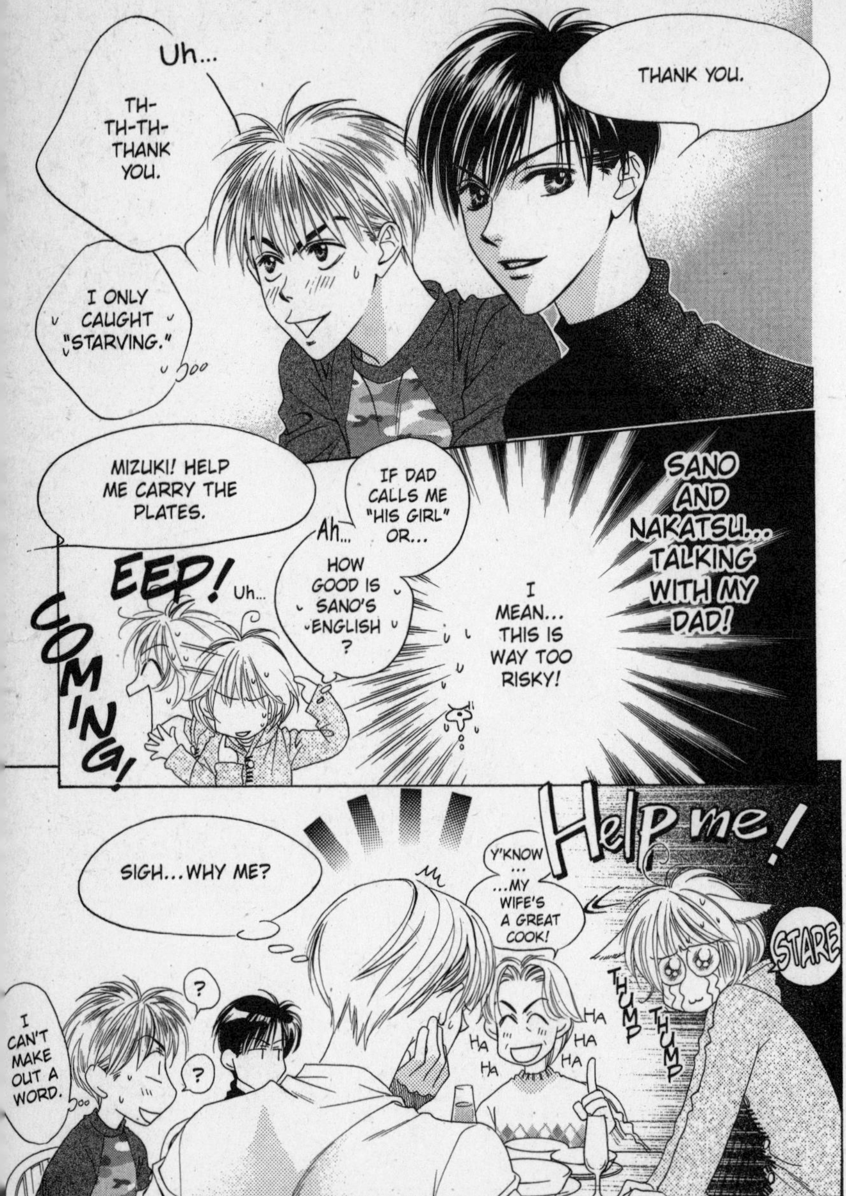
THANK YOU.
Uh...
TH-TH-TH-THANK YOU.
I ONLY CAUGHT "STARVING."
SANO AND NAKATSU... TALKING WITH MY DAD!
I MEAN... THIS IS WAY TOO RISKY!
IF DAD CALLS ME "HIS GIRL" OR...
Ah...
HOW GOOD IS SANO'S ENGLISH?
MIZUKI! HELP ME CARRY THE PLATES.
EEP!
Uh...
COMING!
Help me!
STARE
THUMP THUMP
Y'KNOW... ...MY WIFE'S A GREAT COOK!
HA HA HA HA HA
SIGH... WHY ME?
?
?
I CAN'T MAKE OUT A WORD.

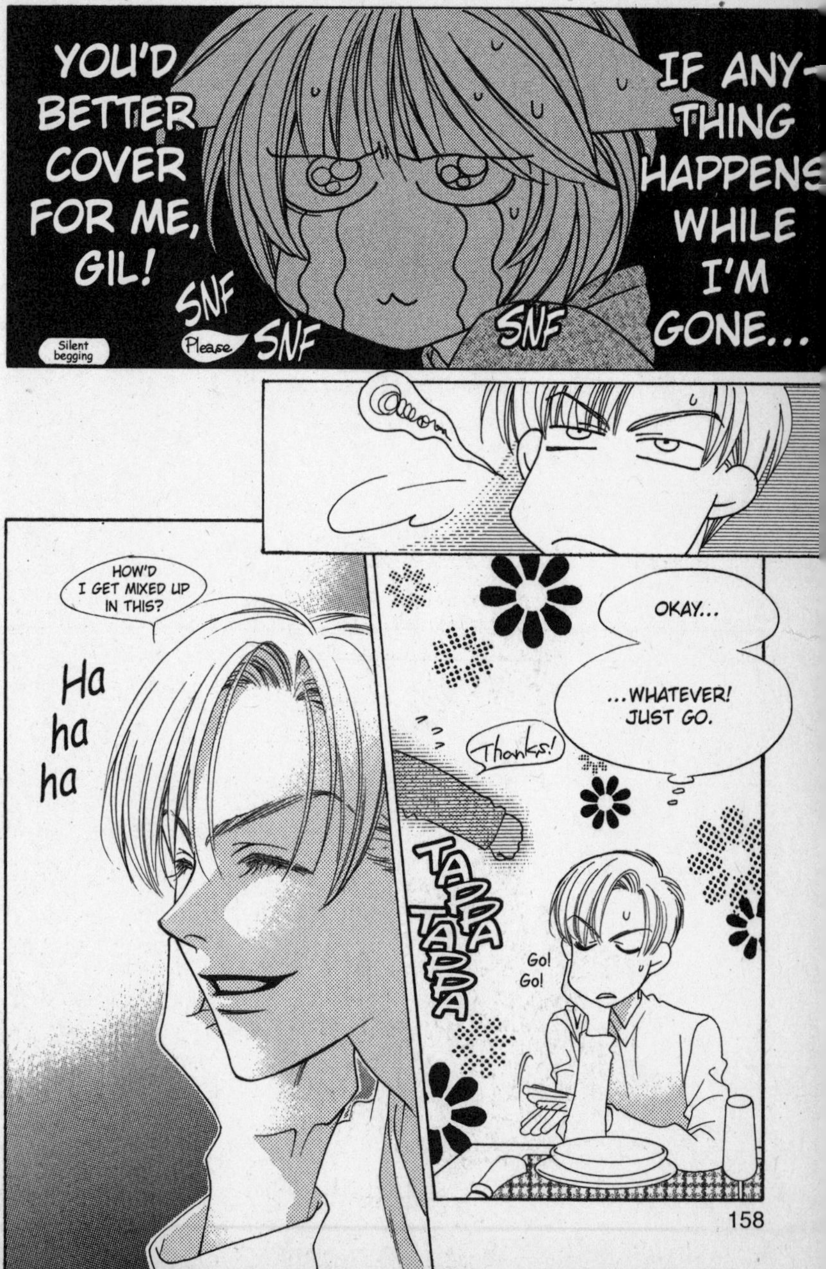
IF ANYTHING HAPPENS WHILE I'M GONE...
SNF
YOU'D BETTER COVER FOR ME, GIL!
SNF
Please
SNF
Silent begging
OKAY...
...WHATEVER! JUST GO.
Thanks!
TAPPA TAPPA
Go! Go!
HOW'D I GET MIXED UP IN THIS?
Ha ha ha

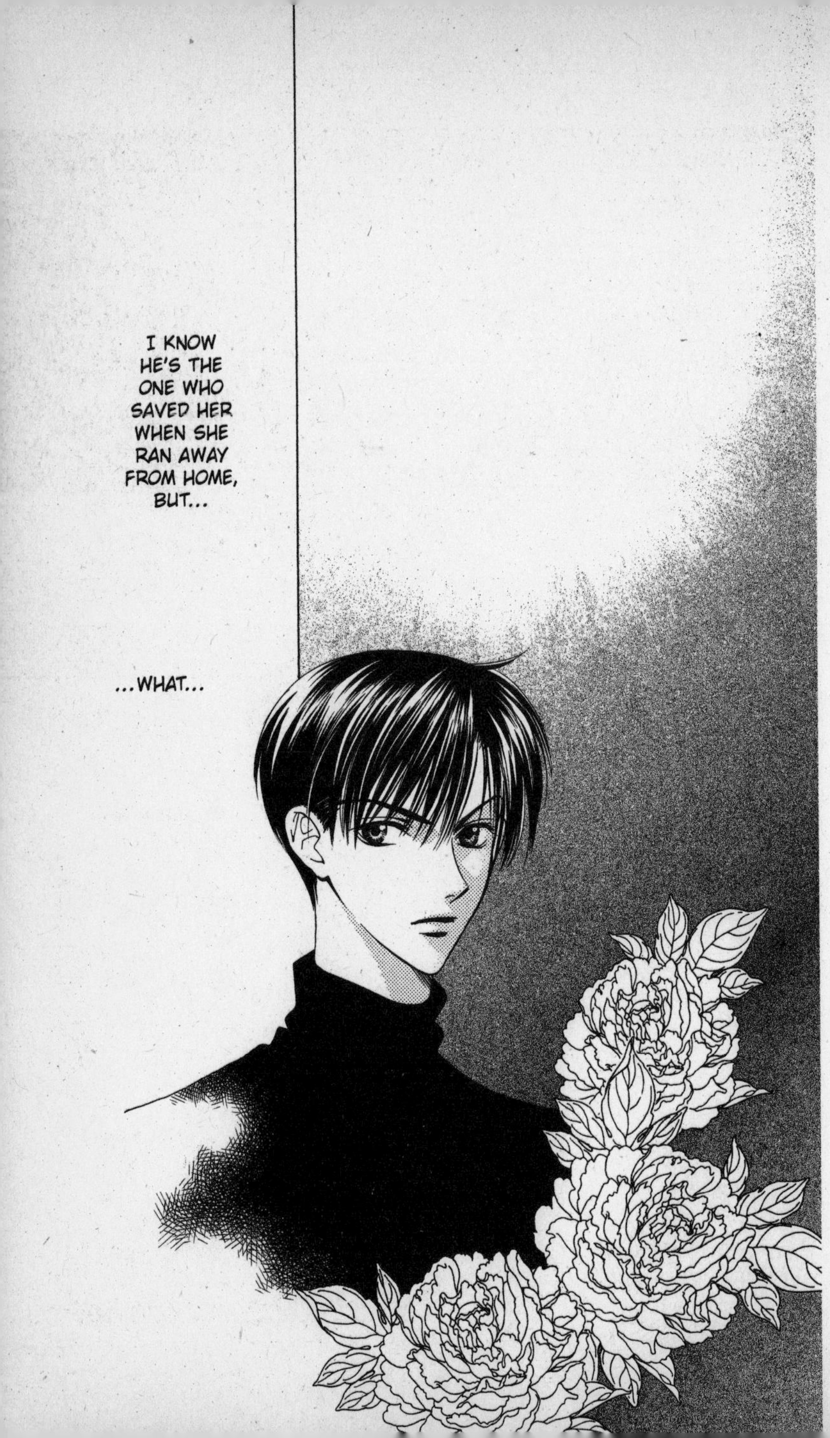
I KNOW HE'S THE ONE WHO SAVED HER WHEN SHE RAN AWAY FROM HOME, BUT...
...WHAT...

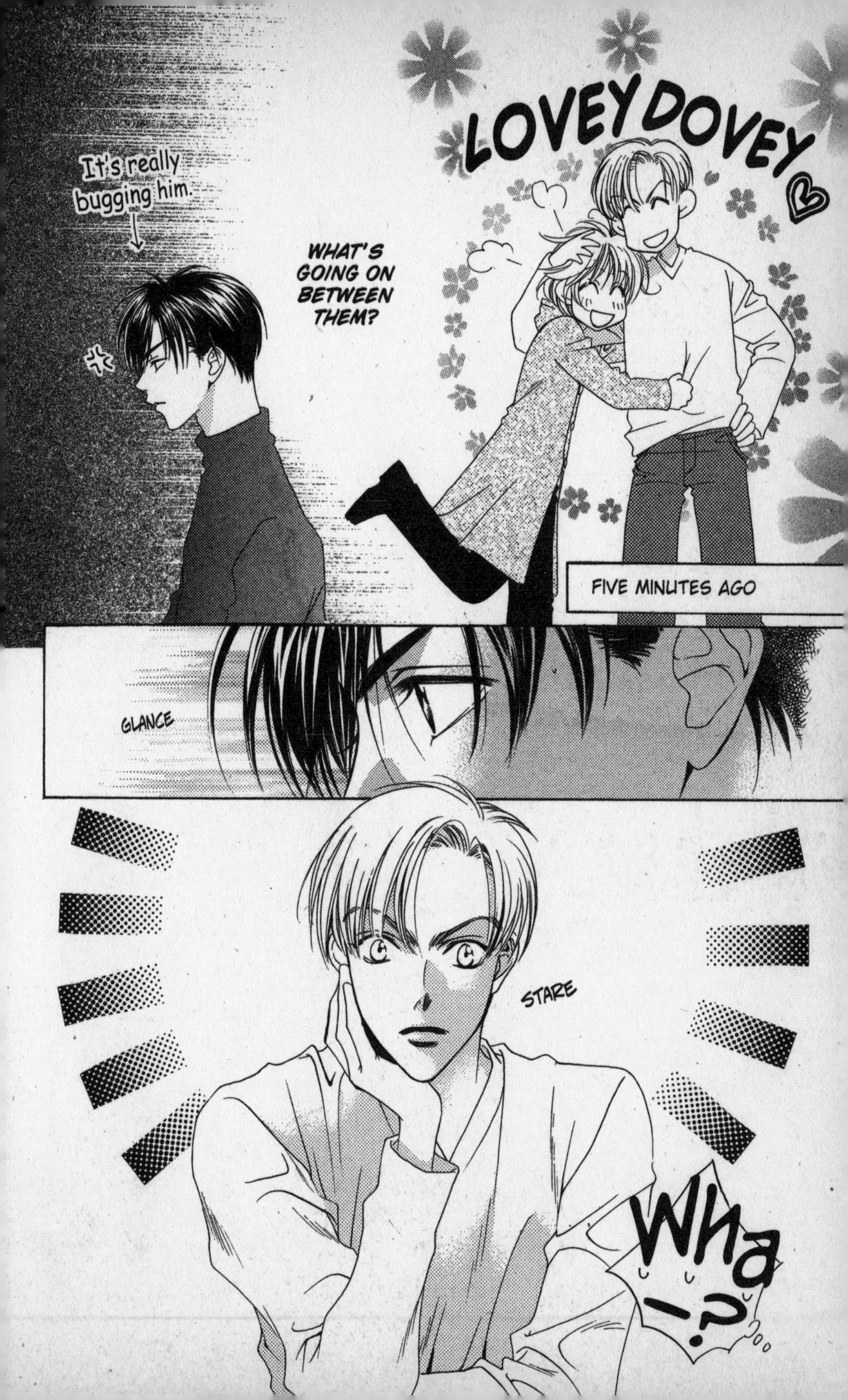
LOVEY DOVEY
FIVE MINUTES AGO
WHAT'S GOING ON BETWEEN THEM?
It's really bugging him.
GLANCE
STARE
Wha--?

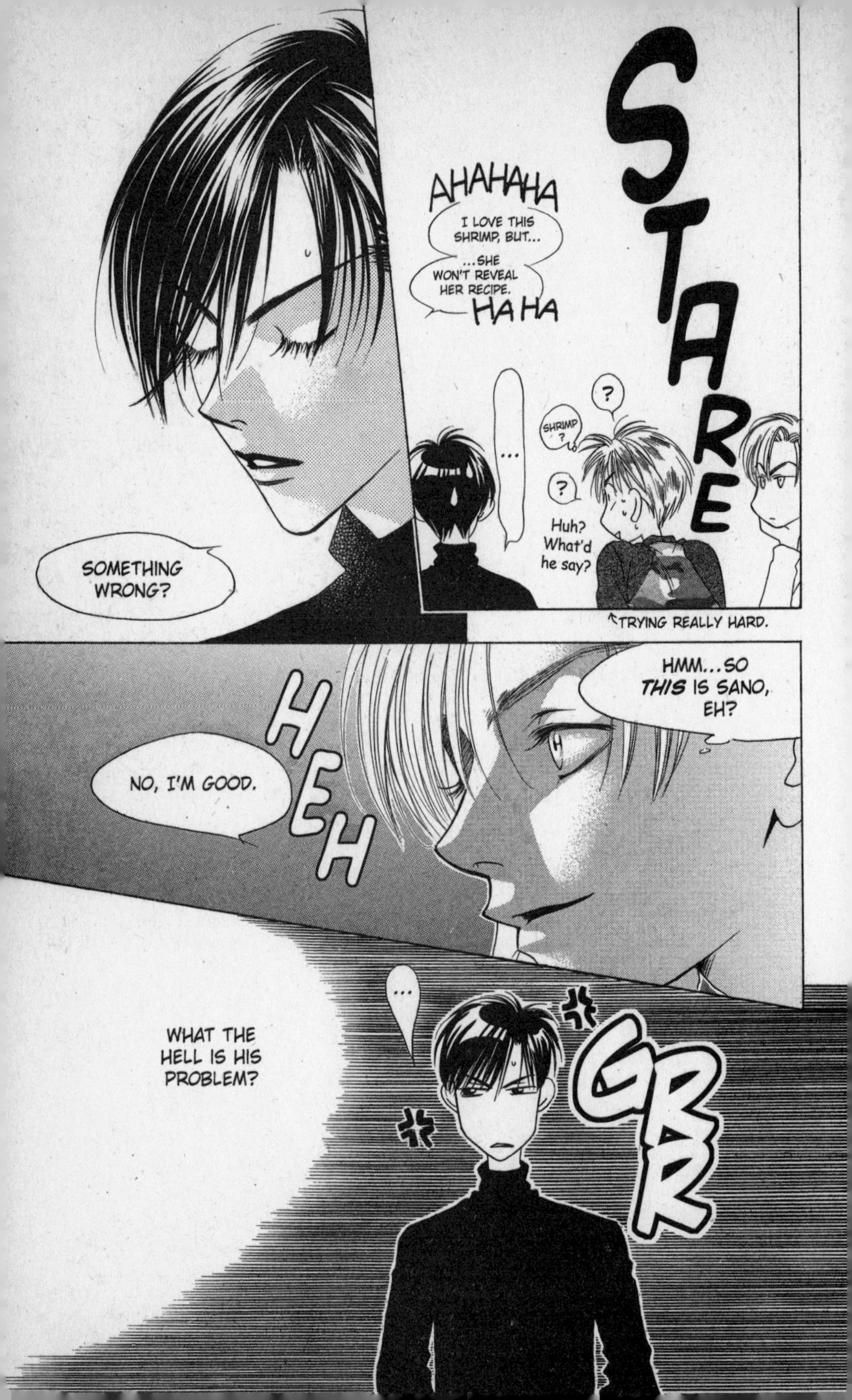
STARE
AHAHAHA
I LOVE THIS SHRIMP, BUT...
...SHE WON'T REVEAL HER RECIPE.
HA HA
?
SHRIMP ?
?
Huh? What'd he say?
...
↖TRYING REALLY HARD.
SOMETHING WRONG?
HMM...SO THIS IS SANO, EH?
HEH
NO, I'M GOOD.
GRR
...
WHAT THE HELL IS HIS PROBLEM?

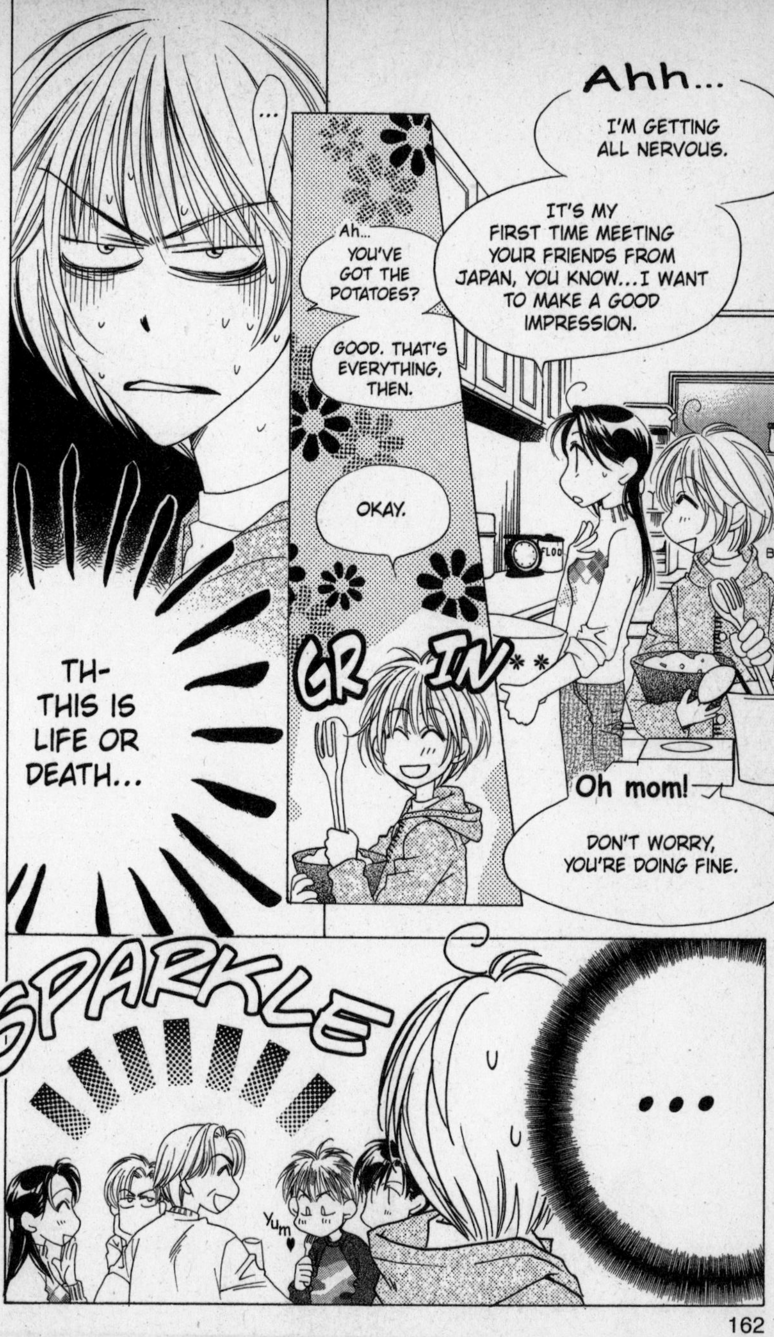
Ahh...
I'M GETTING ALL NERVOUS.
IT'S MY FIRST TIME MEETING YOUR FRIENDS FROM JAPAN, YOU KNOW...I WANT TO MAKE A GOOD IMPRESSION.
Oh mom!
DON'T WORRY, YOU'RE DOING FINE.
BREAD
Ah... YOU'VE GOT THE POTATOES?
GOOD. THAT'S EVERYTHING, THEN.
OKAY.
GR IN
...
TH- THIS IS LIFE OR DEATH...
...
SPARKLE
Yum

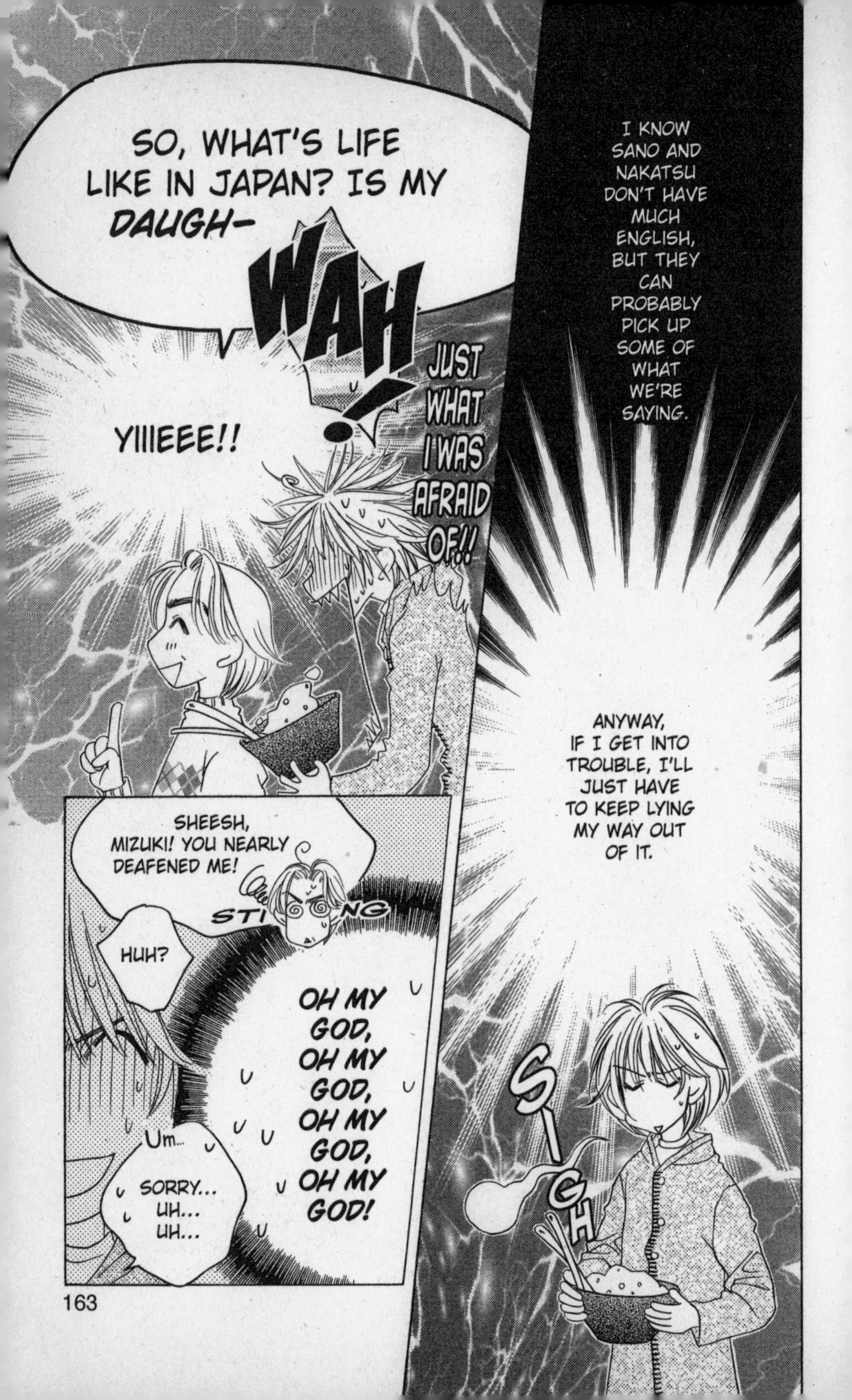
I KNOW SANO AND NAKATSU DON'T HAVE MUCH ENGLISH, BUT THEY CAN PROBABLY PICK UP SOME OF WHAT WE'RE SAYING.
ANYWAY, IF I GET INTO TROUBLE, I'LL JUST HAVE TO KEEP LYING MY WAY OUT OF IT.
SIGH
SO, WHAT'S LIFE LIKE IN JAPAN? IS MY DAUGH-
WAH!
JUST WHAT I WAS AFRAID OF!!
YIIIEEE!!
SHEESH, MIZUKI! YOU NEARLY DEAFENED ME!
STING
HUH?
OH MY GOD, OH MY GOD, OH MY GOD, OH MY GOD!
Um...
SORRY... UH... UH...

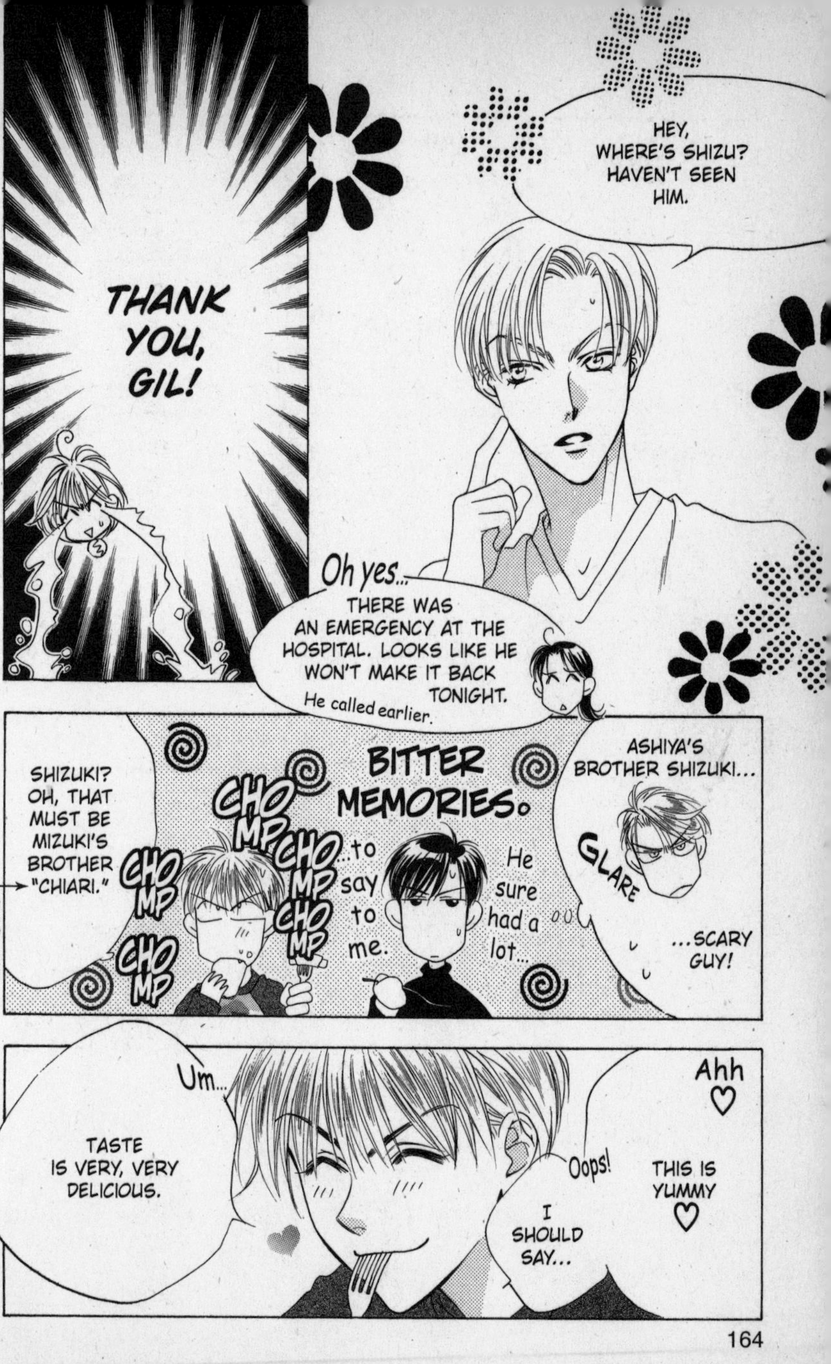
HEY, WHERE'S SHIZU? HAVEN'T SEEN HIM.
Oh yes...
THERE WAS AN EMERGENCY AT THE HOSPITAL. LOOKS LIKE HE WON'T MAKE IT BACK TONIGHT.
He called earlier.
THANK YOU, GIL!
ASHIYA'S BROTHER SHIZUKI...
GLARE
...SCARY GUY!
BITTER MEMORIES.
He sure had a lot...
...to say to me.
CHOMP
CHOMP
CHOMP
CHOMP
CHOMP
SHIZUKI? OH, THAT MUST BE MIZUKI'S BROTHER "CHIARI."
NICKNAME
Ahh ♡
THIS IS YUMMY ♡
Oops!
I SHOULD SAY...
Um...
TASTE IS VERY, VERY DELICIOUS.

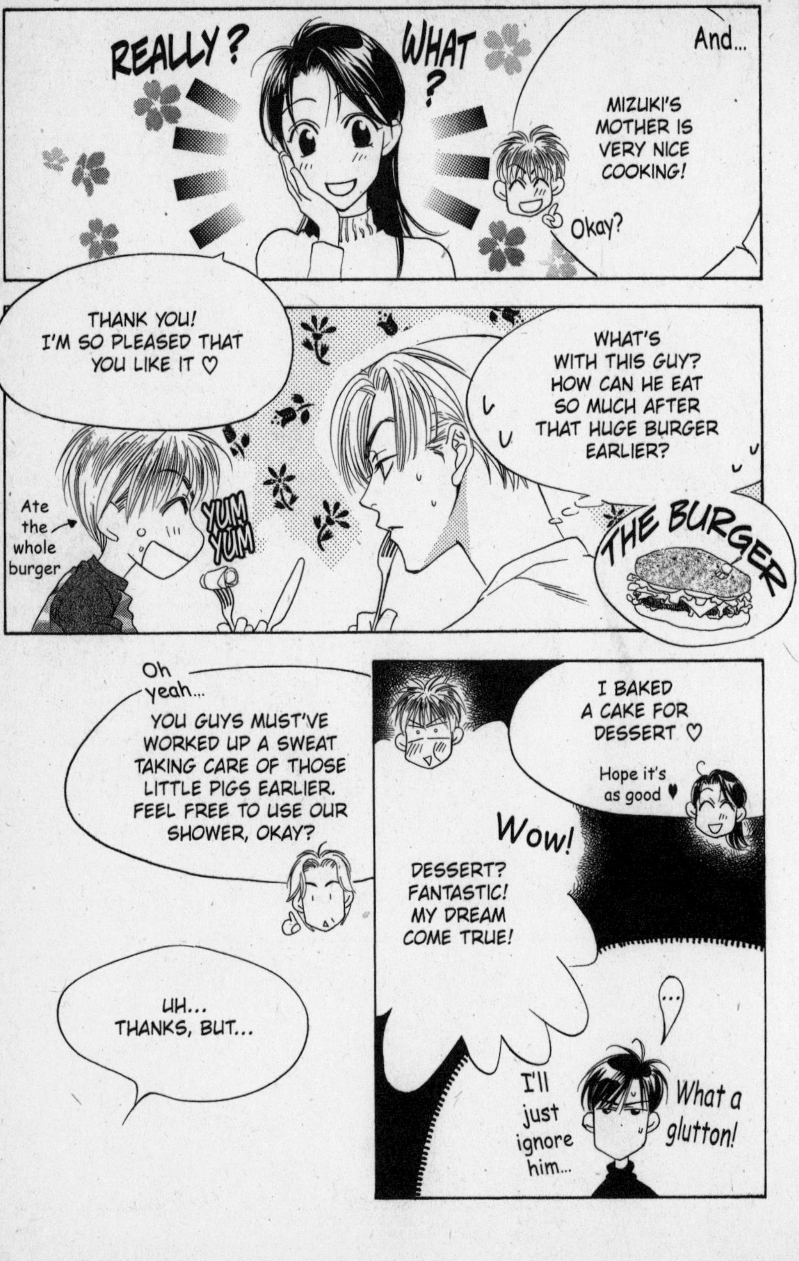
And...
MIZUKI'S MOTHER IS VERY NICE COOKING!
Okay?
WHAT?
REALLY?
WHAT'S WITH THIS GUY? HOW CAN HE EAT SO MUCH AFTER THAT HUGE BURGER EARLIER?
THE BURGER
THANK YOU! I'M SO PLEASED THAT YOU LIKE IT ♡
YUM YUM
Ate the whole burger
I BAKED A CAKE FOR DESSERT ♡
Hope it's as good ♥
Wow!
DESSERT? FANTASTIC! MY DREAM COME TRUE!
...
What a glutton!
I'll just ignore him...
Oh yeah...
YOU GUYS MUST'VE WORKED UP A SWEAT TAKING CARE OF THOSE LITTLE PIGS EARLIER. FEEL FREE TO USE OUR SHOWER, OKAY?
UH... THANKS, BUT...

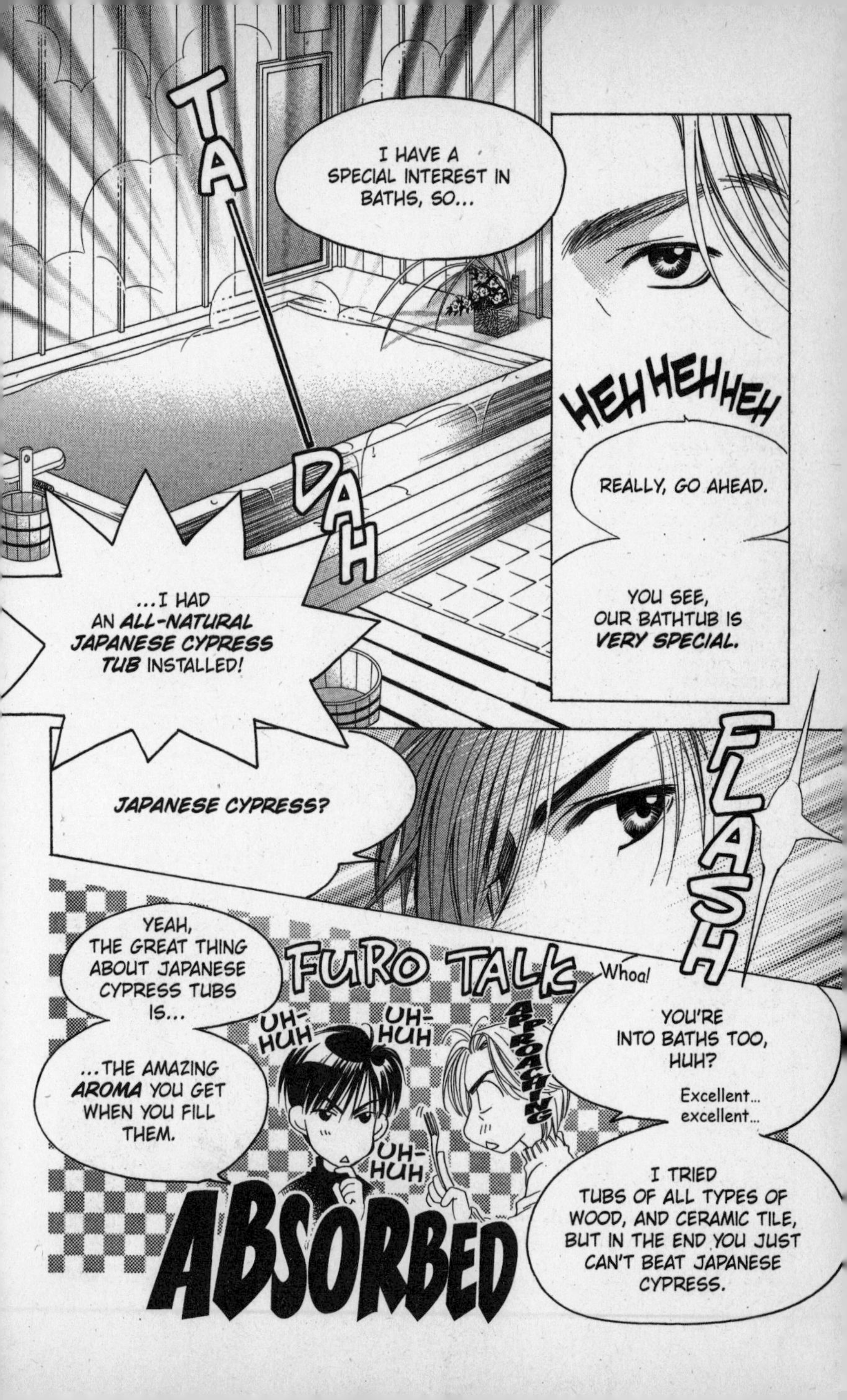

HEH HEH HEH
REALLY, GO AHEAD.
YOU SEE, OUR BATHTUB IS VERY SPECIAL.
I HAVE A SPECIAL INTEREST IN BATHS, SO...
TA
DAH
...I HAD AN ALL-NATURAL JAPANESE CYPRESS TUB INSTALLED!
FLASH
JAPANESE CYPRESS?
Whoa!
YOU'RE INTO BATHS TOO, HUH?
Excellent... excellent...
I TRIED TUBS OF ALL TYPES OF WOOD, AND CERAMIC TILE, BUT IN THE END YOU JUST CAN'T BEAT JAPANESE CYPRESS.
APPROACHING
FURO TALK
YEAH, THE GREAT THING ABOUT JAPANESE CYPRESS TUBS IS...
...THE AMAZING AROMA YOU GET WHEN YOU FILL THEM.
UH-HUH
UH-HUH
UH-HUH
ABSORBED

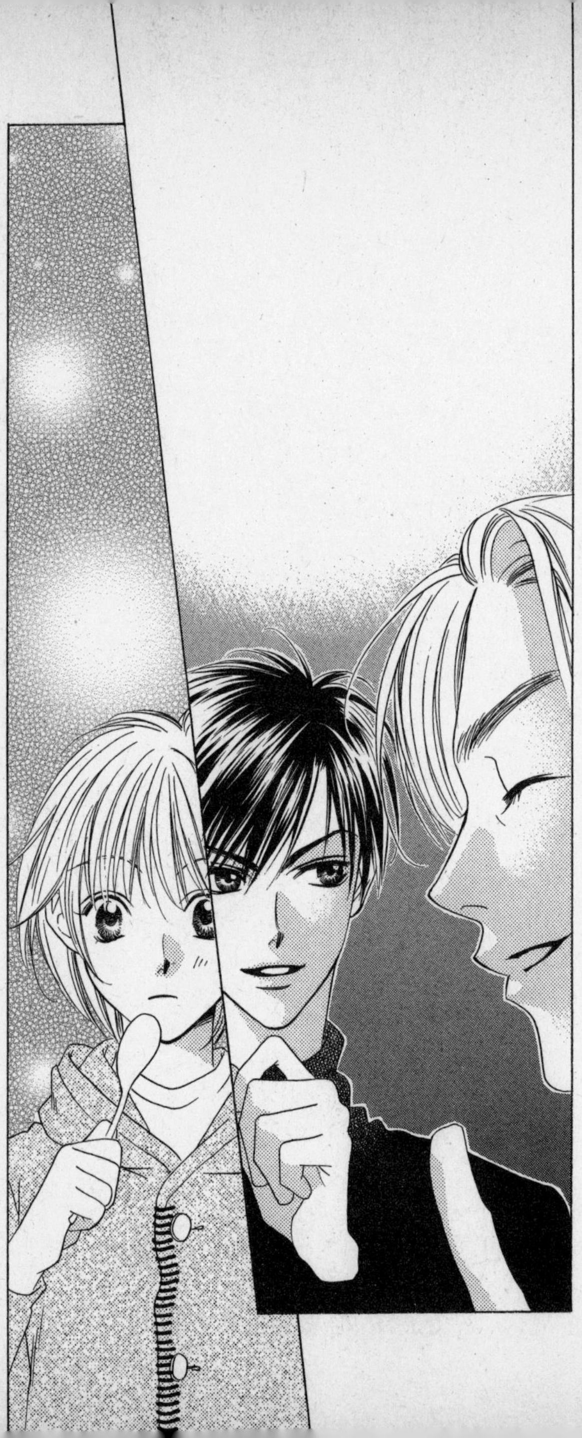

Hanging in there!

I'M SURE YOU'VE NOTICED, BUT THESE QUARTER-PAGE COLUMNS HAVE CHANGED A BIT. (ALTHOUGH THE CONTENTS HAVE STAYED PRETTY MUCH THE SAME.) THANK YOU ALL FOR BEING SUCH AWESOME FANS! I READ ALL OF YOUR LETTERS! I GET DEPRESSED SOMETIMES, BUT WHENEVER I READ YOUR LETTERS, I ALWAYS FEEL MUCH BETTER. THANKS ❤ A LOT!

I REALLY WANT TO THANK ALL THE MALE FANS WHO ALWAYS BUY MY COMICS. I'M SURE YOU FEEL A LITTLE EMBARRASSED AT THE REGISTER, SO I WANTED TO TAKE THIS OPPORTUNITY TO GIVE SOMETHING BACK TO YOU GUYS. TO ALL OF YOU WHO ARE CHASING YOUR DREAMS, GO FOR IT! TO ALL OF YOU WHO ARE BROKEN HEARTED, HANG IN THERE! TO ALL OF YOU WHO ARE BEING PICKED ON, DON'T GIVE UP! TO ALL OF YOU WHO ARE BATTLING A DISEASE, DON'T GIVE UP! TO ALL OF YOU WHO ARE RAISING YOUR CHILDREN, GO FOR IT! TO EVERYBODY...LET'S HANG IN THERE!

JULY 25TH, 2000
HISAYA NAKAJOU

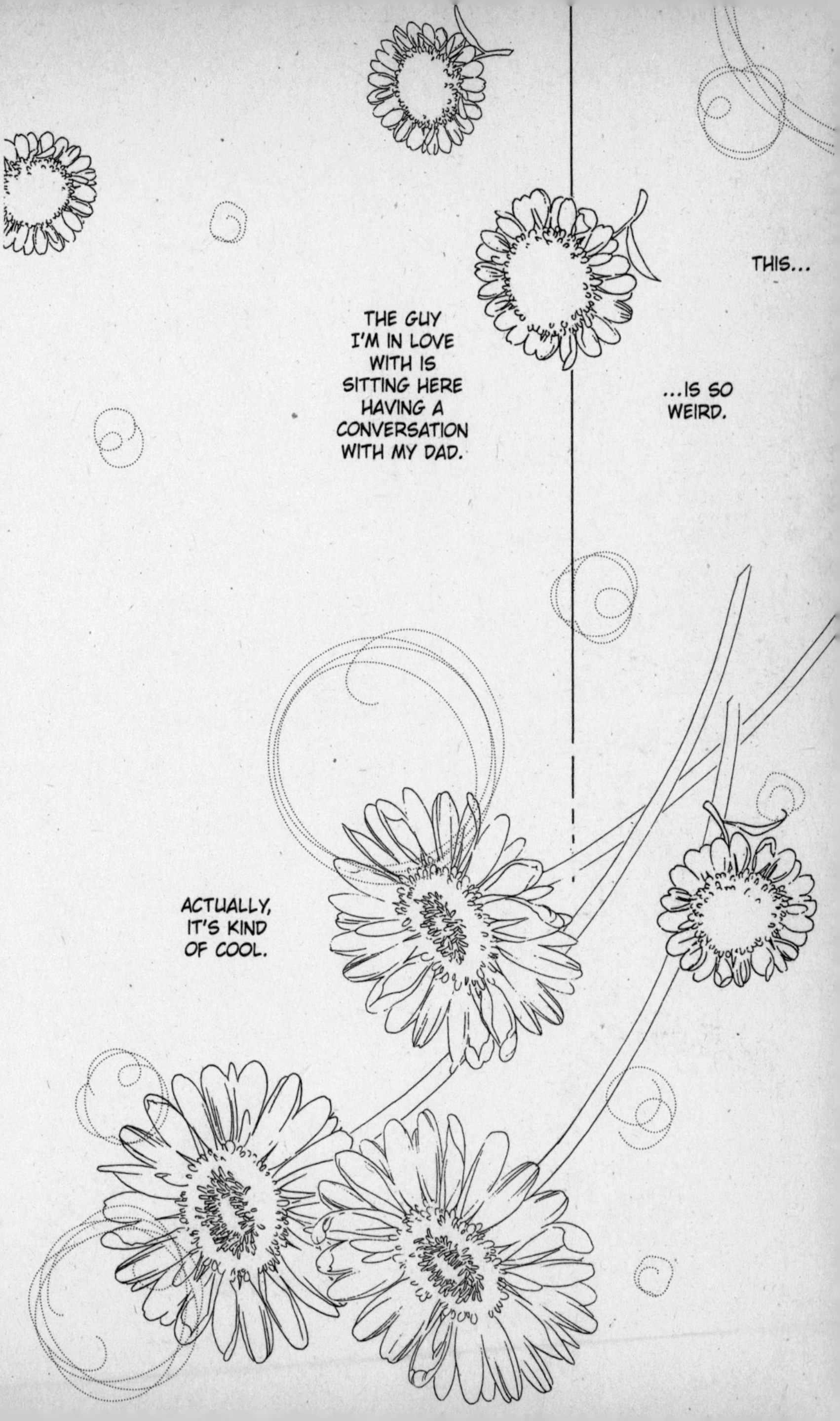
THIS...
...IS SO WEIRD.
THE GUY I'M IN LOVE WITH IS SITTING HERE HAVING A CONVERSATION WITH MY DAD.
ACTUALLY, IT'S KIND OF COOL.

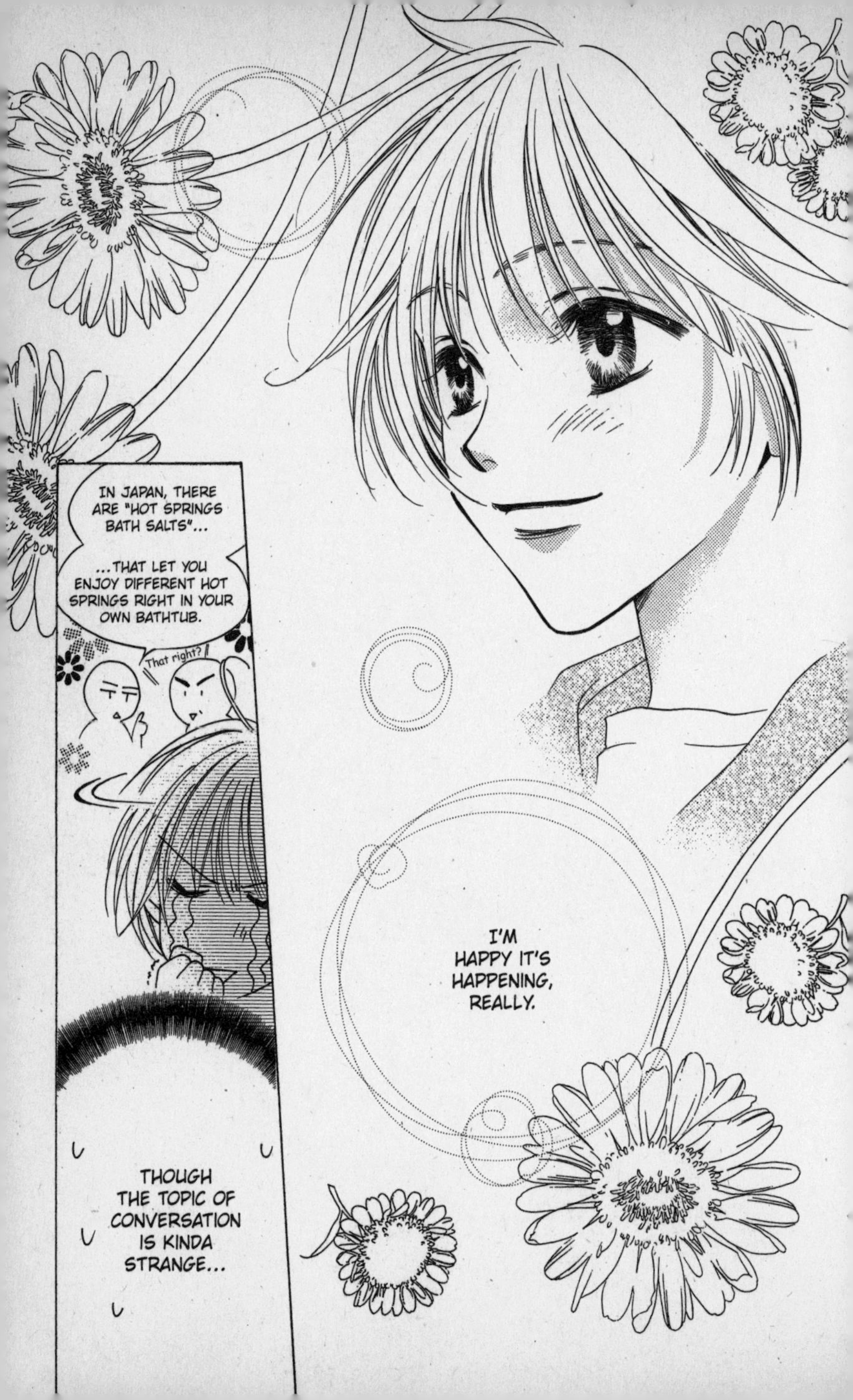
IN JAPAN, THERE ARE "HOT SPRINGS BATH SALTS"...
...THAT LET YOU ENJOY DIFFERENT HOT SPRINGS RIGHT IN YOUR OWN BATHTUB.
That right?
THOUGH THE TOPIC OF CONVERSATION IS KINDA STRANGE...
I'M HAPPY IT'S HAPPENING, REALLY.

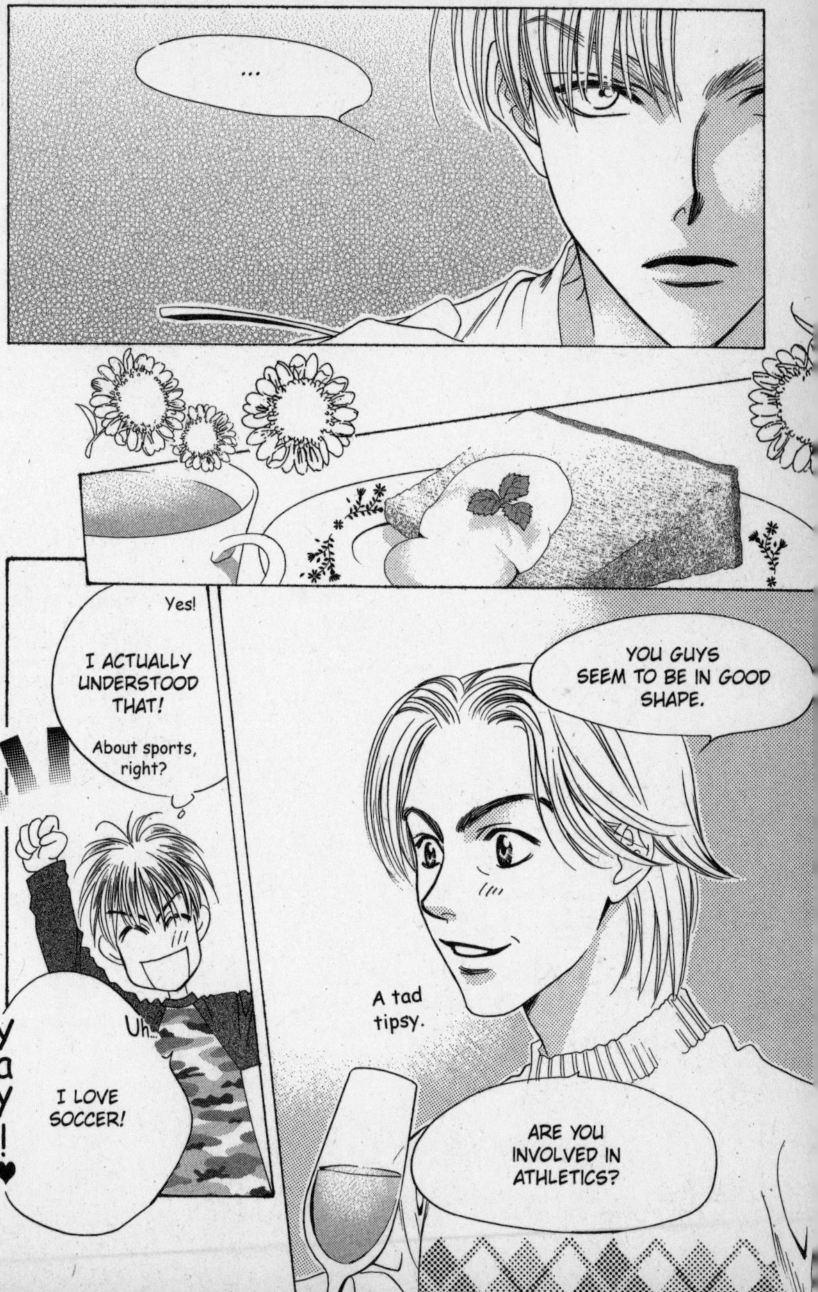
...
YOU GUYS SEEM TO BE IN GOOD SHAPE.
A tad tipsy.
ARE YOU INVOLVED IN ATHLETICS?
Yes!
I ACTUALLY UNDERSTOOD THAT!
About sports, right?
Uh...
I LOVE SOCCER!
Yay!♥

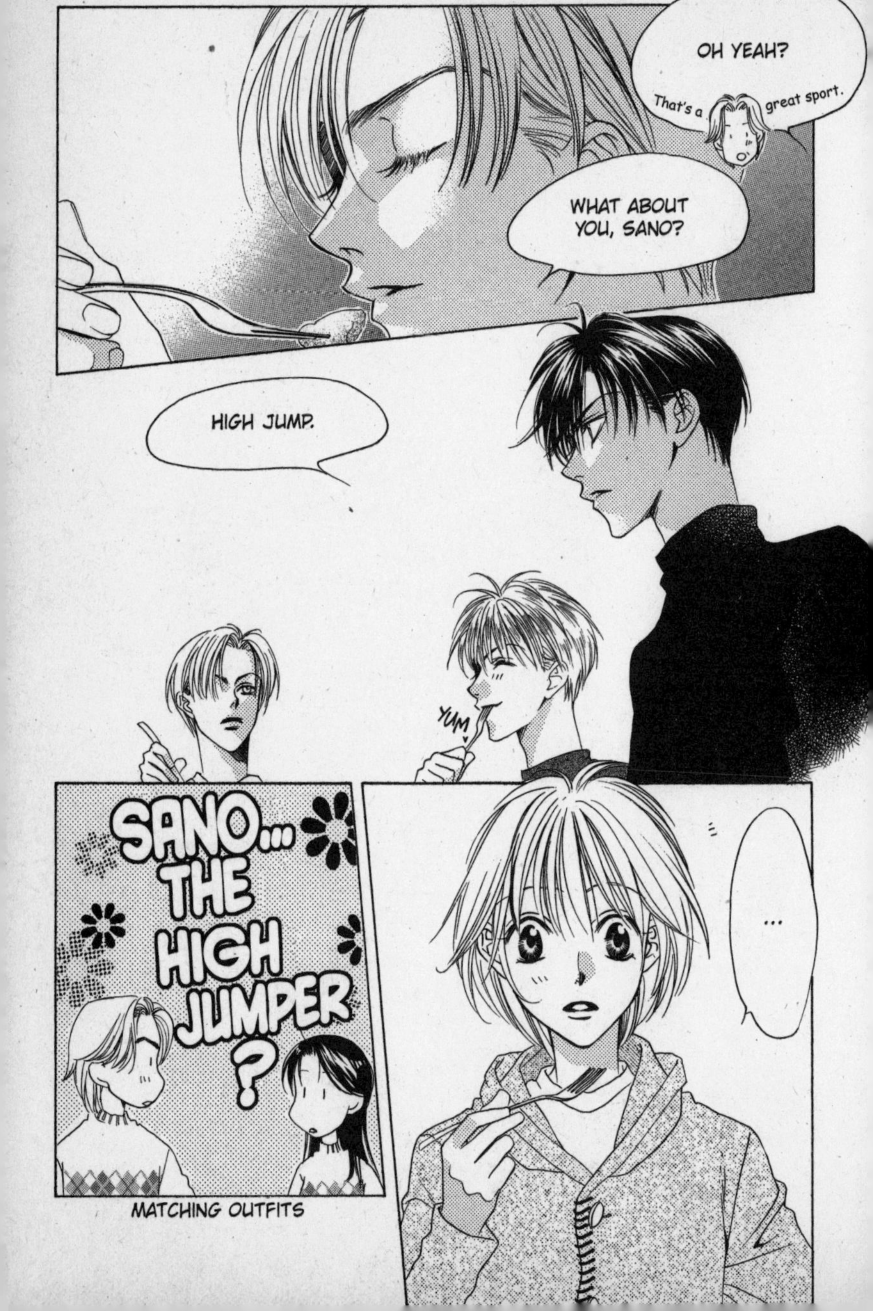
OH YEAH?
That's a great sport.
WHAT ABOUT YOU, SANO?
HIGH JUMP.
YUM
...
SANO... THE HIGH JUMPER?
MATCHING OUTFITS

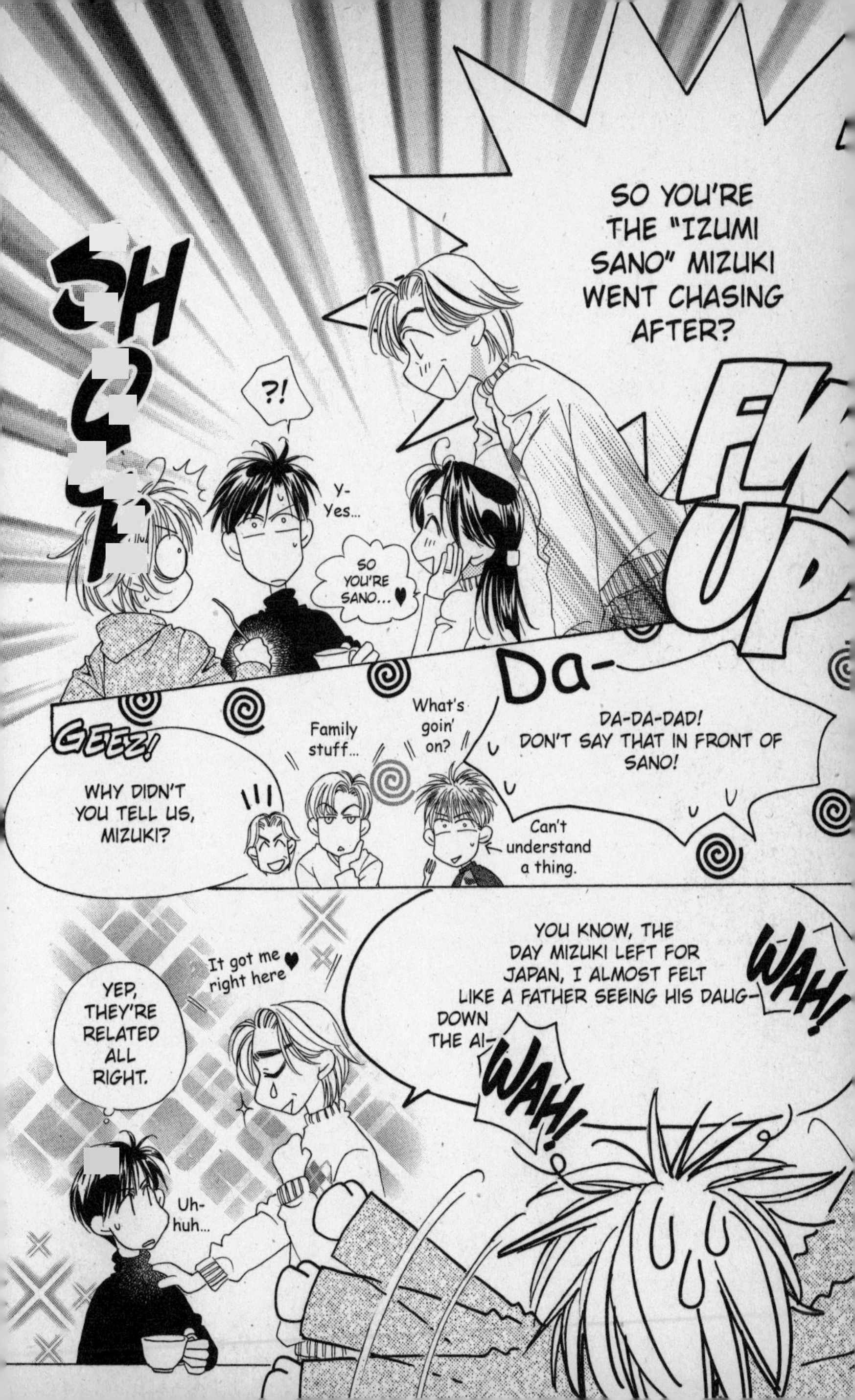
SO YOU'RE THE "IZUMI SANO" MIZUKI WENT CHASING AFTER?
FWUP
?!
Y-Yes...
SO YOU'RE SANO...♥
Da-
DA-DA-DAD! DON'T SAY THAT IN FRONT OF SANO!
What's goin' on?
Family stuff...
GEEZ!
WHY DIDN'T YOU TELL US, MIZUKI?
Can't understand a thing.
YOU KNOW, THE DAY MIZUKI LEFT FOR JAPAN, I ALMOST FELT LIKE A FATHER SEEING HIS DAUG-
DOWN THE AI-
WAH!
WAH!
It got me right here♥
YEP, THEY'RE RELATED ALL RIGHT.
Uh-huh...

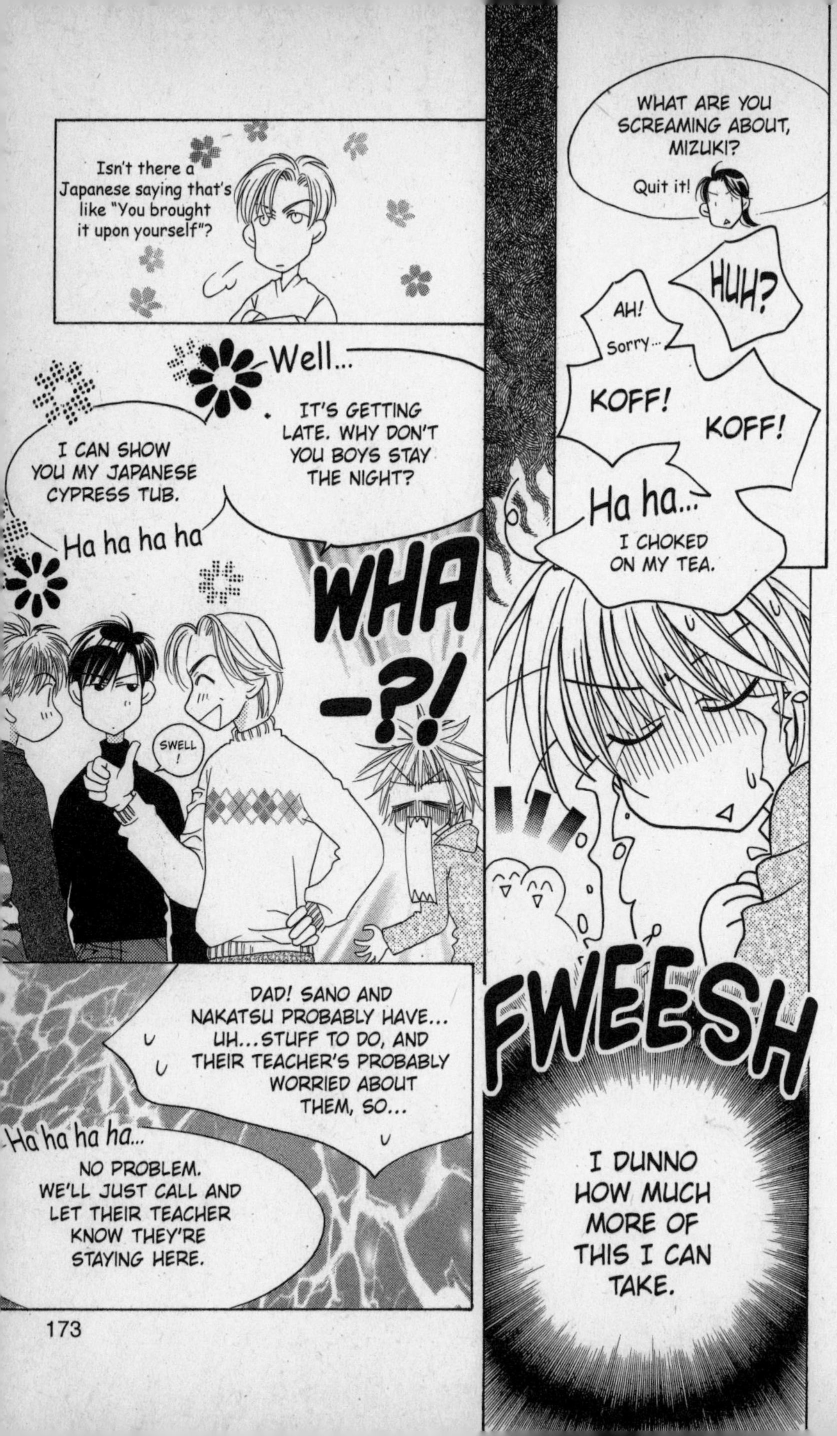
WHAT ARE YOU SCREAMING ABOUT, MIZUKI?
Quit it!
HUH?
AH! Sorry...
KOFF! KOFF!
Ha ha...
I CHOKED ON MY TEA.
FWEESH
I DUNNO HOW MUCH MORE OF THIS I CAN TAKE.
Isn't there a Japanese saying that's like "You brought it upon yourself"?
Well...
IT'S GETTING LATE. WHY DON'T YOU BOYS STAY THE NIGHT?
I CAN SHOW YOU MY JAPANESE CYPRESS TUB.
Ha ha ha ha
WHA-?!
SWELL!
DAD! SANO AND NAKATSU PROBABLY HAVE... UH...STUFF TO DO, AND THEIR TEACHER'S PROBABLY WORRIED ABOUT THEM, SO...
Ha ha ha ha...
NO PROBLEM. WE'LL JUST CALL AND LET THEIR TEACHER KNOW THEY'RE STAYING HERE.

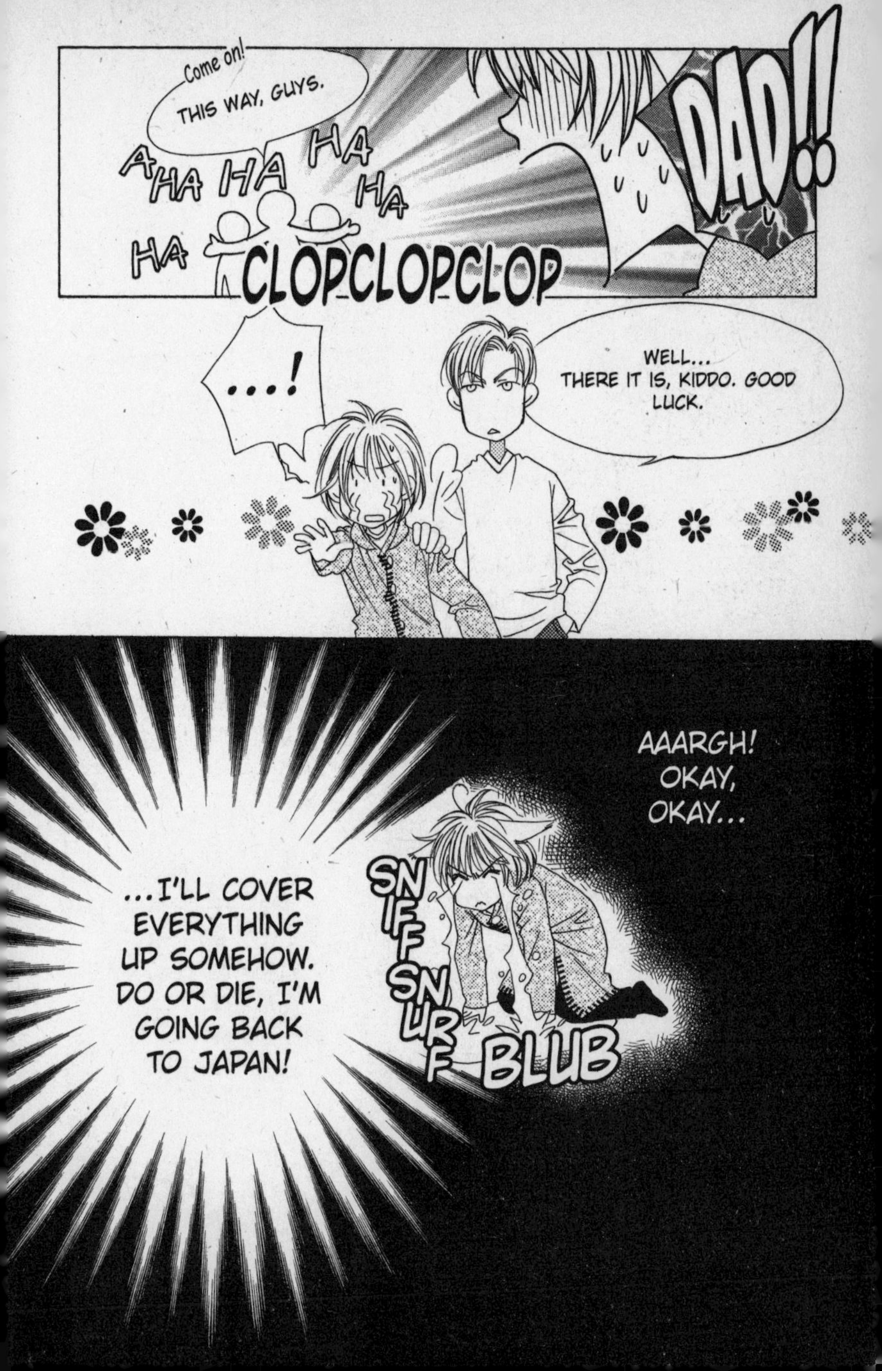
DAD!!
Come on!
THIS WAY, GUYS.
AHA HA HA HA HA HA
CLOPCLOPCLOP
WELL... THERE IT IS, KIDDO. GOOD LUCK.
...!
AAARGH! OKAY, OKAY...
SNIFF SNURF
BLUB
...I'LL COVER EVERYTHING UP SOMEHOW. DO OR DIE, I'M GOING BACK TO JAPAN!

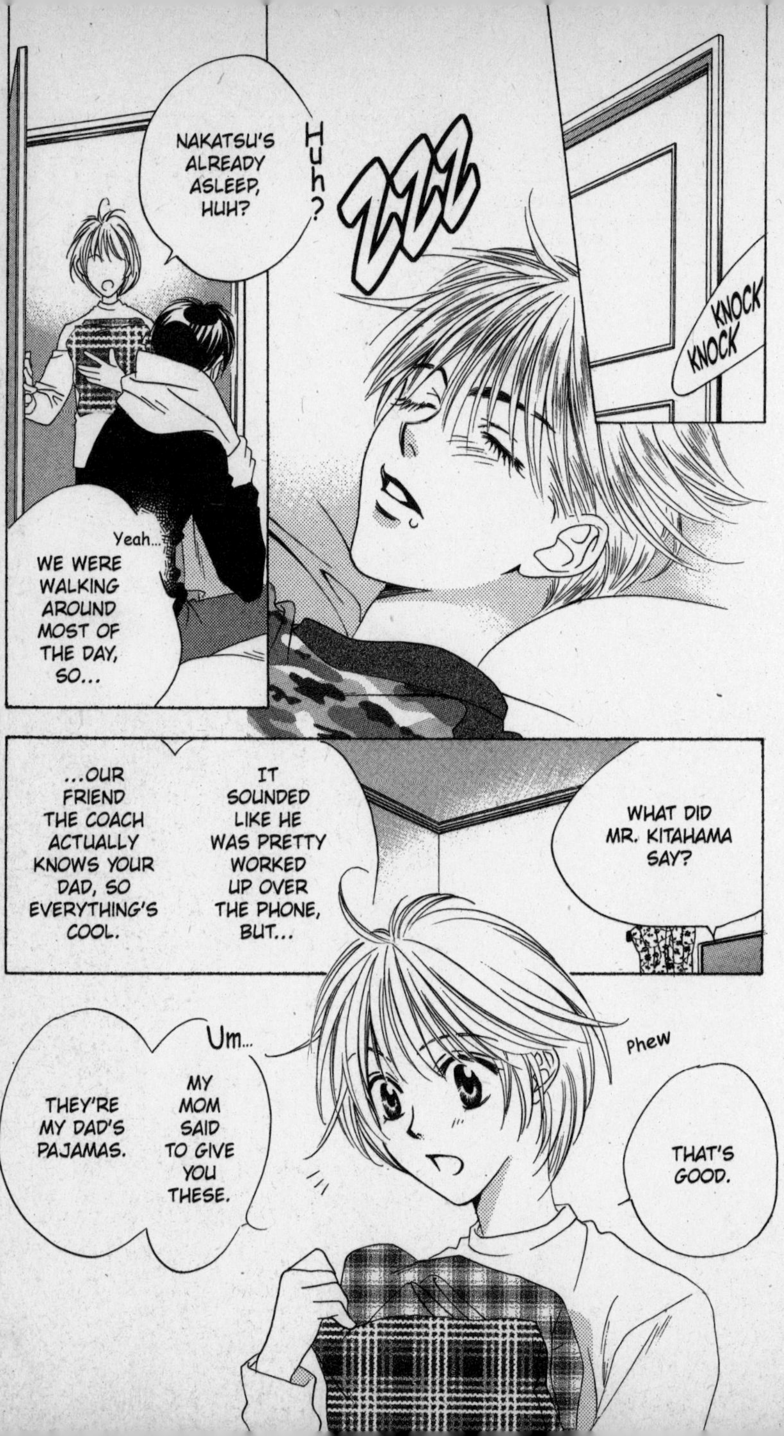
KNOCK KNOCK
ZZZ
Huh?
NAKATSU'S ALREADY ASLEEP, HUH?
Yeah...
WE WERE WALKING AROUND MOST OF THE DAY, SO...
WHAT DID MR. KITAHAMA SAY?
IT SOUNDED LIKE HE WAS PRETTY WORKED UP OVER THE PHONE, BUT...
...OUR FRIEND THE COACH ACTUALLY KNOWS YOUR DAD, SO EVERYTHING'S COOL.
Phew
THAT'S GOOD.
Um...
MY MOM SAID TO GIVE YOU THESE.
THEY'RE MY DAD'S PAJAMAS.

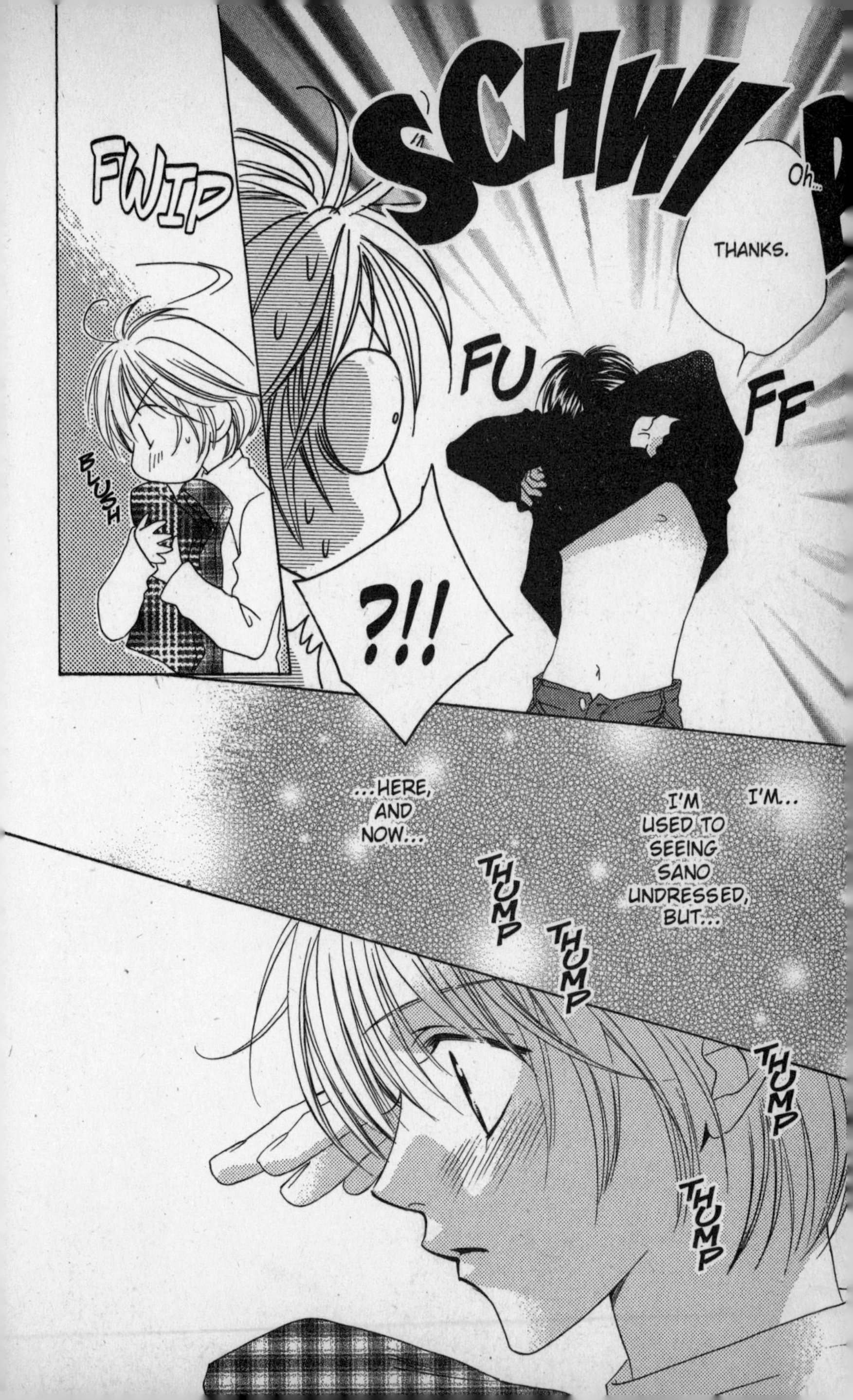
SCHWIP
Oh...
THANKS.
FU FF
FWIP
BLUSH
?!!
I'M...
I'M USED TO SEEING SANO UNDRESSED, BUT...
...HERE, AND NOW...
THUMP
THUMP
THUMP
THUMP

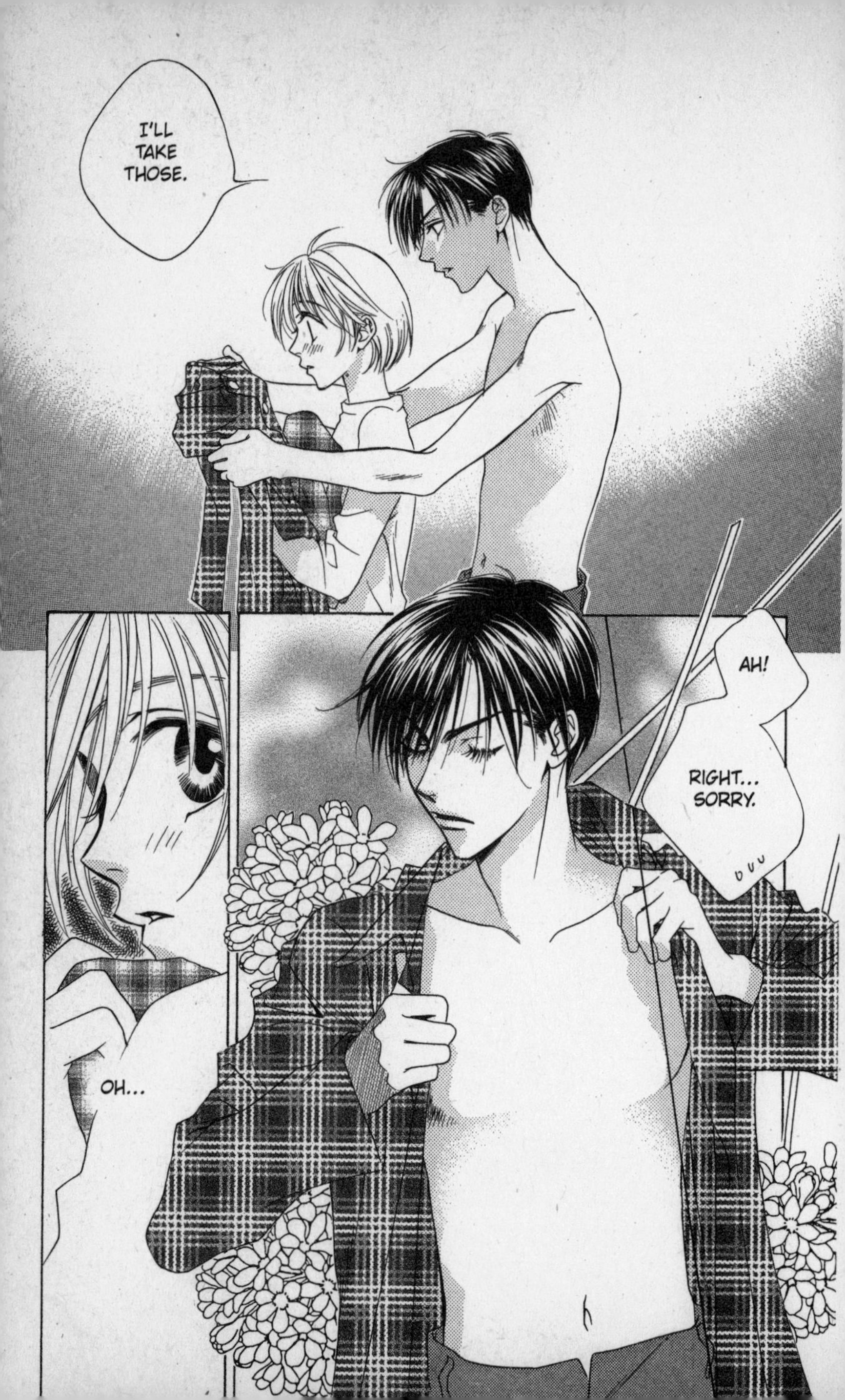
I'LL TAKE THOSE.
AH!
RIGHT... SORRY.
OH...

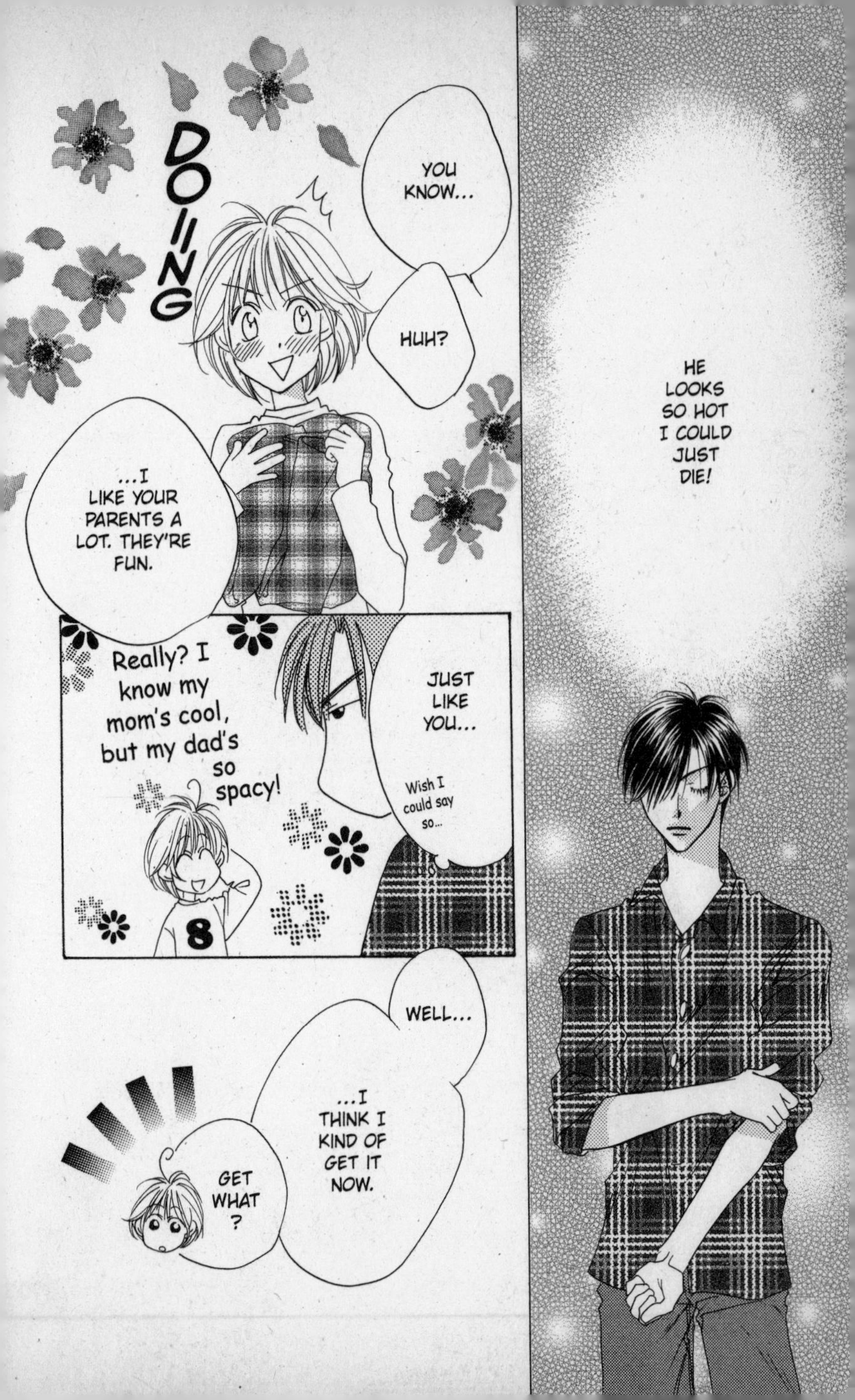
HE LOOKS SO HOT I COULD JUST DIE!
YOU KNOW...
HUH?
DOIING
...I LIKE YOUR PARENTS A LOT. THEY'RE FUN.
JUST LIKE YOU...
Wish I could say so...
Really? I know my mom's cool, but my dad's so spacy!
8
WELL...
...I THINK I KIND OF GET IT NOW.
GET WHAT ?

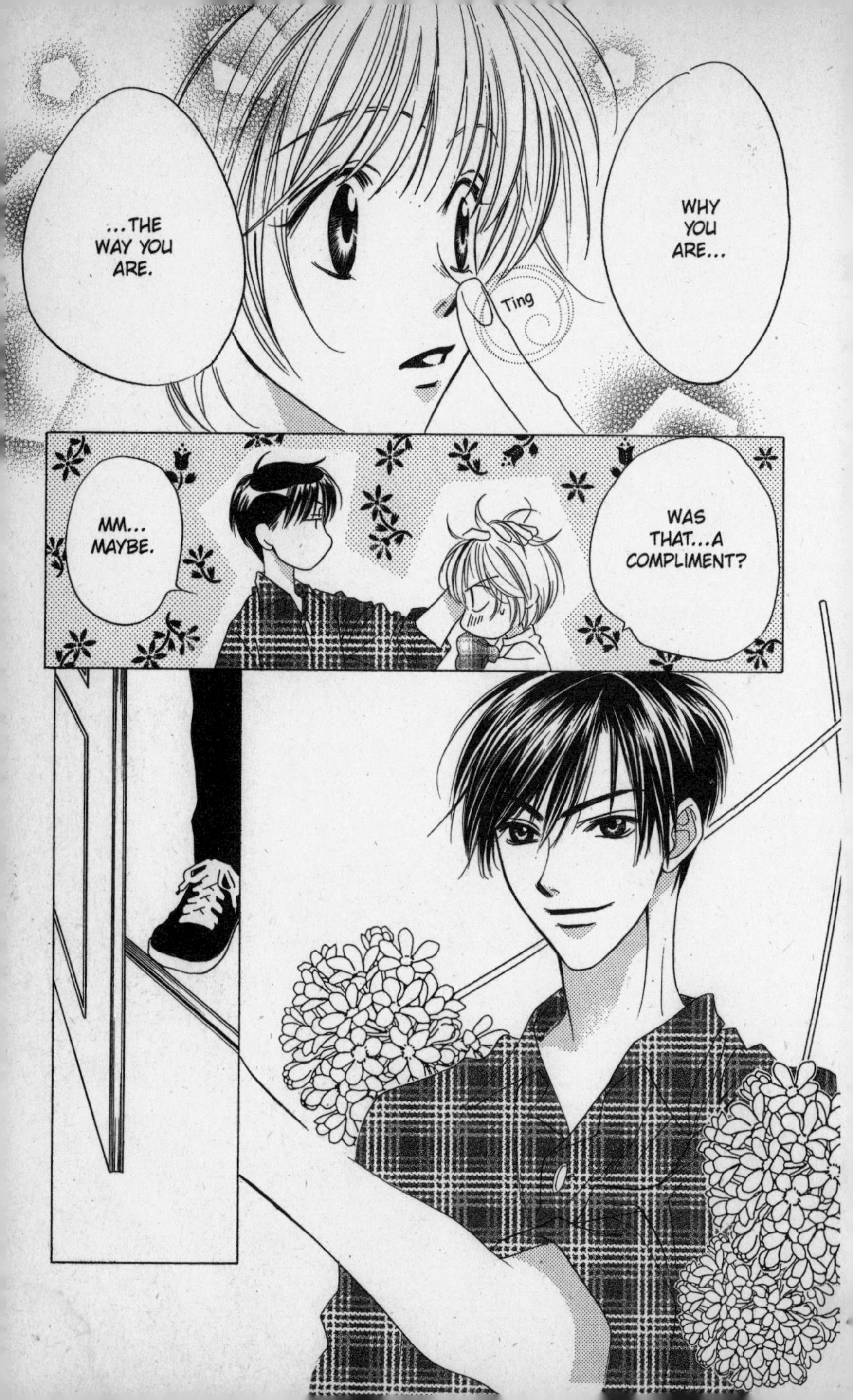
WHY YOU ARE...
Ting
...THE WAY YOU ARE.
WAS THAT...A COMPLIMENT?
MM... MAYBE.

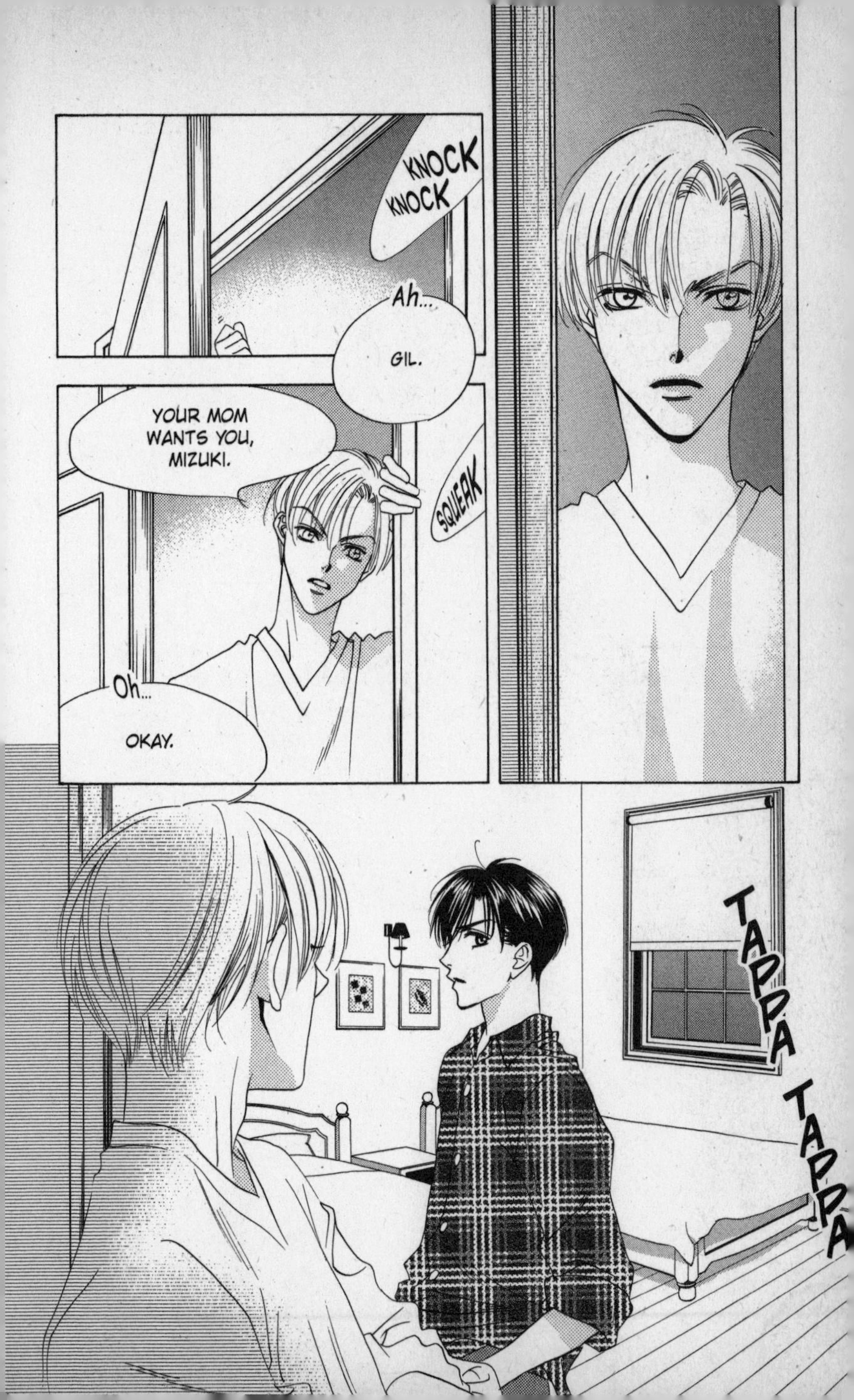
KNOCK KNOCK
Ah... GIL.
YOUR MOM WANTS YOU, MIZUKI.
SQUEAK
Oh... OKAY.
TAPPA TAPPA

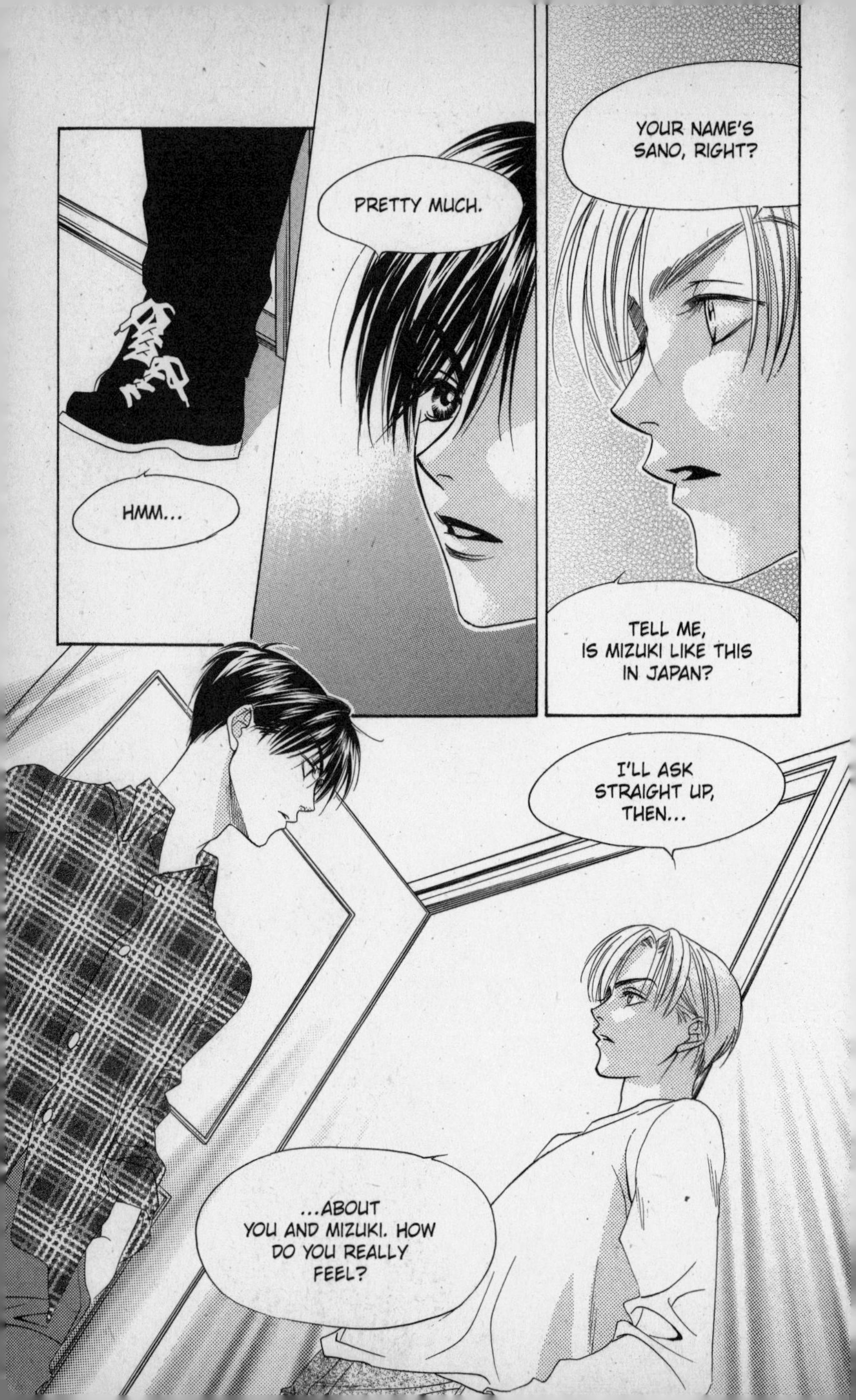
YOUR NAME'S SANO, RIGHT?
TELL ME, IS MIZUKI LIKE THIS IN JAPAN?
PRETTY MUCH.
HMM...
I'LL ASK STRAIGHT UP, THEN...
...ABOUT YOU AND MIZUKI. HOW DO YOU REALLY FEEL?

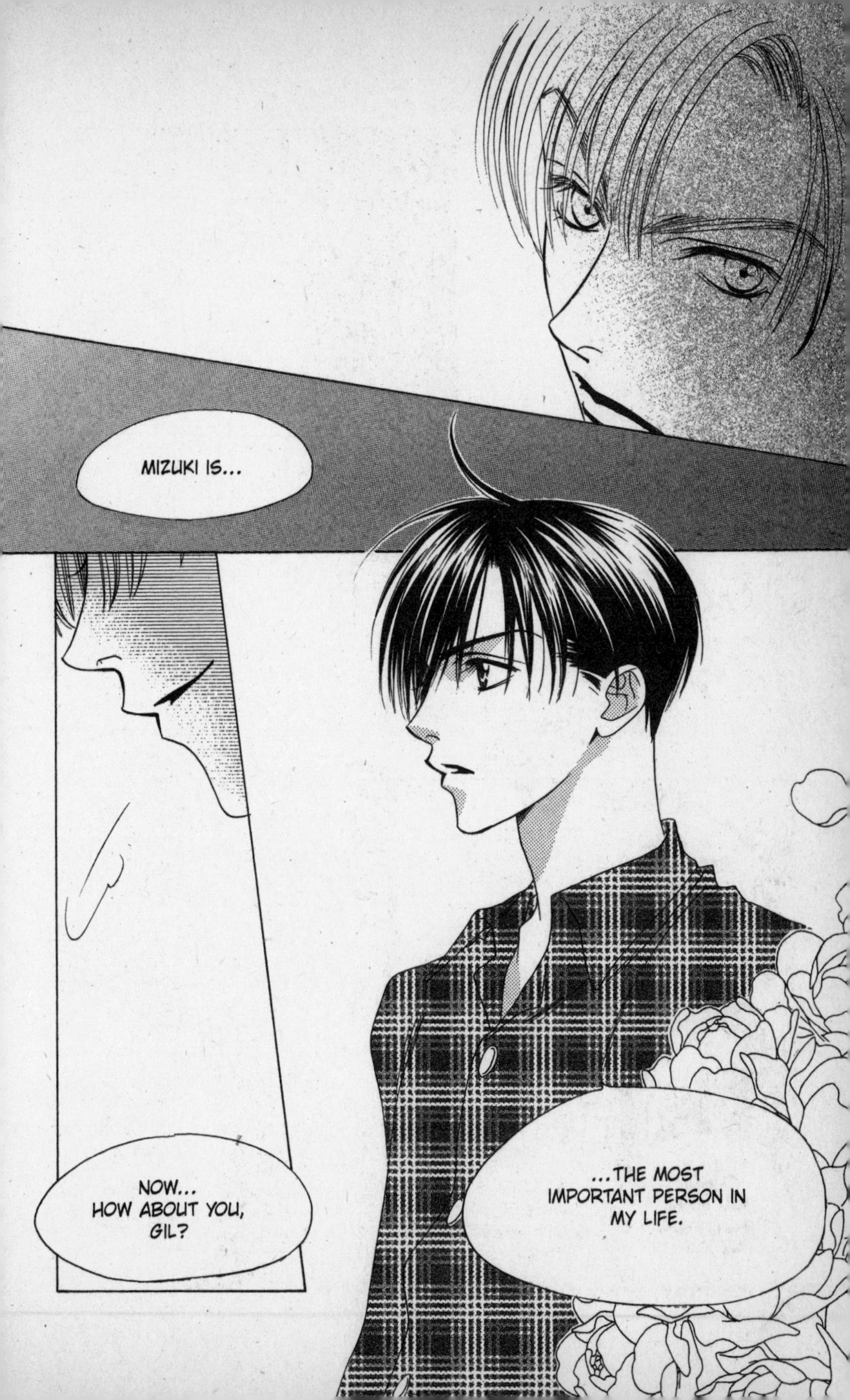
MIZUKI IS...
...THE MOST IMPORTANT PERSON IN MY LIFE.
NOW... HOW ABOUT YOU, GIL?

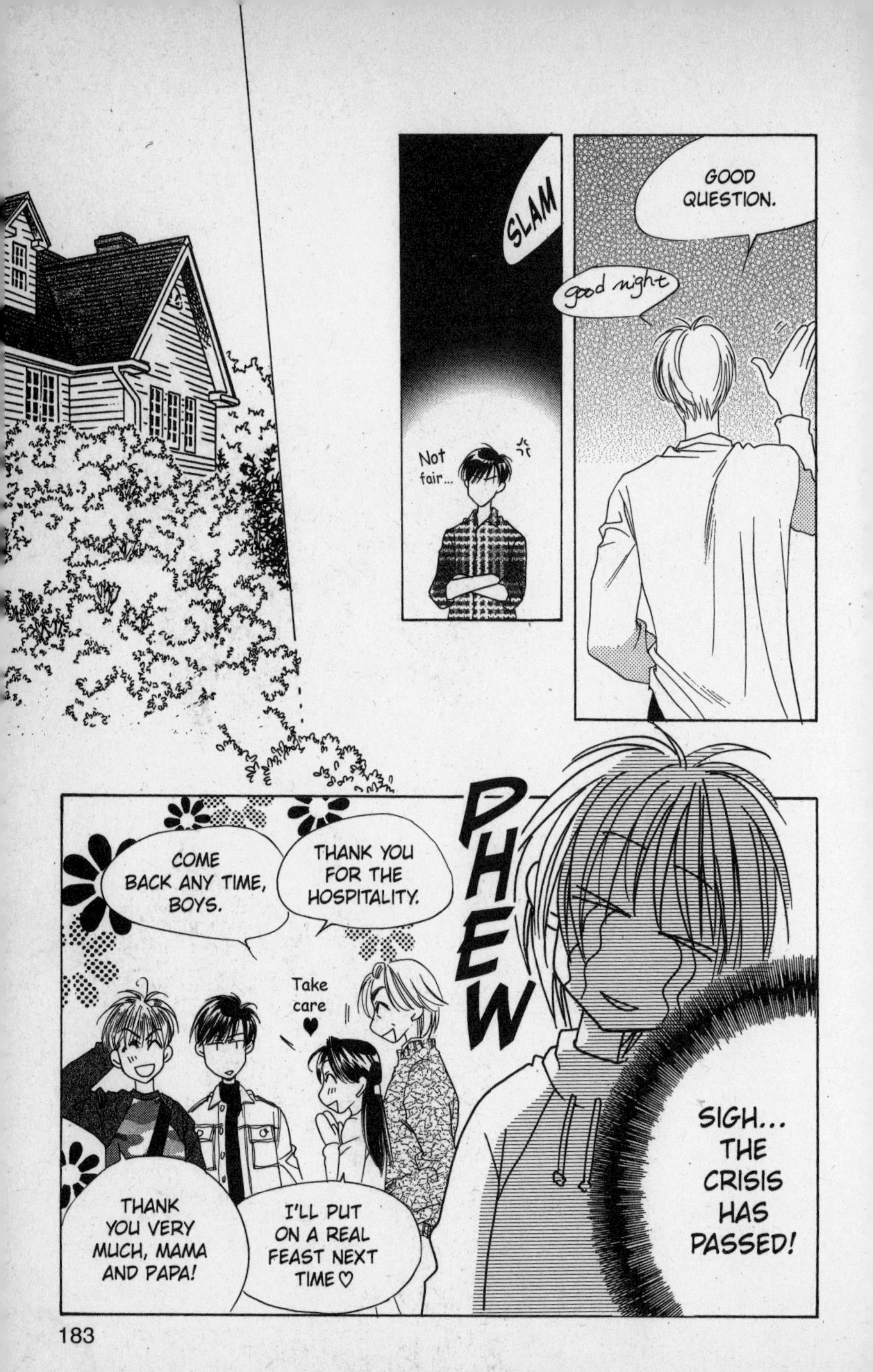
GOOD QUESTION.
good night
SLAM
Not fair...
SIGH... THE CRISIS HAS PASSED!
PHEW
THANK YOU FOR THE HOSPITALITY.
COME BACK ANY TIME, BOYS.
Take care ♥
I'LL PUT ON A REAL FEAST NEXT TIME ♡
THANK YOU VERY MUCH, MAMA AND PAPA!

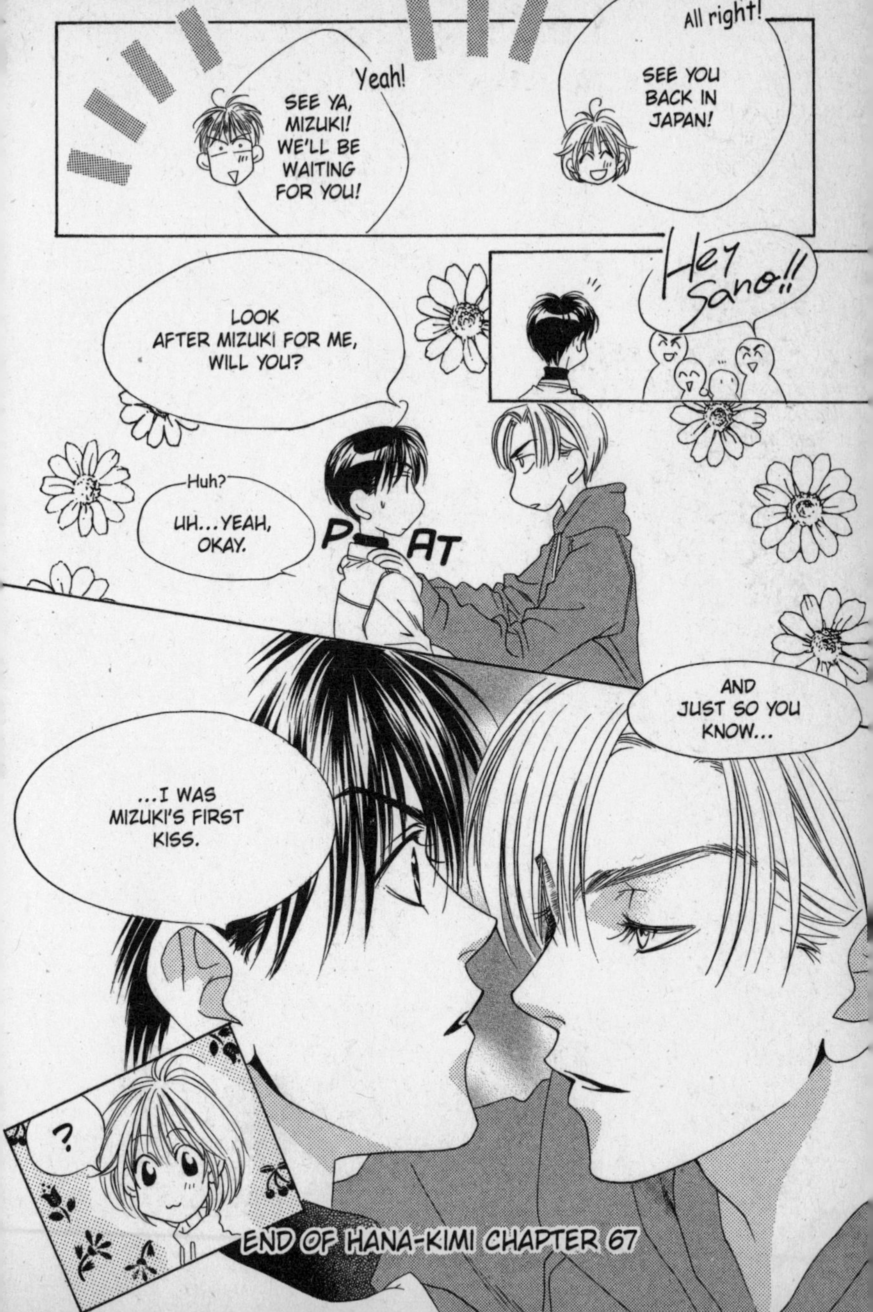
All right!
SEE YOU BACK IN JAPAN!
Yeah!
SEE YA, MIZUKI! WE'LL BE WAITING FOR YOU!
Hey Sano!!
LOOK AFTER MIZUKI FOR ME, WILL YOU?
P—AT
Huh?
UH...YEAH, OKAY.
AND JUST SO YOU KNOW...
...I WAS MIZUKI'S FIRST KISS.
?
END OF HANA-KIMI CHAPTER 67

★Hana-Kimi CD Release Special Report★

Let's go to a voice-over session!

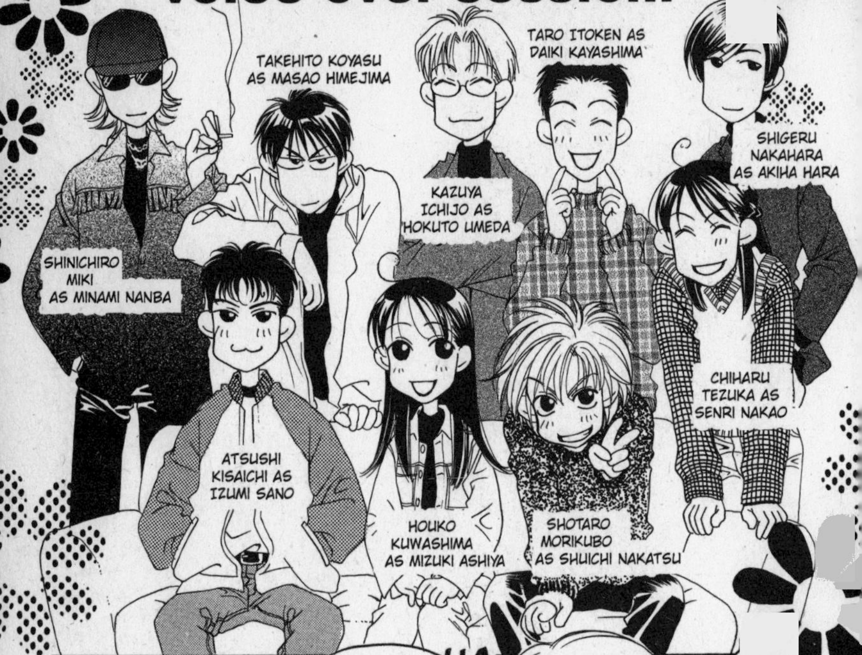
SHIGERU NAKAHARA AS AKIHA HARA
TARO ITOKEN AS DAIKI KAYASHIMA
KAZUYA ICHIJO AS HOKUTO UMEDA
TAKEHITO KOYASU AS MASAO HIMEJIMA
SHINICHIRO MIKI AS MINAMI NANBA
CHIHARU TEZUKA AS SENRI NAKAO
SHOTARO MORIKUBO AS SHUICHI NAKATSU
HOUKO KUWASHIMA AS MIZUKI ASHIYA
ATSUSHI KISAICHI AS IZUMI SANO

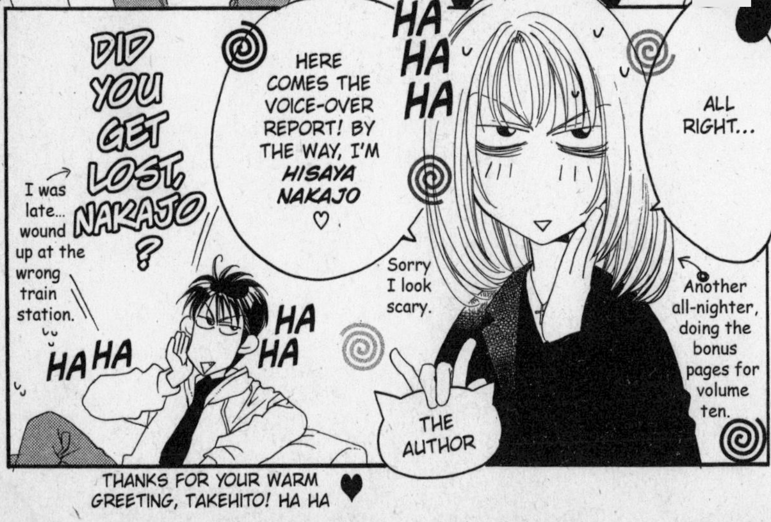
ALL RIGHT...
Another all-nighter, doing the bonus pages for volume ten.
HA HA HA
HERE COMES THE VOICE-OVER REPORT! BY THE WAY, I'M HISAYA NAKAJO ♡
Sorry I look scary.
THE AUTHOR
DID YOU GET LOST, NAKAJO?
I was late... wound up at the wrong train station.
HA HA
HA HA

THANKS FOR YOUR WARM GREETING, TAKEHITO! HA HA ♥

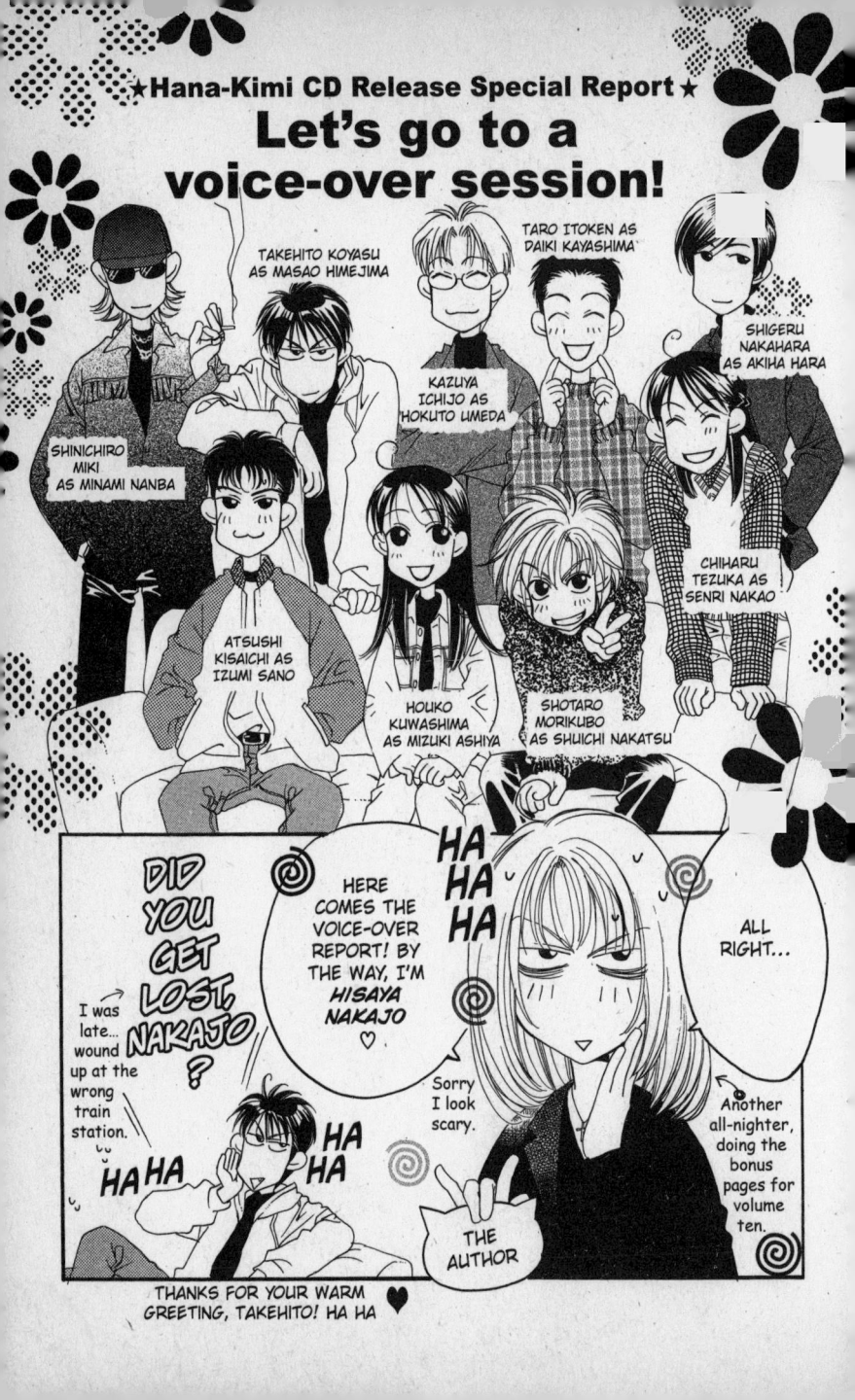

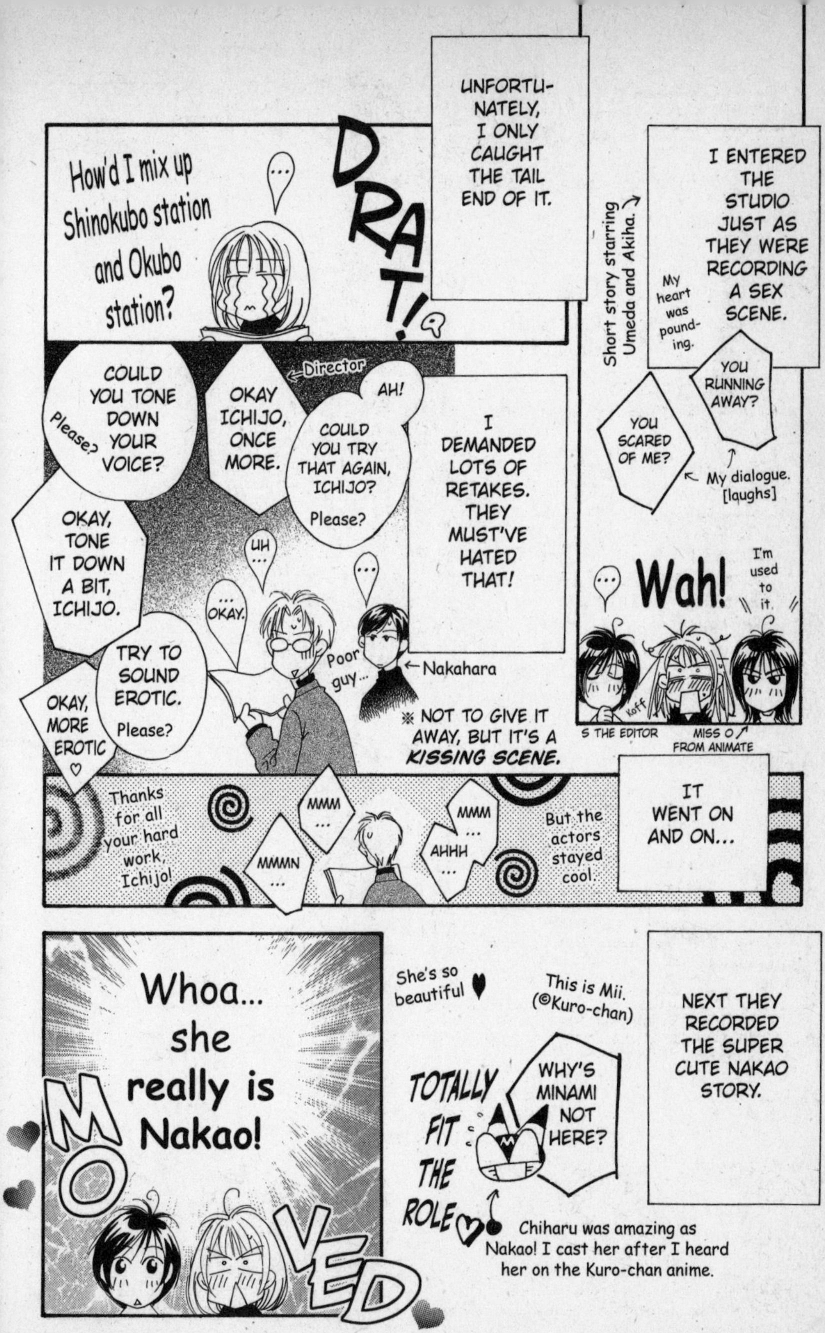
I ENTERED THE STUDIO JUST AS THEY WERE RECORDING A SEX SCENE.
My heart was pounding.
Short story starring Umeda and Akiha.
UNFORTUNATELY, I ONLY CAUGHT THE TAIL END OF IT.
DRAT!
How'd I mix up Shinokubo station and Okubo station?
...
YOU RUNNING AWAY?
YOU SCARED OF ME?
My dialogue. [laughs]
Wah!
I'm used to it.
...
koff
S THE EDITOR
MISS O FROM ANIMATE
I DEMANDED LOTS OF RETAKES. THEY MUST'VE HATED THAT!
COULD YOU TONE DOWN YOUR VOICE? Please?
OKAY ICHIJO, ONCE MORE.
Director
AH!
COULD YOU TRY THAT AGAIN, ICHIJO? Please?
OKAY, TONE IT DOWN A BIT, ICHIJO.
UH ...
... OKAY.
...
TRY TO SOUND EROTIC. Please?
OKAY, MORE EROTIC ♡
Poor guy...
Nakahara
※ NOT TO GIVE IT AWAY, BUT IT'S A KISSING SCENE.
IT WENT ON AND ON...
But the actors stayed cool.
MMM ... AHHH ...
MMM ...
MMMN ...
Thanks for all your hard work, Ichijo!
NEXT THEY RECORDED THE SUPER CUTE NAKAO STORY.
This is Mii. (©Kuro-chan)
She's so beautiful ♥
WHY'S MINAMI NOT HERE?
TOTALLY FIT THE ROLE ♡
Chiharu was amazing as Nakao! I cast her after I heard her on the Kuro-chan anime.
Whoa... she really is Nakao!
MOVED

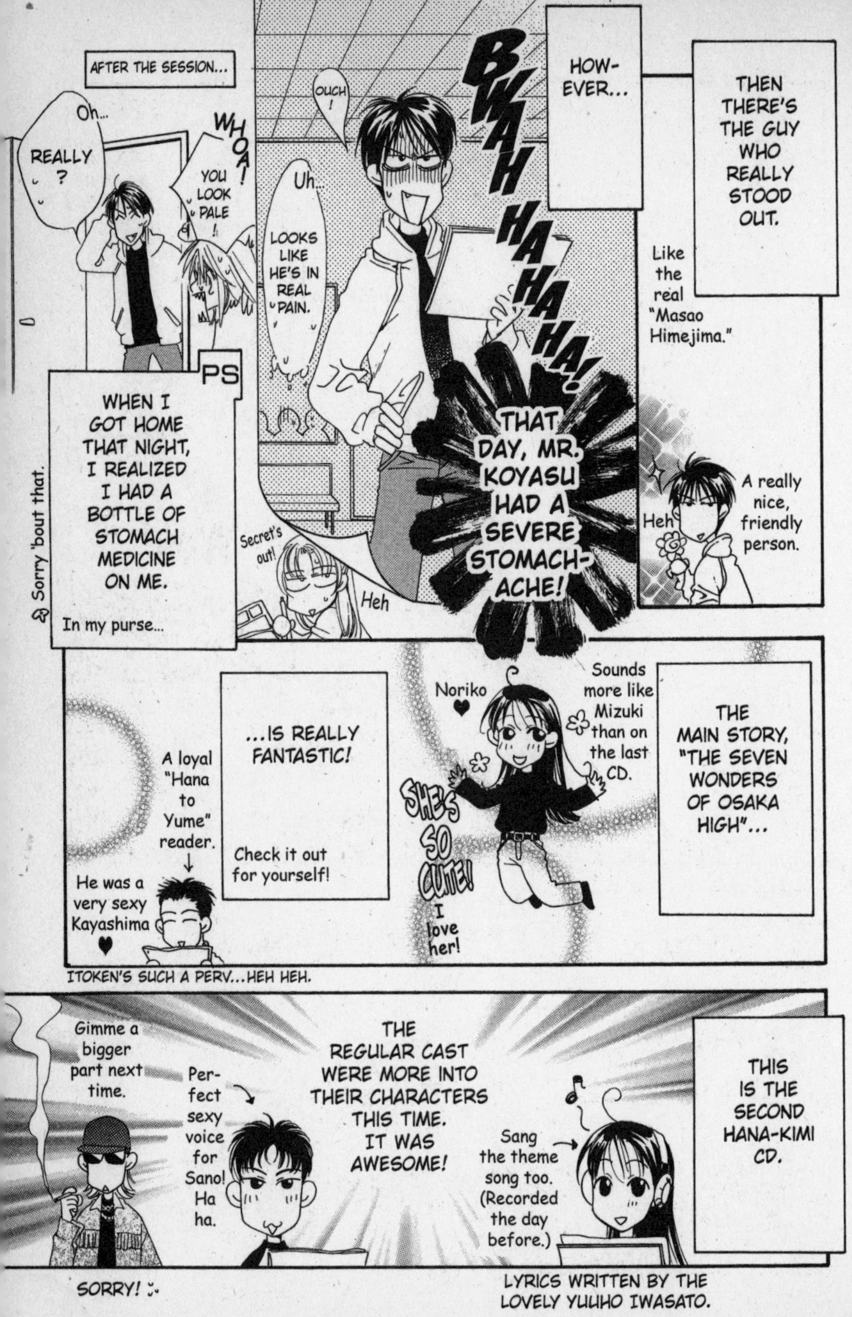
THEN THERE'S THE GUY WHO REALLY STOOD OUT.
Like the real "Masao Himejima."
A really nice, friendly person.
Heh
HOW-EVER...
BWAHHAHAHAHA!
THAT DAY, MR. KOYASU HAD A SEVERE STOMACH-ACHE!
OUCH!
Uh...
LOOKS LIKE HE'S IN REAL PAIN.
Secret's out!
Heh
AFTER THE SESSION...
Oh...
REALLY?
WHOA!
YOU LOOK PALE!
PS
WHEN I GOT HOME THAT NIGHT, I REALIZED I HAD A BOTTLE OF STOMACH MEDICINE ON ME.
In my purse...
Sorry 'bout that.
THE MAIN STORY, "THE SEVEN WONDERS OF OSAKA HIGH"...
Sounds more like Mizuki than on the last CD.
Noriko
SHE'S SO CUTE!
I love her!
...IS REALLY FANTASTIC!
Check it out for yourself!
A loyal "Hana to Yume" reader.
He was a very sexy Kayashima
ITOKEN'S SUCH A PERV...HEH HEH.
THIS IS THE SECOND HANA-KIMI CD.
Sang the theme song too. (Recorded the day before.)
LYRICS WRITTEN BY THE LOVELY YUUHO IWASATO.
THE REGULAR CAST WERE MORE INTO THEIR CHARACTERS THIS TIME. IT WAS AWESOME!
Per-fect sexy voice for Sano! Ha ha.
Gimme a bigger part next time.
SORRY!

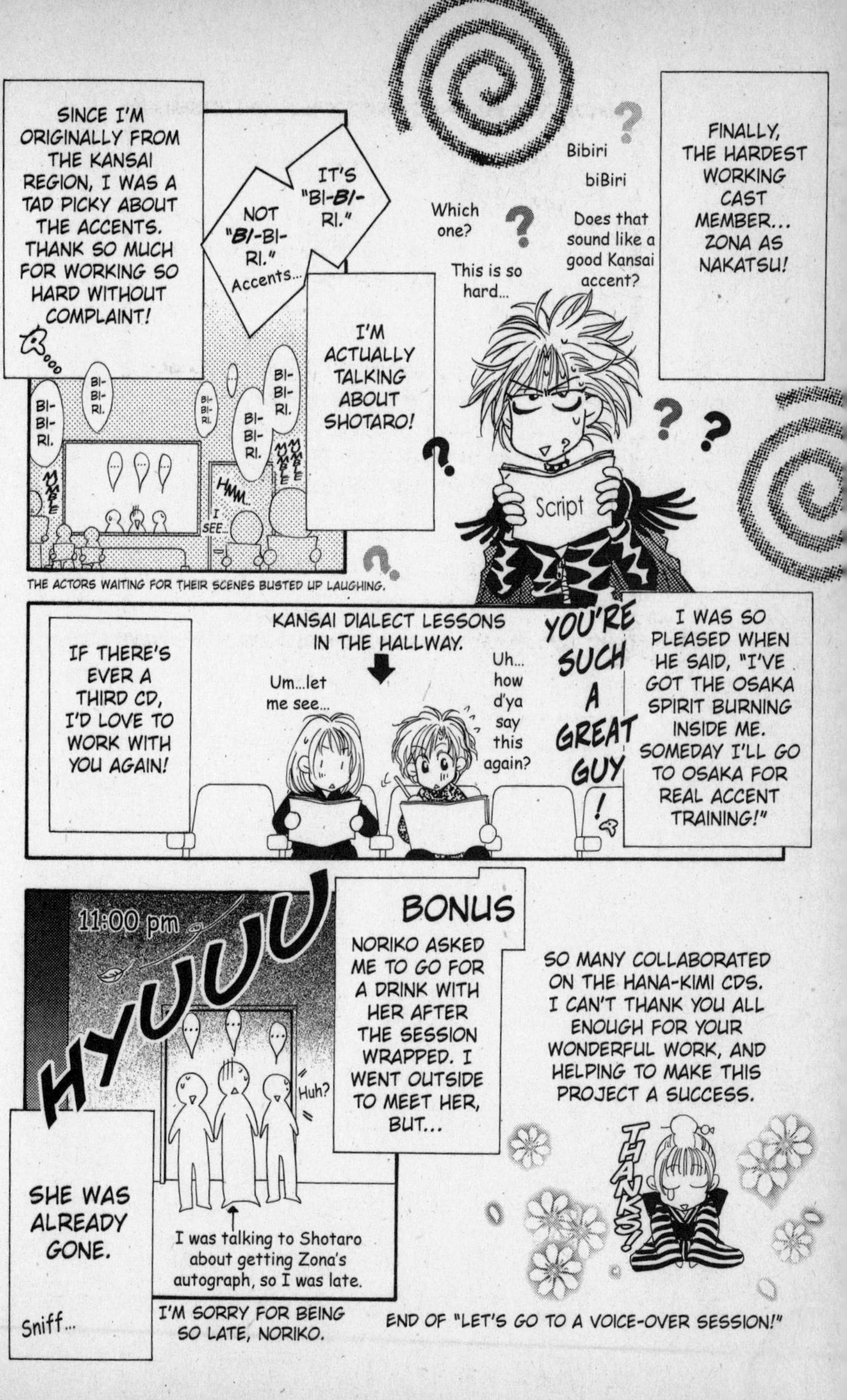
FINALLY, THE HARDEST WORKING CAST MEMBER... ZONA AS NAKATSU!
Bibiri
biBiri
Does that sound like a good Kansai accent?
Which one?
This is so hard...
Script
I'M ACTUALLY TALKING ABOUT SHOTARO!
SINCE I'M ORIGINALLY FROM THE KANSAI REGION, I WAS A TAD PICKY ABOUT THE ACCENTS. THANK SO MUCH FOR WORKING SO HARD WITHOUT COMPLAINT!
IT'S "BI-BI-RI."
NOT "BI-BI-RI." Accents...
BI-BI-RI.
BI-BI-RI.
BI-BI-RI.
BI-BI-RI.
BI-BI-RI.
MUMBLE
MUMBLE MUMBLE
HMM...
I SEE...
THE ACTORS WAITING FOR THEIR SCENES BUSTED UP LAUGHING.
I WAS SO PLEASED WHEN HE SAID, "I'VE GOT THE OSAKA SPIRIT BURNING INSIDE ME. SOMEDAY I'LL GO TO OSAKA FOR REAL ACCENT TRAINING!"
YOU'RE SUCH A GREAT GUY!
KANSAI DIALECT LESSONS IN THE HALLWAY.
Uh... how d'ya say this again?
Um...let me see...
IF THERE'S EVER A THIRD CD, I'D LOVE TO WORK WITH YOU AGAIN!
BONUS
NORIKO ASKED ME TO GO FOR A DRINK WITH HER AFTER THE SESSION WRAPPED. I WENT OUTSIDE TO MEET HER, BUT...
SO MANY COLLABORATED ON THE HANA-KIMI CDS. I CAN'T THANK YOU ALL ENOUGH FOR YOUR WONDERFUL WORK, AND HELPING TO MAKE THIS PROJECT A SUCCESS.
THANKS!
END OF "LET'S GO TO A VOICE-OVER SESSION!"
11:00 pm
HYUUUU
Huh?
I was talking to Shotaro about getting Zona's autograph, so I was late.
SHE WAS ALREADY GONE.
Sniff...
I'M SORRY FOR BEING SO LATE, NORIKO.

ABOUT THE AUTHOR

Hisaya Nakajo's manga series **Hanazakari no Kimitachi he** (For You in Full Blossom, casually known as **Hana-Kimi**) has been a hit since it first appeared in 1997 in the shôjo manga magazine **Hana to Yume** (Flowers and Dreams). In Japan, two **Hana-Kimi** art books and several "drama CDs" have been released. Her other manga series include **Missing Piece** (2 volumes) and **Yumemiru Happa** (The Dreaming Leaf, 1 volume).

Hisaya Nakajo's website:
www.wild-vanilla.com

IN THE NEXT VOLUME ...

Short of funds, Mizuki takes a job with Akiha the photographer, and straight off she manages to spill tea on male diva supermodel "Alex." Relations between them don't improve when Mizuki accidentally discovers the model's most closely guarded secret! Back at Mizuki's school, everyone is distracted by a mysterious food thief who's leaving flowers in place of what's been stolen.

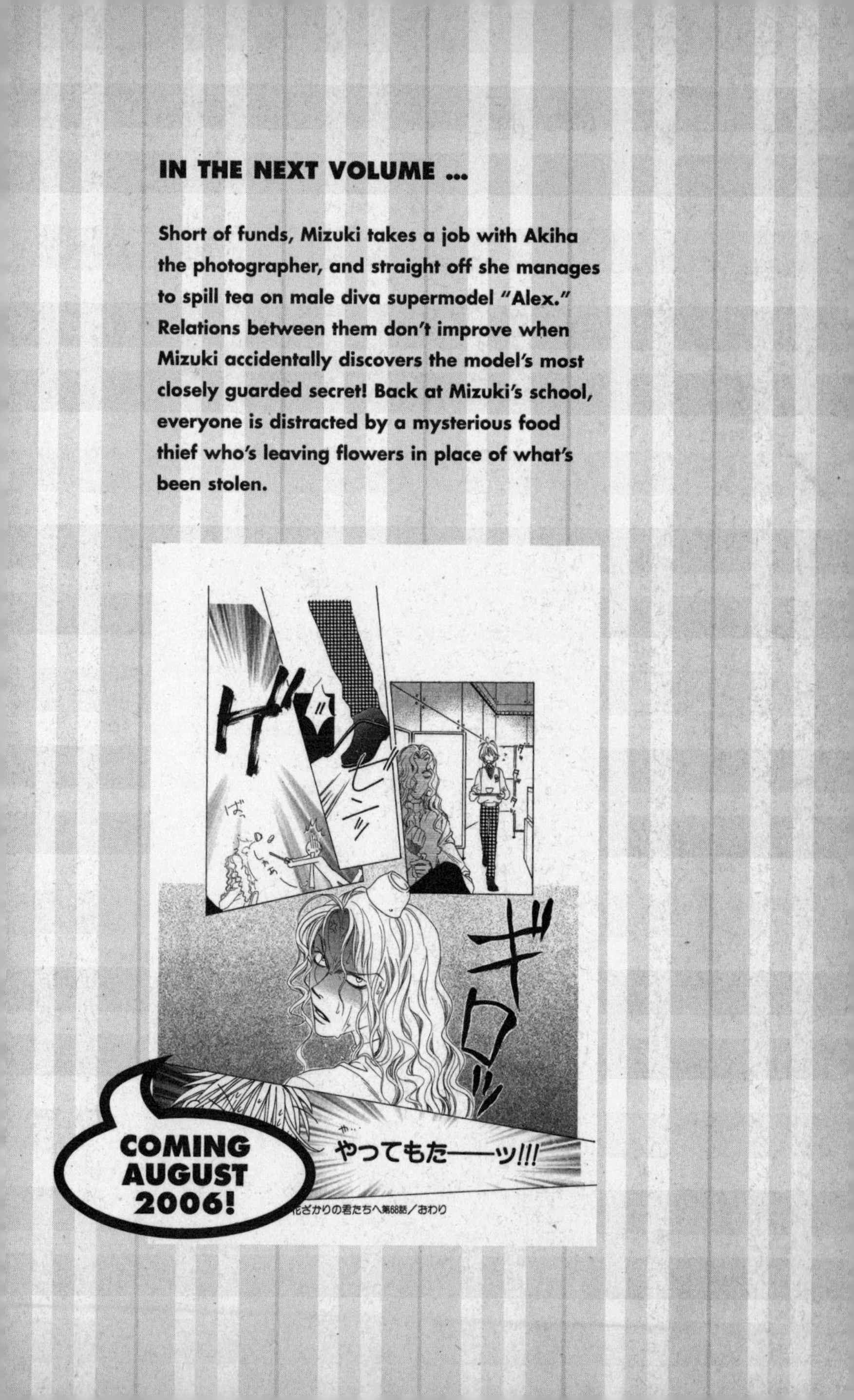
ザ
ギロッ
や…
やってもた――ッ!!!
COMING AUGUST 2006!
花ざかりの君たちへ第68話／おわり

HAPPY HUSTLE HIGH ™

Straight from Japan's top ten sales chart *—start your graphic novel collection today!

ONLY $9.99!

Unfortunately, he doesn't know (or care) that she's alive. What's a rough-neck girl to do?

Hanabi Ozora's always acted like a boy, but she's never actually wanted to date one. That is until her all-girls' school gets mixed with an all-boys' school and she meets Yasuaki Garaku!

TOMBOY, INTERRUPTED!

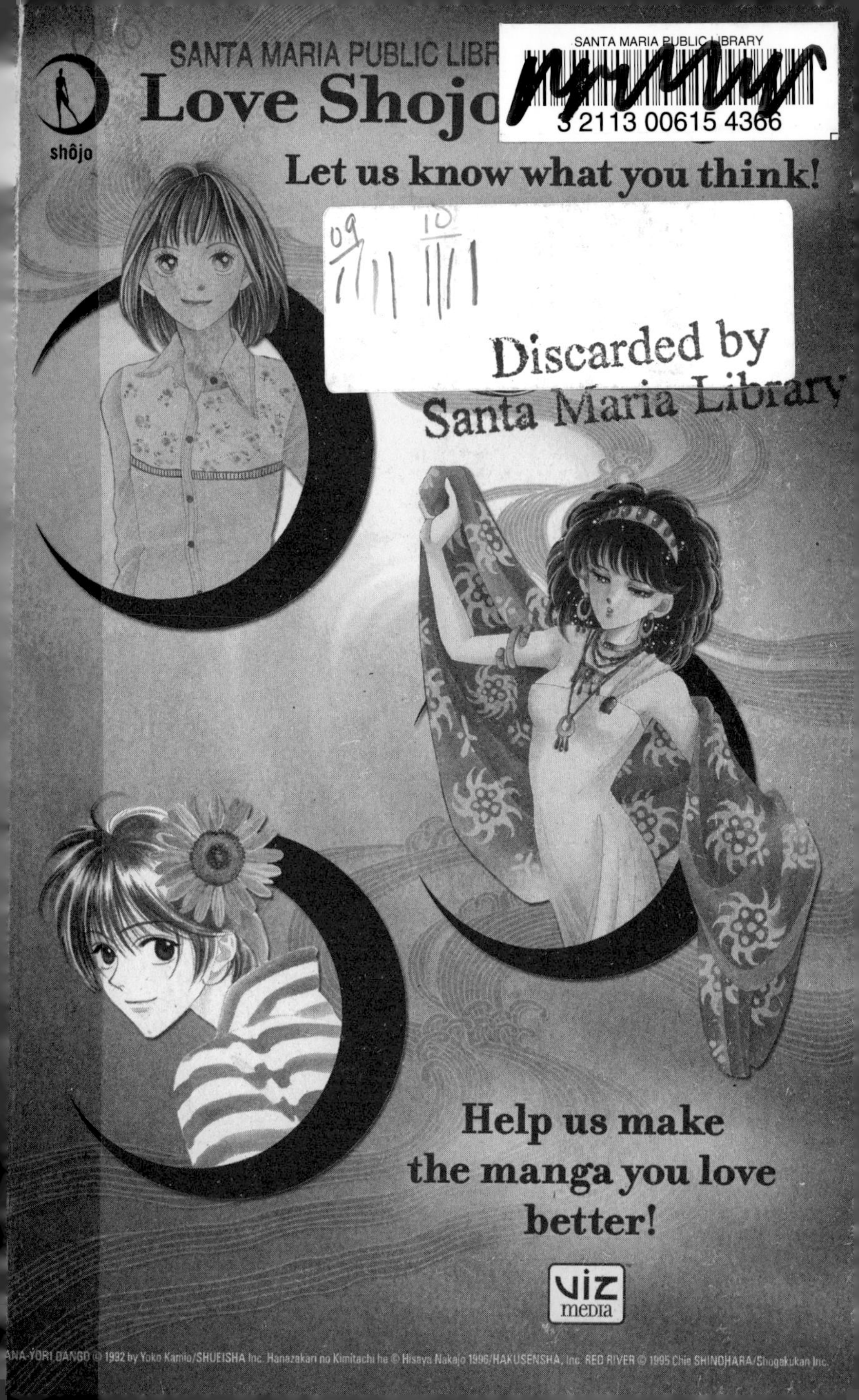
SANTA MARIA PUBLIC LIBR
SANTA MARIA PUBLIC LIBRARY
3 2113 00615 4366
shôjo
Love Shojo
Let us know what you think!
Discarded by
Santa Maria Library
Help us make
the manga you love
better!
VIZ media
ANA-YORI DANGO © 1992 by Yoko Kamio/SHUEISHA Inc. Hanazakari no Kimitachi he © Hisaya Nakajo 1996/HAKUSENSHA, Inc. RED RIVER © 1995 Chie SHINOHARA/Shogakukan Inc.